STUDIES IN HISTORY, ECONOMICS AND PUBLIC LAW

Edited by the
FACULTY OF POLITICAL SCIENCE
OF COLUMBIA UNIVERSITY

NUMBER 222

THE FREE NEGRO IN MARYLAND, 1634-1860

BY

JAMES M. WRIGHT

THE FREE NEGRO IN MARYLAND
1634–1860

BY

JAMES M. WRIGHT

1971

OCTAGON BOOKS
New York

Reprinted 1971
by special arrangement with Columbia University Press

OCTAGON BOOKS
A DIVISION OF FARRAR, STRAUS & GIROUX, INC.
19 Union Square West
New York, N. Y. 10003

LIBRARY OF CONGRESS CATALOG CARD NUMBER: 72-159258

ISBN-0-374-98775-0

Printed in U.S.A. by
NOBLE OFFSET PRINTERS, INC.
NEW YORK 3, N. Y.

TABLE OF CONTENTS

PREFACE

THE free negro class in Maryland sprang up in connection with the institution of slavery. Of slavery in the provincial era the following were the outstanding characteristics: the social status was substantially fixed; the formal legal status was also well-defined, although in practice liberties of varying extent were enjoyed by many slaves; and the economic welfare ranged from the meanest to one as good as that of the average white person. In some respects, therefore, the slave negro's position approximated that of the white citizen, and it was probably improved, at least on the economic side, after the provincial era had passed. The problem here, however, is the rise and condition of the free negro. Formally the first important step was the acquisition by the negro of the property right in his own person and services. In early practice the act of manumission had been designed to effectuate this so completely that no legal obstacle should remain to hinder the progress of self-improvement. If it failed to attain that object, the default was probably due to the peculiarities of the negro himself, i. e. that his racial distinctness from the whites continued to be as marked as that of the slave and that his impotency for organizing to protect and promote his own interests left him both subordinate and very dependent. Thus although manumission did mark him off from the slave, since in the process it created in the population a formally separate class, it seemed thereby to build up a separate and unwelcome institution. This institutional phase was called by some " free-negroism." Another aspect of the situation lay in that, while negro slavery had been a disappointment, " free-negroism " as supplanting it was also not deemed a success.   Something, it was thought, had to be done about that.   The thing attempted was to create and execute a legal status to correspond to the condition of the class itself.   The matter was thrown into state politics, and the status became as ill-defined as was the free negro's position hybrid and anomalous.   The problem has received less exposition than the numbers of the free negroes seem to merit.   The pages that follow endeavor to help fill the void.

The subject of the free negro has not been left untouched. Sidelights on the earlier period are to be found in Mac-Cormac's *White Servitude in Maryland,* and some information occurs in certain of the general and special histories, but in Brackett's *The Negro in Maryland* is found a predecessor in which the space devoted to manumission and the free negroes nearly equals that given to the slaves. Dr. Brackett's faithful chronicle of the formal history has made his work an inevitable help in its field.   Although the present study is narrower in scope, and although in its chapters II, III and X, especially, it retraces many of the steps taken in the preceding work, in chapters II and X, at least, it draws upon lucrative materials from which the earlier work derived nothing mentionable.   It has seemed meet to interweave what these sources yielded with the formal history, and thus to give further account of the following matters : the reasons for the manumission of some negroes and the failure to manumit others, how manumission was understood and executed by the owners of negroes, the territorial distribution of the free negroes and slaves, the genesis, development, retardation and fiasco of the colonization movement and the clash of economic interests over the negro question in state politics.   Furthermore, although Brackett has given the law and some of the other facts about apprenticeship and vagrancy, and although the materials contained in Bishop Payne's *History of the African Methodist Episcopal Church* were indispensable to the chapter on the church, chapters IV-IX (inclusive) attempt to cover ground that had not been previously cultivated intensively.

The work whose results are presented was first undertaken at the instance of the Carnegie Institution of Washington, D. C. A subvention from that source made possible the assembling of most of the materials used. The writer wishes further to make acknowledgments to Mr. Alfred H. Stone, Professor J. C. Ballagh and Dr. B. C. Steiner for assistance and counsel; to the library staffs of the Peabody Institute and the Maryland and New York Historial Societies and to the custodians of state and county archives and of certain church records and business account books for permission to use materials and for assistance during the researches; and finally to his wife who aided for months in exploring many volumes of newspapers and public records.

JAMES M. WRIGHT.

GEORGETOWN COLLEGE.

INTRODUCTION

In the sixteenth and seventeenth centuries several of the European nations founded colonies on the coasts and islands of the Americas. [Their establishment was due to mingled political, commercial, religious and personal causes.] The colonizing powers sought to achieve European ends through American agency, often utterly neglecting or deliberately injuring the interests of their own settlements. [The population of the new lands was to come from the two old continents across the sea, Europe and Africa.] As to the character of the settlers that were to come, each community had its own demands and wishes, which were more or less like those of its neighbors. Had there been a freedom of choice, no doubt each colony would have preferred to receive its population from the best classes of its own mother-land. As it was, each one received such laborers, and other persons, as the statesmen " at home " who regulated its affairs chose to let it have or to impose upon it.

The English province of Maryland, established in 1634, was one of these settlements. Its people were bent on personal enrichment.[1] They found that an ample supply of land was to be had at small cost, but that labor was scarce. Before long too, it was found that men of small means could use the land to raise themselves to a position of comfort, or even of affluence. As a consequence energetic laborers were not content to be other than proprietors, working the land for themselves. Their constant conversion into landholders depleted the ranks of the manual laborers and kept

[1] *Cf.* Gambrall, *History of Early Maryland*, pp. 65-67.

the wages of voluntary laborers high.[1]   The demands for labor were importunate.   The factors determining both the manner of supplying the demand and the character of the supply were external and complex.   The turn taken by events was destined to establish in Maryland population elements similar, as it were, to those of Virginia, on the one hand, and of Pennsylvania on the other.   The outward results of it will be noted in a brief survey of the evolution of the labor system of the colony and commonwealth.

Three different systems of labor—bond servitude, negro slavery and free wage labor—have successively held foremost rank in Maryland industry.   All were found in the early province, and although each one subsequently developed in its own way, it was influenced in its course by the other two: the employers, whenever they were able, choosing that one which seemed to offer the greatest advantages to themselves.   Each new ship-load of laborers that arrived was generally at once absorbed into the working class without satisfying the demand.   But the poverty that impelled many persons in England to seek to come to the province was a bar to their taking passage, until the redemption principle came into vogue.   In the system based upon it, the provisions for simultaneously compensating ship-owners for the costs of affording passage to America, for securing the labor of passengers to provincial landholders for long terms after arrival, and for freeing the laborers after the fulfilment of their contracts opened the door through which employers and workers were brought together.   The indenture contracts binding the parties concerned and fixing the duration and the other terms of service gave to the system the names of "indented servitude" and "bond servitude." The advantages it offered on both sides made it the preferred method of employing labor, until in the last half of the

---

[1] MacCormac, *White Servitude in Maryland*, pp. 33-34.

eighteenth century the more desirable portion of the supply from the mother country was curtailed.[1] Thereafter, although new recruits long continued to come from the continent of Europe,[2] white servitude yielded to negro slavery the predominance in the field of agricultural labor.

[The beginnings of slavery in Maryland were made in the first decade of its history.] [Just when the first negroes were brought in[3] is uncertain, but slaves who were probably negroes were mentioned in two acts of the provincial assembly in 1638-39; and three years later the governor became owner of a gang of slaves.[4] [The increase in numbers was slow and the labor demand so great that for a time the importation of negroes was invited by statute.[5] Forty years afterwards there were in the province according to the best information now available only about 8000 negroes, about 17 per cent of the whole population.[6] A change had set in

[1] MacMormac, op. cit., pp. 107-09. "Spirited" persons and transported convicts were often merged among the redemptioners. According to MacCormac the presence of convicts greatly injured the system. Cf. also Boucher, A View of the Causes and Consequences of the American Revolution, pp. 183-184, 189.

[2] Hennighausen, The Redemptioners, Second Annual Report of the Society for the Study of the History of the Germans of Maryland.

[3] Dr. Brackett, The Negro in Maryland, p. 26, writes: "When, and by whom the first negroes were brought to Maryland, we do not know; but it was soon after the settlement." Inasmuch as it is known that the negroes were there early, the question is of only curious interest. Cf. Kennedy, History and Statistics of Maryland, p. 9.

[4] Archives of Maryland, vol. i, pp. 41, 80; vol. iv, p. 189.

[5] Laws, 1671, ch. ii.

[6] Cf. Browne, Maryland: the History of a Palatinate, pp. 199-200; Brackett, The Negro in Maryland, pp. 38-39; Mereness, Maryland as a Proprietary Province, pp. 130-32. These estimates are probably based upon the list of the population in the Public Record Office in London, mentioned in Stevens, Historical Index, vol. viii. Kennedy, op. cit., ascribes to Maryland only 30,000 people as late as 1715. Cf. also DuBois, Suppression of the Slave Trade, p. 15.

already, however, and the great activity of the British merchants in furnishing negroes to the planters resulted in making the negro population in 1755 about 30 per cent of the total population, notwithstanding that the latter had more than trebled in the interval.[1] In 1755 the slaves were 24.3 per cent of the whole population, the negroes, free and slave, 29.5 per cent and the whites 70.5 per cent. The next generation, closing with the first federal census, witnessed a crucial contest between slave and free labor—perhaps also between negro and white labor. In its course the slaves increased 136.8 per cent, the total of the negroes 145 per cent, and the whites 92.8 per cent, so that in 1790 the three classes respectively were 32.2 per cent, 34.7 per cent, and 65.3 per cent of the whole population. But numerically the increase of the freemen, 106 692, was 79.3 per cent greater than that of the slaves, that of the whites alone 68.7 per cent greater than that of the slaves and 62.2 per cent greater than that of all the negroes, even though in the years 1775-82 the negro increase had exceeded that of the whites by more than 6000.[2] The distribution of these increments was significant. The negroes were settled in all parts of the state, but with considerable advantage to Southern Maryland and the Eastern Shore. The whites, however, were settled chiefly in the northern counties and in Baltimore City, hence the establishment on the respective spheres of predominance of slave and free labor in the state in the nineteenth century.

[1] Calculating on the basis of the United States Census estimates, Kennedy, *op. cit.*, the percentage of negroes in the population in 1756 was 29.9 per cent, and on the figures of the *Gentlemen's Magazine*, 1764, p. 261, it was 29.5 per cent in 1755. The one may have been based upon the same enumeration as the other.

[2] The increase of the negroes after 1790 was confined mainly to that of the freemen, as will be shown below. The maximum ratio of negroes to total population was reached at 38 per cent in 1810. By 1860 it had declined to 24.9 per cent.

Thus it was that negro slavery and white servitude sprang up about the same time; that neither one at any time embraced the whole laboring population; that the former fell into an inferior position, until the avidity of English slave traders brought on its progressive development in the eighteenth century; that it continued to grow rapidly after its rival had begun to decline; that it reached its height at the end of the eighteenth century; and that soon thereafter disintegrating forces, which had already impaired its position, reversed its process of growth and prepared the way for its extinction during the great war between the states.

Some voluntary laborers, it appears, were employed for wages in the early province. " Hired servants " are mentioned in some of the statutes,[1] and in the census of Maryland of 1755, as published in the *Gentleman's Magazine*, hired servants are mentioned, but are merged into the same column with indented servants.[2] The conditions under which their services were to be procured and remunerated, however,[3] linked with that of the profitableness of using involuntary laborers, forbade any great dependence upon them. Their number was obviously small. But in the last half of the eighteenth century the causes that checked the growth of white servitude[4] without correspondingly checking the growth of the white population increased the relative importance of free labor. And, although the manumission of a slave did not in every point of view mean the the addition of a free laborer, the decay of slavery contributed to the same end. These two changes—the decline of slavery and the advance of free labor—left no part of the

---

[1] *Laws*, 1715, ch. xix and ch. xliv, *Archives of Maryland*, vol. xiii, p. 452, vol. xxii, p. 546. *Cf.* Mereness, *op. cit.*, pp. 133-34.

[2] *Gentleman's Magazine*, 1764, p. 261.

[3] MacCormac, *op. cit.*, pp. 33-34.

[4] *Op. cit.*, pp. 107-09.

state unaffected.[1] To carry further the statement of the last paragraph above: the two generations after the first federal census witnessed a loss of 15.38 per cent on the part of the slaves, but gains of 54.06 per cent, 943.6 per cent and 147.2 per cent on the part of all negroes, of free negroes and of the whites respectively. The total free population gained 176.8 per cent of which the free negroes comprised 19.8 per cent. As a consequence the eighth federal census showed in the several classes the following percentages of the total population: slaves 12.7 per cent, free negroes 12.2 per cent, whites 75.1 per cent and total freemen 87.3 per cent. The territorial distribution of the increments of this period, excepting that of the free negroes, was substantially like that of the preceding period.

The import of the above survey at this stage is that in the period of chief interest for this study, that expiring between the close of the revolution and the war of secession, the free negroes constantly increased at the expense of slavery; that owing to manumissions of slaves and the interstate slave trade slavery declined after 1810, until in 1860 slaves and free negroes stood with respect to each other as 50.95 and 49.05; that there was but one section of the state in which slavery was not being rapidly depleted; and that the percentage of excess of the whites over all the negroes which had been 41 per cent in 1755 and 30.6 per cent in 1790 had risen to 50.2 per cent by 1860.

The early free negroes are not to be thought of apart from slave negroes and slave masters. In a formal sense, as possessed of the formal status of freedom, they had been raised above the slaves and had become entitled to the legal

---

[1] It should be noted that Southern Maryland, however, including six counties in 1790, and seven counties in the same bounds in 1860, gained only 194, or 0.39 of one per cent, in its number of slaves between 1790 and 1860, while its number of freemen increased 24.3 per cent.

privileges and immunities of freemen under the common
law. Had other things been equal, and had there been no
specific provisions of law applying to their case, freed
negroes and their descendants would have been placed upon
a par with white freemen. But the shifting from one
legal category to another left negro persons unaltered with
respect to fitness for the station they had thereby attained.
It did not make them independent of doles from the larders
and ward-robes of the whites; it did not essentially change
their occupations, their abodes, or their diversions; it failed
to raise their intellects above those of the slaves, with
whom they continued to associate and consort. Hence in
the economic point of view they were not sharply distinguished, and on the social side still less so, from those whose
status, as the law would have had it, was lower than their
own. Their position was anomalous. They were played
upon by a complex of forces, some of which arising outside
the state, were met and crossed by internal, counter forces.
They themselves were impotent. They went hither and
thither as they were impelled.

The history of the free negroes in Maryland may be
divided into two periods, one before, the other after the
general emancipation of the civil war period.

The formal act of emancipation occurred in Maryland in
1864. The first period was marked by the obscure rise of
free negroes among the slaves of the seventeenth and
eighteenth centuries and by their development in the manner
noted in the above paragraphs. The later period opened
with the merging of all negroes into a common class by the
extinction of slavery, and has witnessed a continued increase in the negro population. It is with the first of these
periods that concern is had here, and unless otherwise indicated, the things said below will be meant to apply to the
Maryland free negroes in that period. This interval may

itself be divided into two periods, the dividing point being the American Revolution. Before that time the forces that had produced slavery held sway, and such free negroes as appeared were only an unmarked incident in the mass of men of their color. After that time slavery was disintegrating, even though until 1810 the number of slaves was growing, and as it declined, the free negroes advanced. The more significant part of this study bears upon things that transpired between the revolution and the great war between the states.

CHAPTER I

The Colonial Period

[Before the year 1634 the territory that is now Maryland was a part of the North American wilderness. Its human occupants were a few hundred Indians.] The Maryland of the nineteenth century became such as it was through the combined efforts of men of the European and African stocks, the former as active, the latter mainly as passive factors in state building. [The Englishmen who founded the province came of their own accord to build their personal fortunes.] They found abundant natural resources suited to their purpose, but a dearth of men to utilize them. They induced some others of their own nation and of kindred nations to follow them. But the need of men was urgent—a condition that in course of time developed rapidly. The best hands to work were most wanted, but in their absence others were usable. To meet the demand there sprang up a traffic in laborers, in which fair methods and foul, persuasion and force, were used to secure recruits for the colony. Abundance of labor was desired. And since for a given number of laborers the abundance of the supply was in direct ratio to the length of the service of each subject, it was desirable to avail fully of the services of each worker. For this purpose they adopted for Europeans a system of servitude,[1] the duration of which for each of its subjects

---

[1] A Relation of Maryland, 1635, in Hall, *Narratives of Early Maryland*, pp. 98-100.

was as long as conditions would permit. And yet in the face of growing demands the number was insufficient.

Some adventurous traders took advantage of the situation to foist an unrelated race and a second system of servitude upon the provincial people.[1] [They knew that Europeans were preferred by the colonists; but they also knew that adventure would make Africans as easily available for the trade as Europeans, and that furnishing the former, who could be sold for life, was more lucrative than carrying Europeans, whose services could be sold only for limited terms. Through their agency Africa also contributed to the peopling of Maryland.] Its contribution consisted of an unwilling body of pioneers, dragged out of a primitive society and rushed without other preparation than the experiences of voyages on slave vessels into the midst of an advanced race, whose physical, mental and moral characteristics differed strikingly from their own. Neither in deciding to leave their old homes nor in choosing their lot in the new one did they have a voice. And in contrast to their European fellow-men they were placed in a position from which no might of their own could extricate them. Such in brief was the manner of supplying the labor for the fields and households of the colonial agriculturists of Maryland. Its results were to fix upon local society the institution of negro slavery and in due course to entail the economic, social and political developments that followed in its train.

The growth of slavery in Maryland has been described by Dr. Brackett[2] in such wise that it need not be repeated in

---

[1] DuBois, *Suppression of the Slave Trade*, pp. 1-5.

[2] *The Negro in Maryland*, pp. 26-46. Dr. Brackett holds that as the provincials had no English precedent for "granting any especial rights and privileges" to negroes, slavery became an incident in the condition of the colonies, and slave codes grew up as a "matter of local law," pp. 26-27. Browne, *Maryland: the History of a Palatinate*, p. 180,

full here. Throughout the history of the province the
need of more labor was urgent, and the futility of depending
on free laborers, or even on bond servants, to do the work
seemed clear. [Therefore negroes who were brought in
almost exclusively as slave laborers, were distributed into
every part of the commonwealth.] These laborers became
a subject for special treatment. The same economic interest that had led to their importation, dictated that the
titles to property in their services should be guaranteed by
law. And for negative reasons social interest, based upon
matters of race, soon added force to the same demand.[1]
The two combined to strengthen the legal foundations of
slavery. It appears that most of the rules employed for
their regulation were based on custom, but in course of
time statutes were also added. [One such measure, enacted
by the provincial legislature in 1664, declared that "all
Negroes and other slaves already within the Province and
all Negroes and other slaves to be hereafter imported into
the Province shall serve Durante Vita. And all Children
born of any Negro or other slave shall be Slaves as their
ffathers were for the terme of their lives."[2] The same

states that slavery existed in the province from its foundations. Time
was required, however, for the more complete definition of the conditions and incidents of the different classes of persons who shared
African blood. [Regarding developments in Virginia, *cf.* Ballagh,
History of Slavery in Virginia, pp. 27-32, and Russell, *The Free Negro
in Virginia*, 1619-1865, pp. 16-21.

[1] These reasons were those tangible and intangible grounds of opposition to the freedom of negroes, who might, as a consequence of becoming free, live among the free whites as citizens.

[2] *Archives of Maryland*, vol. i, pp. 533-34. This act, if literally applied, would have prohibited free negroes as such from remaining
under Maryland jurisdiction. *Cf.* Brackett, *op. cit.*, p. 33, note 1. It
would likewise have made slaves of the issue of white women by negro
men. In view of the later condition of the law touching such issue,
cf. infra, p. 13, it is doubtful whether this act was conclusive as to the
condition of the two classes named.

object was promoted further by an act of 1671 which decided that baptism according to the rites of the Christian
church did not entitle a slave negro to release from slavery,[1]
by other acts of the assembly,[2] and by the rules of the courts
which presumed that persons of African blood were slaves,
and which in freedom suits placed the burden of proof as
to status upon the plaintiffs, not upon their detainers.[3]
There was thus a tendency to cement more firmly the ties
binding slave property to its owners, a tendency that was
distinctly adverse to the emergence of free negroes.

But a contrary movement also began in the seventeenth
century. One part of the act of 1664, mentioned in the
preceding paragraph, would have made slaves for life of all
negroes in the province; another part of it seemed to imply
that at thirty years of age the children of white women by
negro slaves were to be free.[4]   According to its amendment
of 1681, the issue from similar unions contracted at the instigation of " masters or dames" were to be " free and

[1] *Archives of Maryland*, vol. ii, p. 272. The motives for this measure
were twofold: To encourage religious instruction of negroes, and to
prevent depletion of the labor force. *Cf.* Act of 1715, ch. xliv, which
embraced this provision. Also Browne, *op. cit.*, p. 179.

[2] *Laws*, 1681, ch. iv; 1692, ch. xv; 1715, ch. xliv; 1717, ch. xiii; 1728,
ch. iv.

[3] *Md. Appeal Reports*, 4 H. & McH., p. 305; 6 G. & J., pp. 141-44,
388-91; 9 G. & J., pp. 174, 179-80; 5 H. & J., p. 190. Certain documents
in the *Archives of Maryland*, vol. ii, p. 272, and vol. vii, pp. 203-04,
seemed to regard all negroes as slaves.

[4] Its actual provision was that such children should serve their parent's
masters until the age of thirty years. *Archives of Maryland*, vol. i,
p. 534. In that there is a presumption of the slavery of all negroes.
The legislators may have intended here to discriminate and to call the
issue in question " mulattoes" rather than negroes. But whether this
intention prevailed does not matter, because later on both classes of
persons of African blood were deemed " free negroes," or " free persons of color." For the purposes of this study this usage will be followed, and either a free negro or a free mulatto will be considered
as the same before the law.

manymitted."[1] And the same code of laws that protected the title to property in a negro also recognized the owner's power to vest that title in the negro, its object.[2] In spite of certain contrary evidences it is doubtful that that potential right was ever in abeyance, whatever may have been true as to its actual use. There is some doubt as to the administrative policy in the matter before 1690, although in Somerset County the court dealt with one negro as with a freeman in the year 1667.[3] But that doubt is cleared away by the fact that freedom suits were entertained in the courts, by the fulfillment of two promises of manumission, and by an administration account for a negro's estate, all of which fell before the end of the seventeenth century.[4] It appears that thereafter slave-owners were allowed to use at discretion any approved forms of manumitting negroes, and that fraudulent detention of negroes in slavery, when brought into the courts, was declared void. Hence individual negroes could become free, and it was by individual accretions that the free negro class came into being. Its numbers increased much less rapidly, however, than those of the slaves.

The possible ways of adding free negroes to the population were voluntary immigration and coerced importation from

[1] *Op. cit.*, vol. vii, p. 204; *infra*, p. 13.

[2] *Cf.* Hurd, *Law of Freedom and Bondage*, pp. 213-16.

[3] *Somerset Deeds and Judicial Record*, Lib. B, pp. 111-16; *vide infra*, p. 16.

[4] *Provincial Court Judgments*, Lib. 5, p. 579; *Charles Co. Recs.*, Lib. X, p. 51. Also *Provincial Court Recs.*, Lib. C, pp. 162, 361, referred to by Brackett, *op. cit.*, pp. 30, 148. For the administration account, *vide Md. Testamentary Proceedings*, Lib. 17, p. 210. *Cf.* also *Md. Wills*, Lib. TB, p. 12 (1700). What appears to have been a move favoring the prohibition of free negroes in Maryland occurred in 1715, when a member of the legislature reported that no free negro was permitted to remain longer than a specified term in the province of Virginia. *Archives of Maryland*, vol. xxx, p. 16.

without, general emancipation, individual manumission, and natural increase of free negroes. In view of certain well-known conditions the first factor was undoubtedly unimportant, although a few free negroes may have come in from neighboring provinces. Those who were fraudulently imported and enslaved, but subsequently declared free by judicial decree,[1] or otherwise, were likewise not numerous. And no general emancipation occurred until 1864. These things granted, the last two factors remain. In so far as free negroes sprang from the slave class, natural increase was dependent for the most part upon pre-existing free negroes. Within those limits manumissions originated their class and thereafter joined forces with natural increase to swell their numbers. These two factors will now be dealt with in the order mentioned.

The subject of manumissions will be dealt with more at length in the following chapter. The methods employed in manumitting were by word of mouth, by last will and testament and by deed. The first two were formally abolished by statute in 1752.[2] The third, although not much employed up to that time, came into general use at the time of the revolution. In the following paragraphs attention will be devoted mainly to the causes of manumissions, since the causes operating in the province were not quite the same as the more effective causes operating thereafter.

Manumissions in the province were never numerous. For this fact two reasons may be assigned, first, the labor situation had not then reached a fitting stage of development, and second, the other later powerful causes had not yet begun to act. As the motives actuating manumitting

---

[1] *Provincial Court Judgments*, Lib. 13, pp. 108, 193, 615, 618; Lib. 19, p. 118; Lib. 41, pp. 43-44, 46, 49; *Charles Co. Recs.*, Lib. A, no. 2, p. 182; Lib. B, no. 2, p. 667; *Archives of Maryland*, vol. xxxi, pp. 409-10; *Md. Appeal Reports*, 3 H. & McH., pp. 139, 501-02.

[2] *Laws*, 1752, ch. i.

slave-owners were often not stated in their writings we are left in part to inference to determine what they were. However, from assigned reasons in some of the cases direct information may be gleaned. The following chief causes seem to merit discussion: (1) blood relationship to manumittors, or to other white men, (2) good will of masters earned by faithful service, or otherwise.

The reason for regarding blood relationship as a major cause here lies in inferences chiefly. A statute of June, 1692, recited that " forasmuch as diverse freeborn English and white women do sometimes intermarry with and sometimes permitt themselves to be gotten with child by negroes and other slaves " *etc.*[1] Now it does not appear that the offspring of such unions became the objects of manumissions.[2] But the offspring of negro women by white men were often manumitted. They were not the issue of regularly married persons, but appeared as a consequence of the incontinency of negro women and of their coerced deference to the demands of lustful masters.[3] The conclusion stated rests further upon population statistics. According to the census of 1755, given in the *Gentleman's Magazine*,[4] 357, or .84

---

[1] *Archives of Maryland*, vol. xiii, pp. 546-47.

[2] *Infra*, pp. 28-29.

[3] The mention in an act of manumission that the beneficiary was a mulatto, although it may give rise to suspicion, creates no presumption that the benefactor was favoring a child of his own. For it may have been the child of his neighbor, or his father or grandfather, at any rate the child, or grandchild of some white man. For provisions for the manumission of mulattoes *vide Md. Wills*, Lib. CC, no. 3, pp. 482, 508, 831; Lib. 11, p. 312; Lib. WD, no. 21, p. 36; Lib. DD, no. 7, p. 13; *Cecil Land Recs.*, Lib. 4, p. 507 (1749).

[4] 1764, p. 261. This census, although giving many details is not accepted as satisfactory, but only as the best available. But inasmuch as its showing for the aggregate population of all classes corresponds closely to that used in the volume of *History and Statistics of Maryland*, printed by the United States Census, it may probably be regarded as approximately correct.

per cent, in a total of 41,143 negroes, and 1460, or 35.1 per cent in a total of 4158 mulattoes in the population were free. 80.2 per cent of the 1817 free persons of color belonged to the 9.1 per cent who had white blood in their veins. Some of them no doubt were born of free negro and mulatto mothers, some of white mothers, and some may have come in from the outside world; the rest were obviously born in slavery and manumitted. If manumittors had been uninfluenced by ties of kinship, it is probable that, in view of the disparity between the two complectional classes of slaves, at least as large a number of negroes as of mulattoes would have become free.

The other chief reason assigned was that on account of the good will of masters, however gained, manumission was conferred as a favor. Two early deeds, one in Talbot County in 1703 and the other in Somerset in 1709, well illustrate this motive.[1] In the latter the grantor wrote that he was actuated by "divers good and lawful considerations of the trusty and faithful services done me by my negro Sambo and his wife Betty." He therefore made them both free. The larger number of such grants were made by last will and testament.[2] Upon the whole it appears that the rate of recorded manumissions did not exceed the rate of increase in total population, which according to the estimates quoted on page 14 trebled between 1712 and 1755.[3]

[1] *Talbot Deeds*, Lib. RF, no. 9, p. 358; *Somerset Deeds*, Lib. CD, no. 1, p. 416 and Lib. GH, p. 311; Lib. B, p. 85. *Cf.* also *Baltimore Chattel Recs.*, Lib. B, no. G, p. 18 (1762).

[2] For examples *vide Md. Wills*, Lib. CC, no. 2, p. 18; Lib. CC, no. 3, pp. 452, 508, 632, 831; Lib. DD, no. 7, pp. 476, 520, 522; Lib. BT, no. 1, p. 65 and Lib. WD, no. 18, pp. 14, 163, 235.

[3] No doubt there was an improvement in the economic welfare of the planters which would have enabled them to incur the sacrifices of manumitting negro laborers. But there were lacking those benevolent feelings which were felt strongly during the contest with the mother country, and the habit of manumitting negroes did not spring up in the province.

Of natural increase the normal case was that of descent from a free colored mother. But some members of the class were born of white mothers. They early became a subject of concern. The statute of 1664, already cited, tells that some freeborn English women, forgetful of their station, had married negro slaves, and that suits touching their freedom had arisen in the courts. It enacted that in future such offenders and their children by slaves should become slaves of the respective masters of their husband-fathers.[1] Its manifest design here was to prevent the marriage of white women to negro slaves. But the contrary result offered an advantage to any slave master who could bring it about. Hence the terms of servant women were purchased, and the women themselves were married to slaves apparently with a view to invoking upon them the penalties just recited. The legislators returned to the subject in 1681. They left the general rule as it had been before but provided an exemption from its application for cases in which the forbidden marriages had been entered into at the instigation of "masters" or "dames."[2] As such enslavement could only occur as a result of judicial decree,[3] opportunity was afforded to avail of the exemption. But the modification did not do away with this kind of offence. After some further alterations in 1692,[4] the comprehensive negro act of 1715 included free mulattoes with free white women in the inhibition against marrying

[1] *Archives of Maryland*, vol. i, pp. 533-34; *supra*, p. 9; *cf.* also *Md. Appeal Reports*, 1 H. & McH., pp. 372-73.

[2] *Archives of Maryland*, vol. vii, p. 204. Fines were to be imposed upon the owners of slaves and upon the priests who had to do with such marriages. It seems that Lord Baltimore was himself instrumental in securing this change in the law because of a case in which he had personally been interested. *Md. Appeal Reports*, 1 H. & McH., p. 376.

[3] *Md. Appeal Reports*, 2 H. & McH., p. 233.

[4] *Archives of Maryland*, vol. xiii, p. 547.

negro slaves and fixed the terms of service at seven years for mothers and thirty-one years for such offspring.[1]

The province witnessed many instances of the enforcement of these provisions. Enslavement of offending white women and their hybrid children had occurred under the act of 1664.[2] One of these cases, that of Eleanor, called Irish Nell, had aroused the proprietor to take steps to secure the important amendment of the law in 1681,[3] but the victim and her descendants were apparently held as slaves, until one of the latter was adjudged free in 1787.[4] The lighter penalties imposed under the act of 1715 varied considerably. Leaving aside those on mothers, however, we find by implication that after their terms of servitude their children were to become free. In this way two infants in Charles County, who were sold into servitude till thirty-one years of age for 1000 and 200 pounds of tobacco respectively, and three successive children of one mulatto woman in Somerset, sold in the same manner in 1745-60, were to become free ultimately.[5] But except for making

---

[1] *Laws,* 1715, ch. xliv, sec. 25; *cf.* 1717, ch. xiii.

[2] *Archives of Maryland,* vol. vii, p. 204; *Md. Appeal Reports,* 2 H. & McH., pp. 231-33. MacCormac, *op. cit.,* p. 68, writes that there had been "many" such cases.

[3] *Md. Appeal Reports,* 1 H. & McH., p. 376.

[4] *Op. cit.,* 2 H. & McH., pp. 232-33. This case was so decided because there was no evidence from a court of record that Irish Nell had been adjudged to have incurred the penalties of the act of 1664. Without conviction in a court of record neither she nor her descendants could have been legally enslaved. The parents of this successful suitor, both claiming descent from Irish Nell, had been adjudged free by the Provincial Court, but upon appeal the higher court in 1771 reversed the decree on the ground that the exemptions of the act of 1681 had not been designed to apply to offspring of unions contracted prior to its passage. *Op. cit.,* 1 H. & McH., pp. 374, 376; *cf.* 2 H. & McH., pp. 26, 36, 38. Also MacCormac, *op. cit.,* pp. 67-68.

[5] *Charles Co. Recs.,* Lib. Q, no. 2, pp. 518, 520; *Somerset Co. Court Judgments,* June, 1745, pp. 40, 232; 1752-54, pp. 205-06; 1757-60, p. 335.

illegitimate the children thus brought to life, it cannot be said that the execution of this part of the code was successful. The decline of white servitude and the operation of the factors which tended to increase the public disfavor for consortships of whites, especially white women, with negroes and to establish more definite relations between the white and black races were probably more effective than the law. But the important point here is the amount of contribution to the body of free negroes from this source. On this point no reliable estimate can be made as to that arising either from this source, from the issue of free women, or from manumissions of slaves. The public later attached a too exclusive importance to manumission as the origin of the free negroes [1] and frequently referred to them indiscriminately as freedmen. However that may be, it is certain that under the act of 1715 the freedom of the mulatto issue of white women in any case depended merely upon their outliving their terms of service, whereas that of mulatto slave children depended mainly upon the uncertain favor of doting white relatives. And in 1755, 64.9 per

For other cases of the sale of these children *vide* the following: Somerset, *op. cit.*, 1722-24, p. 51; 1724-27, pp. 97, 132; 1730-33, p. 28; 1733-36, p. 198; 1736-38, pp. 2-3; 1738-40, pp. 8, 13; 1740-42, p. 58; 1742-44, p. 132; 1744-47, p. 99; 1747-49, p. 228; 1752-54, p. 122; 1754-57, pp. 64, 109; 1757-60, pp. 3, 4, 40, 63, 118, 146, 236, 335; 1760-63, pp. 76, 88, 100, 130, 145, 252; 1765-66, pp. 26, 27, 90; *Charles Co. Recs.*, Lib. B, no. 2, pp. 211, 244-45; Lib. D, no. 2, pp. 9, 70, 136, 196, 197, 198; Lib. E, no. 2, pp. 207, 255, 301, 304; Lib. I, no. 2, p. 223; Lib. K, no. 2, pp. 127-28, 223, 307; Lib. 39, pp. 450, 627-28; Lib. R, no. 2, pp. 297-98, 475; Lib. T, no. 2, pp. 6, 37, 46, 142, 188, 220; Lib. 42, pp. 603, 604; Lib. F, no. 3, p. 465; Lib. K, no. 3, p. 99. *Dorchester Co. Land Recs.*, Lib. 4½, pp. 157, 165, 176. *Dorchester Co., Court Recs.*, Lib. JP, pp. 88-89; 1754-5, pp. 125-27. *Queen Anne's Co. Court Judgments*, June, 1730, Aug., 1730, Nov., 1730, and March, 1754. *Frederick Judicial Rec.*, Lib. M, p. 323.

[1] Kennedy, *History and Statistics of Maryland*, p. 20; *Preliminary Report on Eighth Census of the United States*, pp. 7, 12; *American Farmer*, 1 ser., vol. i, p. 99.

cent of all the mulatto contingent in the population were still in slavery.

Thus the negroes were passive factors both in entering Maryland and in falling into the niche to which events destined them. Once located, their personal qualities well fitted them to stay put. Their ignorance, although they probably improved somewhat from contact with the whites, doomed them to a narrow outlook upon life; docility, innate and inculcated, inclined them to acquiesce in the arrangements made for them by others; lack of race training left them unfit for any endeavors that could result in distinctive achievement; and appreciation of their own impotence made submission to the whites a choice without alternative. They also lacked inherited property and family connections other than the humblest. They had no power either to make or to unmake. As slaves their energies were under the direction of masters, for whose welfare, so far as they could see, all things existed. Those who became free saw from a slightly different angle that the old inequalities, and the powers that maintained them, still persisted; that in some important points they as non-slaves were still like the slaves. These circumstances, tempered by a modicum of knowledge of the industrial arts, and by the little property tendered them by the whites, represent the bed-rock level upon which the free negroes undertook to play a rôle in society. As a consequence it was in humble capacities, not in those of an active, determinative character, that individual negroes figured. They furnished on the one hand an element of discord by individual crimes and other disorders, and on the other grateful contributions to the ordinary work of every-day life. The latter absorbed the greater part of the negro energy expended.

Although offending against social order was a minor function, it deserves a brief mention here. What is to be said in this paragraph was true substantially of slaves as well of free negroes. It was mainly for petty offences that the latter were arraigned before the courts whose records afford our information. The earliest reference to a free negro I have found was one in Somerset County, in which a culprit "confest" that he with two white companions had stolen some corn from an Indian. And on June 30, 1667 the county court " ordered that the said . . . . [white parties named] and John Johnson, negro, that when the crop of corn is housed they shall deliver two barrels of Indian corn at Manokin Towne to the king of Manokin . . . . and pay all necessary charges." [1] Another in Dorchester in 1690 was ordered to provide for his bastard child by a white woman, and was fined 500 pounds of tobacco for his offence.[2] Such crimes as rape and murder, whose actual number was perhaps over-rated by the whites, were committed by negroes and were in many cases punished vindictively.[3] For these offences slaves and free negroes were apparently treated without distinction. But what the whites most feared from negroes were attempts at insurrection. Although no large number of negroes ever concerted in such movements, the whites suspected them of plotting and were easily alarmed and aroused. To forestall dangerous risings a statute passed in 1723 made each owner of a plantation responsible for all gatherings of negroes on his premises. At the same time it empowered each county court to appoint

[1] *Somerset Judicial Recs.*, Lib. B, pp. 111, 116. It is not stated that this fellow was a free negro. But he was not mentioned as anybody's slave, he had both a Christian and a surname, and he was required to pay his own penalty in property. In the first two of these points it was not usually so with slaves.

[2] *Dorchester Co. Court Judgments, Land Recs.*, Lib. 4½, pp. 157, 165, 176.

[3] *Provincial Court Judgments*, Lib. E, no. 7, pp. 7, 19-20; Lib. 36, p. 490; *Charles Co. Recs.*, Lib. P, no. 2, p. 9; *Somerset Co. Court Judgments*, June, 1763, p. 252; *Archives of Maryland*, vol. xxxii, pp. 91-92, 163, 178-79, 200, 333, 335; vol. xxxi, p. 157.

constables to make periodical visits in the hundreds under its jurisdiction to the haunts of negroes and to disperse all meetings of negroes which had not been duly authorized.[1] Pursuing the course thus laid down constables were appointed to enforce this act in Charles County in 1735 and 1747, in Prince George's in 1740, in Somerset in 1736 and in Queen Anne's in 1754.[2] In the last mentioned county the constables each claimed annually 400 pounds of tobacco for a period of fourteen years for "suppressing tumultuous meetings" of negroes.[3] But no reported disorder seemed to have been difficult to quell. The Maryland negroes were not generally rebellious, and the freemen among their number were not fomenters of discord. Had they endeavored to throw off their yoke, the excess of whites in the population in all parts of the colony was sufficient to have enabled them to put down any incipient uprising that might have occurred.

In the matter of earning their livelihood the free negroes were again both unlike and like their slave brethren. The formal conditions under which they engaged to work were fundamentally different from those of slavery. For apart from the pressure of economic forces they had the power to accept or to reject particular proffers of employment, to collect and expend the earnings of work done, or, if they chose, to attempt to become independent workers of the soil. And yet for potent reasons they drifted into a position unlike that of free laborers. These reasons lay in themselves

[1] Laws, 1723, ch. xv.

[2] Charles Co. Recs., Lib. T, no. 2, p. 93; Lib. 41, p. 189. Archives of Maryland, vol. xxviii, pp. 188-91; Somerset Co. Court Judgments, 1736-38, p. 133; Queen Anne's Co. Court Judgments, Nov., 1754; H. Dels. Journal, 1740, pp. 207, 229, 238, 281, 302.

[3] Recs. of Expenditures on Account of the Levy List, Bounties on Squirrel Scalps, etc., Queen Anne's, 1754-67. Cf. Frederick Judicial Rec., Lib. M, pp. 151, 363.

and in their environment.   As for themselves the handicaps under which they labored inclined them to become suppliants rather than free agents.   To this the conditions of the environment—the rude system of making exchanges, the strong hold of servitude upon white laborers and the customary dependence of negroes upon white employers— committed them all the more.   As a consequence the few free negroes continued to perform the same actual functions in the same manner and to be treated by their employers in substantially the same way as the slaves.   Thus some contracted to work under indentures like those of the white servants.[1]   And inasmuch as in the nineteenth century free negroes continued to work for the farmers under agreements essentially like these indentures, it seems safe to infer that the details were much the same.[2]

Over half of the free negroes of 1755 were persons under fifteen years of age.   Most of the indentures of negroes I have found applied to the cases of children.   Sometimes the apprenticing was done at the instance of parents,[3] or of the children themselves,[4] but more often at that of the county courts or the justices of the peace.   The motives of the latter were to provide for training the negro children as laborers and to keep them from becoming a charge upon the public.   Holding these objects in view the contracts required the masters to maintain, instruct, and upon discharge give " freedom suits " to their apprentices, and the latter to

[1] *Somerset Co. Court Judgments*, 1722-24, p. 142; 1757-60, pp. 209, 226-27; *Charles Co. Recs.*, Lib. P, no. 2, p. 238; *Frederick Judicial Rec.*, Lib. M, pp. 323-24, 377. It should be recalled here also that as a consequence of their peculiar descent some free negroes were bound under indentures.

[2] Chapter on " Occupations and Wages," *infra*, pp. 157-58.

[3] *E. g. Charles Co. Recs.*, Lib. B, no. 2, p. 433; *Frederick Judicial Rec.*, Lib. M, p. 126.

[4] *Somerset Co. Court Judgments*, 1757-60, pp. 226, 227.

be obedient, to render service and abstain from injuring their masters by absconding and by damage to their property.[1] They copied many features of the English system of apprenticeshp and prepared the way for its more extensive employment by the orphans' courts after the revolution. Excepting for the smaller variety of occupations and less stringent rules as to personal conduct these contracts were substantially like the later ones whose details will be set forth more fully in a later chapter.

Turning now from conditions of employment we find that negro property holdings were trifling in amount. They consisted chiefly of movables and small bits of land, part of which was given them by the whites. In three separate cases of administrations on negro estates no property at all was found for administration.[2] The following were some of the things left to negroes by will: outfits of clothing in two cases in 1700,[3] small amounts of tobacco and money,[4] a horse in St. Mary's in 1722, and a heifer and some fowls in Prince George's in 1730.[5] But such tenders were not numerous, and devises of land were still less so. In Somerset in 1709 a life interest in a tract of land together with some cows, calves, pigs, household goods and a year's provisions were deeded to a negro man and wife who were to go free at the donor's decease.[6] Twenty years later a whole

---

[1] *Kent Co. Court Bonds and Indentures*, Lib. JS, no. 20, p. 234; *Somerset Co. Court Judgments*, 1757-60, pp. 226, 224, 227; 1760-63, pp. 62-63, 82, 97, 98, 120, *etc.*; 1747-49, p. 6; *Frederick Judicial Rec.*, Lib. M, pp. 126, 184; *cf.* also *Laws*, 1715, ch. xliv, sec. 10.

[2] *Md. Testamentary Proceedings*, Lib. 17, p. 210; Lib. 22, pp. 355, 451.

[3] *Md. Wills*, Lib. TB, no. 1, pp. 12, 29; *cf.* Lib. CC, no. 3, pp. 565, 766-67; Lib. DD, no. 7, pp. 476, 520, 522.

[4] *Op. cit.*, Lib. CC, no. 2, p. 450; Lib. CC, no. 3, p. 453; Lib. DD, no. 7, p. 293; Lib. WD, no. 18, p. 163.

[5] *Op. cit.*, Lib. WD, no. 18, p. 14; Lib. CC, no. 3, p. 250.

[6] *Somerset Deeds*, Lib. CD, no. i, p. 416.

estate was left to five negroes in St. Mary's County.[1] At least one negro in the province acquired land by deed as apparent purchaser.[2] I have no direct evidence as to what advantages accrued to the recipients of these things. But judging from the character of the articles transferred the donors must have expected generally that their benefactions would not be of long avail. However, two of those mentioned might apparently have been made the basis of family fortunes. It is doubtful that such was the outcome. From documents existing at the court houses of the counties it is impossible to find out how much property was possessed by the negroes of the province. But the records of the general assessment of 1783 lend weight to the conclusion that its total was insignificant.

[1] *Md. Wills,* Lib. CC, no. 3, p. 632; cf. *Laws,* 1845, ch. 327.
[2] *Md. Deeds,* Lib. ED, no. 9, p. 311.

CHAPTER II

THE GROWTH OF THE FREE NEGRO POPULATION

THE fate of the negroes in America was not an apparent issue in the American revolution.[1] The period in which the revolution occurred, however, marked a turning point in the history of the negroes of Maryland. Theretofore fresh supplies of negroes from abroad had been frequently absorbed into the laboring population, and those who bought them appeared to prosper.[2] After the revolution the number of slaves increased 28,140, or 33.7 per cent. But 69.9 per cent of that growth took place before a decade had passed, a decade in which the more important forces that were to disintegrate slavery had already become manifest. The operation of these forces at once increased the rate of manumissions of slaves and the number of free negroes. The last mentioned class reached a total of 8043, or 7.2 per cent of the negro population in 1790, and 33,927, or 23 per cent of the negro population in 1810, notwithstanding that the slaves alone in 1810 exceeded the total of both classes in 1790. From that time until 1860 the conversion of slaves into free negroes continued apace, and acting in conjunction with the interstate slave trade, which drew off many slaves to the south, slowly reduced the slave population to

[1] The importation of negroes in British slave ships had been a subject of protest in the Associations of 1774. MacDonald, *Select Charters of American History*, 1607-1776, pp. 363-64.

[2] *Cf*. Scharf, *History of Maryland*, vol. ii, pp. 46-52, 58-60; Jacobstein, *Tobacco Industry of the United States*, pp. 27-28, 30-31.

78 per cent of its former maximum. Hence the last census before the end of slavery showed that, while the total negro population had increased 17.6 per cent in the half century, the free negroes had gained 147.4 per cent and had become almost equal to the slaves in numbers. Such attention as is to be given to the slave trade will be deferred to a later chapter. This chapter will concern itself with the causes, processes and numerical results of the growth of the free negro class.

The growth of the free negroes was not unimpeded. The choice as between their slavery and their freedom lay with the whites, whose primary object was always to promote the interests of their own race. For that object they were willing to make financial sacrifices, if necessary. The slaves were property, and rights to property were not generally relinquished without compensation. But aside from this, what were to be the consequences of having a body of enfranchised negroes in the population? Might they not form a breadless, half-clad burden upon the whites? Or if they prospered, might they not acquire property, and eventually other things for which property afforded the basis? Knowledge, the ballot, and even political power might fall to their lot! Finally, who could think of treating with them in general social relations, intermarrying with them, *etc.,* as with white persons? Yet on what other terms could their freedom be realized?[1]   But as these objections are to be in evidence at various points in the following chapters, further treatment of them will be waived here and attention given to the causes of the change in the negro population.

Some negroes became free as a result of the operation of the laws against the slave trade. In April, 1783, the legisla-

---

[1] *Cf. Md. Appeal Reports,* 1 H. & McH., p. 382; 2 H. & McH., p. 201; 8 Gill, pp. 318-19; *Md. Col. Journal,* vol. i, pp. 225-26.

ture enacted a law to prohibit any one to "import or bring into this state . . . . any negro, mulatto or other slave, for sale, or to reside within the state," and enacted further that any "person brought into this state as a slave contrary to this act, . . . shall be free." Travelers sojourning in the state were not, however, to be molested on account of domestic servants attending themselves; and citizens of the United States coming into Maryland to settle permanently were allowed to bring with them such slaves as they previously owned, provided that the negroes concerned had themselves been slaves in the United States for at least three years prior to their introduction.[1] As re-enacted in 1796 permission was given to heirs of estates to bring back to Maryland their inherited slaves, in case the latter had been carried away by executors without consent, or during the infancy of those entitled to them.[2] Other acts made further modifications in behalf of those acquiring negroes by certain rights *ex lege* and granted limited exemptions to persons who desired to work their negroes on both sides of the Maryland-Virginia state border.[3] And in 1831 the introduction of slaves for residence was prohibited.[4] Aside from these changes the main principles were adhered to, until in 1849 the privilege of importing negroes for residence was restored.[5] In the meantime the courts had declared that the law applied only to voluntary importations and not to those made involuntarily by refugees from the revolution

[1] *Laws*, 1783, ch. xxiii. In the act of 1792, ch. lvi, the number of domestics allowed to French political refugees from the West Indies was limited to three for an individual and five for a family.

[2] *Op. cit.*, 1796, ch. lxvii.

[3] *Op. cit.*, 1794, ch. 66; 1802, ch. 88; 1804, ch. 90; 1818, ch. 201; 1823, ch. 87; 1832, ch. 317; *Md. Appeal Reports*, 3 H. & J., p. 491; *cf.* Brackett, *The Negro in Maryland*, pp. 60-63, 66-67.

[4] *Laws*, 1831, ch. 323.

[5] *Op. cit.*, 1849, ch. 165.

in St. Domingo,[1] and had set free not only a few non-resident negroes who had been brought in contrary to law,[2] but also certain resident negroes who had been returned after having been employed outside of the state borders with their masters' consent.[3] However, no large increment came to the free negro population from this source.

In 1789-91 the general assembly rejected a bill proposing the gradual emancipation of the slaves by law.[4] In 1790 it restored the long-denied right to set free slaves by will. What it had refused to adopt as a matter of public coercion, it here permitted as a matter of private choice. The exercise of that power of choice became a chief cause of the growth of the free negro class. The other chief cause was natural increase. The influx of free negroes from without was a minor factor. These causes will be discussed in the order in which they have been mentioned.

The establishment of property in negroes had been a result of the pursuit of material interests. The law made that property secure, but permitted its holders to enfranchise the objects of which it was composed. The rapid increase in manumissions was a consequence of fundamental industrial changes which occurred simultaneously with an awakening in the political and ethical ideas of the whites. The staple crop of Maryland agriculture was tobacco. It was an unsteady crop of fluctuating value:[5] its culture exhausted the fertile soils of the province; its product yielded neither food for men nor provender for cattle; and its pro-

---

[1] *Md. Appeal Reports*, 5 H. & J., p. 86.

[2] *Op. cit.*, 3 H. & McH., p. 139; 4 H. & McH., pp. 414-16; 4 H. & J., pp. 282-83.

[3] *Op. cit.*, 3 H. & McH., pp. 168-69; 4 H. & McH., p. 418; 9 G & J., pp. 29-30; *cf.* also 3 H. & J., pp. 491, 493.

• [4] *H. Dels. Journal*, 1789, pp. 64-65; 1791, pp. 19, 31, 38.

[5] Jacobstein, *op. cit.*, p. 23.

per handling occupied labor time that might have been devoted to supplementary crops, had not the tobacco demanded it.[1] Nevertheless the Maryland settlement had increased and the proud aristocracy flourished upon the proceeds of the sales of its staple.[2] The product itself became an early competitor with Virginia tobacco in the English market,[3] and in the year 1740 exports of leaf tobacco from Maryland alone were reported as having totaled 30,000 hhds. of 900 pounds each.[4] Thereafter the normal quantity produced maintained a substantial level until the revolution.[5] During the wars, embargoes and non-intercourse that followed the operations of producing and marketing the crop were greatly disturbed. A temporary revival of the industry in 1790-92 was soon followed by decline and, in the chief tobacco-growing counties of Maryland, stagnation, "a miserable and dreary aspect."[6] Another slow revival raised Maryland's exports of leaf tobacco to 12681

[1] *Archives of Maryland*, vol. vi, p. 38; vol. xix, pp. 540, 580. Sheffield, *Commerce of the American States*, 1784, p. 92; *Amer. Farmer*, vol. i, pp. 99, 264-65; vol. iii, p. 290; Scharf, *op. cit.*, vol. ii, p. 48.

[2] Scharf, *op. cit.*, p. 46, wrote: " The old Province of Maryland rested on tobacco. It owed its existence to tobacco." *Cf.* pp. 46-52; also vol. i, p. 520.

[3] Jacobstein, *op. cit.*, pp. 20-22.

[4] *Tenth Census of the United States, Agriculture*, p. 922; *cf.* Scharf, *op. cit.*, vol. i, p. 520.

[5] According to Governor Sharpe the tobacco exports of 1748 and 1761 amounted to 28,000 hhds. each. *Archives of Maryland*, vol. xxxii, p. 23. Lord Sheffield, *op. cit.*, p. 93 and app. table VI, gives tables showing the exports of tobacco from all the colonies among which Maryland and Virginia were the chief contributors, as 85,000 hhds., valued at £906,637 ..18..1½, in 1770, and as 10,728,000 lbs. in 1775. The average in 1770-75 was variously stated at 85,000 to 100,000 hhds. per annum. *Cf.* also Pitkin, *Statistical View of the United States of America*, 1816, p. 108; Scharf, *op. cit.*, vol. ii, p. 200; Jacobstein, *op. cit.*, p. 33. Maryland apparently contributed about 30 per cent to 35 per cent of the whole product exported.

[6] *American Farmer*, vol. i, p. 99; *cf. 12 Niles Register*, p. 276.

hhds. in 1818, and the total crop to 27157 hhds. in 1820 and about 26000 hhds. in 1825.[1] In 1838, 1849 and 1859 the total product amounted to 24816, 21407 and 38411 thousands of pounds respectively. But this product was confined mainly to five counties of Southern Maryland in which 94.7 per cent of the crop of 1859 was produced.[2]

For the sake of the staple the provincials had established a laboring population of negro slaves. They dwarfed and neglected the production of cereals for which slave labor was less adapted than free labor.[3] By the middle of the eighteenth century, however, the feasibility of cereal crops had been demonstrated,[4] and an alternative provided for those who tired of raising tobacco. A line of cleavage then began to form between tobacco culture and slavery on the one side and other activities and free labor on the other. Notwithstanding the stagnant condition of the tobacco industry, however, slavery continued to grow, although the real progress made in the state was in the industries carried on mainly by free labor.[5] Exports other than tobacco which had amounted to about 10 to 12 per cent of the total exports of native produce in 1747, reached about 26 per cent in 1761, 54 per cent in 1791 and 63 per cent in 1823.[6] In 1849 the tobacco crop constituted 11 per cent

[1] Seybert, *Statistical Annals*, p. 84; *American Farmer*. On the size of the hogshead cf. 33 Cong. 1st Sess., H. Exec. Doc., no. 307, pt. 2, p. 238.

[2] *Eighth Census of United States, Agriculture*, p. 73; *Tenth Census, Agriculture*, p. 922.

[3] Scharf, *op. cit.*, vol. ii, p. 46; Jacobstein, *op. cit.*, pp. 30-31; *Easton Gazette*, Jan. 22, 1842.

[4] Scharf, *op. cit.*, vol. i, pp. 438-39, 520, quoting contemporary documents.

[5] Carey, *Letters on the Colonization Society*, 1832, p. 27; *Md. Pub. Documents*, 1843 M, pp. 44-45; 1852, L, pp. 3-5; *68 Niles Register*, p. 332.

[6] The percentages are given as approximations, based upon figures found in Scharf, *op. cit.*, vol. i, p. 520; MacMahon, *Historical View of the Government of Maryland*, vol. i, p. 316; *Archives of Maryland*, vol. xiv, p. 90; vol. xxxii, p. 23; Seybert, *op. cit.*, p. 84. Also certain numbers of the *American Farmer*.

and in 1859 14[1] per cent of the aggregate agricultural productions of the state. The five counties which produced 94.7 per cent of the tobacco crop of 1859 afforded only 18 per cent of the wheat and 17.5 per cent of the corn grown in the state. Moreover, slave labor contributed but little to the teeming industries of the four chief cities.

After the revolution other developments also tended to weaken the hold of the slave system. Improved facilities for making money payments favored free labor.[2] The growth of population increased the ratio of laborers to the number of places to be filled and relieved the stress upon the existing labor force.[3] Chains became less necessary for the security of labor once contracted for. White servitude went into decay. Moreover, the respective situations and relations of employers and employees influenced greatly the course of events. On the part of the former class the fortunes established in the province had made it possible to sacrifice, wholly or in part, the value of their negroes, if sacrifice was necessary in undertaking manumission.[4] But the extent of these sacrifices can be over-estimated, because they were in part offset. So long as the numbers and the efficiency of the laboring class remained unchanged, social interests were unimpaired by manumissions of slaves. Individual manumittors, however, were affected in a somewhat

---

[1] These estimates for 1849 and 1859 were furnished by F. W. Oldenberg, Extension Agronomist of the Maryland Agricultural College.

[2] *Cf.* Bullock, *Essays in the Monetary History of the United States*, ch. vi.

[3] This statement is based mainly upon a consideration of the general situation. But *cf. Harford Wills*, Lib. JLG, no. A, p. 276. Also *American Farmer*, vol. i, p. 99.

[4] On the wealth of the provincials *cf.* Scharf, *op. cit.*, vol. ii, pp. 13, 21, 45. Scharf wrote: " The makers of deeds surrendering their property, and often their means of subsistence, upon the grounds of conscience simply," *op. cit.*, p. 103.

different way.   When the negroes went free at their master's death, the effect was somewhat like that of an irre-
gularly applied inheritance tax.   When they were to serve
until, or beyond the age of twenty-five years, the value of
their services already rendered at the time of manumission went far towards reimbursing their owners for the
trouble and expense of their rearing.[1]   Again, the rural free
negroes generally engaged themselves to the landholders,
sometimes to their own manumittors,[2] to work under agreements which, apart from small nominal wages, placed them
in a position substantially like that of the slaves.[3]   In so far
as they did so, the grounds for keeping slaves rather than
manumitting them were nearly neutralized, excepting for
those owners who derived benefits from the wages of slaves
hired out to other employers.   Finally, manumission sometimes afforded the owner-employer a means of relief from
the burdens of maintaining aged and infirm slaves, from poll
and property taxes on negroes and from the other special
responsibilities attaching to owners of slaves.

Economic developments thus prepared the way for the
freeing of slaves.   But on account of the deterrents above-
mentioned some weight in determining the rate of manumissions must be ascribed to other impelling causes.   Such
causes were often alleged in the deeds and wills which pro-

[1] This was true irrespective of the manner of manumission.   In all
parts of the state it was possible to bind out negro children of tender
years for their keep until they reached the age of twenty-one years.
Cf. infra, chapter on Apprenticeship.

[2] *Cf. Cecil Land Records*, Lib. JS, no. 10, pp. 269, 310, 369; Lib. JS, no.
11, p. 221; Lib. JS, no. 12, pp. 22-23, 72, 386, 388; *Queen Anne's Land
Recs.*, Lib. STW, no. 4, p. 494; *Somerset Deeds*, Lib. K, pp. 116, 117,
118, 225; *Frederick Land Recs.*, Lib. WR, no. 10, p. 34.

[3] *Infra*, chapter on "Occupations and Wages," pp. 114-16; *cf. Somerest
Deeds*, Lib. K, pp. 117-18, statement that the general use of slaves had
nearly excluded from the labor market persons hiring themselves as
free laborers.

vided for the freedom of particular negroes. Although their character was varied, chief importance was given to the political and ethical views and wishes of the owners. The influence of these things was due chiefly to the political and religious movements that sprang up after the middle of the eighteenth century.

The white people of Maryland had been used to the slave labor system and had adjusted their political views to a program for its maintenance. They joined in the resistance to British policy after 1763 in order to contest the enforcement of obnoxious laws of the British empire,[1] not to reduce their own population elements to a political level. They involved themselves, however, in a formal sanctioning of the political ideas upon the basis of which their course was to be vindicated. Two ideas of especial note were much emphasized in manumitting negroes. The first was that of natural rights. Two deeds recorded in Talbot County in 1770-73, providing for the manumission of eight persons, asserted that negroes had an indisputable right in equity to enjoy freedom.[2] In December, 1782, a manumittor wrote: " Being conscious to myself that freedom and liberty is the inalienable right and privilege of every person born into the world, and that the practice of holding negroes in perpetual bondage and slavery is . . . . inconsistent with the strict rules of justice and equity "[3]. After that time

---

[1] Cf. Gambrall, History of Early Maryland, pp. 164-66; MacMahon, op. cit., vol. i, pp. 423-26; Scharf, op. cit., vol. ii, pp. 104-07, 116-17.

[2] Talbot Deeds, Lib. JL, no. 20, pp. 111, 332. A similar reason was assigned for the freeing of nine other negroes in the Dorchester Deeds, Lib. Old, no. 28, pp. 330, 408 (1781-82). Cf. also Caroline Deeds, Lib. WR, no. B, pp. 184, 197, 440; Somerset Deeds, Lib. H, pp. 30, 457, 487; Talbot Deeds, Lib. BS, no. 23, pp. 60, 61, 183. In the Md. Appeal Reports, 2 H. & McH., p. 228 is the following: " Black people are as much entitled to natural liberty as whites."

[3] Dorchester Deeds, Lib. NH, nos. 2-4, p. 120. The following also

such expressions became much more frequent, especially in the Eastern Shore Counties. The other idea, implied in, but less prominent than the first, was that oppression of the negro was an unwise policy, or according to some, subversive even of law and government.[1]   Moreover, slave-

contain expressions more or less like that quoted: *Anne Arundel Deeds,* Lib. NH, no. 1, p. 377; Lib. NH, no. 2, pp. 151, 213, 328, 393, 414, 471, 531; Lib. NH, no. 4, p. 148; Lib. NH, no. 8, p. 140; Lib. NH, no. 9, p. 142; *Anne Arundel Wills,* Lib. JG, no. 2, p. 220; *Baltimore Chattel Recs.,* Lib. B, no. G, p. 336; Lib. AL, no. A, p. 310; Lib. WG, no. 4, p. 132; Lib. WG, no. 2, p. 40; Lib. WG, no. 11, p. 74; *Caroline Deeds,* Lib. WR, no. B, p. 143; *Cecil Land Recs.,* Lib. 17, pp. 12, 44, 55; Lib. 18, p. 254; *Charles Co. Recs.,* Lib. Z, no. 3, p. 64; *Dorchester Deeds,* Lib. Old, no. 28, p. 330; Lib. NH, nos. 2-4, pp. 120, 281; Lib. NH, nos. 5-8, pp. 354, 355, 357; Lib. HD, no. 2, p. 723; Lib. NH, no. 14, p. 414; *Frederick Land Recs.,* Lib. WR, no. 33, p. 80; Lib. WR, no. 39, p. 57; *Harford Land Recs.,* Lib. JLG, no. C, p. 142; Lib. JLG, no. E, pp. 7, 369; Lib. JLG, no. F, p. 282; *Harford Wills,* AJ, no. 2, pp. 313, 319; *Montgomery Land Recs.,* Lib. D, p. 141; Lib. F, p. 107; *Queen Anne's Land Recs.,* Lib. CD, no. 1, p. 183; *Somerset Deeds,* Lib. G, pp. 520, 531; Lib. H, p. 457; Lib. 1, pp. 156, 673; *Talbot Deeds,* Lib. RS, no. 21, pp. 158, 438, 454; Lib. RS, no. 22, p. 77; Lib. 23, pp. 183, 291-98; Lib. 27, pp. 54, 60, 317, 372, 373; Lib. 46, p. 207; *Talbot Wills,* Lib. JB, no. 3, p. 24; Lib. JB, no. 4, pp. 3-4; *Worcester Deeds,* Lib. L, p. 65.

Certain of the instruments cited refer each to seven, nine, eleven, thirteen and twenty-three negroes as manumitted. Most of them refer to smaller numbers, as one to five each. Two more extracts from deeds ran as follows: From the *Harford Land Recs.,* Lib. JLG, no. E, p. 7 (August, 1782) : " Being conscious to myself that the holding of negroes in perpetual bondage and slavery is repugnant to the law of God and inconsistent with the strict rules of equity and that freedom and liberty is the unalienable right of every person born into the world." The deed freed seven negroes. From the *Anne Arundel Deeds,* Lib. NH, no. 2, p. 213 (Nov., 1784) William McCubbin, manumittor: " Being conscious to myself that the holding of negroes in perpetual slavery and bondage is inconsistent with the pure precepts of the gospel of Jesus Christ, repugnant to the rules of justice and equity and also that freedom and liberty is the right and privilege of every person born into the world."

[1] *Queen Anne's Land Recs.,* Lib. STW, no. 2, p. 85; *Caroline Deeds,* Lib. WR, no. C, p. 116. In the *Dorchester Deeds,* Lib. HD, no. 2, p. 723 (1790), occurred the sweeping declaration that it was " wrong and oppressive to hold negroes in abject slavery, when it is clearly against

holders, participating in the 'glorious revolution,' had helped to establish liberty for the oppressed. Should they themselves after the contest was over choke the fruits of liberty by still enslaving the abject African?[1]

Ethical ideas were indissolubly bound up with these political views. Their demands that slaves should be liberated were strongly impressed upon the slaveholders. Two religious bodies, the Quakers and Methodists, especially insisted upon the moral wrongfulness of slavery. The Quakers in their Yearly Meeting at Baltimore in 1760 took ground against the foreign slave trade.[2] They followed this with declarations against slavery itself, and in 1772 counseled their members to give freedom to their own negroes.[3] In 1776 they further voted that the quarterly meetings should provide books to record manumissions granted by their members,[4] and interested individuals labored to induce slaveholders to manumit. Although success was not instant, the

---

the principles of law and government, the dictates of reason, the common maxims of equality, the law of nature, the admonitions of conscience, and in short the whole doctrine of natural religion."

[1] A Caroline Co. deed, *Deeds*, Lib. WR, no. B, p. 41, providing for the freedom of ten negroes, referred to the unalienable rights of mankind "as well as every principle of the glorious Revolution that has lately taken place in America." *Cf.* also: *op. cit.*, Lib. WR, no. C, p. 116, 198, 201, 358; *Dorchester Deeds*, Lib. nos. 5-8, p. 354; Lib. HD, no. 2, pp. 546, 723; *Queen Anne's Land Recs.*, Lib. CD, no. 1, p. 183; Lib. STW, no. 2, pp. 85, 253; Lib. STW, no. 8, p. 472; *Somerset Deeds*, Lib. I, p. 156; *Talbot Deeds*, Lib. RS, no. 21, pp. 158, 438, 454; Lib. 26, p. 270. Daniel of St. Thomas Jenifer in manumitting was moved "by sentiments of Christian charity and Humanity, as well as by the spirit of the declaration of rights that all men are born free." *Anne Arundel Deeds*, Lib. NH, no. 5, p. 187. *Cf. op. cit.*, Lib. IB, no. 5, p. 268.

[1] *Extracts from the Minutes of the Baltimore Yearly Meeting*, pp. 359, 360.

[2] *Op. cit.*, pp. 359-60, 362.

[3] *Op. cit.*, p. 365. *The Harford Land Recs.*, Lib. HD, no. R, p. 275, contain a deed of manumission dated 1803, for a negro who had been freed in 1779, and the record thereof made in the Quaker records.

" testimony " against slavery led to manumissions in several counties.[1] The Yearly Meeting also supported the proposal to remove the restrictions on manumissions by will, and assisted in vindicating the rights of free negroes against kidnappers and in prosecuting claims of freedom.[2] Certain Quakers too were members of the early anti-slavery societies,[3] where their influence was generally a moderate one.

Methodism was established in Maryland in 1760 and its influence spread rapidly.[4] Its preachers had distinct advantages in having come at a time of great awakening and change, and in not being hampered either by a past like that of the established church,[5] or by present dependence upon livings provided by the state. From the outset they appealed for moral reformation, and soon began to preach to negroes as well as to whites. About the end of the revolution they began to attack the institution of slavery.[6] In

---

[1] *Extracts, op. cit.*, pp. 359, 360, 366. *Minutes of Monthly Meetings, Nottingham 1775-76* (no pagination) ; *Deer Creek 1801-19*, p. 351. *Cf. Asbury, Journal*, vol. i, p. 280; *Talbot Wills*, Lib. JB, no. 3, pp. 24, 60, 100; Lib. JB, no. 4, pp. 3-4, 22; *Talbot Deeds*, Lib. JL, no. 20, p. 481; *Baltimore Wills*, Lib. B, no. 4, p. 392. These several instruments providing for the freedom of sixty-six negroes were made by persons reputed to have been Quakers.

[2] *Extracts, op. cit.*, p. 366. *Minutes for Sufferings 1778-1841*, pp. 82, 86; *Minutes of the Monthly Meeting at Deer Creek*, p. 351.

[3] *H. Dels. Journal*, 1791, p. 83; *cf.* Scharf, *op. cit.*, vol. iii, p. 306.

[4] Scharf, *op. cit.*, vol. ii, pp. 554-55; *cf.* Bangs, *Life of Rev. Freeborn Garrettson*, pp. 20-21.

[5] Scharf, *op. cit.*, vol. ii, pp. 28-34.

[6] Rev. Freeborn Garrettson's conviction of the " impropriety of holding slaves " dated from 1775. He wrote: " My heart has bled, since that, for slaveholders, especially those who make a profession of religion; for I believe it to be a crying sin." Bangs, *op. cit.*, pp. 33-35. Of his own slaves he said: " I told them that they did not belong to me," and " that I did not desire their services without making them a compensation." The name of Freeborn Garrettson appears as manumitter in 1783 in *Harford Land Recs.*, Lib. JLG, no. E, p. 369, and *Anne Arundel Deeds*, Lib. NH, no. 9, p. 143. He freed three negroes by the two

1780 and 1783 their conferences, legislating for the churches of Maryland, warned local and traveling preachers, who were slaveholders, to promise freedom to their slaves, under penalty of suspension for refusal.[1] In 1784 the noted Christmas Conference at Baltimore resolved that slavery was "contrary to the Golden Law of God, on which hang all the law and the prophets, and the unalienable rights of mankind as well as every principle of the Revolution."[2] It adopted a set of drastic rules according to which slave-holding members of Methodist churches were required within twelve months to provide for the liberation of all their negroes within prescribed time limits. And members were forbidden to acquire and dispose of slaves excepting for the purpose of freeing them.[3] Those who declined to comply might withdraw from the communion, or otherwise suffer exclusion. The climax had been reached. The sensitive slave-owners at once resented the action, divided the Metho-

---

deeds. *Rev. Francis Asbury, Journal*, vol. i, p. 280, wrote on June 10, 1778 that some pious Quakers were "exerting themselves for the liberation of the slaves. This is a very laudable design; and what the Methodists must come to, or, I fear, the Lord will depart from them. But there is cause to presume that some are more intent on promoting the freedom of their bodies than the freedom of their souls."

[1] Matlack, *American Slavery and Methodism*, p. 14; *Anti-Slavery Struggle and Triumph in the Methodist Episcopal Church*, pp. 55-57. Both works quote extensively from the Minutes of the Conferences.

[2] *Sunday Service of the Methodists of North America*, 1784, p. 15; *cf.* Matlack, *op. cit.*, pp. 58-59. This formula was repeated in some deeds of manumission; *e. g. Dorchester Deeds*, Lib. NH, nos. 5-8, p. 354 (1786).

[3] *Sunday Service, op. cit.*, pp. 15-16. Slaves of 40 to 45 years were to be free within a year; those from 25 to 40 years within five years; those 20 to 25 years by the thirtieth, and those under twenty years by the twenty-fifth year of age respectively. Unborn infants were to be deemed free from the date of birth. *Cf.* Matlack, *op. cit.*; Stevens, *History of the Methodist Episcopal Church in the United States*, vol. ii, p. 200. The provision with regard to infants did not harmonize with later interpretations of the act of the legislature of 1752, ch. i, *infra*, p. 42.

dists in their attitude towards slavery, resisted the attempt to enforce the provisions, and within a few months forced practical nullification.[1] Heedless attempts to coerce slave-owners by conference action, in which the laity had no direct voice, were henceforth checked by regard for material and social interests. The general attitude of the church towards slavery, however, remained formally unaltered. Denunciation of slavery continued, and compliance with the tenor of the rules was urged by moral suasion.[2]   The Methodist contribution to the progress of manumissions was distinctive.[3]   Other less distinctive moral forces cooperated with these.   They united in inculcating the belief that the liberties of white Americans were not to be vindicated finally, so long as the black Americans were in chains.   As the awakening proceeded, the indefensibility of slavery on moral grounds appeared in clearer light.[4]   The effects of the new teachings were signal.   It is said that the treatment of slaves became more humane than it had been;[5] it

[1] Matlack, *op. cit.*, pp. 59-62; *American Slavery and Methodism*, p. 17. Also Stevens, *op. cit.*, p. 200, and Handy, *Scraps of African Methodist Episcopal History*, p. 23.

[2] Matlack, *Anti-Slavery Struggle and Triumph*, pp. 63-64.

[3] The following occurs in the will of a person who opposed the Methodist position: "As my son ——— is now of a religious profession (called Methodist) and it being common for their professors . . . to manumit their slaves," etc. *Baltimore Wills*, Lib. WB, no. 6, p. 173 (1794). *Cf. E. Shore General Court Judgments*, Lib. 71, pp. 481-82; *Md. Appeal Reports*, 2 H. & McH., pp. 199-201.

[4] Rev. Freeborn Garrettson, brought up in the established church in Baltimore County, had until 1775 "never suspected that the practice of slave-keeping as wrong; I had not read a book on the subject, nor been told so by any." Bangs, *op. cit.*, pp. 17-18; *cf.* also pp. 33-34. Rev. Francis Asbury wrote in 1780: "Spoke to some select friends about slave-keeping, but they could not bear it." Matlack, *American Slavery and Methodism*, p. 17.

[5] *15 Niles Register*, pp. 5-6, also vol. xxxi, p. 25; Seybert, *op. cit.*, pp. 52-53, and the will of Jeremiah Banning, *Talbot Wills*, Lib. JP, no. 5, p. 316.

is certain that generally speaking the intentions of manumitters were humane. In 1768 a resident of Baltimore
County freed a negro woman writing that he had bought
her sixteen years earlier and "soon after grew uneasy
thereat and would fain have returned the girl whence she
came." [1] Before the revolution was over his example was
followed by several others who desired to avoid being " inconsistent with the rules of Christianity," or with other
standards. [2] After the revolution such cases were multiplied, the papers ringing the changes on the inconsistencies

---

[1] The former master of this woman, "being overburdened with those
people refused to take her back as also did the girl to return." She
therefore remained with her new owner, "encumbered" his house with
her hybrid and black offspring, who rambled at night and on Sundays,
until they were often unfit for service at other times. All, however,
were manumitted. *Baltimore Chattel Recs.*, Lib. B, no. G, p. 213;
Harford Land Recs., Lib. JLG, no. A, p. 276 (1776). The latter deed
conferred freedom on the children of the woman.

[2] *Baltimore Chattel Recs.*, Lib. B, no. G, p. 208, a deed affecting nineteen negroes. Also p. 336; *Harford Land Recs.*, Lib. JLG, no. A, p. 8;
Lib. JLG, no. C, p. 444; Lib. JLG, no. D, p. 142; *Dorchester Deeds*, Lib.
Old, no. 22, pp. 254, 255, 308, 309, 356; *Talbot Deeds*, Lib. RS, no. 21,
p. 158. A singular state of agitation seemed to have taken a Harford
County slaveholder. Under the great stress of mind he manumitted
nineteen negroes in 1768 (*vide* first deed cited in this note), but refrained from manumitting others on account of "the many temporal disadvantages they labor under not being looked on or treated by man in
general with equal justice," *etc.* Further: " Yet clear I am the Lord is
risen and pleading their cause with the inhabitants of all the earth, before whom they will shortly appear and to whom they must give account of their stewardship and, oh, breaths (*sic*) my soul, may their
oppressors awake and be roused from their present dream of righteous-
ness and do unto them as they would be done unto that so their cryes
may no longer goe (*sic*) forth and reach the years (*sic*) of omnipotence
against them." *Harford Land Recs.*, Lib. JLG, no. F, p. 59 (1775).
The same name is connected, as co-manumitter, with the liberation
of nine other slaves in 1781. *Harford Land Recs.*, Lib. JLG, no. F,
p. 142; *cf. Anne Arundel Wills*, Lib. JG, no. 2, p. 220; *Somerset Deeds*,
Lib. K, pp. 117-18; also *E. Shore General Court Judgments*, Lib. 71,
pp. 481-82.

of the slaveholders who had revolted against the British oppression, and on their violation of the "precepts of natural religion," of the "Golden Law of God," of the gospel of Jesus Christ which teaches that we should do unto others as we would that they should do unto us, and of the principles of justice and mercy. The conscientious concern to give the negroes their freedom began also to bear fruit.[1]

Several minor causes also deserve mention. The hope of becoming free was gradually implanted in negro minds, and many slaves made successful efforts to redeem themselves, compensating their masters in ways that are to be set forth below.[2] But such compensations were a mere auxiliary factor, whose sole operation would have left the number of manumissions negligible. The inclination to manumit irrespective of monetary consideration was vital. Sometimes its existence was attributed to an appreciation of the merits of the beneficiaries themselves. For instance, in Harford County

[1] *Cf. Anne Arundel Deeds*, Lib. NH, no. 2, pp. 213, 328, 393, 414; Lib. NH, no. 5, pp. 187, 486, 500; Lib. NH, no. 8, p. 140; *Caroline Deeds*, Lib. WR, no. B, pp. 41, 143, 197, 198, 358; Lib. WR, no. C, pp. 116, 201; Lib. WR, no. D, pp. 347, 182; Lib. G, p. 368; *Cecil Land Recs.*, Lib. 17, pp. 12, 42, 44, 55; Lib. 18, pp. 254, 333; Lib. 19, p. 250; Lib. 25, pp. 16, 17; Lib. JS, no. 1, pp. 96, 97; *Charles Co. Recs.*, Lib. Z, no. 3, p. 64; *Dorchester Deeds*, Lib. Old, nos. 2-4, pp. 120, 281, 282, 354, 366, 425; Lib. NH, nos. 5-8, pp. 354, 355, 357; Lib. HD, no. 2, p. 723; Lib. HD, no. 3, p 35; Lib. HD, no. 14, p. 414; *Frederick Land Recs.*, Lib. WR, no. 29, p. 87; Lib. WR, no. 11, p. 57; *Harford Land Recs.*, Lib. JLG, no. D, p. 142; Lib. JLG, no. E, p. 7; Lib. JLG, no. F, p. 282; *Harford Wills*, Lib. AJ, no. 2, pp. 219, 237, 319; *Montgomery Land Recs.*, Lib. D, p. 141; Lib. G, p. 258; *Queen Anne's Land Recs.*, Lib. CD, no. 1, p. 183; Lib. STW, no. 2, pp. 85, 253; Lib. STW, no. 9, pp. 472, 527; *Somerset Deeds*, Lib. E, pp. 156, 673; Lib. G, p. 508; Lib. H, p. 457; Lib. I, p. 156; Lib. K, pp. 117-18; *Talbot Deeds*, Lib. RS, no. 21, pp. 220, 454; Lib. BS, no. 23, pp. 60, 602; Lib. 26, p. 270; Lib. 27, pp. 54, 60, 317, 372, 373; Lib. 46, p. 207; *Talbot Wills*, Lib. JB, no. 4, p. 3; *Worcester Deeds*, Lib. V, p. 416; also *Baltimore Chattel Recs.*, Lib. WG, no. 2, pp. 312, 250, 209, 207; Lib. WG, no. 3, pp. 28, 120, 203.

[2] *Infra*, pp. 74-76.

in 1778, goodwill, faithful services and " divers other good causes" led to the liberation of a female;[1] two deeds manumitting twenty-two negroes in Worcester in 1779-82 state that good behavior and the performance of faithful services were the warrant for their execution:[2] and in 1790 James Earle of Queen Anne's freed the wife and three children of his son's negro, whose services as a foreman had pleased him.[3] A circumstance that determined the action in some cases was the blood relationship, or consortship of negroes with their manumitters or with other whites. But apart from the avowals made by a few French West Indian refugees and by some other persons,[4] direct evidence of the action of this cause is not abundant. From the tenor of some documents it can be suspected rather than established.[5] It had relatively less influence than it had had in

[1] *Land Recs.*, Lib. ALJ, no. A, p. 148.

[2] *Deeds*, Lib. K, pp. 164, 405; *cf. op. cit.*, Lib. L, p. 392; Lib. M, pp. 35, 260, 404, 521.

[3] *Land Recs.*, Lib. STW, no. 1, p. 505; *cf. Anne Arundel Deeds, Lib.* NH, no. 5, pp. 467, 500; Lib. NH, no. 6, p. 63; *Baltimore Wills*, Lib. WB, no. 5, p. 170; *Caroline Wills*, Lib. JR, no. C, p. 474; *Cecil Land Recs.*, Lib. 16, pp. 11, 99; *Dorchester Deeds*, Lib. ER, no. 1, p. 118; *Frederick Land Recs.*, Lib. WR, no. 5, p. 52; *Harford Land Recs.*, Lib. AL, no. 1, p. 368; *Kent Chattel Recs.*, Lib. BC, no. 3, p. 455; *Montgomery Land Recs.*, Lib. D, p. 164; Lib. E, p. 632; *Somerset Deeds*, Lib. K, p. 423; *Worcester Deeds*, Lib. L, p. 392; Lib. O, p. 631; *Washington Land Recs.*, Lib. H, p. 644.

[4] *E. g. Anne Arundel Deeds*, Lib. NH, no. 6, p. 131; *Anne Arundel Wills*, Lib. JG, no. 2, p. 459; *Baltimore Chattel Recs.*, Lib. WG, no. 3, p. 336; Lib. WG, no. 5, p. 379; Lib. WG, no. 27, p. 92; Lib. ED, no. 10, p. 88; *Baltimore Wills*, Lib. WB, no. 11, p. 499; *Frederick Wills*, Lib. GME, no. 2, p. 669.

[5] The manumitter of five mulattoes in 1768 wrote: " I being induced to give the aforesaid molattos their freedom from sundry good and lawful motives ", *Baltimore Chattel Recs.*, Lib. B, no. G, p. 199. A mulatto woman and her children, freed in Anne Arundel County (*Deeds*, Lib. NH, no. 7, p. 84 (1796), were not to go near the city of

the provincial period.   Although the fact that 63.3 per cent
of all the mulattoes in the state in 1850 were freemen
argues that it was not without importance.[1]   But the effec-
tiveness of these minor factors depended upon the negroes'
enjoyment of the favor of their masters, and that of all the
causes depended much upon the state of the public mind,
to whose make-up they all contributed.   The practice of
manumitting slaves grew into a quasi-custom.   It was not
followed as a matter of course, because with some owners
necessity, cupidity, or conscientious doubts about its outcome prevailed against it.   The alternatives were retaining
the negroes as slaves until they died, or selling them to
the traders.   Stagnation of slave labor enterprises partly
discouraged the first, while a rising sentiment against selling
orderly negroes "out of the state"[2] tended to counteract
any recourse to the latter, even when prices were tempt-
ingly high.   Meanwhile the benevolence imputed to honest
manumitters made the imitation of their acts appear to be
an object worthy of emulation in spite of all the reasoning
and prejudice against it.

From causes we next turn to the forms of manumissions.
For more than a century after slavery had been introduced
into the province, so few negroes had been manumitted that

Annapolis.   For other cases, *cf. Baltimore Chattel Recs.*, Lib. WG, no.
10, p. 423; *Lib.* WG, no. 29, p. 377; *Lib.* WG, no. 31, p. 363; *Lib.* TK,
no. 57, p. 155; *Baltimore Wills*, Lib. WB, no. 4, p. 45; *Cecil Land Recs.*,
Lib. 16, p. 361; *Frederick Land Recs.*, Lib. WR, no. 28, p. 413; *Lib.*
WR, no. 30, p. 36.

[1] *Seventh Census of the United States, Mortality*, p. 35.

[2] *Cf. Baltimore Chattel Recs.*, Lib. WG, no. 27, p. 72; *Lib.* AWB, no.
75, p. 12; *Baltimore Wills*, Lib. IPC, no. 29, p. 196; *Caroline Wills*,
Lib. WGN, no. B, p. 47; *Cecil Land Recs.*, Lib. JS, no. 24, p. 196;
Frederick Land Recs., Lib. WR, no. 28, p. 413; *Frederick Wills*, Lib.
GH, no. 1, pp. 262, 374; *Harford Wills*, Lib. TSB, no. 6, p. 328; *Kent
Chattel Recs.*, Lib. JFG, no. 1, pp. 146, 215; *Md. Appeal Reports*,
2 H. & G., pp. 291-95; 6 Md. p., 499; *Md. Historical Mag.*, vol. vi,
pp. 26-28.

but little attention was paid to the manner in which they became free.[1]   The determination of this matter was, as Dr. Brackett observes, left to the slave-owners and the magistrates.[2]   Restrictions upon the former were at a minimum. As a consequence some slaves were allowed by their masters to enjoy a degree of freedom, without any formal change of status, and three formal methods of manumission, by word of mouth, by last will and testament and by deed, came into use.   Now this wide discretion of masters belonged to the old provincial era.   For as population grew and other interests advanced, there arose a demand for the regulation of the exercise of this liberty.   Although this demand was in part reactionary, it looked also to the protection of the public interests.   Its sponsors led the legislature in 1752 to hedge about the slave master's right to manumit with restrictions which with some modification were maintained throughout the later history of slavery in Maryland.

The practice of allowing slaves to go at large and act as free persons was obviously irregular.   The length of time for which it was permitted was limited by a statute of 1787 to ten days in the harvest season, the term being extended to twenty days in 1817.   Excepting the case of well-known pilots, any master's permission to go beyond that limit was to be penalized.[3]   Special provisions were added for four Eastern Shore counties in 1821-22.[4]   But notwithstanding

---

[1] A member of the Assembly reported in 1715 that manumissions were penalized and freed negroes not tolerated in the province of Virginia. He probably was opposed to manumissions in Maryland. *Archives of Maryland*, vol. xxx, p. 16.

[2] Brackett, *op. cit.*, p. 148.

[3] *Laws*, 1787, ch. xxxiii; 1817, ch. 104; cf. *61 Niles Register*, p. 216; *Senate Journal*, 1802, pp. 6, 30, 31; *H. Dels. Journal*, 1802, pp. 89, 96; 1817, p. 47.

[4] *Laws*, 1821, ch. 183; 1822, ch. 115.   In addition to these there were other provisions to prevent the fraudulent use of certificates of freedom by slaves.   *Op. cit.*, 1796, ch. 67, sec. 28; 1805, ch. 66; 1807, ch. 44.

the law, slaves here and there were allowed to hire themselves and collect their own wages outside the harvest time.[1]
Ordinarily their doing so did not affect their owner's rights
of resuming the suspended control at any time, because according to a decree of the appeal court in 1850 a mere abandonment of claim to a slave was not equivalent to a manumission.[2] But in the opinion in which this declaration occurred the court impliedly endorsed an earlier opinion sus-
taining a claim to freedom in a case in which no express
promise of freedom was alleged. The case concerned the
offspring of two women who had been undoubted slaves
in 1784. Subsequently they had lived and reared their
children within three miles of their former owner, had fre-
quented his house, worked for and received wages from
him and had transacted other business as free persons.
Their freedom had not been molested after 1797. The
owner died in 1805. His wife settled his estate and herself died in 1824. Both had known and acquiesced in the
facts recited, and no attempt had been made to prosecute
either of them for violating the law against allowing slaves
to act as free persons. Hence it was held that evidence to
show that they had violated the law was lacking, that the
two negro women had been freed, and that their offspring,
who had been claimed as slaves in 1832, were free persons.[3]

[1] *Baltimore Chattel Recs.*, Lib. WG, no. 1, p. 202 (1816) ; *Cecil Land
Recs.*, Lib. HHM, no. 7, p. 379 (1856) ; Lib. 16, p. 500 (1789) ; *Harford
Land Recs.*, Lib. JLG, no. K, p. 249 (1791) ; *Harford Wills*, Lib. AJ, no.
C, p. 86 (1803) ; *Worcester Deeds*, Lib. P, p. 15 ; *Dorchester Criminal
Appearance Docket*, Jan., 1859 ; *Carroll Criminal Docket*, no. 1, p. 54 ;
Laws, 1860, ch. 322 ; *Md. Gazette*, May 29, 1788 ; *Baltimore American,*
June 5, 1806 ; *E. Shore General Advertiser*, March 24, 1807.

[2] *Md. Appeal Reports*, 9 Gill, pp. 122-23, 135-36 ; cf. published the
recall of a slave's privilege to hire himself, *Md. Journal*, Aug. 3, 1787 ;
also *op. cit.*, Jan. 8, 1795.

[3] *Md. Appeal Reports*, 6 G. & J., pp. 138-44 (1834). It will be noted
that the freedom in this case had lasted thirty-five years without inter-

A belated statute of 1860 declared that in future deeds of freedom were not to be presumed by the courts in behalf of any negroes who had been acting as free persons without formal manumissions.[1]

Manumission differed from the above-mentioned practice in that at its maturity it at once raised the slave to the status of freeman. The forms of manumission have been mentioned above. The simplest one was the verbal order, or promise of freedom. Proof of such an unwritten promise became the ground upon which a mulatto girl was adjudged free in Charles County in 1698.[2] Although the frequency of its use is problematical, it seems to have been adopted as a means of turning out superannuated slaves to burden the community, until its use was prohibited by statute in 1752.[3] Thereafter its effect was substantially the same as that of allowing slaves to go at large without promise of freedom.[4] It secured a temporary freedom to a few negroes who were eventually enfranchised according to recognized forms.[5] And in 1851 the court of appeals sustained a petition for freedom that was based upon a verbal promise. The case was that of a negro child whose mother

ruption. In the case referred to in the last note above the court made much of the fact that the freedom had continued less than twenty years. But it found also that the master had only given a reluctant consent to allow the slave, a female, to live with her free husband, but no consent to deem herself a freed person.

[1] *Laws*, 1860, ch. 322.

[2] *Charles Co. Recs.*, Lib. X, p. 51; *cf.* similar case in *Somerset Co. Court Judgments*, 1722-24, p. 142.

[3] *Laws*, 1752, ch. i.

[4] *Cf. Md. Appeal Reports*, 9 G. & J., p. 136; also 2 H. & McH., p. 201; 6 G. & J., p. 197.

[5] In 1768 a deed manumitting nineteen negroes stated that some of their number had really been freed several years before. *Baltimore Chattel Recs.*, Lib. B, no. G, p. 208; *cf. Baltimore Wills*, Lib. WB, no. 6, p. 480; *Harford Wills*, Lib. AJ, no. C, p. 86.

had been repeatedly told by her master that she was free
and who had been allowed to live as a free woman from
1830 to 1849. The court adjudged the mother free from
the time she had begun to act as free and her child, born
after that time, as freeborn.[1]

Manumissions by written instruments also began in the
seventeenth century. Two wills in Somerset County, one
dated 1680 and the other 1697, each provided for the
freedom of a negro,[2] and in 1696 the Provincial Court
ordered a " mallatto . . . . discharged and set free from
all manner of slavery and servitude" on account of a provision in his master's will.[3] There followed a slow increase in manumissions by will in the first half of the eighteenth century,[4] and in 1752 " many evils " were attributed
to them. Hence a statute of that year enacted that it " shall
not be lawful for any person or persons, within this province, . . . by his, her or their last will and testament, or
by any other instrument in writing, in his, her or their last
sickness, whereof he, she or they shall die, to give or grant
freedom to any slave or slaves." [5] The obvious reason for
this clause was to prevent irrational acts of emancipation.
But at the same time it also restricted the right of disposal of

[1] *Md. Appeal Reports*, 9 Gill, pp. 483-87; *cf.* 8 G. & J., p. 159; 9 G. & J.,
p. 158.

[2] *Somerset Wills*, Lib. EB, no. 5, pp. 128, 137.

[3] *Provincial Court Judgments*, Lib. 5, p. 579; *cf. Charles Co. Recs.*,
Lib. E, no. 2, p. 152 (1712).

[4] *Cf. Md. Wills*, Lib. WD, no. 18, pp. 14, 235, 406 (1722-23) ; Lib.
CC, no. 2, pp. 2, 450, 708 (1725-29) ; Lib. CC, no. 3, pp. 126, 173, 250, 453,
482, 508 (1730-32) ; Lib. DD, no. 7, pp. 13, 18, 27, 50, 260, 358, 492, 520,
532 (1748-53).

[5] *Laws*, 1752, ch. i; *cf.* 1766, ch. i; 1786, ch. 35; 1789, ch. 61; also
Harford Wills, Lib. AJ, no. 2, p. 237. The "many evils" were apparently due to the turning adrift of superannuated and infirm slaves,
and to manumission in general, rather than to manumissions by will in
particular.

a particular sort of property,[1] and thereby supplied a partial check upon the rate of manumissions.   It did not prevent the making of many testamentary provisions for the liberation of negroes from slavery,[2] but it did afford a ground for depriving of liberty every person freed by will before that act was repealed.[3]   After the revolution the Quakers reported that many freed negroes were painfully apprehensive of being reduced to slavery again.   Their memorials initiated a movement which culminated in 1790 in the repeal of the prohibition of testamentary manumissions.[4]   The frequent exercise of this restored right contributed largely to the growth of the free negro population.   The following cases illustrate some of the conditions under which the privileges thus granted were realized.   In 1793 the General Court of the Eastern Shore awarded a year's wages and costs to a negro who had been detained in servitude a year in excess of the time his master's will had decreed he should

[1] *Cf. H. Dels. Journal*, 1790, p. 15.

[2] In Talbot County alone the wills recorded in Lib. JB, no. 3, pp. 19, 24, 60, 73, 82, 100, 154, 189, and Lib. JB, no. 4, pp. 3, 22, 41, 63, 65, 128, admitted to probate while the act was in force, provided for the freedom of negroes.

[3] *Cf. E. Shore General Court Judgments*, Lib. 71, pp. 481-87; *Md. Appeal Reports*, 2 H. & McH., pp. 199-201.

[4] *Laws*, 1790, ch. ix; 1796, ch. 67   On the activity of the Quakers *vide Minutes for Sufferings*, vol. A, pp. 39, 42, 47; *H. Dels. Journal*, 1790, pp. 11, 15, 17.   For details as to the repeal, *vide* Brackett, *op. cit.*, pp. 150-52.

Recurring to note 5, p. 57, above, it may be inquired why those who opposed the multiplication of free negroes permitted this repealing act to pass the legislature, when apparently they could have prevented it. It may have been thought, when the act of 1752 was passed, that self-interest would restrain owners from manumitting, excepting upon approach of death, and that for a time the increase of manumissions was checked by the law.   But after the revolution the manumissions by deed became so numerous that it was useless longer to maintain the ineffective prohibition against those by will.

serve.[1]   Again a will made in Prince George's in 1817, assigned several negroes as slaves to designated persons and freed all the other negroes owned by the testator. The executor attempted to make the freedom of a girl, who belonged to their number, dependent upon a deed executed by her own father, to whom he had sold her. The county court, and in its turn the Court of Appeals, held that the girl had been entitled both to freedom and to a devise of land under her deceased master's will.[2]   But in an instance in which it appeared that it had been left to the executors of a will to fix the time when the freedom of certain negroes was to begin, the higher court in 1846 remanded the case for an equity proceeding in the county court from which it had come.[3]   Manumission by will was again prohibited by statute in 1860.[4]

The last form of manumission was that by deed. It alone was fully recognized by law throughout the history of slavery in the state.[5]   It did not come into common use, until after the use of the other forms had been prohibited by statute in 1752.[6]   The act of 1752 required that each deed of manumission should be attested by the signatures of two witnesses, endorsed by a justice of the peace and recorded in the office of the clerk of the county court within

---

[1] *Judgments*, Lib. 80, pp. 500-05.

[2] *Md. Appeal Reports*, 5 H. & J., pp. 190-95.

[3] *Op. cit.*, 4 Gill, pp. 250-52; *cf.* also 5 H. & J., pp. 310-12; 9 Gill, p. 136.

[4] *Laws*, 1860, ch. 322.

[5] The act of 1860, ch. 322, occurred too late to form a worthy exception to this statement.

[6] Although the list is not given as exhaustive, the following were the principal deeds of manumission discovered by the writer in the counties up to 1753: *Cecil Land Recs.*, Lib. 4, p. 507 (1749); *Somerset Deeds*, Lib. CD, no. I, p. 416 (1709); Lib. GH, p. 311 (1717); Lib. B, p. 85 (1753); *Talbot Deeds*, Lib. RF, no. 9, p. 358 (1703); Lib. RF, no. 12, p. 173; Lib. JL, no. 17, p. 98 (1747).

six months of the date of execution. Furthermore, as was seen above, no such deed was to be valid, if granted during the last sickness of the slaveholder making it.[1] The Court of Appeals seems to have adhered closely to these rules.[2] The legislature, however, passed acts to relieve negroes who, without its intervention would have been barred from freedom on account of defective deeds. Two such acts validated all duly recorded deeds of manumission, if they were lacking only in respect to the signatures required by law,[3] and numerous others were passed to cover similar deficiencies in respect to witnesses and to time and place of recording in individual cases.[4] But the permanent restrictions upon the process were left unchanged.[5]

Aside from the matter of form the chief restrictions upon manumissions had to do with the ages and personal conditions of the manumitted and the financial condition of manumitters. The first provincial statute touching the sub-

---

[1] *Laws*, 1752, ch. i; *cf. Md. Appeal Reports*, 2 H. & McH., pp. 199, 201; also *Laws*, 1796, ch. 67.

[2] *Md. Appeal Reports*, 2 H. & J., pp. 151, 356-59; 5 H. & J., pp. 111-13; 7 G. & J., pp. 253-64.

[3] *Laws*, 1810, ch. xv; 1826, ch. 235. In both instances exception was made for cases which were, or had been, in litigation. *Cf. op. cit.*, 1832, ch. 296; 1833, ch. 284.

[4] *Op. cit.*, 1819, ch. 63; 1820, chs. 113, 115; 1823, ch. 170; 1824, chs. 39, 61, 78; 1826, ch. 208; 1827, ch. 48; 1828, ch. 58; 1830, ch. 60; 1834, chs. 95, 246, 255, 282; 1835, chs. 331, 360; 1836, ch. 194; 1838, ch. 100; 1839, ch. 277. Saving clauses occurred here again for the purpose of preventing conflicts with judicial decrees and with other legal provisions. In 1804 a manumitter in Frederick Co. executed a deed on account of the failure to record the first one made ten years previously. *Land Recs.*, Lib. WR, no. 24, p. 110.

[5] One deed that had been regularly made provided for a negro's freedom to begin in January, 1840. The fellow served in ignorance of the fact till May 12, 1846. The appeal court refused to award him damages for the period he had served beyond his proper freedom day. *Md. Appeal Reports*, 8 Gill, pp. 322-31; *cf.* 7 Md., p. 430.

ject recited that superannuated slaves had been set free by sundry persons to perish from want, or to become a burden upon the community.   Hence it forbade the liberation of any slaves, excepting those under fifty years of age, who were of sound minds, healthy constitutions and ability to labor for the necessaries of life.[1]   The age limits here pre-scribed were preserved in later legislation, saving that that for adults was reduced from fifty to forty-five years in 1796, and removed altogether between the years 1832 and 1858,[2] but in each instance the protective objects of the law were provided for by holding masters liable for the maintenance of their own freedmen, if dependent, unless the latter were otherwise eligible for manumission according to law. In cases of both old and young negroes the Court of Appeals adhered to the statute.   The following cases are in point: in St. Mary's County a will provided for the freedom of a female slave who was above the age of forty-five years and for vesting in her during life the title to her son as a slave, and also the title to some other property, thus attempting to secure to her an independent income.   The county court ad-judged her free, but its decree was reversed on appeal in 1815.[3]   The leading cases affecting children were those involving the issue of female slaves-for-terms-of-years, i. e., slaves who had to serve for fixed periods of time after the execution and before the maturity of the instruments effect-ing their manumission.   In old practice manumitters had

---

[1] *Laws*, 1752, ch. i; *cf.* also 1790, ch. ix.

[2] *Op. cit.*, 1796, ch. 67; 1831, ch. 281; 1858, ch. 307; *cf. Md. Appeal Reports*, 7 Md., p. 465.   In this case the court held that, while a slave of any age could be legally manumitted under the act of 1831, the master was not on that account free from liability for his maintenance, in case he became unable to support himself.

[3] *Md. Appeal Reports*, 4 H. & J., pp. 199-200; *cf.* 5 H. & J., pp. 191-95; 7 Md., p. 405.

sometimes claimed from such issue terms of service similar
to those of their mothers;[1] and in 1809 an act of the legislature empowered manumitters to fix their status, failing
which they were to be slaves.[2]   But to cases arising under
manumissions executed prior to this act the earlier law of
manumission applied.   Such a case was decided in the appeal court in 1823.   A will, made in 1801, had provided that
upon the death of a designated legatee several negroes were
to go free.   A child, born to one of these negroes before
her freedom, petitioned for freedom.   The court held that
he, as the issue, was a part of the use of his mother that had
been transferred by the will, and that at the commencement
of his mother's freedom he had been too young to work for
his own maintenance.   It said; " The policy and object of
the law is to prevent those, who by reason of their tender
years, or of decrepitude, old age, or fixed or permanent
disease, are unable to maintain themselves, from being cast
by emancipation, as a burden upon the community, or
thrown into a state of suffering and want."   The petitioner
was adjudged a slave.[3]   A later will provided for the free-

[1] *Anne Arundel Wills*, Lib. JG, no. 2, pp. 205, 351; *Baltimore Wills*,
Lib. WB, no. 6, pp. 153, 332; *Dorchester Deeds*, Lib. HD, no. 1, p. 348;
Frederick Land Recs., Lib. WR, no. 9, p. 14; Lib. WR, no. 25, p. 140;
Lib. JS, no. 2, pp. 8, 178; *Harford Land Recs.*, Lib. AJ, no. A, pp. 484,
486; Lib. JLG, no. C, p. 268; *Montgomery Wills*, Lib. B, p. 271; *Queen
Anne's Wills*, Lib. WHN, no. 3, pp. 120-21; *Somerset Deeds*, Lib. K,
p. 225; Lib. O, p. 196; *Talbot Deeds*, Lib. BS, no. 23, p. 7; *Talbot Wills*,
Lib. JB, no. 3, p. 60.

[2] *Laws*, 1809, ch. 171.

[3] *Md. Appeal Reports*, 6 H. & J., pp. 16-20; *cf. op. cit.*, p. 526; 5 H. & J.,
p. 431; 8 H. & J., pp. 32-35.   In the last case cited the court said that
" freedom was entirely dependent upon the 'issue's' ability to gain a
sufficient maintenance."   Of the will providing for the freedom it said:
" The intention is express to liberate the issue at its birth, but the
intention cannot be legally perfected, for at the moment of time, when
the freedom is to operate, the petitioner is incompetent to take it; that
is, she was unable to gain a sufficient maintenance."   And her having

dom of both a woman and "her increase" at the age of thirty-six years. The court held that both she herself and every child born to her, before she became free, were to serve as slaves, until each arrived at the age of thirty-six years.[1]

The manumissions thus either took effect at once, or provided for freedom to begin in future. A few, especially in the wills, made the date of maturity dependent upon the death of designated legatees.[2] More often the future date was fixed and the present ages of the negroes were stated. And here some owners took advantage of the latitude allowed them by law. Endeavors were made on the one hand to manumit early enough to allow the freedmen an equal start in life with the freeborn and on the other to make sure of long service before the release took place. The ages usually varied from a minimum of sixteen years to eighteen years for females to a maximum for both sexes at the legal limit, the females being freed at from three to seven years younger than the males.[3] Accordingly there was

acted as free for about ten years meanwhile was of no avail in her behalf.

At least one attempt was made to claim the future issue of a negress, whose freedom was to begin from the date of grant. *Anne Arundel Wills*, Lib. TG, no. 1, p. 52 (1781). It is doubtful that such a claim could have been sustained. *Cf. Md. Appeal Reports*, 14 Md., pp. 115, 118.

[1] *Md. Appeal Reports*, 2 Md., p. 88; *cf. Baltimore Wills*, Lib. WB, no. 6, p. 375.

[2] *Md. Appeal Reports*, 6 H. & J., pp. 16, 20; also *Wills* of: *Anne Arundel*, Lib. JG, no. 1, pp. 321, 329, 344; *Baltimore*, Lib. WB, no. 5, p. 145; Lib. WB, no. 6, pp. 36, 101; *Cecil*, Lib. 10, p. 274; *Frederick*, Lib. GM, no. 3, p. 464; *Kent*, Lib. 6, p. 110; *Queen Anne's*, Lib. TW, no. 1, p. 182. In one case in *Montgomery Wills*, Lib. B, p. 539, the freedom depended upon the future marriage of the widow of the testator. *Cf.* also *Frederick Wills*, Lib. GM, no. 3, p. 578.

[3] The following refer to examples of minimum ages: *Anne Arundel Deeds*, Lib. NH, no. 3, p. 439; *Baltimore Wills*, Lib. WB, no. 4, p. 395;

no ground for legal interference with the results in most cases. Nevertheless, there is reason to believe that this part of the law of manumission was constantly evaded. The decrees of the courts, to be sure, determined what could be done under the law; however, they really regulated only the adjudicated cases, and others in which either the masters, or both parties, determined to follow the rules. Whereas, if both were determined not to follow the rules, the conditions, in the counties at any rate, were such that they might generally have their way. And in view of the arrangements made by benevolent masters for old negroes before the act of 1831, as well as afterwards,[1] of the com-

Harford Land Recs., Lib. AL, no. A, pp. 8, 9; Talbot Wills, Lib. JB, no. 3, pp. 46-47; Somerset Deeds, Lib. G, p. 359. The following refer to high ages of the manumitted: Anne Arundel Wills, Lib. JG, no. 1, 484; Lib. JG, no. 2, p. 86; Baltimore Wills, Lib. WB, no. 5, pp. 30, 493; Lib. B, no. 6, p. 375; Cecil Wills, Lib. 3, p. 153; Lib. BB, no. 4, p. 32; Cecil Land Recs., Lib. 18, p. 242; Frederick Land Recs., Lib. WR, no. 10, p. 84; Lib. WR, no. 18, p. 187; Harford Land Recs., Lib. JLG, no. A, p. 340; Queen Anne's Land Recs., Lib. RT, no. K, p. 453; Lib. RT, no. L, p. 181; Somerset Deeds, Lib. L, p. 216; Worcester Deeds, Lib. N, p. 347.
The following compare ages of males and females, the ages of males preceding in each instance: 21 and 16; Anne Arundel Deeds, Lib. NH, no. 3, p. 439; Somerset Deeds, Lib. G, p. 359. 21 and 18; Harford Land Recs., Lib. JLG, no. F, p. 59; Kent Wills, Lib. 6, p. 166; Montgomery Land Recs., Lib. A, pp. 67, 453, 601; Talbot Deeds, Lib. BS, no. 23, p. 7. 25 and 21; Anne Arundel Deeds, Lib. IB, no. 5, p. 537; Anne Arundel Wills, Lib. JG, no. 1, p. 530. 30 and 25; Anne Arundel Wills, loc. cit., p. 623; Lib. JG, no. 2, p. 68; Baltimore Chattel Recs., Lib. AL, no. A, p. 310; Montgomery Wills, Lib. D, p. 537. 31 and 21; Dorchester Deeds, Lib. HD, no. 2, p. 61. 28 and 25; Baltimore Wills, Lib. WB, no. 5, p. 30. 45 and 35; Cecil Wills, Lib. 4, p. 154; cf. also Baltimore Wills, Lib. WB, no. 4, pp. 404, 543; Dorchester Deeds, Lib. HD, no. 1, p. 348.

[1] E. g., Anne Arundel Deeds, Lib. NH, no. 5, p. 100; Lib. NH, no. 8, p. 455; Lib. IB, no. 1, p. 474; Baltimore Chattel Recs., Lib. WG, no. 1, p. 72; Lib. WG, no. 9, p. 92; Lib. TK, no. 70, p. 200; Lib. ED, no. 10, p. 88; Baltimore Wills, Lib. WB, no. 4, pp. 304-05, 473, 493; Frederick

plaints about turning old negroes adrift, of provisions for the manumission of young children,[1] for giving and selling children to their parents,[2] and of the tolerant attitude of the people towards orderly slaves who acted as free-men without burdening the public for support, there must have been a considerable number both of those too young, and those too old, for manumission who enjoyed many of the essentials of freedom.

Finally there were the restrictions imposed in behalf of the creditors of manumitters. A statute of 1787 had made the real estate and personalty of deceased debtors equally liable for the payment of their debts.[3] The act of manumission of a debtor concerned his creditors, because it involved a transfer of property. The rights of creditors existed independently of the act and suffered no

Wills, Lib. GM, no. 3, p. 362; *Harford Land Recs.*, Lib. JLG, no. P, p. 92; *Montgomery Land Recs.*, Lib. D, p. 637; Lib. E, pp. 117, 657. In the act of 1827, ch. 158, the legislature validated a deed of manu-mission made in behalf of a negress who had passed the age of forty-five years, but provided that the master should bond himself to support her in case of need.

[1] *Anne Arundel Deeds*, Lib. NH, no. 3, p. 52; *Anne Arundel Wills*, Lib. BEG, no. 1, p. 184; *Baltimore Chattel Recs.*, Lib. B, no. G, p. 199; Lib. AL, no. A, p. 320; Lib. WG, no. 10, p. 66; *Baltimore Wills*, Lib. WB, no. 5, p. 170; *Cecil Land Recs.*, Lib. 16, p. 361; *Frederick Land Recs.*, Lib. WR, no. 14, p. 158; Lib. WR, no. 28, p. 186; Lib. WR, no. 39, p. 63; Lib. WR, no. 45, p. 287; Lib. JS, no. 11, p. 395; Lib. JS, no. 21, p. 564; Lib. BGF, no. 1, p. 686; *Montgomery Land Recs.*, Lib. D, p. 539; *Kent Chattel Recs.*, Lib. TW, no. 1, pp. 7, 134; *Somerset Deeds*, Lib. H, p. 507; *cf. Laws*, 1826, ch. 236. A statute of 1858 prohibited the manumission of children under the age of ten years. *Laws*, 1858, ch. 307.

[2] *Anne Arundel Deeds*, Lib. NH, no. 2, p. 649; Lib. NH, no. 9, pp. 55, 73, 664; Lib. NH, no. 11, pp. 363, 500; Lib. NH, no. 6, p. 161; Lib. 16, p. 106; Lib. WSG, no. 1, p. 42; *Kent Chattel Recs.*, Lib. TW, no. 1, pp. 42, 203, 233, 264, 282, 362, 377; Lib. TW, no. 2, pp. 92, 172, 190, 262, 396, 413, 414, 457, 471.

[3] *Laws*, 1785, ch. 72; *cf. Md. Appeal Reports*, 6 Gill, p. 299. Also Bradford, *Laws of Maryland*, p. 155-58, act of April 26, 1715 (D).

diminution because of it. Therefore the validity of the act was conditioned upon the previous satisfaction of those rights. For this reason the restoration of the right to manumit slaves by will in 1790 was made upon condition that no such manumission was to be "effectual to give freedom to any slave or slaves, if the same shall be in prejudice of creditors." [1] Now the incipient rights of manumitted persons were derived from the acts of manumission executed on their behalf. If the acts were valid, the rights were established, but if voided, they were extinguished. The situation gave rise to a conflict in which the attempt to maintain property rights was repeatedly attacked in the name of human liberty. The courts affected no favor for either side.[2] To them the slaves were "both by the letter and policy of the law, property, and subject to the same rules of law as other personal property, unless in cases where discriminations have been made by the statutes of the state." [3] Their chief problems were, as cases arose, to declare the rights of the parties in interest; to show creditors whether, when and how they were to attach, or exempt, manumitted slaves in satisfying their claims; and to point out to petitioners for freedom the means of ascertaining whether the available assets of estates, excluding manumitted negroes, were adequate to pay the debts of their departed owners. In adjudicating petitions for freedom the appeal court evolved an interesting body of rules for the relief of both creditors and petitioners in applying the

[1] *Laws*, 1790, ch. ix; 1796, ch. 67.

[2] In 1849 the Court of Appeals, quoting the statutes of 1752, ch. i, and 1796, ch. 67, said that the design of the laws authorizing manumission had been to gratify slave-owners by enlarging their privileges in the disposal of their property. And that it was not the policy of the state to encourage these things, nor to attempt to destroy slavery. *Reports,* 8 Gill, p. 219 (319).

[3] *Ibid.*, 6 Gill, pp. 388-91.

principles here stated. We first give attention to the side
of creditors.

A will in Somerset County provided for the freedom of
a negro at the age of twenty-eight years. The widow of
the deceased renounced the will and claimed her third of
the estate. The orphans' court permitted her to take the
negro as a slave for life, on the ground that after paying
her husband's debts, the residue of the estate, exclusive of
the negro, was insufficient to afford her her dower. At the
end of the term designated in the will the negro petitioned
for freedom, but was denied it both in the county court and
in the Court of Appeals.[1] A testator in Kent County attempted to manumit his twelve negroes. He ordered that
his personal estate should be first applied in the discharge
of his debts, and thereafter so much of his real estate as
should be necessary for the purpose, "so as to leave my
negroes free as before stated." But the personal estate, even
including the negroes, was not sufficient to satisfy the valid
claims. The negroes, being detained as slaves, sued for
freedom. But since at the time of trial the value of the
real estate had not been duly ascertained, it was not known
whether even the whole estate would satisfy the creditors.
Hence the petition was denied and the judgment affirmed
on appeal.[2] In the next leading case it appeared that the
petitioner had been at liberty under a deed of manumission
for about six years, when he was included as a slave in the
inventory of his master's estate. The appeal court here
stated that in satisfying their claims the creditors must first
exhaust the personal estate, but that in case the latter pro-

[1] *Op. cit.*, 5 H. & J., pp. 59-60.

[2] The three judges in the higher court gave different opinions as to
the grounds of the decree, but all substantially agreed that a testator
could not compel his creditors to look for payment of their claims to
any particular fund, or portion, of the estate specified by himself.
Op. cit., 2 H. & G., pp. 1-8 (1827).

ved inadequate for the purpose, they could resort to the real estate also. A deed of manumission was not " operative, and available, if made to the prejudice of the creditors." But creditors had to prove their own cause. For that purpose they had a remedy in an equity proceeding, which could assemble all the assets of the estate, real and personal, of the deceased, determine whether or not their value, exclusive of the manumitted slaves, was adequate to satisfy their demands, and if not, decree the sale of the slaves for terms of years, or for life, to make up the deficit. That was a sufficient remedy to protect their interests.[1] Reiterating much of the foregoing in 1848 the court added that a testator's exemption of any part of his estate from liability for use for debt payment could not bar a creditor's suit against his executor, and that in chancery an executor's testimony as to the sufficiency of real estate to satisfy debts would not be effective to secure such exemption. Furthermore, negroes manumitted by will were to be entered at full value in the inventory of an estate returned by an executor. Their liability to be appropriated for debt payment was not at an end, until upon full warning creditors had filed their claims, and the executor by settlement of his accounts had satisfied the orphans' court that the other assets of the estate were sufficient to pay the debts. If the orphans' court found it necessary to sell them, their terms of service were to be limited only by the requirements of the debts of their master.[2]

[1] *Op. cit.*, 7 G & J., pp. 96-108; *cf.* 6 Gill, p. 299; also 12 Md., pp. 274-80, in which a similar proceeding was finally declared in 1858 for negroes in behalf of freedom petitions. On the onus of proof, *vide* 17 Md., pp. 92-104 (1861).

[2] *Op. cit.*, 6 Gill, p. 299 (1848). In 1844 the legislature passed an act imposing a tax of two and a half per cent on every hundred dollars worth of property passing to legatees. A Howard County manumitter objected to paying the tax on his manumitted slaves. *Howard*

On the side of petitioners for freedom the evolution of rules was striking. At the outset the court declined to allow any preference of real estate to manumitted slaves for settling vested claims against estates.[1] In the second case cited, however, it was hinted that, if the value of the real estate had been duly ascertained before the trial, it might have been first exhausted in favor of liberating the negroes.[2] The judges expressed commiseration for the hardships resulting to the petitioners but pointed out no way to discover the final merits of the case. In the next case which came up, however, (1835) it was held that the act of manumission was "operative and effectual to give freedom to the slave, unless the rights of creditors are injured by it," and that in the act of 1796 the legislature had intended neither

to make it incumbent on the slave to prove, as a condition precedent to effective manumission, that the residue of his master's property was sufficient for the payment of his debts, . . . nor to suspend the operation of such grant of freedom, until it had been ascertained . . . that it would not operate to the prejudice of creditors.

Further that the law charges the whole of the

Orphans' Court Minutes, Lib. WG, no. 1, pp. 352-61. The case was carried to the Court of Appeals, where the bequest was deemed a taxable legacy in the meaning of the taxing statute. Reports, 6 Gill, pp. 388-91 (1848).

In one will in Frederick County, Lib. GH, no. 1, p. 194, provision was made for the payment of the collateral tax out of the estate to which the manumitted negro had belonged.

[1] Md. Appeal Reports, 5 H. & J., pp. 58-60 (1820).

[2] Op. cit., 2 H. & G., pp. 1-8. The ground chosen by the court was apparently the only safe one on account of the unknown factor, the value of the real estate. In a later case, reported in 6 Gill, pp. 299-342, it was said that in a freedom trial in a court of law evidence as to the value of real estate could not be legally submitted to a jury or form a subject for its determination.

manumitter's property with the payment of his debts, in favor of his manumitted slaves, because the act of manumission is to be effectual, if not done in prejudice of creditors; which plainly and necessarily implies that the residue of his property is to be appropriated to the payment of his debts, before the manumitted slaves can be made liable therefor.

Two years later a petitioner, who in an earlier appeal had been declared a slave, was sustained on the ground that the accruals of assets to the estate after the manumitter's death had made it possible to satisfy the creditors without avoiding the bequest of freedom.[2]   And in 1848 the court held that, if a freedom suit was barred because the value of the real estate of the manumittor had not been ascertained, equity would suspend the proceedings at law, which had prevented doing justice, would decree the sale of the real estate charged with the payment of debts and apply the proceeds to their satisfaction.   After the debts had been paid, the manumitted slaves could prosecute their claims to freedom.[3]   In the same year the chancellor held that in a pro-

[1] *Op. cit.*, 7 G. & J., pp. 96-108; *cf.* 1 Md. Chancery, p. 296.   It would appear that the ruling here as to the suspension of the grant of freedom, until the creditors' interests had been secured, was reversed in the case reported in 6 Gill, p. 299 (1848).   *Cf.* last cited case in preceding paragraph.

[2] *Op. cit.*, 9 G. & J., pp. 158-64.   The court said here that the claim urged against the petitioner that her freedom "must depend upon the sufficiency of the personal assets of the deceased at the moment of her death to pay all her debts, has nothing in reason or law to support it." Conversely, if the assets of the estate, even though at first adequate, had through no fault of the administrator subsequently become inadequate for the payment of the debts, the right of freedom would no longer have existed.   For the first appeal, *cf.* 8 G. & J., pp. 160-66.

[3] *Op. cit.*, 6 Gill, p. 299.   The opinion in this case contained criticisms of an opinion by the United States Supreme Court interpreting the Maryland act of 1796, ch. 67, as bearing on this point.   In 1858 the court said that the manumitted slaves had a right in equity to discover the condition of, and their own relation to, the estates of their masters. 12 Md., pp. 274-80.   This decision was based upon that of 1848 just referred to.

ceeding to determine the "invalidity" of a deed of manumission, as in prejudice of creditors, the "negro manumitted is entitled to the assistance of the heir at law, or the
person holding the real esate, in taking account of the
amount thereof, before the insolvency of the deceased manumitter can be legally ascertained." Furthermore, an act
of manumission "though in prejudice of creditors is valid
against the manumitter himself and his legal representatives,
and the negroes manumitted are not assets for the payment
of debts."[1] Investigations of these matters could only
cause short delays to parties in interest, and would guarantee the preservation of the "rights of a helpless class, if
any rights they have."[2]

In addition to the restrictions thus imposed by law, manumitters themselves sometimes laid down conditions, compliance with which they purposed to regard as necessary to
the freedom of their negroes. Fulfillment was to be sometimes before, sometimes after, the beginning of freedom.
The former involved chiefly continued fidelity in service,
abstention from running away, losing time and other misconduct, until the time of final release.[3] Provisions of this

---

[1] 1 Md. Chancery, pp. 296-306; *cf. Appeal Reports*, 7 G. & J., pp. 96-108.

[2] *Op. cit.*, 12 Md., pp. 274-80 (1858). The allusion here to the great
question of contemporary law and politics, upon which a federal judge
from Maryland had then recently given an opinion, will not pass un-
noticed.

[3] *Anne Arundel Wills*, Lib. JG, no. 2, p. 163; *Baltimore Chattel Recs.*,
WG, no. 3, p. 405; *Baltimore Wills*, Lib. WB, no. 6, pp. 416, 512; *Caro-
line Land Recs.*, Lib. H, p. 159; *Caroline Wills*, Lib. WAF, no. A, p.
141; *Cecil Wills*, Lib. 9, p. 293; *Dorchester Wills*, Lib. LLK, no. 1, p. 1;
Frederick Wills, Lib. GM, no. 3, p. 150; *Harford Land Recs.*, Lib. JLG,
no. A, p. 276; *Harford Wills*, Lib. AJ, no. 3, p. 466; *Montgomery Land
Recs.*, Lib. H, p. 481; Lib. O, p. 410; *Queen Anne's Land Recs.*, Lib.
RT, no. L, p. 181; *Queen Anne's Wills*, Lib. SC, no. 7, p. 276; *Somerset
Deeds*, Lib. K, p. 116; *Talbot Deeds*, Lib. RS, no. 21, p. 220; *Talbot
Wills*, Lib. JP, no. 9, p. 268; *Worcester Deeds*, Lib. U, p. 245.

kind were authorized by statutes of 1715 and 1833, the latter of which enacted that extensions of service might be made in order to penalize absconding slaves-for-terms-of-years;[1] and they were apparently upheld by the courts.[2]

The conditions to be fulfilled after freedom began were of two kinds chiefly. Certain of them required service or money payments to the manumitters' estates, or to designated beneficiaries thereof.[3] A few others, made in aid of the attempts to effect the expatriation of the Maryland negroes, forbade those whom they liberated to reside in the state as freemen.[4] Now the appeal court held that, if the

[1] Laws, 1715, ch. xliv; 1833, ch. 224.

[2] Cf. Md., Appeal Reports, 6 G. & J., pp. 292-98; 1 Gill, pp. 395-403; 13 Md., p. 181; 7 Gill, pp. 213-16; Baltimore Orphans' Court Minutes, Lib. 25, pp. 305, 320; Lib. 26, pp. 67, 150; Lib. 27, pp. 142, 402; Lib. 28, pp. 1, 424; Lib. 29, pp. 78, 112, 161; Lib. 30, pp. 181, 429; Baltimore Co. Orphans' Court Mins., Lib. JLR, no. 1, pp. 115, 189, 157, 274, 279, 316, 413, 437; Harford Orphans' Court General Entries, Lib. BHH, pp. 155, 158, 159, 201, 202, 269; Howard Orphans' Court Mins., Lib. WG, no. 1, pp. 272, 339, 342, 347, 363, 383, 404; Lib. TJ, no. 2, pp. 22, 58, 59, 67, 104, 136, 145, 199, 213, 295.

In 1858 the appeal court said that the master might make the freedom of a negro dependent on "a contingent event. If the event does not happen the negro remains a slave." Reports, 14 Md., pp. 115-18; cf. op. cit., pp. 118-121; also 17 Md., pp. 413-19 (1861).

[3] Anne Arundel Deeds, Lib. NH, no. 4, p. 269; Baltimore Wills, Lib. DMP, no. 14, p. 212; Cecil Wills, Lib. 6, p. 76; Dorchester Deeds, Lib. ER, no. 4, p. 358; Dorchester Wills, Lib. THH, no. 1, pp. 197, 363; Harford Wills, Lib. AJ, no. C, p. 12; Talbot Wills, Lib. JP, no. 9, p. 54; Worcester Wills, Lib. TT, no. 8, p. 58; cf. Anne Arundel Wills, Lib. JG, no. 1, p. 47; Frederick Wills, Lib. GH, no. 1, p. 311; also infra, chapter on "Property of Negroes," pp. 136, 138.

[4] Baltimore Chattel Recs., Lib. TK, no. 70, p. 200; Lib. TK, no. 55, p. 307; Baltimore Wills, Lib. DMP, no. 16, p. 503; Lib. DMP, no. 17, p. 479; Lib. DMP, no. 19, p. 448; Lib. DMP, no. 21, p. 177. On the expatriation policy, cf. Laws, 1831, ch. 281, and chapter on "Colonization," infra.

A peculiar condition recorded in the Anne Arundel Deeds, Lib. NH, no. 8, p. 84, was that a mulatto woman and her child were not to go near the City of Annapolis.

freedom depended upon a contingent event, it could not be realized so long as the event had not occurred.[1] But in a case in which a will had warned a manumitted negro that he would be liable to re-enslavement, if found inside of Maryland after the lapse of thirty days from the beginning of his freedom, it was held that the power of a testator to control his negro ceased, when the act of manumission took effect, and that the " conditions subsequent " of the bequest were not enforceable. The manumitter had no power to restore the state of slavery, when once it had been ended.[2]

Manumitted slaves also enjoyed protection against detention beyond the terms they were entitled to serve.[3] An act of the legislature in 1783 extended this protection to cases of slaves-for-terms-of-years brought to Maryland from other states:[4] in 1790 the abduction of any such persons for sale or other purposes was prohibited under heavy penalty;[5] in 1810 selling them for terms longer than their legal servitude, and in 1817 selling them to agents of non-residents, was prohibited, and special formalities were required for the transfer of all negroes who were to be re-

[1] *14 Md. Appeal Reports*, pp. 115-18.

[2] *Op. cit.*, 8 Gill, pp. 315-21 (1849) ; *cf.* 3 Md., pp. 119-27; 12 Md., pp. 274-80; 14 Md., pp. 109-16. This principle was enacted into a statute in the act of 1858, ch. 307; *cf. H. Dels. Journal*, 1854, pp. 196, 604, 605.

[3] The following refer to cases in which damages were given to negroes on account of too long detention: *Provincial Court Judgments*, Lib. 13, pp. 615-18 (1712) ; Lib. 35, pp. 347-49, 350-56; *General Court Judgments, E. Shore*, Lib. 74, p. 225 (1787) ; Lib. 80, pp. 500-05 (1793) ; Lib. 82, pp. 321, 448-53 (1793) ; *W. Shore*, Lib. 67, pp. 487-90 (1781) ; *Somerset Co. Court Judgments*, 1774-75, pp. 214-15; 1798-99, p. 572; 1804-05, pp. 348-50.

[4] *Laws*, 1783, ch. xxiii; *cf.* also 1796, ch. 67, in which a fine of $800 was provided for violators of this clause.

[5] *Op. cit.*, 1790, ch. ix. The fine of $800 was superseded by sentence to the penitentiary by the act of 1809, ch. 138.

moved outside of Maryland.[1] Finally in 1858 negroes
serving on account of conviction of crime were likewise
given partial protection.[2]   In the case of a manumitted girl
who had been sold to a resident of Virginia the legislature
passed a special act to require the purchaser to secure a
resident of Maryland as his bondsman to guarantee her
release at the end of her legal term.[3]   More than a decade
later there arose two cases of negroes both of whom had
continued to serve beyond the time set for their freedom to
commence.   The first one became aware of his title to freedom about six years after it should have become effective.
The other was detained by his master, who acting in good
faith had deemed him a slave.   Both alike were freed, but
were denied compensation for their excess of service.[4]

It was stated above that the manumission of negroes in
Maryland was encompassed chiefly by the whites.   Accordingly the majority of manumissions were ostensibly
gratuitous.   Even when the freedom resulted from the combined efforts of slaves and their masters,[5] the instrumentality
of the latter often predominated.   Nevertheless the negroes
contributed towards securing their own freedom, first by
self-redemption, and secondly, by manumitting other negroes

---

[1] *Op. cit.*, 1810, ch. xv; 1817, ch. 112; *cf. Baltimore Chattel Recs.*,
Lib. WG, no. 27, p. 72. In a late case the appeal court decided that
no new act of manumission was necessary to secure the freedom of a
slave-for-term-of years who was sold. *Reports*, 8 Md., p. 386.

[2] *Laws*, 1858, ch. 324.

[3] *Op. cit.*, 1840, ch. 111. In another case the buyer of a female slave
contracted not to remove her from the state of Maryland. He, however, sold her to a third party with permission to carry her to another
state. The Court of Appeals decided that the second sale was fraudulent, and that the first seller had a right to damages against the second.
Reports, 2 H. & G., pp. 291-95.

[4] *Op. cit.*, 8 Gill, pp. 322-31; 7 Md., p. 430.

[5] *E. g., Kent Chattel Recs.*, Lib. TW, no. 2, pp. 396, 413.

that had come into their possession as property. In many instances money payments were mentioned as partial, or total, consideration for the execution of deeds of manumission. Some of them were obviously intended to cover only the cost of record,[1] and many that were larger than these were still merely nominal. From this they ranged up to sums equal to the market prices of slaves for life.[2] Sometimes the receipt of the money was mentioned in the instruments.[3] But generally the negroes had only their hire with which to redeem themselves, and several expedients were employed in order to enable them to meet the obligations incurred. Some were allowed to give word or bond to pay the sums agreed upon, and to labor as freemen financially obligated to their manumitters as creditors.[4] Some again engaged themselves to labor under indentures, whose tenures

[1] *Cf.* the following, in each of which 5s. currency was paid: *Frederick Land Recs.*, Lib. WR, no. 14, p. 158; Lib. WR, no. 17, p. 153; Lib. WR, no. 24, p. 110; *Charles Co. Recs.*, Lib. S, no. 3, p. 430.

[2] One negro in Somerset was freed for 5 l, currency, equal to $13.33, *Deeds*, Lib. G, p. 28. One in Queen Anne's paid 15 l, *Land Recs.*, Lib. STW, no. 2, p. 390. In the following cases $400 each was paid: *Baltimore Chattel Recs.*, Lib. WG, no. 12, p. 41 (1806); *Frederick Land Recs.*, Lib. JS, no. 3, p. 415; Lib. JS, no. 18, p. 101; *Montgomery Land Recs.*, Lib. P, p. 54 (1810). In the following $500 each was paid: *Baltimore Chattel Recs.*, Lib. ED, no. 6, p. 433; *Frederick Land Recs.*, Lib. JS, no. 10, p. 138. Most of the payments were not large.

[3] *E. g. Anne Arundel Deeds*, Lib. NH, no. 5, p. 36; *Baltimore Chattel Recs.*, Lib. WG, no. 27, p. 24; *Cecil Land Recs.*, Lib. 16, pp. 334, 361; Lib. 17, p. 544; *Frederick Land Recs.*, Lib. JS, no. 4, p. 577; *Montgomery Land Recs.*, Lib. G, p. 330; Lib. N, p. 260; Lib. O, p. 284; Lib. P, pp. 54, 537; Lib. T, p. 121; Lib. U, p. 8; Lib. X, pp. 148, 573; *Worcester Deeds*, Lib. WET, no. 2, pp. 90, 120.

[4] *Baltimore Chattel Recs.*, Lib. WG, no. 11, p. 374; Lib. WG, no. 12, p. 41; *Dorchester Deeds*, Lib. HD, no. 17, p. 506; *Frederick Land Recs.*, Lib. WR, no. 21, p. 463; Lib. WR, no. 40, p. 69; Lib. no. 42, p. 63; *Queen Anne's Wills*, Lib. WHN, no. 2, p. 183; *Somerset Wills*, Lib. EP, no. 23, p. 61; *Talbot Wills*, Lib. JP, no. 5, p. 263; *Washington Wills*, Lib. D, p. 110.

were deemed adequate to the purposes in view.[1]   Others, finally, fixed as the conditions of release sums which were to be defrayed by continued service as slaves at agreed rates of wages, until their debts were respectively discharged.[2] In each case freedom was to follow the fulfillment of the conditions laid down in the agreement.

Negroes who were already free devoted much energy to the redemption of slaves.   In doing so they adopted many of the same expedients for the complete or partial indemnification of owners that slaves employed in redeeming themselves.   Making payment at or before the time of transfer and giving mortgages upon those transferred were the chief means of securing possession of slaves thus purchased.[3]

[1] Cf. citations in note 3, p. 71, supra; Anne Arundel Deeds, Lib. NH, no. 7, p. 179; Baltimore Chattel Recs., Lib. WG, no. 3, pp. 208, 405; Cecil Wills, Lib. 5, pp. 33-34; Frederick Land Recs., Lib. WR, no. 47, p. 236; Kent Chattel Recs., Lib. TW, no. 1, p. 652; Somerset Deeds, Lib. I, p. 555; Lib. K, p. 116; Lib. P, p. 434; Worcester Deeds, Lib. U, p. 611; Lib. AU, pp. 1-5; Worcester Wills, Lib. TT, no. 8, p. 58.

[2] Cf. Caroline Land Recs., Lib. WR, no. E, p. 516; Dorchester Deeds, Lib. HD, no. 12, p. 421; Frederick Land Recs., Lib. WR, no. 16, p. 28. The following were joint bills of sale and manumissions: Baltimore Chattel Recs., Lib. WG, no. 2, p. 462; Lib. WG, no. 18, p. 48; Lib. WG, no. 29, p. 88; Lib. AI, no. 48, p. 339; Lib. TK, no. 52, p. 77; Frederick Land Recs., Lib. WR, no. 28, pp. 186, 413; Lib. JS, no. 38, p. 91; Harford Land Recs., Lib. JLG, no. M, p. 563; Cecil Land Recs., Lib. 17, p. 43; Lib. 19, p. 174; Lib. 18, p. 52.   The joint bills of sale and manumissions were particularly numerous in Baltimore, Cecil and Frederick counties.   Some of the negroes so disposed of were taken by Pennsylvania masters.

[3] In Frederick County Richard (X) Richardson gave a mortgage for 100 l. currency on a woman named "Hager."   Three years and eight months later the mortgage was released and the slave manumitted by the mortgagor. Land Recs., Lib. WR, no. 30, p. 460 (1807); Lib. WR, no. 38, pp. 484, 621-22.   In Washington Co. in 1847 Thomas (X) Bell paid one dollar for his wife and children four. Land Recs., Lib. IN, no. 2, pp. 633, 645; cf. Anne Arundel Deeds, Lib. NH, no. 6, p. 161; Lib. NH, no. 12, p. 175; Lib. NH, no. 13, p. 531; Lib. NH, no. 16, pp. 106, 328; Lib. WSG, no. 1, p. 42; Lib. WSG, no. 2, p. 566; Lib. WSG,

The prices paid varied widely and often bore no particular relation to the values of the slaves transferred. Thus two Eastern Shore negroes who purchased wives paid, the one one cent, while the other engaged to pay twenty pounds Maryland currency and besides to weave a hundred yards of woolen cloth for the seller.[1] In Frederick County in 1841 a woman paid $200 for her son, aged six years, and four years later a man who had himself just been manumitted paid two dollars for two women of fifty-six and fifteen years of age respectively.[2] Slave-holding by negroes for purposes of gain was not common in Maryland. Indeed the instruments conveying slaves to negroes at times either

no. 3, p. 406; *Kent Chattel Recs.*, Lib. JNG, no. 4, pp. 90, 92, 119, 143, 145, 156, 160, 163, 170, 204, 206, 221, 267, 269, 330, 350.

The following two contain curious expressions, which, however, seem to suggest experiences that others also may have had: In *Caroline Land Recs.*, Lib. G, p. 248 (1801) : " Know all men by these presents that Maryland Troth of Caroline County in the State of Maryland, Laborer, like good old Jacob the father of the children of Israel, having served three years for an wife, and have her in peaceable possession," do manumit, *etc.* And in Lib. H, p. 367 (1803) : Negro (X) Harkless manumitted his wife, " to pay for which I have lost many drops of grease." He declared her " to be as fully and freely entitled to her freedom as I myself am, and continue to be so until the metropolis of Caroline County shall be rent in pains by the explosion of cannon announcing the erection of dry-docks for the preservation of ships of war."

[1] *Caroline Land Records*, Lib. M, pp. 500-1; *Talbot Deeds*, Lib. 26, p. 221. For prices paid by others in these counties, *vide* for the former: *op. cit.*, Lib. O, p. 83; Lib. P, p. 538; Lib. Q, p. 233. In the last one cited $1000 was paid for a wife and five children. Also Lib. S, pp. 214, 346. For the latter county: *op. cit.*, Lib. 27, pp. 78, 151, 160, 242, 485; Lib. 47, p. 65. In Kent in 1834 a woman gave her sons, aged nine and seven years, to serve until each became twenty-one years of age for the freedom of her husband. *Chattel Records*, Lib. JNG, no. 2, p. 170. It appeared that sometimes the slave consort assisted the free partner in executing the financial part of the plan for redeeming.

[2] *Frederick Land Records*, Lib. HS, no. 4, pp. 68-69; Lib. WBT, no. 2, p. 408.

manumitted them,[1] or less frequently stipulated that the grantees were themselves to manumit.[2] But those not so bound were free to do as they chose, and some of them held consorts, or children, or both as slaves for long periods of years.[3]

Nevertheless the chief reason for these purchases was to give freedom to the negroes so acquired. Accordingly the first concern was to secure possession of the buyers' consorts and offspring who were slaves. After these, parents, brothers, sisters and more distant relatives benefited in direct ratio to the nearness of their relationship. And acquisition of those whose kinship was not mentioned was not unknown.[4] In manumitting negroes used the same

[1] *E. g. Anne Arundel Bills of Sale,* Lib. JHN, no. 1, pp. 30, 53, 82, 256; *Baltimore Chattel Records,* Lib. WG, no. 13, p. 472; Lib. WG, no. 16, p. 59; Lib. WG, no. 17, p. 135; Lib. WG, no. 42, p. 127; Lib. WG, no. 43, pp. 238, 396, 398; Lib. WG, no. 44, p. 46; Lib. AI, no. 48, p. 165; Lib. AWB, no. 79, p. 256; *Cecil Land Records,* Lib. RHC, no. 3, p. 580; Lib. RHC, no. 4, p. 154; *Kent Chattel Records,* Lib. JNG, no. 3, pp. 165, 318; Lib. JNG, no. 4, pp. 8, 19, 28, 61, 62, 92, 330; *Queen Anne's Land Records,* Lib. STW, no. 9, p. 490; Lib. STW, no. 10, p. 32. Many of these were joint bills of sale and manumissions.

[2] *Baltimore Chattel Records,* Lib. AL, no. A, p. 412; Lib. TK, no. 52, p. 95; Lib. AWB, no. 74, p. 168; Lib. ED, no. 4, p. 251; *Harford Chattel Records,* Lib. HDG, no. 2, p. 24; *Kent Chattel Records,* Lib. JR, no. 1, pp. 390, 391; *Talbot Deeds,* Lib. 60, p. 258.

[3] *E. g. Baltimore Chattel Records,* Lib. WG, no. 20, pp. 113, 168; Lib. WG, no. 22, p. 373; Lib. WG, no. 29, p. 48; Lib. WG, no. 31, p. 362; Lib. WG, no. 43, p. 246; Lib. TK, no. 60, p. 167; Lib. AWB, no. 74, p. 230; Lib. AWB, no. 81, p. 103; *Frederick Land Records,* Lib. WR, no. 20, p. 495; Lib. JS, no. 5, p. 723; Lib. JS, no. 14, p. 293; Lib. HS, no. 14, p. 69; Lib. ES, no. 9, p. 568; Lib. WBT, no. 2, p. 12; Lib. WBT, no. 3, pp. 634, 675.

In a few cases the legislature passed special acts to set free families whose heads as owners had died intestate.

Laws, 1834, ch. 246; 1835, ch. 266; 1852, ch. 207; 1853, ch. 413. Other acts authorizing negroes to manumit slaves were: 1835, chs. 68, 290; 1836, ch. 167; 1838, ch. 385; 1844, ch. 193; *cf. Frederick Land Recs.,* Lib. JS, no. 47, p. 186.

[4] *E. g. Baltimore Chattel Recs.,* Lib. WG, no. 14, p. 464; Lib. GES, no.

forms of deed and will as the whites. At least one negro manumitted his family before the revolution,[1] and a boy bought by his father in 1764 was manumitted in 1782.[2] After 1783 others followed their example. By the end of the century negroes had become manumitters in at least twelve of the eighteen counties of the state. Their participation in the movement fairly kept pace with the development of the free negro population. In Kent and Baltimore counties instruments made by negroes providing for the freedom of at least two hundred and eighty-one other negroes had been recorded before the beginning of the year 1826, while considerable numbers had been manumitted in like manner in Anne Arundel, Frederick, Harford, Dorchester, Queen Anne's and Talbot countties. Still others not yet freed had become the property of their negro relatives or friends. The laws restricting the manumission of negroes were constantly evaded by transferring slaves to negro ownership.[3]

The second important cause of the growth of the free negro population was natural increase. It must have had a minor effect prior to the war of 1812-14, because even a doubling by birth of the 8043 free negroes of 1790 would still have left more than two-thirds of the increase in the two following decades to be accounted for on other

17, pp. 210, 381; Lib. GES, no. 22, p. 579; Lib. GES, no. 26, p. 385; *Caroline Deeds*, Lib. S, pp. 214, 346; *Kent Chattel Recs.*, Lib. BC, no. 4, pp. 115, 308; *Queen Anne's Land Recs.*, Lib. STW, no. 8, p. 324; *Talbot Deeds*, Lib. 25, p. 349.

[1] *Queen Anne's Land Recs.*, Lib. RT, no. H, p. 56 (1767).

[2] The price paid in this case was 52 *l.* currency. *Baltimore Chattel Recs.*, Lib. AL, no. A, pp. 298-99.

In 1778 one James Perry of Montgomery County, manumitted the daughter of his slave, James, who had purchased the girl from her owner in Fairfax Co., Virginia. *Montgomery Land Recs.*, Lib. A, p. 167; *Cf. Queen Anne's Land Recs.*, Lib. STW, no. 3, p. 289.

[3] *Cf.* interesting article by Calvin D. Wilson, entitled "Negroes who owned Slaves," *Pop. Sci. Mon.*, Nov., 1912, pp. 483-94.

grounds.[1] After that time the rate of manumissions, although still high, had obviously slackened, and dependence upon it mainly to explain the succeeding decadal increases, excepting that of 1820-30, was no longer necessary;[2] a normal growth of the free negroes might well have produced at least half of them. The truth as to the relative contributions made by each of these two factors would lie in a comparison of vital statistics with those of manumissions. For that purpose the data are incomplete. But from sources—official and unofficial—it appears that in 1820-30 the death-rate among the free negroes of Baltimore City and County was greatly in excess of that among the slaves,[3] while in the years 1849, 1850, 1852 and 1859 it was actually less. According to the United States Census the death-rate of the negroes of the city in thirty-six of the years between 1818 and 1863 had been 3.1 per cent and that of the whites 2.49 per cent.[4] Again, in the year ending June, 1850,

[1] The increase in the two decades was 25 844, bringing up to 33 927 whole number in 1810. *Cf.* table IV, *infra*, p. 88.

[2] The following table shows the increase per decade of free negroes in Maryland and in the whole United States, 1790-1860 :

	Maryland	U.S.		Maryland	U.S.
1790–1800	..... 143.5%		1830–1840	..... 17.26%	20.87%
1800–1810	..... 73.2		1840–1850	..... 19.44	12.46
1810–1820	..... 17.1	25.23%	1850–1860	..... 12.00	10.97
1820–1830	..... 33.24	36.20			

History and Statistics of Maryland, Seventh Census of United States, p. 20. *Preliminary Report of Eight Census of United States,* p. 7. The total increase for the half century was 147.4 per cent.

[3] Griffith, *Annals of Baltimore,* p. 233; *Niles Register,* vol. xxv, p. 339; vol. xxxvii, p. 340; vol. xlii, pp. 432, 451; vol. xliii, p. 2. Some of the data in *Niles Register* consists of reports of the Board of Health.

[4] *Eighth Census of United States, Mortality and Miscellaneous Statistics,* p. 280. The rates for several other cities, north and south were:

	Negroes	Whites		Negroes	Whites
Boston	.... 7.03%	2.72%	Philadelphia	..... 3.61%	2.32%
Providence	...... 3.70	2.20	Washington	..... 2.21	1.98
New York	...... 4.09	3.13	Charleston	...... 2.69	2.61
Buffalo	.... 2.16	2.56	New Orleans	.... 5.21	5.96
Average	.... 3.47	2.75			

Cf. Preliminary Report of Eight Census of the United States, p. 6.

in which an epidemic had occurred, 1293 free negroes and
1509 slaves had died, while 2015 living free negroes and
2446 living slaves under one year of age were enumerated.[1]
These facts indicate no permanent excess of deaths over
births in Baltimore County, where, if at all in Maryland,
such an excess should have appeared.   It remains to inquire whether the whole increase was probably due to manumissions.   In accordance with the colonization act of 1831
the county officials reported to the state commissioners on
colonization 4199 manumissions between March 1, 1832 and
January 1, 1851.[2]   In 1830-50 the free negroes increased
21875, or pro rata for nineteen years 20776.   Now, if we
should assume that only a third of the manumissions were
reported, we should yet have to account for an increase of
8179, or 38.1 per cent of the total gain of the free negro
population in that interval.   Less than 17 per cent of this
gain was made up of persons born outside of Maryland.[3]
The rest must have been born of free mothers in Maryland.

Several other factors also affected the growth of the free
negro class.   One which added to their number was migration from without.   Of the 74,723 free negroes of 1850
1.47 per cent had been born in the United States outside of
Maryland, and 0.34 per cent in foreign and unascertained
places.   Some of these had doubtless come in as slaves and
hence owed their status to manumission.[4]   But their

---

[1] *Compendium of the Seventh Census of the United States,* pp. 70, 88.

[2] *Debates of the Constitutional Convention of 1850,* vol. ii, p. 221.
Another report gave a slightly different number, 3943.   *Cf. Laws,* 1831,
ch. 281; *Md. Pub. Docs.,* 1834, p. 3.

[3] Estimate based upon figures in the *Compendium of the Seventh
Census of the United States.*

[4] On the nativity of the negroes *vide, Compendium of the Seventh
Census of the United States.*   After the Civil War the *Compendium
of the Ninth Census,* pp. 388-92, showed 4.46 per cent of the negroes as
born outside of the state.

number had been nearly offset by the migration of resident negroes to Liberia.[1] Still other negroes migrated to the free states. Moreover, the growth of the free was also indirectly affected by the escape of slaves to free territory,[2] and by the sales of others to the traders to the southern markets.[3]

The results produced by the above-mentioned causes were far-reaching. The numerical relations of the several classes of the people underwent striking changes. According to the census of 1755, as given in the *Gentleman's Magazine of London*,[4] the total population of Maryland was 153494. By 1790 it had grown to 319728, a gain of 108.3 per cent, and by 1860 to 687049, a gain of 114.8 per cent over the number of 1790. Of the population of 1755 45301 had been negroes. By 1790 their number had risen to 111079, a gain of 145 per cent, by 1810 to 145429, a new gain of 30.9 per cent, and by 1860 to 171131, a gain of 17.6 per cent. over the last-named figure. Their share of the total

---

[1] These emigrants numbered 1011 in the period 1831-51. *Debates of the Constitutional Convention of 1850*, vol. ii, p. 222. They grew to 1241 by 1856; *infra*, chapter on " Colonization," p. 241.

[2] *The Preliminary Report of the Eighth Census of the United States*, p. 137, gives that in the year 1850 279, or one in every 374, and in 1860 115, or one in every 758 of the slaves belonging to Maryland masters had been reported as fugitives; *cf. Laws*, 1833, ch. 224.

[3] *Cf. 45 Niles Register*, p. 180. This paper stated that the sales of slaves for the southern markets checked the increase of the slaves in Maryland; *cf. Md. Col. Journal*, vol. ii, p. 206; *Genius of Universal Emancipation*, 2 ser., vol. ii, p. 44. One report had it that about 30,000 negroes were sold from Maryland to the southern markets in 1830-40.

[4] 1764, p. 261. Although to be taken perhaps with reserve, the aggregates of population shown in this census harmonize well with those of the other estimates of the population. *Cf. History and Statistics of Maryland, Eighth Census of United States*, p. 50; McMahon, *op. cit.*, vol. i, pp. 313-14; *Maryland, its Resources, Industries and Institutions*, p. 442. Its exhibit of the distribution of numbers corresponds well with what is known about population developments from other sources.

population which had been 29.5 per cent in 1755, became 34.7 per cent in 1790, 38.2 per cent in 1810, and 24.9 per cent in 1860. The free negroes, numbering 1817 in 1755, advanced to 8043 in 1790, a gain of 334 per cent, to 33927 by 1810, a gain of 321 per cent, and to 83 942, a new gain of 147 per cent by 1860. The free portion of all the negroes which had been 3.98 per cent in 1755, was 7.24 per cent in 1790, 23.3 per cent in 1810 and 49.05 per cent in 1860, while the negro portion of all the freemen advanced from 1.64 per cent in 1755 to 3.24 per cent in 1790, 12.6 per cent in 1810 and to 16.3 per cent in 1840, and 13.9 in 1860.

The year 1810 marked the highest percentage of negroes in any census. The correlative changes in the positions of other negroes and other freemen may be obtained by simple subtractions, using the figures given. The free gained in every county of the state in both 1775-90 and 1790-1860. On the whole the whites gained, but after 1790 they lost numbers in nine counties, in five of which the losses were not recovered by 1860, while the slaves lost in fifteen of the counties without any marked tendency to recovery.[1]

The population developed at unequal rates in the different parts of the commonwealth. The census of 1755 had it that 37 per cent of the free negroes and 39 per cent of all the slaves resided in the counties of the Eastern Shore, 42 per cent of each class in the five counties of Southern Maryland, the remainder in Baltimore and Frederick counties and that nearly a third of those in Southern Maryland were in Charles County alone. By reference to Table VI it will be seen that in 1755-90 the several sections named gained re-

---

[1] The most marked losses of the slaves were in Cecil, 72.1 per cent. Caroline, 64 per cent, and Kent, 53.8 per cent. All were on the Eastern Shore, where slavery was obviously marked for extinction. Cecil County gained 106 slaves and 295 free negroes in 1850-60. For the percentage increases of the free negroes decade by decade, *cf. supra,* p. 55, note 2.

TABLE I

ACCOUNT OF MARYLAND POPULATION IN 1755[1]

County	Whites Free — Men	Servants Men hired or indented	Servants Men convicts	Mulattoes Free — Men	Mulattoes Free — Women	Mulattoes Slaves — Men	Mulattoes Slaves — Women	Blacks Free — Men	Blacks Free — Women	Blacks Slaves — Men	Blacks Slaves — Women	Whites Clergy	Whites Men poor	Whites Women	Whites Hired or indented	Whites Convicts	Mulattoes Free	Mulattoes Slaves	Blacks Free	Blacks Slaves
	Taxable Persons over Sixteen Years of Age											*Persons not Taxable*								
Anne Arundel[2]	1534	438	184	16	22	25	11	8	4	1472	1060	3	64	1539	93	51	4	15	6	92
Baltimore	2630	595	472	36	21	25	16	2	2	1144	833	4	58	2587	200	87	14	4	8	47
Calvert	609	124		24			4		1	550	519	2	20	639			2	15	7	39
Cecil	1345	390	47		12	120	86		2	256	216	1	33	1186	282	8			2	13
Charles	1929	173	205	60	36	48	33	3	1	1196	950	4	51	1777	106	78	17	5	2	32
Dorset	1950	172	7	9	7	9	22	7	3	624	514	3	44	2097	126		8	8	2	44
Frederick	2775	216	94	23	4	10	24	45	26	437	314	1	45	2213	163	32	6	2	4	13
Kent	1454	365	82	8	13	7	9	10	5	690	523	2	34	1448	181	12	9	9	6	35
Prince George's	1515	255	73	17	21	37	43	3	3	1278	151	3	44	1680	55	27	8	7	2	88
Queen Anne's	1745	284	287	18	20	33	32	16	9	643	572	3	31	1843	159	73	3	6	3	32
St. Mary's	1561	194	29	16	17	38	27	4	5	822	761	3	61	1806	164	13	16	14	3	49
Somerset	1348	31	1	23	16	15	15	12	3	637	571		61	1446	37			1	2	37
Talbot	1223	294	25	24	18	72	63	1	3	647	595	2	34	1296	160	4	10	1	4	30
Worcester	1768	45	1	31	32	3	7	1	2	401	359	1	57	1964	37	1	1	10	7	44
Totals	23386	3576	1507	(307)	(247)	442	392	(119)	(69)	10827	7938	35	637	23521	1824	386	(95)	99	(58)	595

[1] Gentleman's Magazine, 1764, p. 261.

[2] Order of presentation is here changed to alphabetical.

TABLE I—(Concluded)

ACCOUNT OF MARYLAND POPULATION IN 1755

Persons under Fifteen Years of Age.

County.	Whites Free Boys	Whites Free Girls	Hired or indented servants Boys	Hired or indented servants Girls	Servant convicts Boys	Servant convicts Girls	Mulattoes Free Boys	Mulattoes Free Girls	Mulattoes Slaves Boys	Mulattoes Slaves Girls	Blacks Free Boys	Blacks Free Girls	Blacks Slaves Boys	Blacks Slaves Girls	Free Negro Totals
Anne Arundel	1913	1705	82	26	16		28	35	31	23	10	5	1314	1321	138
Baltimore	3115	2951	126	49	6	6	63	62	28	43	3	1	959	1041	212
Calvert	861	745	48	28			30	31	15	17			671	645	103
Cecil	1506	1372	55	20	1	1	10	4	89	108	5		275	252	37
Charles	1681	1799	228	41	16	7	69	57	52	51	7		1145	1197	252
Dorset	2347	2222	54	17		2	12	22	35	32	6		666	681	77
Frederick	3246	3105	80	56	9	1	22	23	19	19	3	1	465	473	157
Kent	1527	1423	134	76	4	1	16	19	9	20	8	3	650	653	94
Prince George's	1840	1674	33	10	1		42	26	46	55			1340	1239	122
Queen Anne's	2037	1864	82	44	9		31	24	57	58	2	4	621	603	122
St. Mary's	1845	1764	29	24	5	3	24	22	94	98	13	17	862	839	149
Somerset	1230	1232	12	9			24	19	21	25	1	1	875	891	93
Talbot	1322	1197	57	12			20	19	74	81		1	579	657	111
Worcester	2067	2083	28				28	29	7	8	13	6	561	511	150
Totals	26637	25136	1048	412	67	21	(419)	(392)	577	638	(71)	(40)	10983	11003	1817

TABLE II

SLAVE POPULATION OF THE STATE OF MARYLAND, 1790-1860

County.	1860	1850	1840	1830	1820	1810	1800	1790
Allegany.......	666	724	812	818	795	620	499	258
Anne Arundel ..	7332	11249	9819	10347	10301	11693	9760	10130
Baltimore	5400	6718	7595	10653	11077	11369	9673	7132
Calvert	4609	4486	4170	3899	3668	3937	4101	4305
Caroline	739	808	752	1177	1574	1520	1865	1057
Carroll.........	783	975	1122	......	......	......	......	......
Cecil	950	844	1352	1705	2342	2467	2103	3407
Charles	9653	9584	9182	10129	9410	11435	9558	10085
Dorchester	4123	4282	4227	5001	5168	5032	4566	5337
Frederick	3243	3913	4445	6370	6685	5671	4572	3641
Harford....	1800	2166	2643	2947	3320	4431	4264	3417
Howard........	2862	......	......	......	......	......	......	......
Kent ......,....	2509	2627	2735	3191	4071	4249	4474	5433
Montgomery....	5421	5114	5377	6447	6396	7572	6288	6030
Prince George's.	12479	11510	10636	11585	11185	9189	12191	11176
Queen Anne's...	4174	4270	3960	4872	5588	6381	6517	6674
St. Mary's ,.....	6549	5842	5761	6183	6047	6000	6399	6985
Somerset	5089	5588	5377	6556	7241	6975	7432	7070
Talbot	3725	4134	3687	4173	4768	4878	4775	4777
Washington	1435	2090	2546	2909	3201	2656	2200	1286
Worcester	3648	3444	3539	4032	4551	4427	4398	3836
Total	87189	90368	89737	102994	107327	111502	105635	103036

spectively 471 per cent, 181 per cent, and 439 per cent in free negroes, while in 1790-1860 the first two gained respectively 623 per cent and 542 per cent, Baltimore County 3126.6 per cent and the rest of Western Maryland 1015.6 per cent. Furthermore it appears that, although the two first-named sections continued to be the chief centers of negro population, the several sections witnessed changes in their respective proportions of the total free negro and slave classes. Of the former in 1755-90 the Eastern Shore and Western Maryland gained respectively 10.9 per cent and 4.4 per cent, and Southern Maryland lost 15.4 per cent, while in 1790-1860 the Eastern Shore and Southern Maryland lost respectively 14.6 per cent and 10.2 per cent, and

TABLE III

SHOWING WHITE POPULATION OF COUNTIES OF MARYLAND, 1790-1860

County.	1860	1850	1840	1830	1820	1810	1800	1790
Allegany	27215	21633	14663	9569	7664	6176	5703	4539
Anne Arundel..	11704	16542	14630	13872	13482	12439	21030	11664
Baltimore.....	231242	174853	105331	92329	72635	57233	45050	30878
Calvert	3997	3630	3585	3788	3711	3680	3889	4211
Caroline......	7604	6096	5334	6241	7144	6932	6759	7028
Carroll	22525	18667	15221	......	......	......	......	......
Cecil	19994	15472	13329	11478	11923	9652	6542	10055
Charles.......	5796	5665	6022	6789	6514	7398	9043	10124
Dorchester....	11654	10747	10629	10685	10095	10415	9415	10010
Frederick.....	38391	33314	28975	36703	31997	27983	26478	26937
Harford	17971	14413	12041	11314	11217	14606	12018	10784
Howard	9081	......	......	......	......	......	......	......
Kent	7347	5616	5616	5044	5315	5222	5511	6748
Montgomery ..	11349	9435	8766	12103	9082	9731	8508	11679
Prince George's	9650	8901	7823	7687	7935	6471	8346	10004
Queen Anne's..	8415	6936	6132	6659	7226	7529	7315	8171
St. Mary's	6798	6223	6070	6097	6033	6158	6678	8216
Somerset	15332	13485	11485	11371	10384	9162	9340	8272
Talbot	8106	7084	6063	6291	7387	7249	6070	7231
Washington...	28305	26930	24724	21277	19247	15591	16108	14472
Worcester	13442	12401	11765	11811	11232	11490	11523	7626
Totals....	515918	417942	318204	291108	260223	235117	216326	208649

Baltimore City and Western Maryland gained respectively
24.1 per cent and .7 per cent. Of the latter in the first
period the Eastern Shore and Western Maryland lost respectively 2 per cent and 3.4 per cent, and Southern Maryland gained 5.2 per cent, while in the second period Southern and Western Maryland gained respectively 8.8 per cent
and .7 per cent, and the others lost as follows: Eastern
Shore 8.8 per cent, Baltimore County .8 per cent. The table
also gives the numerical changes of both the free negro and
slave populations and the proportions of the negroes in
each section that were slave and free. Attention is moreover called to the rapid growth of the free negroes of
Baltimore County, to the resulting proportional loss of

TABLE IV

FREE COLORED POPULATION OF MARYLAND, 1790–1860

County.	1860	1850	1840	1830	1820	1810	1800	1790
Allegany	467	412	215	222	195	113	101	12
Anne Arundel	4864	4602	5083	4076	3382	2536	1833	804
Baltimore	29911	29075	21453	17888	12489	7208	4307	927
Calvert	1841	1530	1474	1213	694	388	307	136
Caroline	2786	2788	1720	1652	1390	1001	602	421
Carroll............	1225	974	898	......	......	......	......	.....
Cecil	2918	2623	2551	2249	1783	947	373	163
Charles	1068	913	819	851	567	412	571	404
Dorchester	4684	3848	3987	3000	2496	2661	2365	528
Frederick	4957	3760	2985	2716	1777	783	473	213
Harford...........	3644	2777	2436	2058	1387	2221	1344	775
Howard	1395	......	......	......	......	......	......	.....
Kent	3411	3143	2491	?266	2067	1979	1786	655
Montgomery.......	1552	1311	1313	1266	922	677	262	294
Prince George's	1198	1138	1080	1202	1096	4929	648	164
Queen Anne's......	3372	3278	2541	2866	2138	2738	1025	618
St. Mary's.	1866	1633	1393	1179	894	636	622	343
Somerset	4571	3483	2646	2239	1954	1058	586	268
Talbot	2964	2593	2340	2483	2234	2103	1591	1076
Washington	1677	1828	1580	1082	627	483	342	64
Worcester.........	3571	3014	3073	2430	1638	1054	449	178
Totals	83942	74723	62078	52938	39730	53927	19587	8043

nearly 25 per cent of the same class in the Eastern Shore and Southern Maryland and to the retarded rate of change in the last named.

Table VI also shows that, while the gains of the free negroes in both numbers and percentages were large, their proportion of the total increase of freemen was relatively large only in the Eastern Shore and Southern Maryland in 1790-1860. And the gains of the white population of the Eastern Shore were mainly at the extremes, viz., in Cecil in the north and Somerset and Worcester in the south.

TABLE V.   SHOWING CHANGES IN SECTIONAL DISTRIBUTION OF NEGROES

| | Totals: | | | | | | Percentages of: | | | | | |
| | Negro Population. | | | Free Negroes. | | | All Negroes free. | | | All free Negroes of the State. | | |
	1755	1790	1860	1755	1790	1860	1755	1790	1860	1755	1790	1860
Eastern Shore . . .	17826	42498	53414	684	3907	28277	3.8	1.19	53.2	37.6	48.5	33.6
Southern Maryland. .	19210	50856	62689	764	2145	13784	3.9	4.1	21.9	42.	26.6	16.4
Baltimore County* . .	{8275	8059	35311	{369	927	29911	{4.4	11.5	84.7	{20.4	11.5	35.6
Western Maryland . .		9666	19717		1064	11970		11.0	59.7		13.3	14.0

| | Percentage: | | | | | | | | | Slave Population. | |
| | No. of Slaves. | | | Of Negroes Slave. | | | Of Slaves in State. | | | Gain. | Loss. |
	1755	1790	1860	1755	1790	1860	1755	1790	1860	1755-90	1790-1860
Eastern Shore . . .	17142	38591	24957	96.2	90.8	46.8	39.4	37.4	28.6	125	34.6
Southern Maryland. .	18446	48711	48905	96.1	95.9	78.1	42.0	47.2	56.0	164	†0.13
Baltimore County . .	{9723	7132	5400	{95.6	88.5	15.3	{18.6	6.9	6.1	{61.8	24.2
Western Maryland . .		8602	7927		89.0	40.3		8.3	9.0		7.7
Whole State. . .	43494	103036	87189	96.0	87.4	50.95				136.8	15.3

* The reason for not distinguishing Baltimore County in 1755 was that at that time it embraced much of what later became Harford and Carroll counties. Further its negro population was not metropolitan then, as it tended later to become. Other counties erected in that section were Washington, Allegany and Garrett.   † Gain.

Table VI. Comparing Increase of all Freemen with that of the Free Negroes

	Number of Freemen.			Number of Free Negroes.			Per cent Increase.				Negro per cent of total.		Negro per cent of Freemen.		
							Freemen.		Free Negroes.						
	1755	1790	1860	1755	1790	1860	1755–1790	1790–1860	1755–1790	1790–1860	1755–1790	1790–1860	1755	1790	1860
Eastern Shore	50364	69048	120171	684	3907	28277	37.0	74.0	471.0	623	18.8	47.6	1.35	5.65	23.43
Southern Maryland	34486	58043	72159	764	2145	13784	67.7	24.3	180.7	542	5.8	82.4	2.21	3.69	19.08
Baltimore County	} 25291 {	31805	261153	} 369 {	927	29911	} 254.0 {	721.1	} 439.0 {	3126.6	} 2.5 {	12.6	} 1.45 {	2.91	11.4
Western Maryland		57796	146377		1064	11970		153.0		1015.6		12.3		1.84	8.18
Whole State	110141	216692	599860	1817	8043	83942	96.7	176.8	342.0	943.6	5.8	19.8	1.64	3.71	13.99

This growth of the free negro population was not confined to Maryland alone. Measures designed to extinguish slavery had also been undertaken in many other places. The people in the states north of Maryland adopted the plan of compulsory gradual emancipation,[1] those of Delaware, and, for a few decades, Virginia, adopted essentially the same neutral attitude as Maryland, while those of the other great slaveholding states, after nursing the emancipation sentiment for a time, yielded but sparingly to its influence. Free negroes, however, appeared in all the states.[2] The first federal census numbered in the whole country 59527 free negroes and 697897 slaves, the eighth census 488070 free negroes and 3950531 slaves, increases respectively of 719.9 per cent and 466.53 per cent. The total free population increased 747.6 per cent in the interval. Of the free negroes of 1790 68.6 per cent and of those of 1860 61.1 per cent resided in the six states of New York, Pennsylvania, Delaware, Maryland, Virginia and North Carolina. Among these states Virginia stood first in point of numbers, and Maryland second, until at the third federal census their positions were reversed. But Virginia was like North Carolina in both advancing free negro and slave classes, while Maryland, like Delaware, was marked by an advancing free negro, and a declining slave class.[3] Maryland and Virginia combined had 35.1 per cent of the nation's total of free negroes in 1790 and 28.8 per cent in 1850. Next to them stood two northern states, Pennsylvania and New York, which had in 1790 18.8 per cent and

---

[1] *Cf. Preliminary Report of Eighth Census of United States*, p. 10.

[2] *Op. cit.*, pp. 124-31.

[3] The situation in Delaware was remarkable, since there 30.5 per cent of the negroes were free in 1790, 82.8 per cent in 1830 and 91.6 per cent in 1860. It was far in advance of the Eastern Shore counties of Maryland with which it had so much in common.

TABLE VII. SHOWING FREE NEGRO POPULATION IN CERTAIN OF THE UNITED STATES

| | 1860 | | 1830 | | 1790 | | Per cent of nation's total of Free Negroes. | | | Per cent of native Free Negroes. |
	Free Negroes.	Slaves.	Free Negroes.	Slaves.	Free Negroes.	Slaves.	1860	1830	1790	1850
United States.	488070	3950531	319599	2009043	59527	697897	.	.	.	.
Maryland	83942	87189	52938	102994	8043	103036	17.2	16.5	13.5	98.17
Virginia	58042	490865	47348	469757	12866	293427	11.6	14.8	21.6	99.02
Pennsylvania	56949	.	37930	403	6537	3737	.	.	.	70.43
New York	49005	.	44870	75	4654	21324	.	.	.	76.58
North Carolina	30463	331059	19543	245601	4975	100572	.	.	.	.
Ohio	36673	.	9568	6	1899*	.	.	.	.	49.
Delaware	19829	1798	15855	3292	3899	8887	4.06	4.9	6.5	93.69
Louisiana	18647	331726	16710	109588	7585*	34660*	0.71	.	.	.
Georgia	3500	462198	2486	217531	398	29264	.	.	.	.
Alabama	2690	435080	1572	117549	.	.	.	.	.	.
Mississippi	773	436631	519	65659	240*	3489*	.	.	.	.

* Population at Third Census, 1810.

in 1860 21.7 per cent of that total. Ohio stood sixth in point of numbers in 1850 and fifth in 1860. In the three last-named states, as will be seen by reference to Table VII, only 70.43 per cent, 76.58 per cent and 49 per cent of the respective negro populations of 1850 were of native birth. The rest had been recruited mainly from voluntary emigrants from the other states and from fugitive slaves. In contrast to the large numbers in all these states were those of the great slave states of Georgia, Alabama and Mississippi. That of the first which had 11.69 per cent of the slaves was only .71 per cent of the free negroes of the whole United States. The others had still less. Louisiana stood in an intermediate position.

CHAPTER III

LEGAL STATUS OF THE FREE NEGROES

IN the early province of Maryland there were apparently no separate rules of law applying to the free negroes alone. Until such rules had been created, therefore, their freedom was as unqualified as that of the European part of the population. But the change of slaves to the legal status of freedom did not alter the marks of race nor raise the social station of the negroes. As freemen they continued to live substantially like the slaves lived,—to associate with slaves, and apart from formal rights to be indistinguishable from slaves. They tended to reflect the feelings and thoughts of slaves towards the white master class, and were themselves regarded by the latter with no less suspicion and depreciation than the slaves. Some early statutes mentioned " all negroes and other slaves " as subject to the same provisions of law. But it was manifestly impossible to treat both classes alike. Hence a few separate provisions were early made for free negroes, and when the " evil " of their numbers increased the statutory provisions affecting their activities increased also. These statutes endeavored (1) to protect property and personal rights from infringement by means of negro freemen, (2) to prevent the free negroes from becoming a financial burden to the state, and (3) to prevent servile insurrections. (4) A fourth object, probably, was that of preventing the growth of the free negro class, irrespective of its consequences. The complex restrictions covered a part

94

of the field of legal relations, in the rest of which free
negroes were governed like the whites. This chapter will
deal chiefly with that part, viz. the exceptions to the
ordinary rules made on account of the free negroes.

The legislature of Maryland did not intend that the
negro's freedom from slavery should become a freedom
from labor. The feeling that he was falling short in industry led to repeated efforts to correct his failing in that
point. The statute of 1796 provided that any free negro
who should be found by a magistrate guilty of going at
large and living without visible means of support might be
compelled either to give a bond for thirty dollars for his
own good behavior or leave the state within five days. If
he refused to comply, or if he complied and returned within
six months, he was to be liable to imprisonment, and if he
failed to pay his prison charges within twenty days, to be
sold into servitude for six months.[1] In 1825 the term allowed for leaving the state was increased to fifteen days,
and as an alternative the offender might hire himself to a
responsible citizen to work. Any aged or infirm free negro,
who could not labor, was to be supported by the county,
if in want.[2] Further changes were made in 1839. In a
county where there were no local magistrates, jurisdiction
over vagrancy was vested in the orphans' court. This
court like the magistrate was empowered to summon witnesses and take testimony as to accused parties; and upon
proof that a negro had neither visible means of support

[1] *Laws*, 1796, ch. 67, sec. 20; *cf.* act of 1804, ch. 96, authorizing the
Criminal Court of Baltimore County to commit to hard labor in the almshouse as vagrants all persons living without employment, all beggars,
prostitutes, jugglers, fortune tellers, common gamblers, vagabonds, *etc.*
Also acts applying to Annapolis and Georgetown; 1796, ch. xxx; 1797,
ch. 56; and *Acts of 1811*, ch. 212; 1818, ch. 169.

[2] *Op. cit.*, 1825, ch. 161. The constables were here enjoined to be
vigilant in apprehending vagrants and idlers.

nor habits of industry, it might order him sold as a slave for the remainder of the year. From the proceeds of the sale the costs were to be defrayed, and the residue turned over to the offender at the end of his term of service. But if he offended again, he was to be liable to a renewal of the same penalty.[1] It was a habit of agitators to prate and to petition the assembly about the " idle and vagrant habits of a large portion of the free negroes." [2] The law was applied, however, with discrimination. Strange negroes were dealt with, as will be shown below, under the fugitive slave and immigration laws. Those who were thievish were prosecuted as criminals. Those who did not keep themselves employed were commonly first warned to get to work. If they declined, they might be apprehended and fined. But in Baltimore County, for a time at least, commitment of offenders to the alms-house under the general vagrancy act was apparently preferred to selling them into servitude.[3] Elsewhere the penalty was invoked in extreme cases, but in any event its consequences did not differ strikingly from the conditions under which the rural free negroes constantly

[1] *Laws*, 1839, ch. 38. Amendment of conduct was effective to avoid a repetition of penalty. In 1842 jurisdiction over this offence was also vested in justices of the peace. *Laws*, 1842, ch. 281; *cf. Md. Col. Journal*, vol. vi, p. 236.

[2] *E. g. Md. Pub. Docs.*, 1841, H, p. 4; 1843, M, pp. 45-47; *H. Dels. Journal*, 1852, pp. 99, 619; *cf. Md. Col. Journal*, vol. x, p. 138, for a comment on this habit.

[3] *Reports of Baltimore Co. Almshouse, Appendices to Ordinances of Baltimore City*, 1851-60; *cf.* also same for 1835, 1836; Brackett, *op. cit.*, p. 221; *Laws*, 1831, ch. 58; 1854, ch. 116.

For cases in the counties *cf.* the following: *Baltimore Sun*, July 31, 1855; Cecil Whig, Jan. 29, 1853, a negro was sold for $22.50; *Dorchester Criminal Appearance Docket*, no. 19, July, 1860; *Frederick Orphans' Court Mins.*, April, 1845, negro fined $20 and costs; *Md. Col. Journal*, vol. vi, p. 236; *Washington Orphans' Court Mins.*, 1835-46, pp. 238, 247; *cf.* also *Dorchester Co. Court Mins.*, April 14, 1857; *Howard Criminal Docket*, no. 12, Sept., 1841.

labored.   The manner in which the children of free negroes
were trained for labor will be taken up in a subsequent
chapter.[1]

Aside from the coercion of the vagrancy laws the free
negro enjoyed a wide liberty in getting a living.   He had
a right to engage in agriculture, in the mechanical trades,
in business, or to hire himself to any employer whom
he could serve and to collect and expend his earnings.[2]
The law barred him wholly from no legitimate callings
saving politics, and military service, and according to
the code of 1860 peddling.[3]   That his energies were confined mainly to manual labor was due to his disqualification
for other things to which he has since attained.   But the
law restricted his exercise of certain other callings with a
view of promoting fair dealing.   These restrictions had to
do with navigating the waters of the state, with service
contracts and buying and selling.

Vessels traversing the navigable waters of Maryland
afforded means of escape to absconding slaves.   Hence a
special regulation was passed by the legislature in 1753 forbidding concealment or employment of any slave or servant on board a vessel within the province without his
master's consent.[4]   Another act of 1824 required ships'
masters to keep careful registers of all colored persons
employed on their vessels and prohibited them from carrying out of the state any negro or mulatto who did not have
an authenticated certificate of freedom issued by a clerk of a

[1] Governor Hicks in his inaugural address stated that there was more
negro vagrancy in the lower counties on both shores than in the rest
of the state. *Senate Journal*, 1858, app., p. 13.

[2] Regarding certain of his rights *vide Md. Appeal Reports*, 9 G. & J.,
pp. 19, 27 and 12 Md., p. 464.

[3] *Code of Laws of Maryland*, 1860, art. 56.

[4] *Laws*, 1753, ch. x.

county court or register of wills.[1] A decade later it was objected that negroes were engaged in an illicit trade on Chesapeake Bay, and especially that some vessels were commanded by negro captains and manned by negro crews;[2] and that the efforts of slaves to abscond were facilitated thereby. Upon 'this there followed a new statute requiring that a white person above the age of eighteen years should be chief navigator on each vessel navigating or working in the waters of the state. But in the counties of Baltimore and Anne Arundel this act was not operative between the years 1837 and 1853.[3] To these general laws other local laws were added at the instance of certain of the counties. From Worcester County it was reported that free negro participation had become an injury to the oyster industry, and from Charles and Prince George's Counties arose complaints against negroes boating on the Potomac River and its creeks. Accordingly in 1852 negroes engaged in the oyster industry in Worcester were especially restricted, and after one unsuccessful attempt in 1856 a law applying to boating on the Potomac in the latter two counties was passed. Of slaves it required their master's permits to have or use boats; of free negroes it required a magistrate's license issued only upon proof of good character by the word of two or more respectable landholders, and revocable without remedy upon their recommendation.[4] Oral reports have it that the state-wide law against negroes acting as chief navigators was generally observed, although a merely nominal compliance

[1] *Op. cit.*, 1824, ch. 85. This act was especially aimed at those who might attempt to carry away slaves to Hayti.

[2] *H. Dels. Journal*, 1835, pp. 66, 180.

[3] *Laws*, 1836, ch. 150; 1837, ch. xxiii; 1853, ch. 446.

[4] *Op. cit.*, 1852, ch. 57; 1858, ch. 356; *Senate Journal*, 1856, pp. 161, 474; *cf. Laws*, 1861, ch. 57; *H. Dels. Journal*, 1838, pp. 35, 196; 1858, pp. 35, 639.

with its terms was sometimes permitted. At least two Eastern Shore negroes ran their own vessels in trade to Baltimore without molestation.

The legislation directed against negro competition in trade was of minor importance. In 1836 a committee of the House of Delegates was ordered to inquire whether licenses to trade and to keep ordinaries should not be withheld. In 1840 a bill to withhold from negroes retailers' licenses failed of enactment.[1] But in 1852 such a bill applying to the counties of Anne Arundel, Somerset and Worcester was passed. As suggested above it excluded negroes from the liquor trade. In order to sell any other merchandise the negro was to be required to get at least twelve respectable free-holders of the vicinity of the proposed shop to recommend to the circuit court the issuance of a dealer's license to himself. No license was to be given a white person to enable him to trade in partnership with a negro, and no white merchant was to employ a negro as clerk or salesman in a retail shop.[2] This law did not exclude negroes from the trade in any of the counties, however.

Beginning about 1825 a long-sustained effort was made to exclude the negroes by law from certain occupations.[3] It was not successful. In 1836 began a movement to pass another act requiring negroes to fulfill the labor contracts to which they were parties.[4] It led to the statute of 1854 which declared any free negro who quit service before the end of the term of his contract guilty of a misdemeanor.

---

[1] *H. Dels. Journal*, 1840, pp. 85, 296. For other such proceedings *vide* Brackett, *op. cit.*, pp. 209-10; also *H. Dels. Journal*, 1837, pp. 25-26.

[2] *Laws*, 1858, ch. 288.

[3] *Genius of Universal Emancipation*, 2 ser., vol. ii, p. 10; *H. Dels. Journal*, 1840, pp. 209, 325; 1844, pp. 257, 261, 379; 1847, p. 145; 1860, pp. 292, 309.

[4] *H. Dels. Journal*, 1837, pp. 25-26, 108, 173; 1845, p. 11; 1853, pp. 260, 923-24.

He might be compelled by a justice of the peace to serve the rest of his term, to lose the wages for the time lost and to pay the costs of his trial. If his contract was in writing, he was to be bound to render the service called for. Upon refusal to comply he was to forfeit to his first employer 40 per cent of his wages earned from any other employer. And the second employer was to be liable to pay damages, if he hired any negro against whom he know such a judgment had been rendered. But such redress of the first employer was barred, if not sued for within a month after the offence.[1] Two years later the provisions were extended to verbal contracts in which a portion of the stipulated wages had been paid in advance.[2] Negroes who were treated in a cruel or improper manner by employers were probably denied redress excepting such as came from the moral reprobation of the neighbors of their employers.[3]

Slaves frequently bought and sold articles without fraud, although they could have claimed no legal right to do so.[4] The general statute of 1715 forbade all persons to deal with servants, whether hired, indentured or slave, without the consent of their masters.[5] An act of 1747 forbade the sale of liquors to servants, negroes and other slaves within three miles of any Quaker meeting in either Talbot or Anne Arundel County.[6] Such provisions thus applied to the free negroes, excepting those who were working for other persons. In the nineteenth century their number was increased. As

[1] Laws, 1854, ch. 273.

[2] Op. cit., 1856, ch. 252.

[3] I have found but little evidence bearing upon the application of this act by the justices' courts.

[4] Md. Appeal Reports, 9 G. & J., p. 27 (1837).

[5] Laws, 1715, ch. xliv; cf. Act of 1692, Archives of Maryland, vol. xiii, p. 455.

[6] Op. cit., 1747, ch. 17.

applied to free negroes they had in view two objects: (1) to protect the interests of property holders, and (2) to prevent disorders on the part of negroes under the influence of rum.

In 1805 it was reported that free negroes had been selling farm products which they had received from the hands of slaves. A statute of that year denied to any free negro the right to sell corn, wheat or tobacco without having first procured from a justice of the peace a license stating that the seller was an orderly person of good character. The license was to be renewed annually, and any such sale without a valid license was to be punished by a fine of five dollars on the seller and double that amount on the purchaser.[1] An attempt was later made to amend this act with more detailed provisions. It led the legislature in 1825 to authorize a fine of a hundred dollars on any purchaser of tobacco from a negro, unless the latter had a justice's certificate stating the quantity and quality of the produce to be sold. But the justice was to issue the permit therefor only on proof by a respectable citizen that the seller had acquired the tobacco by honest means.[2] In the act of 1831 the whole law was restated. It was made also to apply to sales of bacon, beef, pork, oats, and rye and required the vending negro, if a slave, to have his master's permit, but if a free negro, a certificate as before from either a justice of the peace, or three respectable persons, stating that he had probably come into possession of the articles honestly. Other clauses noticed elsewhere were to regulate the sale of spirits, powder, shot and lead to negroes.[3] These general provisions survived as such until the civil war

---

[1] *Laws,* 1805, ch. 80; cf. *H. Dels. Journal,* 1805, p. 80; *Senate Journal,* 1805, p. 37; also *Laws,* 1817, ch. 227, sec. 5.

[2] *Laws,* 1825, ch. 199; cf. *H. Dels. Journal,* 1807, pp. 28, 29, 36.

[3] *Laws,* 1831, ch. 323.

period. The notable additions to them were that of 1842, according to which a free negro convicted of trafficking in stolen goods might be sold to serve as a slave outside of the state for a term of five to ten years, and that of 1856 prohibiting the sale of lottery tickets to free negroes.[1] Further protection was extended to certain localities from which came special complaints of lawlessness. It was first granted for Kent County in 1818,[2] but the act granting it was repealed in the following year. And in 1841-45 the county courts of four Southern Maryland counties, or in their recesses the justices of the peace, were authorized to revoke the licenses of traders who were guilty of dealing with negroes contrary to law.[3] These restrictions, wherever they were enforced, subjected negro farmers to a certain inconvenience, yet without great apparent obstruction to legitimate enterprise. For disregarding them some negroes and some whites were prosecuted.[4] But in dealing with negro offenders the county courts obviously concerned themselves with the initial offence of stealing rather than with that of the subsequent disposal of the produce stolen. It can hardly be doubted that the free negroes were credited with an undue share of the blame for the traffic in question.

The second object stated was that of counteracting the in-

---

[1] *Laws*, 1842, ch. 279; 1856, ch. 195. A negro sold out of the state under this act of 1842 was not to be allowed to return to the state to reside after serving out his term.

[2] The act declared it unlawful for any one to sell to or buy from any unlicensed negro any cereals, bacon, or merchandise between sunset and sunrise. Licenses were to be for twelve months each, and to be kept on record by the magistrates granting them. *Op. cit.*, 1818, ch. 170; *cf.* repeal of this act 1819, ch. xiv.

[3] *Laws*, 1841, ch. 273; 1845, chs. 131, 281.

[4] *E. g. Dorchester Criminal Presentments*, Oct., 1795, no. 11; Oct., 1850, no. 8; Oct., 1851, no. 4; *Harford Criminal Docket*, 1846-51, p. 71; *Howard Criminal Docket*, I, nos. 15, 16; *Somerset Co. Court Judgments*, 1821-22, p. 438; *Baltimore Sun*, Jan. 17, 1853.

fluence of rum upon the negroes.   Expedients were devised
to prevent or discourage their efforts to buy the stuff.   In
1817 it was made a penal offence for a retailer of liquors
to allow a negro, without leave from the latter's master or
employer, to visit his shop at night.   The act authorizing
it extended to the counties of Anne Arundel, Calvert and
St. Mary's.[1]   At the next session after this had been passed,
a similar provision applying to the sale of liquors between
sunset and sunrise and on Sundays was enacted for the
counties of Charles, Dorchester, Prince George's, Somerset
and Talbot.   But in 1819 both provisions were repealed,
so far as concerned the counties of Dorchester and Talbot
and the City of Annapolis.[2]   By the act of 1831 no retailer
was to sell any liquors to any negro anywhere in the state,
unless the purchaser bore a permit for the purchase, signed
by a justice of the peace and directed to the seller, or if the
purchaser was a slave, a written permission from his
master.[3]   And after this two local acts were passed, one to
apply to seven counties, and the other to Annapolis City
and its environs.[4]   The first practically revived the act of
1818, while the second attempted to bar sales of liquor to
any negroes who could not get a certificate of good character
and temperate habits.   Finally, a discrimination was made
against negroes entering the liquor trade.   In 1827 any
negro who might be found dispensing spirits or wine within

---

[1] *Laws*, 1817, ch. 227; *cf*. act of 1747, ch. xvii.

[2] *Op. cit.*, 1818, ch. 184, 1819, ch. 18.   The inclusion here of a provision
to penalize persons who bought produce from negroes without permits
authorizing them to sell, seemed to strike at the reputed sale, or barter,
of stolen produce by negroes for rum.   *Cf*. acts of 1854, ch. 194, 1818,
ch. 170.

[3] *Laws*, 1831, ch. 323, sec. 10.

[4] *Op. cit.*, 1854, ch. 194; in this the counties mentioned were Anne
Arundel, Calvert, Charles, Howard, Prince George's, St. Mary's and
Somerset, and 1858, ch. 55.

a mile of a camp-meeting became liable to thirty-nine stripes, which were to be inflicted at least a mile away from the meeting-place.[1]   In 1831 the power of granting licenses to negroes to retail liquors was limited to the respective county courts and the city court for Baltimore City, and precautions in conferring them were further enjoined.[2] And in 1852 this power was taken away altogether from the courts of Anne Arundel, Somerset and Worcester.[3]

During the legislative session of 1832 a member of the lower house said that the rule passed in the preceding session to govern the sale of spirits to negroes had been a complete failure.[4]   The Committee on the Colored Population was instructed to look into the matter and report, but no definite action was taken as a result.[5]   Some persons, both colored and white, were prosecuted for illegal practices in selling liquors.   For instance, two negroes in Carroll County were fined in 1847 for "selling liquor without License," and at Baltimore in 1855 a person was fined for selling to negroes who had no permit to buy.[6]   But the determination to use the law to keep liquor from the negroes was not general.   Repeated enactments did not strengthen it permanently.

Notwithstanding the above-mentioned restrictions the negroes still had the right to acquire and dispose of prop-

---

[1] *Laws*, 1827, ch. 29.

[2] *Op. cit.*, 1831, ch. 323, sec. 11.

[3] *Op. cit.*, 1852, ch. 288. For one year a negro's name was to be regarded as having no weight when signed to a saloon petition in Kent County. *Op. cit.*, 1818, ch. 170; 1819, ch. xiv.

[4] *H. Dels. Journal*, 1832, p. 55; cf. *op. cit.*, 1834, p. 499.

[5] *Op. cit.*, 1833, pp. 110, 197-98; also 1834, p. 499.

[6] *Carroll Criminal Court Docket*, no. 1, pp. 105, 111; *Baltimore Sun*, Mar. 30, 1855; cf. *Carroll Criminal Docket*, no. 1, p. 14, no. 2, p. 4; *Howard Criminal Docket*, 1, no. 20; *Somerset Co. Court Judgments*, 1821-22, p. 194.

erty. In doing so they could employ any of the common methods of effecting transfers employed by other citizens. It will be noted that none of the statutes referred to applied to transfers of any kind of property by the law of descents or to real estate transfers, whether to negroes or from negroes. In 1817 the appeal court held valid a devise of real property to a negro girl,[1] and in two later cases in which manumitted negroes were to be supported out of the rents of real property whose possession was to be vested in white persons, it held that they were entitled to receive the benefits intended for them.[2] If a negro died intestate and devoid of heirs born in lawful wedlock, his estate could not be taken by any other person claiming under him. Several acts were passed by the legislature to empower particular negroes to transmit property to heirs in cases in which it had been

---

[1] *Md. Appeal Reports*, 5 H. & J., pp. 191-95; *cf.* 12 Md., p. 450.

[2] *Op. cit.*, 5 Md., pp. 137-40; 12 Md., pp. 87-96. In the latter case the court said: " It is certain that their being devisees of real estate, will not give them any rights not enjoyed by others, but as long as they are allowed to remain in the state, why may they not have land of their own? If set free without any such devise in their favor, they might hold land acquired in any other way, and if they remove, the title to the land would remain in them."

In 1831 the act had passed forbidding any negro manumitted thereafter to remain in the state without the permission of the orphans' court of the county wherein he resided. *Laws*, 1831, ch. 281. A will executed in 1843 freed several slaves, ordered that out of the assets of the estate a house should be built, and devised such a house and two acres of land adjoining it to them and their heirs forever. It appeared subsequently that after making certain money payments to the heirs, including the negroes, the personal assets of the estate were insufficient to build the house as specified in the will. It was held in chancery in 1848 that the testator had not intended that the house should be built out the assets arising from the realty; hence the house could not be built, there could be no two acres of " adjoining land," and the devise was void. I *Md. Chancery,* pp. 355-58. At the end of the report of the opinion it was stated that no appeal was taken in the case.

alleged they were incompetent to do so.[1] But in response to an application for similar action in another case the House of Delegates took the view that the existing laws did not " preclude free negroes from holding and transmitting real estate to their legitimate descendants." [2]

The legislature also passed two acts to validate titles to real estate.[3] But this did not mean that other titles were incomplete without such validation.[4] Free negroes enjoyed the right to hold property by all of the common methods of possession and ownership. The sole exceptions to this rule in point of either kind or quantity were found in the restrictions on keeping dogs and guns.

The general act of 1715 forbade any negro or other slave without his master's consent to carry a gun or other offensive weapon, when away from his master's premises.[5] In 1806 in response to petitions for further regulations the legislature prohibited the keeping of either a dog or a gun by a slave. It also enacted that a free negro going at large with a gun was liable to forfeit the same and to payment of costs, unless he had a magistrate's certificate stating that he was an orderly person. Such a certificate was valid for his protection for only twelve months.[6] Subsequent petitions called for more legislation so insistently that from

[1] *Laws*, 1834, ch. 187; 1856, ch. 337; 1858, chs. 75, 296, 408; cf. *Md. Appeal Reports*, 1 H. & McH., pp. 559-63.

[2] *H. Dels. Journal*, 1835, pp. 68, 356, 357. The committee here referred to the act of 1825, ch. 156.

[3] *Laws*, 1834, ch. 112; 1854, ch. 52.

[4] The legislature several times declined to take final action upon proposals to take away titles to real estate from free negroes. *H. Dels. Journal*, 1836, pp. 23, 243; 1849, p. 416; *Senate Journal*, 1838, pp. 14-15; *Md. Pub. Docs.*, 1845 G., p. 2; cf. *Md. Appeal Reports*, 12 Md., pp. 462-64.

[5] *Laws*, 1715, ch. lxiv, sec. 32.

[6] *Laws*, 1806, ch. 81.

1824 to 1831 the privilege of keeping firearms was entirely denied to negroes.[1] But this stringent provision was relaxed by the act of 1831. This act allowed the free negro to keep powder, lead, a fire-lock, or military weapon, but only on condition that he procured a license therefor from the court of the county or corporation wherein he resided: his license was to be renewed annually and was liable to be recalled sooner. Moreover, he was liable to forfeit any such articles found in his possession without license, and for a second offence to be whipped with not exceeding thirty-nine stripes.[2] In the following year remuneration was voted to negroes for arms taken from them up to that time and not yet forfeited to the informers,[3] but sentiment did not recoil in favor of a restoration of the privilege denied. As for keeping dogs the act of 1806 provided that a free negro might procure a license yearly from a justice of the peace allowing him to keep only one dog which anybody might kill if found at large.[4] The law remained at this, with the exception that in 1854 an act applying to Kent County created a dog tax, added a fine for a free negro who kept a dog without a license, and a treble fine for keeping a bitch in any case.[5] Under these laws some guns were seized. In 1859-60 for a time the privileges granted were revoked in some counties and special searches made for weapons.[6] On complaint also negroes' dogs were

---

[1] *Op. cit.*, 1824, ch. 303; *cf. H. Dels. Journal*, 1813, pp. 62, 98, 99.

[2] Dealers were likewise to be penalized, in case they sold any of these forbidden articles to negroes who had not special magisterial permits for the purchase. *Laws*, 1831, ch. 323, sec. 7; *cf. Md. Republican*, Nov. 12, 1831.

[3] *H. Dels. Journal*, 1832, p. 84.

[4] *Laws*, 1806, ch. 81.

[5] *Op. cit.*, 1854, ch. 262; *cf H. Dels. Journal*, 1838, pp. 271, 422, 690.

[6] *Annapolis Gazette*, Oct. 18, 1860; *Baltimore Sun*, Nov. 17, 1859; *Easton Gazette*, Dec. 3, 1859; *Somerset Union*, Jan. 5, 1860; *cf. Baltimore Clipper*, Jan. 6, 1849.

killed by the constables, when they increased beyond the numbers permitted by the law. But as a rule these regulations were well enforced only in and near the cities and towns, while in the more remote rural districts there was less interference with violations of the law.

The early prohibition of marriages between negroes and whites was referred to in the chapter on the provincial period. It was there noted that according to a law of the year 1663-64 both white women who married negro slaves and their children by slave husbands were to be condemned to slavery. This provision was also extended to marriages with free negroes.[1] After some later modifications an act of 1717 provided that a free negro or free mulatto marrying a white person should become a slave for life, saving that, if the mulatto offender was a child of a white woman, he was to serve only seven years.[2] A minister or magistrate solemnizing such a marriage was to be fined. This statute became a permanent part of the code.[3] But as the relations between the races became more definitely fixed, intermarriage between whites and negroes became much less frequent and the uninvoked prohibition practically became a dead-letter. Free negroes formed unions with persons of their own color, either slave or free, subject to the same conditions as those governing the whites, saving that the legal incapacity of slaves affected the results materially in many cases.

The vexed question of the system of involuntary labor was that of keeping the workmen at home. In Maryland the masters and officials generally cooperated in intercept-

---

[1] *Archives of Md.*, vol. xiii, pp. 546-47; vol. xxii, p. 552.

[2] *Laws*, 1717, ch. xiii. For penalties on the offspring, *vide*, 1717, ch. xliv; *cf.* also 1790, ch. ix.

[3] *Code of 1860*, art. 30, secs. 127, 128; *cf.* secs. 151, 152, on white women guilty of fornication with negroes.

ing and returning absconders to their places, and the law endeavored to facilitate their efforts. Restrictions on the freedom of negroes which were designed to protect masters' interests were passed by the legislature. The earliest statutes referring to negroes had to do with their running away.[1] They dealt mainly with the unfree, but they also concerned indentured free negroes who ran away and freemen who aided or harbored fugitive servants.[2] But besides this the free negroes were hampered in going from place to place on their own account. Although they were generally protected, so long as they remained among those who knew they were free, once outside the circle of such acquaintances they were liable to be suspected and to be treated as fugitive slaves. According to the act of 1715 they could be arrested, and if unable to prove satisfactorily that they were not runaways, returned to their masters, or sold into servitude to pay the costs of their detention and trial.[3] Delays in the trial of causes led to accumulation of such expenses. In order to cover them the terms for which the prisoners were sold were sometimes long.[4] To free negroes who had

[1] *Laws*, 1641, ch. vi; 1649, ch. v; 1654, ch. xxx; *cf.* also 1671, ch. ii; 1676, ch. ii.

[2] For the last named offence the penalties were, according to the act of 1641, ch. vi, death and forfeiture of land and goods; according to that of 1715, ch. xliv, a fine of a thousand pounds of tobacco, or in default of payment a term of servitude; and according to the act of 1748, ch. xix a hundred pounds of tobacco for every hour the fugitive was harbored.

[3] *Laws*, 1715, ch. xliv. For a few cases of such detentions, *vide* advertisements in the *Md. Journal*, Dec. 15, 1786; Aug. 21, 1789; Feb. 9, May 11, June 11, Aug. 3, Sept. 24, 1790; June 3, 1791; Nov. 15, 1793; July 15, 1793; May 16, Aug. 8, Oct. 13, 1796; *Baltimore Chattel Recs.*, Lib. WG, no. 14, p. 454; Lib. WG, no. 20, p. 233; Lib. WG, no. 23, p. 142.

[4] *Niles Register*, vol. 21, p. 32; vol. 31, p. 25; also *Baltimore Chattel Recs.*, as in the last note.

offended only by coming into a community this seemed an unmerited hardship. In 1817 therefore the legislature enacted that in future the counties were to meet the expenses thus incurred from other sources.[1] But its act of justice to free negroes left upon the counties a financial burden for which no revenue was now forthcoming. This was particularly true in Baltimore County, to which many negroes came from the rest of the state. To relieve its embarrassment another statute was passed requiring justices who committed negroes to jail to produce the names and places of residence of supposed owners and to state the grounds upon which commitment had been made, in order that final disposition of their cases might be made within forty-eight hours from time of commitment. Only those recommitted after examination were to be advertised as suspects.[2] According to an act of 1828 the expenses incurred on account of those who were finally released without penalty were provided from the state treasury.[3]

The general negro act of 1715 impliedly sanctioned the use of passes by servants sent on errands for their masters.[4] Similarly free negroes sometimes secured from their manumitters, or often from county officials and magistrates, papers to enable them to go about without interference.

[1] *Laws*, 1817, ch. 112.

[2] *Op. cit.*, 1824, ch. 171.

[3] *Op. cit.*, 1828, ch. 98; *cf. H. Dels. Journal*, 1828, p. 609; *Washington Orphans' Court Minutes*, 1850-52, pp. 18, 69; 1855-59, pp. 338, 536, 681. In 1826 such fees had been paid by the county. *31 Niles Register*, p. 25. The act of 1840, ch. 237, provided that the county should pay the prison fees and remit the fine of a free negro imprisoned at Frederick.

Rev. Charles T. Torrey wrote in 1844 that he thought he had broken up "the old, but now illegal practice of imprisoning men of color who were free, and then selling them for their jail fees," while he was imprisoned at Annapolis. Lovejoy, *Memoir of Rev. Charles T. Torrey*, p. 130; *cf.* also 131.

[4] *Laws*, 1715, ch. xliv.

Within proper limits this practice would have been a great convenience to all concerned. But after the revolution its use spread too rapidly, certificates were counterfeited and transferred and no longer served as a sure means of identification of persons. The ruses thus employed enabled slaves to escape when otherwise they would have been detained,[1] and eventually gave rise to doubts about the genuineness of many bona-fide freedom papers. They injured the interests of both masters and negroes entitled to freedom. In order to correct the confusion and the other evils that resulted, the legislature in 1796 enacted a provision that any free negro who should give or sell a certificate of freedom, issued to him by a magistrate or clerk of a county court, and should thereby enable a slave to escape from service, should be liable to fine of a hundred and fifty dollars, one half of which was to go to the offended slave-owner.[2] It was a time of rapid growth of the free negro population. " Great mischiefs " still arose from the possession of freemen's certificates by slaves. In 1805, therefore, another act was passed to confine the issuance of freedom certificates to the clerks of the county courts, registers of wills and local magistrates of the counties where the manumissions of parties were recorded, and in 1807 this function was limited to the first two classes of officers. Stipulations were made that certificates were to be recorded and that applicants for them

---

[1] For mention of such papers, *cf. Baltimore Gazette*, May 13, 1829; *Cecil Whig*, July 24, 1858; *Md. Gazette*, Oct. 28, 1790; May 15, 1788; *Md. Journal*, Jan. 7, 1783; June 14, 1793; *Md. Republican*, Oct. 8, 1825; Nov. 11, 1828; Oct. 7, 1817. They were often mentioned in connection with advertised runaways. Copies of such passes may be found in *Md. Land Recs.*, Lib. DD, no. 6, p. 566 (1781). And *Somerset Land Recs.*, Lib. K.

[2] *Laws*, 1796, ch. 67, sec. 28. In the code of 1860 this fine was given as $300, art. 30, sec. 154. *Cf. Cecil Whig*, Nov. 10, 1860; also *Md. Pub. Docs.*, 1850, pp. 264, 395.

were to give satisfactory evidence of their titles to freedom and satisfactory account of papers alleged to have been
lost. Papers were moreover to contain particular descrip-
tions of the persons, the ages, times of manumission and
places of origin of their bearers. Freeborn negroes might
secure papers similar to these saving the reference to manumission.[1] Any grants of such certificates excepting by
those so authorized were to be severely penalized. The
volumes of copies of these papers, as " Records of Freedom
Certificates," or " Records of Free Negroes " in the several
counties,[2] show a literal compliance with the tenor of these
provisions. Later proposals to require annual or periodical
renewal of freedom papers by all free negroes were rejected
by the general assembly.[3]

The laws restricting the introduction of slaves into Maryland were mentioned in the preceding chapter. Their object had been to check the growth of the negro population,
and their enactment had come at a time when none could
have foreseen the results of the manumission movement.
The subsequent growth of the class of freedmen at home and
in the neighboring states aroused fears that the coming of free
negroes might defeat the ends of the exclusion policy. A new
barrier was, therefore, raised by a statute of 1807 which made
it an offence to be penalized by a fine of ten dollars a week
for any non-resident free negro to come into the state and
remain there longer than two weeks. In default of payment of the fine the intruder was to be sold into servitude
to pay his fine and costs. Exception was to be made only
for sailors, and for waggoners and messengers in the actual
service of non-resident employers.[4] This law failed to be

[1] *Laws*, 1805, ch. 66; 1807, ch. 164.

[2] *Cf.* Bibliography, *infra*, p. 12.

[3] *H. Dels. Journal*, 1835, pp. 39, 48; 1843, pp. 145, 552, 649; 1853, pp.
37, 755, 1038.

[4] *Laws*, 1806, ch. 56.

effective and attempts were made to strengthen it. Finally in 1823 a supplementary act was passed mainly on account of reports about conditions in the counties bordering on the Potomac River. It refused exemption to offenders without respect to the length of their residence in Maryland and to those found in the state after having been penalized and required especial vigilance in executing the law in nine of the counties.[1] The provisions were reaffirmed in 1831 and 1839, and heavier penalties were added to their violation. First the period of sojourn of the non-residents without penalty was reduced to ten days, and the fines to be imposed for their remaining beyond that limit were quintupled, and in the case of those who harbored or employed them doubled;[2] while the second act made the mere inward crossing of the state boundary finable, and raised to five hundred dollars the penalty for either a refusal to leave the state within five days after having been fined, or for re-entry after expulsion.[3] The federal district, however, afforded a loophole through which negroes continued to come in, claiming immunity on the ground that the place from whence they came was not outside of Maryland. The whites in the neighboring quarters of Maryland were annoyed and " greatly injured " by it. Hence in 1845 the provisions of the act of 1839 were extended to apply to negro residents of the District of Columbia.[4]

In outward aspect these laws created a Chinese wall

---

[1] *Op. cit.*, 1823, ch. 161. The nine counties were Allegany, Anne Arundel, Calvert, Charles, Kent, Montgomery, Prince George's, Somerset and Worcester. *Cf. H. Dels. Journal*, 1823, pp. 52, 70, 88.

[2] *Laws*, 1831, ch. 323.

[3] *Op. cit.*, 1839, ch. 38. Thus far, it appears, there had been no further penalty for refusal to leave the state after conviction of a first offence. *Md. Appeal Reports*, 12 G. & J., p. 335.

[4] *Laws*, 1845, ch. 153.

which mounted ever upward. Under them some offenders
were penalized.[1] But with the increase of the free negro
population the immigrant's facility in escaping detection by
those who would be likely to report him was increased. In the
case that came before the Court of Appeals in 1842 it was
declared by counsel whose view the court upheld that any
proceeding to lay a fine had to be instituted within twelve
months after the alleged offence had been committed.[2] In
some cases negroes could stay about unobserved for a
year, or until they seemed from long residence to belong
where they were. The whites on their part, although sometimes vigilant, hardly loathed their coming enough to
favor a stringent execution of the exclusion policy.[3] Complaints that they were apathetic, or that the law was ineffective, did not avail to create a consistent demand for better
enforcement. And the legislature, although maintaining
the enactments in the manner indicated above, passed other
acts making exceptions to its own cherished policy. To be
sure, it rejected or ignored the majority of the petitions
asking that the law should be waived on behalf of individuals, but it found sufficient, special pretexts for heeding

[1] *Baltimore Gazette*, Jan. 1, 1831; *Carroll Criminal Docket*, no. 1, p.
85, no. 2, p. 76; *Cecil Land Recs.*, Lib. JS, no. 11, p. 181; *Cecil Whig*,
Oct. 22, 1859; Jan. 12, 1861; E. *Shore General Advertiser*, Mar. 24, 1807;
Easton Star, Oct. 30, 1849; *Frederick Orphans' Court Proceedings*, April
9, 1845; *Howard Orphans' Court Minutes*, Lib. TJ, no. 2, p. 48; *Washington Criminal Appearance Docket*, no. 8; *Washington Orphans' Court
Minutes*, 1835-46, pp. 208, 289; 1852-55, pp. 72, 261, 360, 559, 563; 1855-59,
pp. 174, 336, 649. No doubt some of the negroes taken up as runaway
slaves and sold for jail fees, or discharged without penalty, were immigrant free negroes. Some of them claimed to be such.

[2] *Md. Appeal Reports*, 12 G. & J., pp. 335-36; cf. preceding paragraph,
act of 1823, ch. 161. The act referred to by this advocate was one of
the year 1777, ch. vi.

[3] E. g. H. *Dels. Journal*, 1823, pp. 52, 70, 88; *Republican Star and E.
Shore General Advertiser*, July 16, 1822.

others.[1] Even after the penalties had reached their extreme height in 1839, three such petitions were granted.
But in two of them restrictions as to the place of residence
were imposed.[2] And in another case a negro resident of
the District of Columbia was permitted to go under bond
to visit his wife in Prince George's County for periods of
four days at a time.[3]

Another form of exclusion appeared as a part of the
colonization scheme. As a complement to the provision
requiring manumitted negroes to leave the state, one of the
hydra-headed laws of 1831 enacted that, if a resident negro
should spend a period of thirty or more days outside the
state, he should be regarded as having established a domicile
there, unless he should have signified in writing to the clerk
of the court before leaving both the object of his journey
away and his intention to return to Maryland. Exception
was again made for sailors, waggoners and hired domestics
in the employment of non-residents.[4] Thirteen years later
one act repealed the clause regarding the written statement
to the clerk of the court; and a second act of the same session explained that the first was not to be construed to prevent colored residents from going and staying outside longer
than thirty days between the first of May and the first of
November each year, provided they procured the required
permits from the orphans' courts. But no such permit
was to be had without the endorsement of three " respectable" white persons.[5] Up to that time negroes had been

[1] *Laws*, 1807, ch. vi; 1816, ch. 211; 1822, ch. 54; 1826, chs. 120, 121, 166;
1827, ch. 169; 1837, chs. 117, 345. Brackett records that out of twenty
petitions offered eight were granted in the years 1806-31. *The Negro
in Maryland*, p. 177.

[2] *Op. cit.*, 1847, ch. 133; 1854, ch. 261; 1858, ch. 364.

[3] *Op. cit.*, 1847, ch. 103.

[4] *Op. cit.*, 1831, ch. 323.

[5] *Op. cit.*, 1844, chs. 16, 283. For specimen permits, *vide Kent Chattel*

allowed to sojourn outside the state for periods of less than thirty days each and to return at will. Complaints came from certain Eastern Shore counties that that privilege had been abused by negroes running to and from Delaware. In response the legislature in 1849 enacted that free negro residents of Cecil, Kent and Queen Anne's counties, who should return after having once left the state, should be liable to the high penalties of the act of 1839 against immigrating free negroes.[1] This measure, however, went too far, and soon a modification of it was desired. Accordingly in 1853 it was so changed as to allow the return of free negro employees of white persons in Cecil County from business errands across the state border within twenty-four hours of the time of their going out,[2] and three years later the same privileges were extended under like conditions for ten-day periods to colored employees hired by the month to white farmers of the two counties of Cecil and Kent.[3]

The observance of these restrictions was subject to the same condition as that of the immigration laws. The people willingly countenanced some vigilance in regard to the movements of the negroes. But they did not generally favor interference with innocent travel. Many permits to leave Maryland and return were given in some of the counties,[4]

Recs., Lib. JGN, no. 2, pp. 396, 431, 529, 531, 535; Lib. JGN, no. 3, pp. 15, 461, 462; Washington Orphans' Court Minutes, 1835-46, pp. 303, 310, 315, 355, 356, 362 and passim.

[1] Laws, 1849, ch. 538, supra, pp. 78-79.

[2] Op. cit., 1853, ch. 177.

[3] Op. cit., 1856, ch. 161.

[4] Supra, p. 81, note 2; Cecil Land Recs., Lib. JS, no. 31, pp. 43, 119; Lib. GMcC, no. 8, p. 145; Somerset Deeds, Lib. LH, pp. 121, 289, 381; Washington Orphans' Court Minutes, 1850-52, pp. 103, 260, 261, 264, 270, 275, 278, 279, 282, 296, 307, 411, 412, 426 and passim; 1852-55, pp. 147, 164, 196, 197, 198 and passim.

and it appears that the special restrictions applying to the
three Eastern Shore counties were for a time enforced,[1] but
complete enforcement of the statewide law did not follow.
The legislature also made exceptions to its rules. It voted
to grant immunity from penalities to negroes who visited
Trinidad, Guiana and Liberia with a view to migrating from
Maryland.[2] In doing so it could plead obvious necessity in
facilitating the execution of the colonization plan. But aside
from this it allowed the merits of certain individual appli-
cations for re-entry to outweigh considerations of that
public policy: it passed acts in 1854-60 permitting the return of at least eleven negroes, whom the act of 1831 would
have barred.[3]

The free negro had the right to maintain actions at law
in the Maryland courts. Notwithstanding that this had
been the practice, a doubt about it, or a wish that it had not
been true, lurked in some minds until late in the history of
slavery. A case in point came up in the Court of Appeals
in 1858. It was contended that a negro could not sue without first having proved that he was of free condition. The
court, on the contrary, held that not only was it not necessary
for the free negro to prove his freedom in such a case but
that he need not even declare himself a " free negro " in
his pleadings. Reciting the cases in which the negro suffered disqualification on account of his color, it further
stated that in all other cases legal policy and social welfare
alike required that he should be allowed to defend his
person and his property in the courts. The denial of these
rights could confer no benefit upon others, while their pro-

[1] *Cecil Whig*, Aug. 7, 14, 1858; *Baltimore Sun*, June 10, 1859, report of
slaveholders' convention.

[2] *Laws*, 1839, ch. v; *Md. Col. Journal*, vol. iii, p. 354; vol. iv, p. 17;
infra, chapter on " Colonization," p. 284.

[3] *Laws*, 1854, ch. 66; 1856, chs. 37, 84, 229, 271; 1860, ch. 345.

tection would become the incentive to thrift and respectability.[1]

In respect to giving evidence in the courts, however, the rights of negroes were limited. A statute of the year 1717, declaring that " dangerous consequences " would follow an unrestricted admission of negro evidence, enacted that no negro or mulatto slave, free negro, or mulatto born of a white woman during the servitude appointed by law, should be accepted as " good and valid evidence " in law in any matter depending before a magistrate or a court of record, wherein a Christian white person was a party.[2] In 1846 the provision was extended to the cases of whites who were not Christians.[3] But in a case involving the interests of free negroes in which other competent testimony was lacking, this evidence might be introduced, provided it was not a cause involving life or limb. The logical consequences of the act are thus set forth by Dr. Brackett: " The child of a white man and a mulatto slave would be during life incapable of witnessing against a white; the child of a black man and a white woman . . . . would be so disqualified during the limited term, only, for which he was put to service. A free mulatto was good evidence against a white person." [4] An act of 1796 excluded from freedom trials the testimony of negroes freed according to the terms of the act of 1783;[5] beginning in 1801 slaves were permitted to testify against

[1] *Md. Appeal Reports*, 12 Md., pp. 450-51, 462-64. The cases of disqualification were that of incompetency to testify in a suit to which a white person was a party, and that of assuming the burden of proof in any suit involving a negro's own liberty.

[2] *Laws*, 1717, ch. xiii.

[3] *Op. cit.*, 1846, ch. 27; cf. H. Dels. Journal, 1852, p. 19; 1856, p. 127.

[4] Brackett, *The Negro in Maryland*, p. 191; cf. *Md. Appeal Reports*, 3 H. & J., p. 97.

[5] *Laws*, 1796, ch. 67, sec. 5.

free negroes who were charged either with stealing, or receiving stolen articles from others, and in 1808 the restrictions upon the use of negro evidence in criminal prosecutions
of negroes were entirely removed.[1] In the test cases
brought before its bar the appeal court upheld the principles
set forth in these statutes.[2]

Under the constitution of 1776 white persons and negroes
were allowed to vote at elections for members of the lower
house of the legislature without discrimination on account
of color. For those negroes who were freed before the
year 1783 this privilege was continued for another quarter
of a century, and those who were otherwise qualified had a
part in political life.[3] But a statute of 1783 denied to
persons manumitted thereafter the privileges of office-hold-
ing, voting at elections, giving evidence against white persons, and all other rights of freemen excepting those of
acquiring and holding property and obtaining redress at
law and equity for injuries to person and property.[4] But
this law did not affect the position of free negroes residing
in Maryland prior to its passage. Their privileges were,
however, regarded with jealousy, and an ineffectual attempt
to bar them from voting for members of the House of
Delegates, for the electors for state senators and for sheriffs

[1] *Op. cit.*, 1801, ch. 109; 1808, ch. 81; *cf.* also 1820, ch. 88.

[2] *Md. Appeal Reports*, 3 H. & J., pp. 97-98, 491; *cf. op. cit.*, p. 158;
1 H. & J., p. 750; 5 H. & J., p. 51; 12 Md., p. 274; *Baltimore Sun*, Dec.
19, 1856. *Vide* attempt to disparage the testimony of a white who, it
was alleged, "associated and kept company with negroes." *Md. Appeal
Reports*, 3 H. & J., p. 241.

[3] It was alleged that James McHenry availed of free negro support
in agitating for the ratification of the federal constitution by the convention of Maryland, *Md. Journal*, Sept. 30, 1788; *cf.* election notice in
Md. Journal, July 10, 1775.

[4] *Laws*, 1783, ch. xxiii. Substantially the same provisions were re-
enacted in the act of 1796, ch. 67.

was made in 1802.[1] It was followed by the constitutional amendment of 1810 which took away their rights and limited the suffrage in local, state and national elections to white persons.[2] Subsequent legislation wrought no changes in their behalf. The right of petition for redress of grievances remained and was frequently availed of, although it was asserted that its existence did not diminish the legislature's power to make such disposition of the free colored population as seemed good to it.[3]

The next question is that of holding negro assemblies. The perpetuation of the relations existing between the white and black races in Maryland society was conditioned upon the indisputable control of affairs by the former. Efforts were made by the whites to organize themselves to maintain that control. The same end was also held in view in the endeavors to make sure of an absence of organization on the part of the negroes. The chief measure taken was that to prevent rebellious action by negro assemblies. The acts passed for this purpose in the eighteenth century did not provide for separate penalties for slaves and free negroes. But those laws became the basis for the later legislation affecting the free negroes. An act against the frequent assembling of negroes was passed in 1695.[4] It was followed in 1723 by an act authorizing constables to flog negroes found in tumultuous meetings without permission,[5] in 1725 by special prohibitions of both tumultuous

[1] Official publication in the *Herald* and *E. Shore Intelligencer*, May 4, 1802.

[2] Kilty, *Laws of Maryland*, vol. iii, p. xxxviii; *cf. Laws*, 1809, ch. 83, secs. 1, 2, 4.

[3] *Cf.* Declaration of Rights in *Constitution of 1850-51*. Also *Md. Pub. Docs.*, 1845 G, pp. 3, 4, 5, and Brackett, *op. cit.*, p. 187.

[4] *Laws*, 1695, chs. 6, 26.

[5] *Op. cit.*, 1723, ch. 15. *Cf.* chapter on Colonial Period, p. 32.

meetings and the sale of spirituous liquors within three miles of any of the Quaker meetings in Anne Arundel and Talbot counties, and later by acts enjoining the bailiffs of Easton and certain other towns to prevent tumultuous meetings of negroes, slaves and " other disorderly and dissolute persons within the limits" of their authority.[1] But in re-enacting the provisions of the old general law in 1806 it was added that any free negro found in a tumultuous meeting was to be fined or imprisoned, if he had been disorderly, but if not, to be bonded for good behavior and for appearance in the county court.[2] Under the authority of these laws the constables had deputized citizens to assist in their searches. In four of the counties in 1820 the law was extended to enable the justices of the peace, on complaint of three persons, to organize companies which were to be composed of fifteen persons of military age in each instance, to search for and break up " riotous and unlawful " meetings of negroes and to bring actual and suspected offenders before the magistrates for trial. These companies, or patrols, were to have power to search negro dwellings and other buildings by force and were to make especial marks of negroes away from their own homes and offenders against negro exclusion laws. The law was first enacted for four counties of Southern Maryland,[3] and was later extended to Calvert, Frederick and Kent counties.[4] The patrols were first designed chiefly to keep slaves at home

---

[1] *Laws*, 1725, ch. 6; 1747, ch. 17; 1790, ch. 14; 1796, ch. 30; 1804, ch. 70.

[2] *Laws*, 1806, ch. 81. In 1809, ch. 38, the offence of raising an insurrection, which had long been a capital crime for slaves, cf. act of 1737, ch. 7, was expressly made capital for free negroes also.

[3] *Laws*, 1820, ch. 200. Cf. *Amer. Farmer*, vol. i, pp. 98-99, letter from a whilom resident of Southern Maryland.

[4] *Op. cit.*, 1822, ch. 85; 1826, ch. 210; 1856, ch. 177; cf. also 1842, ch. 281, sec. 5.

at night, but were used against free negroes as well as against slaves, and according to common report too often degenerated into the use of undue violence without salutary results.[1]

The act of 1806 had not been directed against innocent assemblages. Although there had been some jealousy of the independent African church, its meetings were generally unmolested. But the religious services held in an old meeting house at Piscataway in Prince George's County excited the displeasure of the whites. They reported that they were a nuisance and induced the legislature to prohibit all meetings there excepting on Sunday and on Easter and Whit-Monday between the hours of seven o'clock a. m. and five p. m. Free negroes who violated the prohibition were to be fined, slaves striped.[2] These restrictions were local and comparatively mild. Three years later the legislators were seized by the frenzy that followed the Southampton insurrection in Virginia and by reports of a similar plot in Anne Arundel County, Maryland. They then enacted that outside of the cities of Annapolis and Baltimore free negroes were not to assemble nor to attend any religious meeting which was not conducted either by a licensed white preacher, or by some respectable white person of the neghborhood. In the two excepted cities white ministers were authorized to grant permits to negroes to hold meetings before the hour of ten o'clock p. m., and slave owners could permit like meetings on their own premises. Negro meetings not thus authorized were liable to be dispersed and those in attendance to be punished.[3] In 1844 camp and bush-meetings

---

[1] Cf. Md. Republican, April 16, 1817; Nov. 12, 1831; Somerset Union, Nov. 8, 1859.

[2] Laws, 1828, ch. 151.

[3] Laws, 1831, ch. 323, secs. 7 and 8. Cf. Md. Republican, Nov. 29, 1831.

and all other meetings of negroes excepting those held in regular and appointed houses of worship according to the act of 1831 were prohibited. But in the following session an amendment confined this prohibition to camp and bush-meetings,[1] and stated that the negroes might attend the camp-meetings held by the whites of any of the religious sects.

The act of 1831 seemed inadequate to cover the cases of fraternal and benevolent societies. Hence another act was passed in 1842 prohibiting free negroes to become members of any secret societies, or to allow meetings for such purposes to be held on their premises. The penalty for violation of this provision was to be a fine of fifty dollars to be paid, or satisfied, by servitude of the offender, and for a second offence slavery for life outside of the state of Maryland. White persons furnishing meeting-places for such societies were to be liable to terms of service in the state penitentiary.[2] But the facility of interference here afforded struck at the charitable and burial societies of the " honest, industrious and peaceable " colored people of Baltimore City. White friends of these enterprises interceded in their behalf. In response to their appeal the legislature amended the act so as to allow the mayor of Baltimore to grant annual permits to free colored residents of that city, who paid five dollars, or more, each in taxes, to form charitable societies and hold meetings to promote their objects. But a police officer was to attend each meeting, to sit throughout and to report to the mayor upon its doings.[3]   In

---

[1] *Op. cit.*, 1845, ch. 94, and 1846, ch. 166. *Cf. H. Dels. Journal*, 1844, pp. 40, 105, 265; 1845, pp. 8, 22, 163. Also *Senate Journal*, 1845, p. 1, and *Md. Republican*, Nov. 29, 1831.

[2] *Laws*, 1842, ch. 281. *Cf. Senate Journal*, 1842, p. 142. *H. Dels. Journal*, 1841, pp. 222, 226.

[3] *Op. cit.*, 1845, ch. 284.

1846 an act withheld from the free negroes the privilege of incorporating lyceums, masonic and other lodges, fire companies, and literary, dramatic, social, moral and charitable societies.[1]

The negroes had warmly cherished the privilege of holding assembles. They regarded its curtailment with deep regret and yet with submissiveness. The more repressive restrictions had been enacted at a time when alarmist whites had apprehended negro violence. They had been advertised, until they became as well known as any part of the negro code. Possessing this knowledge the negroes in general preferred to observe the restrictions rather than provoke the wrath of the whites by breaking them. In this endeavor they enlisted the assistance of whites, many of whom desired to mitigate the hardships resulting from the laws. Negro meetings led by white preachers fulfilled the law to the letter. Those led by negroes were legitimized by the presence of whites acting as " protectors." In carrying out the law the scrutiny of negro conduct varied considerably. Forbearance was often shown towards omissions. But if there were fears of disorder, systematic interference was sure to follow. Aside from the churches there were in the counties some colonization societies and a few short-lived schools, all of which were tolerated only so long as they were not suspected of sinister designs. In Harford County in 1860-61 three negroes were prosecuted and fined " for being members of a secret association."[2]

The negroes of the city of Baltimore had a variety of negro organizations, whose managers apparently conformed well to the demands of the law. The whites there were more tolerant than those of the rural counties, but in cases of violation of the law the police supported by the courts

[1] *Op. cit.*, 1846, ch. 323.
[2] *Harford Criminal Docket*, Lib. WG, pp. 52-53.

interfered to restore order.[1] The rules regarding negro assemblies constituted an eminent infringement of the fundamental rights of freemen.

The provincial laws of Maryland exempted the negroes from the duty of serving in the militia.[2] But in the fall of 1780, when a draft was authorized in order to secure a thousand additional soldiers for three years service, slaves and freemen alike were to be admitted. And in the following year it was added that " every free male idle person, above sixteen years of age, who is able-bodied, and hath no visible means of an honest livelihood, may be adjudged a vagrant by the lieutenant, and by such adjudication he is to be considered as an enlisted soldier." [3] Beginning again in 1793 the militia service was confined to the whites.[4] But in 1814 the negroes of Baltimore were both invited and " required " by the committee on vigilance and safety to aid in constructing fortifications for the defence of the city.[5]

Property holders in Maryland without distinction as to color contributed to the ordinary public revenues. In providing for public roads and free schools, however, the negro became the subject of certain discriminations. It was held that many free negroes paid no taxes and performed no military duty, and that it was but reasonable that they should contribute to repairing the public roads. Accord-

---

[1] *Cf. Baltimore Clipper*, Feb. 24, 26, 1849; *Baltimore Sun*, Mar. 10, 1854; Jan. 1, 1857; July 26, 1858; May 11, 12, 1859; Oct. 3, 1860; Payne, *History of the A. M. E. Church*, pp. 231-32. *Cf.* also Brackett, *op. cit.*, pp. 204-05.

[2] *Laws*, 1715, ch. 43; 1722, ch. 15; 1733, ch. 7. *Cf.* 1777, chs. 3, 17.

[3] *Laws*, November, 1780, ch. 43; May, 1781, ch. 15. The quotation here given is from the abstract of the act given in the *General Laws*, published in 1787.

[4] *Laws*, 1793, ch. 53.

[5] *Baltimore American*, Sept. 12, Oct. 29, 1814. *Cf.* also *Laws*, 1822, ch. 58.

ingly the public road act passed for Caroline County in 1822 authorized each road supervisor to call upon any free negro over eighteen and under fifty years of age residing in his district to work upon the roads for one day in each year.[1] The act for Talbot in 1825 laid a similar burden upon non-tax-paying free negroes and able-bodied slaves;[2] while that for Worcester two years later required three days labor of free negroes, and two days labor of whites who paid no taxes.[3] These statutes virtually imposed poll taxes upon negroes, although they were not wholly discriminatory. In respect to the schools, of which the negroes did not have common use, a few discriminations were made in the opposite direction. An act applying to the first election district of Baltimore County made all white persons above the age of twenty-one years, who were not otherwise taxable, subject to a personal tax for school purposes, but omitted all references to negroes who paid no property taxes.[4] The exemption of the property of negroes from school taxes was authorized in the act of 1834 applying to Kent, in that of 1838 applying to Montgomery, and in the code of 1860 as applying to Anne Arundel.[5]

The penal clauses of the negro code were of varied char-

[1] Laws, 1822, ch. 58.

[2] Op. cit., 1825, ch. 196. Cf. 1827, ch. 96.

[3] Op. cit., 1827, ch. 56. Cf. 1826, ch. 73. Also 1849, ch. 534, act applying to Anne Arundel, Charles, Kent, Montgomery, and Prince George's. It authorized the calling upon free negroes who were not employed by white persons by the year, or who had no taxable estates in excess of $150 each.

[4] Laws, 1826, ch. 263. By the act of 1829, ch. 146, the free whites over twenty-one years of age were designated as those who were to vote on the question of establishing free schools in districts in which they held real estate.

[5] Op. cit., 1834, ch. 263; 1838, ch. 327. Code of 1860, art. 2, sec. 157. Cf. Kent Co. Levy List 1860.

acter.   According to the provincial laws death had been the
penalty for negroes committing, or attempting to commit,
the crimes of raising insurrection, of murdering or poison-
ing whites, arson and the rape of white women.[1]   The
penalties on slaves for perjury were flogging and cropping
the ears, and for absconding and rambling abroad at night
either flogging, branding on the cheek, or cropping the ears.[2]
But a change in the direction of less severity began in 1809.
It was attended also by some discriminations between slaves
and free negroes.   The penalty for attempted insurrection
by any negro freeman then became service in the penitentiary for not less than six nor more than twenty years,
while for this and for other non-capital crimes by slaves the
courts were at liberty to decree either service in the penitentiary, or flogging, or banishment to a foreign country.[3]
And after 1817 the minimum term for which any negro
could be sentenced to the penitentiary was one year, after
1825 two years, until in 1839 it was again altered to eighteen
months.[4]   For offences which seemed to merit lighter pains
than such services, fines, flogging or jail sentences were to be
substituted, as the courts deemed most fitting.   After 1818
slaves were to be excluded from commitment to the penitentiary—their offences being thenceforth penable by flogging
on bare back, by banishment from Maryland, or by transportation abroad.[5]   And for the interval between two sessions of the legislature in 1825-1826 the same thing was true

---

[1] *Laws*, 1751, ch. 14.   *Cf. Session Laws*, 1729, ch. 24; 1737, ch. 7;
1740, ch. 7; 1744, ch. 18; 1747, ch. 16.   Also *Archives of Md.*, vol. xxxi,
p. 157; vol. xxxii, pp. 91-92, 163, 178-79, 200, 246-48, 333.   Death was
the penalty for burglary also.   *Op. cit.*, pp. 178-79.

[2] *Laws*, 1851, ch. 14.

[3] *Op. cit.*, 1809, ch. 138.

[4] *Op. cit.*, 1817, ch. 72; 1825, ch. 93; 1839, ch. 37.

[5] *Laws*, 1818, ch. 197.   *Cf.* also 1819, ch. 159.

of free negroes, saving that they were never to be sold to serve for terms in excess of those set for whites to serve in the penitentiary for similar offences. But on account of fears that this might entail life servitude upon those who were to be sold out of the state an act of 1826 restored the penalty of service in the penitentiary, which was to be followed on release by banishment from the state. Any negro found in the state later than sixty days after such release was to be liable to be sold into slavery for a term equal to his original prison term.[1] In 1831 the courts were again given the option of decreeing banishment of free negroes to foreign countries for non-capital offences in lieu of other penalties at home.[2] And in 1835 it was enacted that the criminal courts were to ascertain whether free negroes found guilty of crimes had previously served terms in the penitentiary. Those who had so served were to be liable to be sold out of the state as slaves for terms of years.[3]

The common law was not regarded as adequate to give nice justice to the free negro. Courts and executive officials were often embarrassed with the problem of what to do with him. Their labors were often lightened by assistance from two sources. One was that of the negro's " next friend," generally a white man, who undertook to vouch for him. The other was the passing of statutes by the legislature to cover defects in the law. Now some of the statutes enacted were probably obstacles to the course of justice. Others, however, served to enhance the highest political privileges of the citizen. The laws, although curtailing the privileges of the negro, still guaranteed to him many of the fundamental privileges of citizenship. It was

---

[1] *Op. cit.*, 1825, ch. 93; 1826, ch. 229.

[2] *Op. cit.*, 1831, ch. 323.

[3] *Op. cit.*, 1835, ch. 200. *Cf.* also 1838, ch. 69, on the distribution of the returns from such sales.

claimed by some that he fell short of legal equality with the whites but little more than the ignorant, unenfranchised rural laborer of contemporary Europe fell short of equality with his landlord.   He was protected in his essential rights and was permitted to improve his own condition.

CHAPTER IV

THE APPRENTICESHIP OF NEGRO CHILDREN

THE function of the negro in Maryland was to do manual labor. The rules of the negro code were designed mainly to facilitate the use of him in that capacity. The laws referred to in the preceding chapter had to do mainly with adult negroes. Provision was also made for the training of negro children to take up the work of the various trades, as they grew to manhood. Reference has already been made to the practice of binding out children to labor as apprentices under the supervision of the county courts of the province.[1] The same general policy was continued by the orphans' courts to whose hands the execution of the law was transferred during the revolution. The county courts had bound out white and colored children almost without discrimination on account of color. But because of the rapid growth of the free negro population the orphans' courts made a significant departure from that course. In certain of the counties they began early in the nineteenth century to omit the provision for education of negro apprentices. This innovation was copied in other counties, was sanctioned by statute in 1818, and thereafter tended to prevail outside of the city and county of Baltimore and Harford County.

The free negroes generally lacked knowledge of affairs, social prestige and power to command the use of material

---

[1] Chapter on the Colonial Period, p. 18.

resources for their own betterment. To some extent they also lacked the opportunities and other stimuli necessary to the endeavor to acquire these things. Those who prospered in spite of adverse circumstances were sometimes able to look well to the needs of their children. Those who tended to exert themselves only to the extent necessary to acquire a mean living generally fell short in rearing their offspring. From the latter number came most of the negro children who were bound out by the county officials to learn to labor.

Various reasons were assigned for apprehending them. The mother of an Anne Arundel County boy was a " complete pauper : " he was naked and breadless. The mother of another had died, and his father was a slave.[1] Two women left their children in Talbot County; one went to Baltimore and the other to Philadelphia.[2] Some others were mentioned as orphans in " entire destitution," some were taken from the county alms-houses, and some were illegitimates, and were without visible means of support.[3]

[1] *Anne Arundel Orphans' Court Minutes*, Lib. 216, pp. 112, 245. *Cf. op. cit.*, pp. 257, 269, 270, 274; Lib. 217, pp. 368, 369-75, 377; *Talbot Indentures*, Lib. 3, p. 340; Lib. 6, pp. 29, 136, 137. The last cited refers to a boy whose father was a slave and whose mother was serving a term in the state penitentiary.

[2] *Talbot Indentures*, Lib. 4, pp. 332, 468. *Cf. op. cit.*, p. 9; *Anne Arundel Orphans' Court Minutes*, Lib. 217, p. 321; *Baltimore Co. Indentures*, Lib. JLR no. 1, p. 118.

[3] *Anne Arundel, op. cit.*, Lib. 216, pp. 277, 294; Lib. 217, pp. 12, 35, 36, 370-77; Lib. 218, p. 15; *Baltimore Co. Indentures*, Lib. JLR no. 1, pp. 8, 17; *Carroll Indentures*, Lib. JB no. A, pp. 29, 53; *Orphans' Court Minutes* 1854-56, pp. 95, 367; *Frederick Orphans' Court Minutes*, May 22, 1826; Lib. R, p. 165; *Dorchester Orphans' Court Minutes*, Lib. THH no. 2, pp. 53, 280; *Harford Orphans' Court General Entries*, Lib. AJ no. 3, pp. 38, 114, 154, 216, 271, 277, 283; Lib. TSB no. 2, pp. 74, 178, 182, 205, 260, 276; *Talbot Indentures*, Lib. 3, pp. 18, 160; Lib. 4, p. 230; Lib. 6, p. 127; *Washington Indentures*, Lib. 3, pp. 121, 163, 244; Lib. 5, p. 319.

Again it was alleged of some that they were the children of "lazy and worthless free negroes," that they lacked "good and industrious habits," or were not at service or learning trades.[1] Waiving consideration of other consequences to these unfortunates, were nothing done for their relief, their growing up without learning to work was to be deplored.[2] Slaveholders and others voluntarily saved some of them from destitution without compensation. The rest were fit subjects for the apprenticeship system.

A general act of the legislature, passed in 1794, ordered that the Orphans' Courts in the several counties " shall and may bind out as an apprentice every orphan child, (the increase of profits of whose estate . . . . is or are not sufficient for maintenance, support and education, of the said child,) to some manufacturer, mechanic, mariner, handicraftsman, or other person . . . . until such orphan child, if a male shall arrive to the age of twenty-one years, or if a female, to the age of sixteen years."[3] The powers here conferred were sometimes exercised by the justices of the peace. Contracts that had been so sanctioned were validated by a statute in 1826, provided they conformed to the law in other points.[4] Prior to this, however, the legislature had begun to enact special laws dealing with colored children

---

[1] Anne Arundel Deeds, Lib. WSG no, 16, p. 49; Baltimore Co., op. cit., p. 8; Carroll Orphans' Court Minutes, 1854-56, p. 367; Cecil Indentures, Lib. 3, p. 331; Dorchester, op. cit., p. 256; Howard Chattel Recs., Lib. 2, p. 336; Orphans' Court Recs., Lib. WG no. 1, p. 133; Talbot Indentures, Lib. 4, p. 279. In this one it was stated that "The income and profits of her estate not being sufficient for her education, support and maintenance," etc. Also, Worcester Deeds, Lib. EDM no. 7, p. 8.

[2] Cf. expressions of this sentiment, in Anne Arundel, op. cit., Lib. 216, p. 153; Lib. 217, p. 21.

[3] Laws, 1793, ch. 45.

[4] Op. cit., 1826, ch. 155.

alone and at each succeeding step extended the provisions
for disposing of them.   According to an act of 1808 any
child of a lazy, indolent or worthless free negro could be
bound out as an apprentice on the order of the orphans'
court, or in its recess by the trustees of the poor.[1]   But an
act of 1818 made the condition of the child the occasion for
the action.   Accordingly any free negro child who was not
at service, or working at home, became liable to be apprenticed to learn a useful trade.   The parents of such child were
only to be consulted as to the choice of a master.[2]   In 1825
it was made the duty of the officials to inquire as to the welfare of negro children who were not properly fed and
clothed and to apprentice them.[3]   And in 1839 the orphans'
court was given power to summon before it any negro
child in the county, to inquire whether his parents were able
and willing to support him and train him in habits of industry, and if not, to bind him out to a white master.[4]   This
was followed seven years later by a special act applying to
Harford County alone.   It provided for warning free negro
parents to employ or bind out their children, and in case
they failed to do so, made it the duty of the constables and
justices of the peace to apprentice them.   Failure on their
part was to be a misdemeanor.[5]

The parties to the apprenticeship contract were quite

[1] *Op. cit.*, 1808, ch. 54.

[2] *Op. cit.*, 1818, ch. 189.

[3] *Op. cit.*, 1825, ch. 161.   The trustees of the poor had already been
empowered to bind out negro children in their care.   *Op. cit.*, 1824,
ch. 87.

[4] *Op. cit.*, 1839, ch. 35.   A female bound under this act was to serve
only till the sixteenth year of age, but under the act of 1849, ch. 341,
till the eighteenth year of age.   For indentures under this act, *vide*
Carroll Chattel Recs., Lib. JS no. 2, pp. 272, 319, 374; Lib. JBB no. 3,
p. 262; Lib. JBB no. 5, p. 53; *Howard Chattel Recs.*, Lib. 2, p. 336;
Orphans' Court Minutes, Lib. WG no. 1, p. 133.

[5] *Ibid.*, 1846, ch. 355.

unequal. A recurrence to conditions of virtual slavery was prevented by the formation of specific contracts establishing between masters and apprentices mutual obligations which were to be fulfilled under the supervision of the public authorities. With the master, as the major party in each case, rested the chief responsibility for fulfilment. He was bound to maintain his apprentice, give him industrial training and moral discipline and provide such instruction, and at the end of the term, such freedom dues as the indenture called for. But it is necessary to look at the indenture from the other side also in order to get a correct idea of its character. The apprentice was bound to subordinate himself to his master's lawful commands, to be faithful in service, to protect his master's interests and to refrain from conduct that was hurtful either to his master's good name, or to his good character. We first give attention to the obligations of masters and then to those of the apprentices.

Throughout their terms of service apprentices were to be maintained by their masters. The indentures set forth with varying fulness the minimum accommodations that were to be provided for that purpose. Sometimes there was merely a general statement that the supply should consist of such fit and convenient things as were generally enjoyed by persons of the class to which apprentices belonged,[1] a reminder of the allowance system of slavery. Sometimes good and sufficient food and clothing, or comfortable clothing and maintenance were required.[2] Again a mention was made of sufficient meat, drink, clothing, washing, lodging and other necessaries.[3] And some indentures stipulated

[1] E. g. Anne Arundel Deeds, Lib. NH no. 1, p. 521.

[2] Dorchester Co. Court Judgments, Lib. HD no. 5, p. 264; Howard Chattel Recs., Lib. WG no. 1, p. 84; Queen Anne's Orphans' Court Minutes, Mar. 18, 1800.

[3] Caroline Indentures, Lib. IT no. E, p. 17; Frederick Orphans' Court Minutes, Apr. 14, 1801. Cf. Laws, 1793, ch. 45.

that apprentices were also to be cared for in sickness, that medicines and medical aid were to be provided.[1]

But the matter of chief concern in apprenticeship was the training of a labor force. The apprentices were to be taught how to work for their own support and, as far as possible, to be disciplined in habits of industry.[2]   Regular employment was to be afforded.   In many cases it was left to the parties to choose the " useful " and " lawful " trades in which training was to be given.[3]   Common labor was the lot of some.   Generally, however, the occupations were specified, the leading part being taken outside of Baltimore by farming for boys and domestic service in its several departments of cooking, washing, ironing, knitting, sewing and spinning, for girls.[4]   A few girls in Montgomery

[1] *Baltimore Co. Indentures,* Lib. JLR no. 1, pp. 16, 18, 80; *Carroll Indentures,* Lib. JB no. A, pp. 23, 53; *Cecil Indentures,* Lib. 2, p. 455; *Harford Orphans' Court General Entries,* Lib. TSB no. 2, p. 35; *Kent Bonds and Indentures,* Lib. 6, p. 35; *Talbot Indentures,* Lib. no. L, p. 138; *Washington Indentures,* Lib. 2, p. 388.   In 1794 an indenture in Anne Arundel provided for the inoculation of a negro boy against the small-pox. *Deeds,* Lib. NH no. 7, p. 179.   An indenture recorded in Baltimore County after 1850 provided that a negro apprentice was to be decently interred in case of death. *Indentures,* Lib. JLR no. 1, p. 80.

[2] *E. g. Anne Arundel Orphans' Court Minutes,* Lib. 216, pp. 44, 153, 250, 290.

[3] *Cf. Harford, op. cit.,* Lib. BHH, pp. 131, 178, 183, 192, 208, 240, 241, 278; *Kent, op. cit.,* Lib. 3, pp. 32, 168; Lib. 6, pp. 520, 539, 540; *Somerset Orphans' Court Minutes,* 1811-1823, pp. 70, 71.   In Anne Arundel a girl was apprenticed to do " such work as colored women usually do in country places." *Orphans' Court Minutes,* Lib. 218, p. 26.   The indenture in *Washington Indentures,* Lib. 6, p. 156, merely pointed to a " useful calling".

[4] *E. g. Baltimore Co. Indentures,* Lib. JLR no. 1, pp. 8, 11, 51, 52, 97, 125, 140, 148, 153, 161, 168, 179, 181, 182; *Kent Bonds and Indentures,* Lib. 6, pp. 20, 33, 34, 520, 532, 636, 665; *Talbot Indentures,* Lib. 1, pp. 235, 268; Lib. 3, pp. 32, 147, 210, 243, 256, 290.   Work about the house was variously designated as domestic vocations, house-keeping, house-service, house-work, house-wifery, *etc.*

County were bound to " house and field work," a few elsewhere to farm work, and some boys to house service.[1]   Un-
skilled labor was thus to claim the energies of the majority
of negro children bound out.   But there was also a goodly
number of candidates for the skilled trades.   Among them
chief importance was attached to blacksmithing, with shoemaking and cordwaining in second place.[2]   Outside of
Baltimore City the other chief trades represented were
butchering, carpentry, coopering and tanning.   And scattered among the counties were one or more candidates for
each of the following: baker, barber and hair-dresser,
brewer, brick-maker, cabinet-maker, caulker, confectioner,
distiller, hatter, jackscrew-maker, manufacturer, mason,
miller, plasterer, ropemaker, seamstress, tinner, spinster,
weaver, well-digger, pump-maker, wheelwright, whip-saw-
yer, and whitesmith.

The statute of 1793 required that, so far as was practicable, apprentices should be taught to read and write.   Following the practice established in the province the orphans'
courts continued to require in a part of the indentures of
negroes that some such instruction should be given.[3]   And

[1] *Montgomery Land Recs.*, Lib. JGH no. 5, pp. 195, 296, 456, 489, 626;
Lib. JGH no. 6, p. 347; *Anne Arundel Testamentary Proceedings*, 1787-
1808, pp. 525, 559; *Queen Anne's Orphans' Court Minutes*, May 23, 1804,
and Apr. 18, 1812.

[2] Cordwaining was mentioned frequently in Southern Maryland, and
especially on the Eastern shore. *E. g. Anne Arundel Orphans' Court
Minutes*, Lib. JHH no. 2, pp. 218, 241, 499; Lib. 216, pp. 72, 124, 150;
Lib. 217, p. 13; *Kent Bonds and Indentures*, Lib. 6, pp. 13, 292, 477;
Lib. 12, pp. 66, 73, 152; *Somerset Co. Court Judgments*, 1791-94, p. 306;
Orphans' Court Minutes, June 14, 1822, Mar. 5, 1828.

[3] For indentures requiring education in the province, *vide Anne Arundel Deeds*, Lib. PK, p. 220 (1697); *Frederick Judicial Rec.*, Lib. M,
pp. 126, 184; *Kent Bonds and Indentures*, Lib. JS no. 20, p. 234;
Somerset Co. Court Judgments, 1757-60, pp. 224, 226; 1760-63, pp. 63,
82, 97, 98, 120. For later contracts in which education was required,
vide Harford Orphans' Court Minutes, 1778-97, pp. 53, 64, 129, 139, 140,
146; *Kent Bonds and Indentures*, Lib. 3, pp. 102, 103, 203, 221, 225,
326, 342; Lib. 6, pp. 140, 154, 159, 165, 168, 194, 201, *etc.*

although the provision was not made universal, the number of negroes so to be taught was greatly increased. The specific provisions as to education were of two kinds, (1) those which required school attendance for stated periods of time, and (2) those in which the instruction was to result in definite attainments. Thus a boy of thirteen years in Washington County was to be schooled for one or two months, two in Cecil for six months each, and one in each Cecil and Kent for nine months,[1] and another in Cecil for two months in each of seven years.[2]   The attainments substituted for school attendance were chiefly to teach to read, to read and write, or " to read, write and cipher as far as the rule of three." [3]   Three orphans in Montgomery County were to have a " reasonable education " in reading and writing.[4]   In Kent in a few instances it was enjoined that the master should not only provide instruction but, as stated in one case, keep the child " to it so that he may retain his learning when at age." [5]   Two negro children in Cecil County were to receive their instruction in the public schools,[6] while in certain cases in Talbot and Kent the ful-

---

[1] *Washington Indentures*, Lib. 2, p. 462; *Cecil Indentures*, Lib. 1, pp. 346, 375. The last referred to called for six months in a public school. *Op. cit.*, p. 400. *Kent Bonds and Indentures*, Lib. 4, p. 231. The following referred to a year's schooling, which probably meant not more than nine months in aggregate: *Cecil, op. cit.*, pp. 88, 140; *Harford Orphans' Court General Entries*, Lib. AJ no. A, p. 349; *Kent, op. cit.*, Lib. 4, p. 337.

[2] *Cecil, op. cit.*, p. 365. The following required each eighteen months schooling: *Harford, op. cit.*, p. 414; *Kent, op. cit.*, Lib. 3, p. 32.

[3] *E. g. Anne Arundel Orphans' Court Minutes*, Lib. JHH no. 2, pp. 197, 217, 218, 233, 241, 244, 485; *Talbot Orphans' Court Minutes*, 1787-95, pp. 225, 273, and Aug. 14, 1798; *Indentures*, Lib. 2, p. 66; *Cecil Indentures*, Lib. 1, pp. 15, 277, 315, 329, 347, 354; *Somerset Co. Court Judgments*, 1791-94, pp. 101, 305, 306.

[4] *Orphans' Court Minutes*, Lib. D, p. 485.

[5] *Bonds and Indentures*, Lib. 1, p. 66. *Cf.* Lib. 3, pp. 168, 207, 326; Lib. 4, p. 246; Lib. 6, pp. 156, 466.

[6] *Indentures*, Lib. 1, pp. 375, 400.

filment of the obligation to educate was conditioned upon the discovery of teachers who " could be prevailed upon to undertake such teaching on common reasonable terms." [1] Although the attendance of negro children at the rural day schools was not common, it was not unknown. But generally those apprentices who were taught at all, were taught in private either by tutors or by members of the households of their masters.

The education provision did not become universal at any time. Its insertion in the indentures without distinction of racial lines was encouraged by the progress of the doctrines of natural rights and of political equality of all men. As a consequence the orphans' courts for about a generation after their establishment tended to give the negroes a square deal in respect to education. But the spread of anti-free negro sentiment with its objections to educated negroes brought about a change. The orphans' court of Talbot County in binding three boys to a farmer in 1804 expressly absolved their master from the obligation to teach them to read. Similar proceedings were recorded in Anne Arundel in 1803, and in Kent in 1805.[2] The courts in several other counties also soon followed their example, the notable exception being Baltimore. But in the counties of Frederick, Carroll, Harford and Cecil contrary forces long impeded the progress of the change. All these counties were advancing in wealth and population, all lay on the Pennsylvania border, and all felt the pressure of the influences from across that border. In Frederick about a third of all the

---

[1] *Talbot Indentures*, Lib. 2, p. 337; *Kent Bonds and Indentures*, Lib. 6, p. 141; Lib. 12, p. 62. According to the act of 1793, ch. 45, this condition might have been made general.

[2] *Talbot Orphans' Court Minutes*, Dec. 11, 1804; *Anne Arundel Orphans' Court Minutes*, Lib. JHH no. 2, pp. 312, 315, 316; *Kent Bonds and Indentures*, Lib. 6, pp. 140, 154, 159, 165, 168 (1805); 194, 201, 203, 214, (1806).

negroes apprenticed before 1830 were to receive some
" learning," but thereafter the proportion was lower. In
Cecil nine negroes were appointed in 1832 : three of them
were to have education. In Southern Maryland and the
Eastern Shore, however, the movement prevailed to such
an extent that, saving when parents or other friends were
instrumental in fixing the terms, the education provision
was generally omitted.

Meanwhile the provisions for white apprentices continued without apparent change. Equal treatment for
those of both races seemed to demand that some indemnification should be made for the loss. At first no such indemnification was made, but the statute of 1818 already referred to, contained a clause stating that the orphans' court
might require that a negro apprentice should be taught to
read and write, or in lieu thereof paid a sum of money not
in excess of thirty dollars in addition to the freedom dues
allowed by law.[1] Six years later similar powers were
vested in the trustees of the poor in binding out children
from the alms-houses.[2] But in neither case was it man-
datory to adopt either of the two courses. The result was,
therefore, chiefly to cause payments to be required in lieu
of education, another practice that failed also to become
universal. It was followed in Washington and Caroline in
1819 and in Montgomery and Kent in 1821-22.[3] It prevailed in Kent to a greater extent than in any other county
visited by the writer. It was common in Caroline until
about 1830, became common in Frederick and Washington
after 1832, in Carroll from the date of its formation in

---

[1] *Laws*, 1818, ch. 189.

[2] *Op. cit.*, 1824, ch. 87.

[3] *Washington Indentures*, Lib. 3, pp. 143, 184; *Caroline Indentures*,
Lib. IT no. E, pp. 102, 138, 139; *Montgomery Orphans' Court Recs.*,
Lib. M, p. 426; *Kent Bonds and Indentures*, Lib. 10, pp. 84, 122.

1837, and in Anne Arundel after 1845. In Cecil and Harford it was almost unknown. In a few cases masters were allowed the option of education or making the money payments as they chose.[1]

Trade discipline and school training were designed to develop the power to labor. It was desired also to inculcate in the negro laborers respect for social conventions and especially for the laws of the state. Masters were thus everywhere expected to assume the duties of controlling the conduct of apprentices and of teaching them submission to law and at least something of the other principles of morality.[2] Going beyond this an Anne Arundel indenture required teaching the Christian conception of duty to God and one's neighbors.[3] In Cecil and Harford counties much emphasis was laid upon religious instruction. In the former a mulatto, apprenticed in 1807, was to be taught the Lord's prayer, the creed and the shorter catechism,[4] and at least half of the negroes indentured between 1794 and 1860 were to be "brought up in Christian faith."

Besides what has been already indicated, two kinds of material obligations were assumed by masters, (1) freedom dues, payable upon discharge at the end of the term, and (2) other payments as compensation for service. Dues of the first class were customary in the early province

[1] *Baltimore Co. Indentures*, Lib. JLR no. 1, p. 13; *Howard Orphans' Court Minutes*, Lib. WG no. 1, pp. 41, 56; *Washington Indentures*, Lib. 3, p. 238.

[2] A boy in Caroline, for instance, was to be taught morality and good conduct, "if capable to learn." *Indentures*, Lib. WAF no. A, p. 181.

[3] *Anne Arundel Deeds*, Lib. NH no. 7, p. 602 (1795). Cf. *Harford Orphans' Court General Entries*, Lib. TSB no. 1, p. 139.

[4] *Cecil Land Recs.*, Lib. JS no. 3, p. 356. Cf. *Harford, op. cit.*, Lib. BHH no. 5, p. 57; also *Records*, 1828-33, pp. 115, 141, 152. A slave girl, hired out by her owner in Carroll in 1842, was to have the privilege of church attendance "every other Sunday during her term of servitude." *Indentures*, Lib. AJ no. A, p. 23.

and later became almost, if not quite, universal. The obligation to pay them did not depend upon contract, and mention of them was sometimes omitted from indentures.[1] The act of 1715 concerning servants and slaves provided that every male servant " at the expiration of his servitude " was to be allowed and given " one new hat, a good suit; that is to say, coat and breeches, either of kersey or broadcloth, one new shift of white linen, one new pair of French fall shoes, two hoes and one axe, and one gun of twenty shillings price; " and every woman servant " a waistcoat and petticoat of new half-thick, or pennistone, a new shift of white linen, shoes and stockings, a blue apron, two caps of white linen and three barrels of Indian corn." [2] These clauses, enacted at a time when those discharged from servitude were mostly white persons, furnished the standard for the legal and customary freedom dues after adult white servitude had declined.[3] And although various forms of payment were allowed, the principle of freedom dues was adhered to consistently by the orphans' courts. The indentures which they sanctioned generally enumerated the articles that were to be tendered, but sometimes in the later decades of the period under consideration stated only the values of the outfits required. Accordingly we find in them lists of particular articles of apparel,[4] in imitation of

[1] E. g. Harford Land Recs., Lib. JLG no. L, p. 88; Lib. HD no. Q, pp. 128, 129, 130; Harford Chattel Recs., Lib. ALJ no. 2, pp. 159, 163; Dorchester Orphans' Court Minutes, 1845-54, pp. 76, 77.

[2] Laws, 1715, ch. 44, sec. 10. Cf. Archives of Maryland, vol. xxii, p. 548.

[3] Cf. Anne Arundel Testamentary Proceedings, Lib. IG no. 1, p. 426; Anne Arundel Deeds, Lib. WSG no. 11, p. 83; Baltimore Co. Indentures, Lib. JLR no. 1, pp. 4, 11; Cecil Indentures, Lib. 1, p. 14; Lib. 2, p. 323; Harford Orphans' Court Minutes, 1778-97, p. 139.

[4] E. g. Kent Bonds and Indentures, Lib. 2, pp. 11, 66; Lib. 3, pp. 168, 207; Lib. 4, pp. 217, 219; Talbot Indentures, Lib. 1, p. 146; Orphans' Court Minutes, 1787-95, p. 254; Cecil Indentures, Lib. 1, pp. 332, 379, 420, 421.

the statute, and mention of one or two suits to a single apprentice, of working and Sunday suits,[1] of clothing of a
stated money value,[2] of payments partly in clothing and
partly in money, of options to contracting parties to choose
between clothing and money payments,[3] of cash in lieu of
all other freedom dues,[4] and finally of presentation of
tools such as axes, malls and wedges, spades and grubbing
hoes.[5]

Dues of the second class were of but little importance
until late, and even then recurred only in a minority of contracts. The contracts in which they occurred often
amounted to virtual sales of children into slavery for terms
of years.[6] If the apprenticeship laws were to take their
course, parents were entitled to such compensation for the
use of the children whom they had reared. In order to
secure them that benefit, a special act was passed by the
legislature in 1856 to apply to four counties on the Eastern
Shore. It provided that the orphans' courts in apprenticing

[1] *Anne Arundel Orphans' Court Minutes*, Lib. 217, pp. 186, 201, 360,
368; *Baltimore Co. Indentures*, Lib. JLR no. 1, pp. 14, 15, 48, 58, 66,
78, 103, 104, 108, 126; *Cecil Indentures*, Lib. 3, pp. 230, 286; *Kent Bonds
and Indentures*, Lib. 12, pp. 62, 177, 337.

[2] *Caroline Indentures*, Lib. GAS no. F, pp. 31, 47, 58, 60, 128, 153, 182,
186, 187; *Harford Orphans' Court General Entries*, Lib. AJ no. 3, p.
152; Lib. TSB no. 2, pp. 65, 71, 74, 107, 158, 176, 178.

[3] *Caroline Indentures*, *op. cit.*, pp. 23, 59, 61, 65, 144, 151, 164, 188, 215,
224, 249, 250; *Talbot Indentures*, Lib. 3, pp. 80, 86, 93, 109, 115, 124,
130, 139.

[4] *Dorchester Orphans' Court Minutes*, 1845-54, pp. 187, 284; Lib. THH
no. 2, pp. 150, 152, 157, 160, 201; *Washington Indentures*, Lib. 2, pp.
232, 271; *Frederick Land Recs.*, Lib. BGF no. 1, p. 715.

[5] *Frederick Orphans' Court Minutes*, Jan. 8, 1821; *Queen Anne's
Deeds*, Lib. JT no. 3, pp. 464, 465, 466, 468, 659; *Washington Indentures*, Lib. 2, p. 466. *Cf.* also *op. cit.*, Lib. 3, pp. 95, 120, 121.

[6] The following refer to sales of children by their parents: *Kent
Chattel Recs.*, Lib. WS no. 1, p. 192; *Caroline Land Recs.*, Lib. S, pp.
347, 377; Lib. T, pp. 118, 128, 236, 381; Lib. U, p. 371.

children might require such amounts to be paid as would
reasonably and justly indemnify parents for expenses incurred on their account.[1] The amounts thus to be paid
varied as wages vary. A Cecil County indenture provided
for the payment of seventy-five cents a month throughout the term, one in Kent for thirty shillings a quarter,[2]
another in Kent for fourteen pounds currency in ten annual
instalments, one in Washington for twenty dollars, and one
in Anne Arundel for thirty dollars a year.[3] The periodical
payments were generally to be in equal amounts, and their
continuance was apparently conditioned upon continuance in
service. Lump sum payments which at once satisfied all
demands, were employed no less than instalments. Thus
thirty-five dollars was paid in one case in Howard County,
and a hundred and seventy-five in a case in Frederick.[4]

Under the statute of 1715 a master was liable to be fined
either for failing to provide sufficient meat, drink, clothing
and lodging for his servant, for unreasonably burdening

---

[1] *Laws,* 1856, ch. 87. The four counties were Caroline, Kent, Somerset and Worcester. In Washington County in 1842 an apprentice was
assigned one-half of the payment to be made on his contract. *Indentures,* Lib. 5, p. 302.

[2] *Cecil Indentures,* Lib. 3, p. 579; *Kent Bonds and Indentures,* Lib. 4,
p. 231. *Cf.* Baltimore County Indentures, Lib. JLR no. 1, p. 30, op.
cit., p. 167, a requirement of a dollar a month for three years, and thereafter two dollars a month for a period of two years. The apprentice
was a girl of two years at the date of the indenture.

[3] *Kent Bonds and Indentures,* Lib. 4, p. 217; *Washington Indentures,*
Lib. 6, p. 145; *Anne Arundel Orphans' Court Minutes,* Lib. 217, p. 173.
Cf. op. cit., Lib. 218, p. 63; *Baltimore Co. Indentures,* Lib. JLR no. 1,
p. 138, requirement of $140, one-fourth to be paid down and the rest in
annual instalments of $13.12½ each, *Kent, op. cit.,* Lib. 6, p. 507;
Talbot Indentures, Lib. 6, p. 176; *Washington, op. cit.,* p. 169.

[4] *Howard Orphans' Court Minutes,* Lib. WG no. 1, p. 9; *Frederick
Land Recs.,* Lib. BGF no. 4, p. 648. *Cf.* also *Anne Arundel Orphans'
Court Minutes,* Lib. 218, p. 18; *Harford Chattel Recs.,* Lib. ALJ no. 2,
p. 159; *Kent Bonds and Indentures,* 1849-59, pp. 220, 249.

him with labor, debarring him from necessary sleep and rest, or for beating excessively or otherwise abusing him. For a third offence he could be deprived of further use of the aggrieved servant,[1] who was himself to be set at liberty. But the act of 1793 substituted for this grant of liberty, transference to another master. By the latter act also a master was forbidden to carry an indentured servant out of the state. And upon information of such designs justices of the peace were empowered to demand securities that no such action should be taken.[2] Selling apprentices out of the state, excepting under decrees of competent courts, was prohibited, and after 1793 the sales of terms of apprenticeship belonging to the estates of deceased persons were to be legalized only by the sanction of the orphans' courts.[3]

It was stated above that the obligations of masters and apprentices were mutual. Those of the latter were mainly submission to and compliance with the wills of their masters. They were to show honor and respect to their masters and to the members of their master's families,[4] to obey their masters' lawful commands, to be faithful and honest in service, and in all things to demean themselves as good apprentices ought to do.[5] They were to render such reasonable service as their masters required, a duty

---

[1] *Laws*, 1715, ch. 44, sec. 21.

[2] *Op. cit.*, 1793, ch. 45, secs. 7, 11. *Cf. op. cit.*, 1840, ch. 111. Also *Md. Appeal Reports*, 2 H. & G., pp. 291-95.

[3] *Laws*, 1793, ch. 45. *Cf.* 1839, ch. 35; 1844, ch. 247; 1856, ch. 78.

[4] *E. g.* Carroll, *Orphans' Court Minutes*, 1845, p. 3; *Indentures*, Lib. JB no. A, p. 4; Montgomery, *Orphans' Court Recs.*, Lib. M, p. 232; *Land Recs.*, Lib. JGH no. 6, p. 186.

[5] *Caroline Indentures*, Lib. IT no. E, p. 17; Lib. JR no. D, p. 332; Carroll, *Orphans' Court Minutes*, Oct. 1845, p. 3; 1848, p. 18; Lib. JB no. A, p. 8; Lib. JB no. I, p. 52; *Baltimore Co. Indentures*, Lib. JLR no. 1, pp. 18, 21, 138; *Kent Bonds and Indentures*, Lib. 1, p. 76; *Somerset Land Recs.*, Lib. 1, p. 355; Lib. GH no. 3, p. 259; *Washington Indentures*, Lib. 2, pp. 271, 374; Lib. 5, p. 302.

which outside of the towns might have included service
in the harvest fields for artisan apprentices.[1] They
were to be loyal to their masters' interests, to keep their
secrets, not to waste or destroy their goods, not to lend, buy
or sell such goods without due leave, not to embezzle them,
and neither themselves to injure, nor suffer any other
person to injure, their masters' interests without notice
or interference.[2] Moreover, they were to refrain from
injuring the good names of their masters and injuring
their own characters by immoral conduct. Thus some
indentures forbade the apprentices to swear, to drink in-
toxicating liquors, to play cards, throw dice or engage in
any other " unlawful games," forbade them to frequent
taverns, ale and play-houses and gaming places, and finally
forbade them to commit fornication or contract matrimony.[3]
But it appears that the sanctions of the sumptuary restrictions were chiefly moral suasion and community demands for average decency.

According to the act of 1715 complaints arising between
masters and servants were to be heard and settled in the
provincial courts and the county courts. In 1793 jurisdiction over such matters was given to county and criminal
courts and in 1842 transferred to the orphans' courts with a
right of appeal to the county courts. Servants were subject to correction by their masters for minor offences, but
no servant was to be given more than ten lashes for any

[1] *Laws*, 1793, ch. 45, sec. 13.

[2] *E. g. Baltimore Co. Indentures*, Lib. JLR no. 1, p. 138; *Caroline
Indentures*, Lib. JR no. D, p. 332; *Kent Bonds and Indentures*, Lib. 4,
p. 222; *Talbot Indentures*, Lib. 1, pp. 138, 217; Lib. 6, p. 217.

[3] *Anne Arundel Orphans' Court Minutes*, Lib. 217, p. 343; *Caroline
Indentures*, Lib. IT no. E, pp. 284, 385; *Cecil Indentures*, Lib. 2, pp.
394, 397; *Harford Orphans' Court General Entries*, Lib. AJ no. 3, p.
304; *Howard Orphans' Court Recs.*, Lib. WG no. 1, p. 29; *Montgomery
Orphans' Court Recs.*, Lib. D, p. 285; *Queen Anne's Deeds*, Lib. JB no.
1, p. 138; *Talbot Indentures*, Lib. 6, p. 217.

one offence without a previous hearing before a justice of the peace.[1] After 1793 servants guilty of ill behavior or incorrigible tempers were liable to be transferred to new masters and their former masters awarded compensation for the loss of service incurred. For running away or being absent from service the " satisfaction " to be rendered under the act of 1715 was additional service of not more than ten days for each day's absence. Under the act of 1793 the form of satisfaction was to be " either by service or by payment of money as justice and equity may require." In 1804 it was added that such compensation was to be made only in case it appeared that the absconding was not due to ill-conduct or mistreatment by the master.[2] Injunctions against absconding were also frequently inserted in the indentures,[3] and the courts consistently compensated masters who suffered by it by extending the terms of their offending employees. In Harford County, for instance, occurred additions of three, five and ten years respectively, in cases brought before the orphans' court.[4] Flagrant misconduct and insubordination were sometimes penalized by selling the unexpired terms of service to non-residents.[5]

[1] *Laws*, 1715, ch. 44; 1793, ch. 45; 1842, ch. 25.

[2] *Op. cit.*, acts of 1715 and 1793; also 1804, ch. 90. *Cf.* also 1839, ch. 35, sec. 4.

[3] *E. g. Baltimore Co. Indentures*, Lib. JLR no. 1, pp. 21, 138; *Cecil Indentures*, Lib. 1, pp. 381, 411, 412, 413; *Harford Orphans' Court Recs.*, 1828-33, p. 151; *Worcester Deeds*, Lib. K, p. 187; Lib. AC, p. 158.

[4] *Harford Orphans' Court General Entries*, Lib. TSB, p. 289; Lib. BHH, pp. 145, 155. *Cf. op. cit.*, pp. 120, 158, 159, 201, 202; also *Dorchester Orphans' Court Minutes*, 1845-54, pp. 286, 395; *Howard Orphans' Court Minutes*, Lib. WG no. 1, pp. 339, 342, 347, 383, 404; Lib. TJ no. 2, pp. 145, 199, 213, 295, 324, 326.

[5] *Baltimore Orphans' Court Minutes*, Lib. 25, p. 305; Lib. 27, pp. 142, 402; Lib. 29, p. 78; Lib. 30, p. 429; Harford, *op. cit.*, Lib. BHH, p. 155; *Howard, op. cit.*, Lib. WG no. 1, p. 404; Lib. TJ no. 2, p. 58; Lib. TB no. 2, p. 339.

If the apprentice was convicted of a finable offence, his master might himself pay the fine and be indemnified by the extension of the term of the offender.[1] The unexpired terms of apprentices were transferable, the sole results of the transfers being that the unfulfilled obligations of the grantors were to be assumed by the new masters.[2]

With the few exceptions noted above the old forms of indentures survived to the end. In their fulfillment a great deal depended upon the manner in which the respective functions were performed. Judging from what appears in the court records of several counties, masters fell short of their obligations less frequently than did apprentices. The supervision of the county courts and the orphans' courts attempted to enforce such an observance of the terms of the indentures as custom demanded. The free negroes lived and worked like the slaves, and in the public mind their lot was associated with that of the slaves. What the public desired, therefore, was that negro apprentices should be treated about as well as slaves were treated, that they should be so subjected to authority, so fed, clothed, housed and attended when sick, so employed, and so trained for labor in the trades to which they had been apprenticed.[3] In this way the apprenticeship system collaborated with

---

[1] *Laws*, 1793, ch. 45. According to the act of 1797, ch. 54, such an offender in Baltimore City was to be striped, unless his master consented to pay the fine.

[2] For cases of transfers, *vide Anne Arundel Deeds*, Lib. WSG no. 11, p. 517 (1826); *Cecil Indentures*, Lib. 2, p. 219 (1822); Lib. 3, pp. 118, 230, 419; *Washington Indentures*, 1835-46, p. 184; *Orphans' Court Minutes*, 1855-59, p. 520; *Worcester Deeds*, Lib. AP, pp. 445, 446, 447; Lib. EDM no. 2, p. 313.

[3] Obviously the inquiry of the Queen Anne's Orphans' Court, *cf. Minutes*, Jan. 4, 1791, as to whether apprentices were being taught their trades, or rigorously turned to common labor with axe and hoe referred mainly to the condition of white apprentices.

slavery in training up those who were to become free negro laborers. Its leading contributions were farm and household laborers, and among skilled workmen smiths and shoemakers in the counties and smiths, barbers and caulkers in Baltimore City.

CHAPTER V

OCCUPATIONS AND WAGES OF FREE NEGROES

THERE was no question as to the occupations in which the free negroes worked. But as to their industrial capacity and the reasons why they held an inferior position there were two opinions between which one must steer carefully in order to get at the truth. One view was that they were rather systematically excluded from the most desirable occupations and that in the rest they were subjected to oppressive conditions. And further that but for the injustice thus done them, they should have risen much above the level upon which they were working. This view was mainly held, or implied in the utterances, by persons residing outside of the state who were not fully conversant with the actual conditions. And although an unguarded reading of certain statutes and legislative documents would create the impression that it was true, it lacked much of being entirely correct. The other view was that the negroes were essentially inferior, degraded, lazy and improvident beings, and that instead of using liberty to provide well for themselves and their families, they often deliberately went unemployed and depended upon gratuities and stolen stuffs to supply what they lacked. As a consequence they tended progressively to want and depravity: they were " an incubus upon the land." [1] This view was put forward in Maryland

---

[1] *Md. Col. Jour.*, no. 19 (1838). *Cf. op. cit.*, vol. ix, p. 279; vol. x, p. 34; *Genius of Universal Emancipation*, Sept. 16, 1826; *Frederick Examiner*, March 24, 1858; *Easton Gazette*, Nov. 13, 1858; *Baltimore Sun*, Jan. 7, 1856; *Letter of General Harper to E. B. Caldwell*, p. 8. *Letter of R. S. Reeder to Dr. Dent*, p. 18.

by those who had an interest in disparaging both negro activity and negro prospects in the future. Its propagators too often suppressed many facts that were available and argued from those whose magnification suited their purposes.[1] It was a one-sided view also, but excepting for its insistence upon the retrogression of the negroes who were not slaves, it lay nearer the truth than the first.

The negroes who were brought to Maryland had been abducted from a life that was probably in either the hunting or the pastoral stage of economy. They were then two or three cultural stages behind the whites whom they had come to serve. At the close of the revolution very few of their families were farther than three generations removed from that primitive life, and the majority were not so far. Their experience as slaves had been one of forced labor. They were treated as laboring machines, not as children who were to be carefully educated and prepared for the role of citizens. They had not had time either to grasp the white man's point of view or to adjust themselves to the white man's orderly methods of getting a living. They were fitted for manual labor but too often loathed it because of its irksomeness and because of the stigma attaching to it. To such as held this idea the hope of freedom was cherished as a refuge from strenuous toil.[2] The living as freemen was to be had without it somehow. Moreover, the slave wages of food, raiment and shelter had been no stimulus to achievement.[3] It was on a low plane, therefore, that all manumitted negroes, excepting a favored few, began to do for themselves in the world.

[1] Cf. *Genius of Universal Emancipation*, loc. cit.; *Md. Col. Jour.*, vol. iii, p. 290; vol. x, p. 138.

[2] Cf. *Frederick Examiner*, March 24, 1858.

[3] Cf. *Md. Col. Jour.*, 1838, p. 82, on the inadvisability of offering certain incentives to slaves.

We have seen that certain rules of the negro code were designed to keep the free ngroes from being idle, and that others debarred them from the callings of peddling, politics, public service and soldiering. They were excluded also from the learned professions and the other " higher pursuits " only as a result of the conditions in the market for personal service. Over such conditions the state exercised no control.[1] One must avoid laying too much emphasis upon the callings from which the negroes were excluded. For after all there was a large variety of outlets for negro talents. As freemen they did not forfeit the kinds of work in which they had engaged as slaves, and besides engaging in manual labor as employees, they went into farming and several kinds of business as managers of their own concerns. Moreover, some men found their livelihood in preaching and teaching their own people, and a few others devoted at least a part of their time to attending to affairs from which were derived independent incomes. In none of these enterprises were they subjected to special taxes, and they had but few other restrictions to which the whites were not also subjected. There was left then no mean liberty for earning, collecting and expending or accumulating the fruits of their labor.[2] Attention will now be given in turn

---

[1] Had there been no other differences between white men and black men than mere color of skin, it seems reasonable to say that there would probably have been no differences or preferences in respect to occupations. Remarks of a "colored physician of Baltimore." *Cf.* also *Md. Col. Jour.*, vol. vi, p. 74.

[2] *Cf.* remarks of Reverend R. J. Breckenridge in *Md. Col. Jour.*, vol. iii, pp. 174-75. Contemporaries said and wrote a great deal that did not harmonize with the view here stated. *Cf. Genius of Universal Emancipation*, vol. ii, p. 10; *The Maryland Scheme of Expatriation Examined*, p. 8; *Letter of R. S. Reeder to Dr. Dent*, p. 13; *Md. Col. Jour.*, vol. ii, p. 206; vol. vi, pp. 6-7; *Frederick Examiner*, March 24, 1858; *H. Del. Journal*, 1844, pp. 257, 261, 379.

to the participation of the negroes in common labor, skilled labor and agriculture and business affairs in the order mentioned.

The energies of the negroes that were turned to industry were devoted chiefly to common labor for which some thought they had been providentially intended. As slavery declined and the population increased, an increasing proportion of the work to be done fell to the hands of freemen. In some places the whites took the major portion of this work, but everywhere the negroes divided it with them, and in parts of Southern Maryland and the Eastern Shore took over almost the whole of it.[1] Negro women everywhere cooked, washed and ironed the linens, did housework, served as nurses, as body servants, sometimes as midwives[2] and often worked also in the fields. Negro men also served as domestics and hostlers and as general menials, where obsequious devotion was required. Free negroes were allowed to bear the brunt of heavy work, such as leading the gang in cradling wheat and lifting heavy burdens. In Baltimore City they long took the lead as carters, draymen and carmen, as hod-carriers and assistants to building tradesmen, as stevedores, grain-measurers, coal-handlers and as warehousemen.[3] They were not less conspicuous as teamsters and cab- and hack-drivers throughout the state. At the factories and foundries they served as forge-men, bar-

[1] Cf. Somerset Union, Feb. 14, 1859, and Feb. 21, 1860; 27th Annual Report of Amer. Anti-Slavery Society, pp. 209-10; Governor Hicks's Inaugural Address, p. 13; Md. Col. Jour., vol. i, p. 201.

[2] Cf. Ledger A of Zachariah MacCubbin, 1789-1800; Md. Journal, Jan. 6, 1795.

[3] Cf. Annapolis Republican, Nov. 2, 1819; Genius of Universal Emancipation, vol. ii, p. 10; Md. Col. Jour., vol. ii, pp. 103, 206; vol. iii, p. 5; vol. vi, pp. 71, 73; Maryland Scheme of Expatriation Examined, p. 9; H. Del. Journal, 1840, p. 325; Md. Pub. Docs., 1847, no. 5, pp. 3-4; Hall, Baltimore, pp. 235-36.

row-men and firemen and as helpers.[1]   And they were
sometimes employed in the mines, the tanneries, frequently
in the fisheries and on vessels as common sailors.[2]   In the
rural districts their labor was regarded by the slave-holders
as supplementary to that of the slaves.   They were thus
employed as wood-cutters and extra harvest hands.   But
to many non-slaveholders they were of primary importance,
because to them there was often no other choice but their
hire.[3]   This became conspicuously true of Caroline County.
Between 1790 and 1860 its total negro population had increased 36.7 per cent and its white population 8.1 per cent,
but its slaves had fallen from 83 per cent to 20.9 per cent of
all its negroes.   In several of the counties in the last years
before the civil war the labor supply was insufficient to meet
the demand, although no doubt in places the failure was
partly due to unwillingness of negroes to do all that was
asked.[4]

For skilled labor no less than common labor the people
depended upon the negroes.   In the provincial era the mechanical trades had been carried on by white men and by
negroes who were mainly slaves.[5]   But with the growth of

---

[1] *Cf. Patuxent Iron Works Journals* A and B, 1774-85; *Elk Forge
Ledger G*, 1812-13; *Cornwall Furnace Journal* M, 1760-62.

[2] *Md. Col. Jour.,* vol. vi, pp. 71-72; *68 Niles Register*, p. 332.

[3] *Cf. Baltimore American*, June 9, 10, 1859; *Somerset Union*, Feb. 21,
1860; *27th Annual Report of Amer. Anti-Slavery Society*, p. 210;
Cross, *A Few Thoughts to Mr. Jacobs*, p. 4; *Easton Gazette*, May 7,
1859.

[4] *Cf. Governor Hicks's Inaugural Address*, p. 13.   Also letter from
"East Maryland" in *Easton Gazette*, May 7, 1859.   The writer of this
letter complained that "during the busy season of the year the farmers
are compelled to procure laborers from the cities at enormous expense
of time and money, for these negroes can not be induced to work," so
long as they could live by other means.

[5] A slave carpenter was freed in Queen Anne's in 1749.   Another
negro in St. Mary's was freed two years earlier and endowed by his

the slave population the proportion of whites apparently declined excepting in Baltimore and Western Maryland. Some of the slaves " hired their time " and worked as freemen, and some were able by self-purchase and by grace of their owners' favor to become legally free. Within two decades after the revolution at least fourteen such negroes had been freed in eight of the counties,[1] and still others were added to their number by means of the training dispensed under the apprenticeship system.

The city of Baltimore was the chief labor market of the state. Its varied employments and higher wages attracted laborers from all of the counties. But through apprenticing negro children to the trades it also trained up artizans from its own population. Between 1794 and 1820 about one-third of all the colored children bound out by the county orphans' court were assigned to the skilled trades.[2] Thereafter the proportion among new apprentices was somewhat reduced, but the change did not of itself affect the training and subsequent activities of those already bound out. The city directories from the year 1819 onward,[3] although not conclusive as to numbers engaged in any trade, show both

master with all the "carphindor's . . . showmaker's (sic) . . . and cooper's tools " with which he had been accustomed to work. *Maryland Wills*, Lib. DD no. 7, pp. 476, 520.

[1] *Anne Arundel Wills*, Lib. TG no. 1, p. 55; Lib. JG no. 1, pp. 221, 361; Lib. JG no. 2, p. 144; *Cecil Wills*, Lib. 6, p. 239; *Harford Wills*, Lib. 6, p. 239; *Harford Wills*, Lib. AJ no. 2, p. 183; *Montgomery Land Records*, Lib. E, p. 632; *Queen Anne's Wills*, Lib. WHN no. 3, p. 191; Lib. SCT, p. 183; *Queen Anne's Land Recs.*, Lib. SCT no. 5, p. 31; *Somerset Wills*, Lib. EB no. 5, p. 60; *Talbot Wills*, Lib. JB no. 3, p. 297; Lib. JB no. 5, p. 318; *Dorchester Deeds*, Lib. HD no. 6, p. 23; *Md. Jour.*, Aug. 3, 1787.

[2] *Cf. e. g. Indentures*, Lib. WB no. 1, pp. 171, 236, 269, 328, 330, 353, 427; Lib. WB no. 2, pp. 276, 350, 422, 498, 539, 578, 637.

[3] The Directory for 1819 was apparently the first that attempted to classify occupations of persons with names listed.

a wide and an enlarging range of negro activities, and in certain branches increases in numbers that more than kept pace with the growth of the city's negro population. Among them were to be found

barbers,	cigar-makers,	ship-carpenters,
blacksmiths,	comb-makers,	ship-joiners,
a brass founder,	coopers,	shoemakers,
bricklayers,	mantua-makers,	a stone-mason,
butchers,	milliners,	a stone-cutter,
broom-makers,	musicians,	tailors,
brush-makers,	painters,	a wheelwright,
cabinet-makers,	plasterers,	a whip-maker,
carpenters,	a plumber,	a sawyer and
caulkers,	rope-makers,	a whitesmith.
cordwainers,		

The following table is compiled from the city directories:

	Number in Trade at Date Given				
	1819	*1831*	*1840-41*	*1856*	*1860*
Blacksmiths	8	13	18	29	30
Barbers	18	12	45	86	117
Caulkers	14	37	38	75	74

The numbers in each grew to some extent according to the demand but were also affected by the increasing competition of the whites, from whose labor organizations the negroes were sometimes excluded.[1] As ship-carpenters, brick-masons, coopers, cordwainers and shoemakers the negroes played a useful part. But they were most prominent in barbering, blacksmithing and caulking. In the first and last of these it is said that they furnished nearly all the labor, until the middle of the nineteenth century,[2] that they were unexcelled as horse-shoers and that they retained a considerable share in the general trade of blacksmithing.

---

[1] *Cf. Baltimore Charter Records*, Lib. ED no. 2, p. 413.
[2] Hall, *Baltimore*, pp. 235-36.

The relative importance of negro mechanics and skilled workmen was greater in the counties than in the city. This was particularly true in Southern Maryland and the Eastern Shore, where the dependence upon negro labor in general was greatest. In these counties the demands were smaller, the variety of trades was correspondingly narrower, and there was a tendency to promote versatility rather than specialization. A few individuals attained proficiency in several trades each. Thus in Talbot County a certain negro who was a shoemaker by trade at times turned boat-builder, wagon-maker, wheel-wright and general wood-workman. Anne Arundel, Cecil and Kent each had a nearly similar case. Many more persons practised each a single trade with a second as accessory, combining, for instance, blacksmithing and wagon-making, carpentry and cabinet-making or carpentry and shoemaking. The trades most commonly represented were barbering, blacksmithing, shoemaking, carpentry and in the southern part of the Eastern Shore whipsawing.[1] In some places the shoemakers worked in fixed places. In the country districts, however, they often went from farm to farm, making at each place the supply of shoes from leather furnished by the master of the premises. A group of five shoemakers, all members of one family, worked in Talbot County.[2] At Chestertown and Cambridge the principal butchers just before the war were negroes. There were negro plasterers in nearly every part of the state and negro ship-wrights and caulkers at the ship-yards in the tide-water districts. At Ellicott's Mills a negro cooper

---

[1] *Cf. Queen Anne's Land Records*, Lib. STW no. 7, pp. 31, 201, 214; *Wills*, Lib. SCT, p. 183; Lib. TCE no. 2, p. 12; *Orphans' Court Minutes*, Dec. 4, 1813; June 10, 1815, and Jan. 10, 1824; *Talbot Land Recs.*, Lib. 33, p. 105; Lib. 39, p. 10; Lib. 49, pp. 204-05; Lib. 50, p. 527; *Md. Col. Jour.*, vol. i, p. 319.

[2] They were a father, two sons and two sons of one of the latter. Their reputed capacity was thirty-seven pairs of shoes a week.

made the barrels for the flour and grist of the miller and two negro harness-makers received a liberal patronage among all classes of users of harness. Other trades represented here and there were brick-laying, hewing and whip-sawing.

In some trades owing to the nature of the service independent negro laborers worked under the piece system. This was true, for instance, of many barbers, of some blacksmiths and other mechanics, of wood-cutters and whip-sawyers and of some foundry-men and forge-men. But it was otherwise where continuous employment at the same work was demanded. Freedom seemed to imply as great a voice for negroes as for white men in engaging their service. But in communities served almost wholly by slaves very little was known about free labor conditions by either negroes or whites.[1] There were then no truly free labor customs to serve as a guide for the freed negroes. In fact the environment seemed to foster the preservation of the conditions existing before they became free. It was particularly tenacious in the agricultural sections which made up most of the state. The land-holders also had an advantage of which they made liberal use to secure their own interests when employing free negroes. They offered arrangements which were strikingly like those of involuntary servitude and which could not be lightly avoided by the workmen. The negroes on their part felt that they were no longer to be treated as slaves, but their lack of tactical advantages left them impotent in bargaining.[2] They needed to be supplied with the means to live, they would not strike out to the frontiers to get them, they cherished the con-

---

[1] A sidelight on this view is seen in the instrument recorded in the *Somerset Land Records*, Lib. K, pp. 117-18.

[2] *Supra*, pp. 30 and 130.

tinuance of the doles and other things they had been accustomed to receive at the hands of the whites and they preferred to trust to the whites to help them to get on. Accordingly they acquiesced in the terms that were offered. Some of their number, to be sure, attempted to take time off and quit their contracts without sufficient cause. Thereby they put their employers to inconvenience and caused much wrath but failed to change the customs governing their working conditions. Free labor customs, therefore, compromised with, rather than supplanted, those of slavery, until other outside factors were introduced.

For the slaves the duration of service was for life, or less if the masters so willed it. For the bond servants it was for terms of years, although subject to termination earlier for sufficient cause. The contract laborers, however, were bound to work only so long as they had agreed to work. The objects of such contracts, as seen by employers of free negroes, were to assure the use of the labor throughout the crop and harvest seasons. Hence on the farms both free negroes and hired slaves were commonly employed from " Christmas to Christmas," or as in Cecil County for terms of nine or ten months each. But extra hands at harvest time and other busy seasons were hired for shorter terms, as by the day, or week, or until the crop had been put away. In the eighteenth century foundrymen and forge-men were likewise hired and paid for shorter terms.[1]   As to the other features of contracts, as constancy in service, attendance during sickness, time of payment and subordination to authority, the treatment of adults was not far different from that of apprenticed children and of slaves also.

[1] Cf. Elkridge Furnace Journal CC, pp. 4, 56, 74, 79; Cornwall Furnace Journal N, pp. 77, 83, 85, 107, 266, 270, 283, 322; Hopewell Forge Journal T, pp. 63, 103, 122.

Regarding the quality of negro labor it was difficult to speak without racial bias. Some facts about it seem clear nevertheless. In the provincial period it was deemed inferior to that of the whites[1] but for reasons already given it was strongly established in place of white labor. After the revolution had passed it won the highest favor it ever enjoyed, as emancipation sentiment was being asserted strongly and it was purposed to give the freed negroes a chance to carry on the trades and by their industry to demonstrate the wisdom of the policy of free manumission. The results were significant. As tonsorial artists negroes were hardly surpassed by any in the state. In the counties they continued doing repair work as blacksmiths, as rough carpenters— building gates, fences and out-buildings—and making into shoes the rough leather of the native tanneries in cases where fit and finish were not the most exquisite. Sometimes they performed the nicer work of the different trades.[2] In course of time they were superseded in part by the whites.[3] They probably made slow progress in what was left to them, but they were confined chiefly to farm, household and common labor. Their partial success as a labor force resulted in causing a vacating of pursuits by the emigration of whites[4] which continued to deplete the white population of some of the counties until as late as 1850. In the counties on the Pennsylvania border and in Somerset and Worcester, however, such depletion as occurred from this cause came before 1820, and excepting in Harford and Worcester, before 1810. These counties, especially those in

[1] *Supra*, pp. 7-8.

[2] *Cf. Md. Col. Jour.*, vol. iii, p. 80; vol. v, p. 361.

[3] *Op. cit.*, vol. i, pp. 225-26; vol. vi, pp. 71, 73, 74; *Md. Pub. Docs.*, 1852 L, p. 4; *34th Ann. Report of American Colonization Society*, p. 57.

[4] *Cf. History and Statistics of Maryland, Seventh Census of United States*, p. 20.

the north, together with Baltimore City, prospered in industry, while the rest of the state complained of stagnation
and retrogression.[1]   The increasing quantities of both skilled and common labor were done largely by the whites.
Their progressive agriculture which abandoned the ancient
staple tobacco and their other industries, for whose products Maryland had formerly looked to outside sources, were
established and carried on mainly by white labor.   The
reason for the course taken in these things was apparently
that white labor was superior in the competition between
races.

The absence of free labor customs left the determination
of the compensation of negro laborers to the factors that
were present.   Custom had rewarded the slave with maintenance, and the bond-servant with maintenance, freedom
dues and sometimes with the payment in addition of a
nominal wage or redemption money.   The occasional gratuities in the case of either could hardly have been regarded as
compensations.   A few negroes voluntarily submitted themselves to a nominal slavery,[2] and others were subjected to
temporary "slavery" by orders of the courts.[3]   This
slavery, however, was apparently very like indentured servitude, many of whose features were copied in the long-term
contracts of the free negroes.   The basic thing in making
compensation was maintenance, while in compensating rural
workers and domestic servants about equal emphasis was laid

---

[1] *Md. Pub. Docs.*, 1841 H, pp. 3-5.

[2] *Dorchester Deeds*, Lib. ER no. 6, pp. 5, 175; *Worcester Deeds*, Lib.
K, p. 187; Lib. GMH no. 3, p. 537; Lib. GMH no. 9, p. 261. The last
cited refers to a case of submission to life slavery in consideration of
the negro's debts. *Cf.* also *Kent Bonds, Indentures etc.*, Lib. 10, p. 152.
Montgomery Land Records, Lib. BS no. 2, p. 226.

[3] *Cf. supra,* chapter on Legal Status, pp. 35-37; *Baltimore Sun*, Feb.
20, 1860.

Table I. Showing Wages Paid to Negroes, 1760–1830.

	Unskilled.				Skilled (Month).			Piecework.	
	Day.	Month.	Year.	Harvest.	Forge men.	Collier.	Mechanic.	Iron, per ton in anconies.	Wood cutting per cord.
1760–1770 . .	1s. 7d. 2s. 6d.	35s. to 41s. Female 25s.	£18 to £25	. . .	40s. to 80s.	40s. to 75s.	40s.	40s.	2s. to 2s. 3d.
1783–1795 . .	1s. 5d. 2s.	30s. 35s.	. . .	. . .	45s.	. . .	60s.	. . .	2s.
1815–1820 . .	19c. to 37c.	Farm $7 Waggoner $9.91	$50.16 $58.56	. . .	$18.55 $18.66	$21	. . .	$5.33	50c.
1830	21c. to 40c.	$4 to $12	. . .	50c. to $1.25 day.	. . .	. . .	. . .	. . .	50c.

TABLE II.   SHOWING WAGES PAID IN CERTAIN MARYLAND COUNTIES, 1850-1866.

(*Cf.* History and Statistics of Maryland, Wages Table.)

	Day.	Month with Board.	Year, with or without "Victuals and Clothes."	Harvest per day.	Wood cutting per cord.	Mechanic per day.
Anne Arundel	. . . . .	$8 to $10	. . . . .	. . . . .	. . . . .	Whip-sawyer $2 to $3 $12 to $18 per month.
Baltimore	50c. to 75c. in warehouse. $1 or $4 a week.	$8 to $10	$65 to $70 with.	$1 In 1861 $1.50	45c. to 50c. Late 75c. *	$1 to $1.50 †
Caroline	25c., 33c., 37c., 50c.	$5 to $7	$35 to $60 with. Female $18 with.	$1 for leader. 67c. for others. 33c. for binder.	50c.	. . . . .
Carroll	50d.	. . . . .	$100, rent and summer firewood.	$1 to $1.25 high $1.50	37c. to 50c.	. . . . .
Cecil	50c. for good laborer.	$10 average.	. . . . .	. . . . .	50c. for oak. 75c. for hickory. 37c. to 40c. (3 levies.)	. . . . .
Dorchester	. . . . .	$6 to $12	$40 to $60 with $75 for the best negroes.	. . . . .	. . . . .	. . . . .
Frederick	40c. to 75c. $1 in town.	$10 to $12	$100 or less with board.	$1.25 or less.	. . . . .	. . . . .
Harford	50c.	$7 to $10 Some $12 Female $4 to $5 with board and clothes.	$80 to $100 with board for 10 months or a year.	$1 to $1.50 Leader more. 1861 $2	. . . . .	. . . . .

TABLE II.—Concluded.

	Day.	Month with Board.	Year, with or without "Victuals and Clothes."	Harvest per day.	Wood cutting per cord.	Mechanic per day.
Howard	75c. to 80c. in rock quarry, 1846. $1.10 in 1861.	$10 Teamster $12			45c. to 50c.	
Kent.	25c. to 33c. 37c. to 50c. with board.	$7.50 to $10 Females $2 to $2.50	$30 to $50. In 1860 $60 to $80 with.	$1.25 to $1.50 Leader 25c. additional.	50c. pine. 75c. oak. $1 hickory.	$1.50 for hewer.
Montgomery. Queen Anne's.	. . . . . . 25c., 33., 50c.	$12 to $15 $6 to $7 and victuals and clothes.	$115 to $120 with board. $20 to $30 Female $30 or less with.	$1 or less.	50c.	
Somerset .	50c. with board.		$75 to $100 in 1861. Less theretofore.			
Talbot .	40c. to 50c.	$8 to $10	$50 or less. A few $80 with.		50c. to 60c.	75c. to $1 $8 to $10 a week.
Washington .	40c. to 50c. with board.	$10 to $12		$1 to $1.25 Binder 75c.		
Worcester.	37c. with board. Female 25c.		$40 to $50 with.			

* Oyster shucking 15c. a gallon. † One mechanic $290 a year.

Variations in different counties will be noted.

upon maintenance and nominal wages. Thus we find the col-
loquial "victuals and clothes" of the Eastern Shore counties.
With these as a partial reward for their work the free negroes
were fed, housed and clothed much like the slaves. Accordingly they ate and slept at the houses of their employers, or if
their numbers were too large for that, in "quarters" where
they received the contractual or customary allowances. A
bushel of meal and fifteen or twenty pounds of meat
formed a mean monthly allowance for food for a laborer.
The clothing allowed for a man, as for instance in Worcester
County, consisted of a winter suit, hat, pair of shoes, two
shirts and pair of trousers; and in Queen Anne's, of Kersey
coat and trousers, summer trousers, hat, two Oznaburg
shirts, a pair of shoes and pair of stockings. Additional
articles were to be purchased out of earnings or awarded as
gratuities. It was usual to give out a considerable part of
the clothing and to pay any remainder of unpaid wages
owing just before the Christmas holidays.

The rates of nominal wages are indicated in the tables
just given. The data given is incomplete for the period expiring before 1850. It indicates, however, a considerable
variation in the wages paid in different parts of the state
and a higher scale of money wages in the middle of the
nineteenth century, especially in the northern and western
counties, than at the close of the revolution.[1] The rise in
the currency value of labor was in part offset by a like
rise in that of other things.

The diversity of wage conditions was partly due to the
differences in natural resources in different parts of the
state but perhaps mainly to the differences in the character
of the laboring population. Laborers of either race seem
to have drawn substantially the same wages for work of

[1] Cf. Carey, Slavery in Maryland, pp. 31-32; Md. Pub. Docs., 1843 M,
and 1845 G.

the same kind and amount.   Both the two races nowhere
stood together long on a par with each other.   The changes
that occurred in either wages or other relations in progressive industries generally turned out to the advantage of the
whites.   And as a consequence of their efficiency they received higher wages than the negroes.[1]   Now it may be
questioned whether the helpless free negroes were pecu-
liarly oppressed in their labor.   It is undeniable that the
whites often took advantage of their superior position to
practice frauds upon them and treated them with injustice.[2]
They often acted so towards white men as well.   Moreover, some labor organizations, savings associations and
building and loan associations extended their benefits to
white persons only.[3]   Again negro evidence was not fully
available against whites in redressing injuries in the courts,
and in seeking justice in general the negroes were subject
to the same disadvantages that have been common to the
humbler classes.   But the proposals deliberately to hamper
negro enterprise by statutory exclusion of negroes from
certain trades, by avoidance of their land titles or by general
re-enslavement either failed to pass the legislature, or such
as were passed went the way of the colonization fiasco.
Such narrowing of the field of their activities as occurred in
manual employments seemed to be due to the preference
of employers for the more efficient white labor, while in
clerical and professional capacities it was mainly due to the
same cause and only secondarily to racial bias.   In this

[1] *Letter of General Harper to E. B. Caldwell*, pp. 8-10.   Hall, *Address
to the Free People of Color of Maryland*, p. 3; *Md. Col. Jour.*, vol. vi,
pp. 70-71; *Md. Pub. Docs.*, 1834, pp. 8-9, and 1843 M, p. 47.   *Genius of
Universal Emancipation*, vol. ii, p. 10.   *Somerset Union*, Feb. 21, 1860.

[2] *Cf. Somerset Union, loc. cit.*

[3] *Baltimore Charter Record*, Lib. ED no. 1, pp. 232, 240, 245, 252, 272,
319, 322, 419, 455; Lib. ED no. 2, p. 451; Lib. GES no. 4, pp. 13, 17, 23,
29, 60, 99, 107.   Brackett, *Negro in Maryland*, p. 188.

course the Maryland employers were following the lead of those of the northern states.

It was stated above that free negroes sometimes engaged in business affairs on their own account. The callings thus entered were chiefly farming, trading, catering and shop-keeping, most important of which in point of numbers engaged was the first. They carried on truck-gardening and farming both as proprietors and as tenants of other proprietors. They followed the example of the whites both in the choice of crops and in the methods of cultivation, and their imitations here succeeded to about the same extent as they succeeded in competing with white laborers when working for wages. In nearly every county a few of them prospered. Some built up good estates. The number who thus rose above the shiftless multitude increased considerably between 1800 and 1860.[1]

Notwithstanding their lack of material resources and credit the negroes played a small role in business affairs which was much heralded among the whites. They engaged in two forms of trading, selling farm and truck produce, and huckstering and marketing. They were often accused of foul practice in both, but more especially in the former. In fact it was reputed that there was a constant traffic in stolen farm produce in which negroes were credited with a large part.[2] The scenes in which it originated were chiefly the forest-shrouded bays and inlets of the tide-water districts. Here water-craft stole into appointed recesses at night-fall, dropped anchor, received their freights from

---

[1] Cf. infra, pp. 174-75, chapter on Property Holdings. In the Baltimore City directories are indicated for 1819 two negro gardeners, in 1824 six, in 1831 twelve, in 1841 and 1850 four each, and in 1860 five.

[2] Letter of General Harper to E. B. Caldwell, p. 10; H. Del. Jour., 1844, p. 106. Supra, pp. 101-02, chapter on Legal Status. Also Amer. Farmer, vol. i, p. 99. Oral tradition also relates much about this trade.

persons on land and steered themselves away before day-
break. The operations were facilitated by the cooperation
of slaves who helped to smooth the way to their masters'
store-houses from which the spoils were taken. Attempts
at preventive legislation failed to check the growth of the
practice. It seems, however, that reports grossly exag-
gerated the extent of such trade, and of such as was
carried on much was no doubt done with the help or
at the instigation of white men who reaped the major part
of its profits. Kidnaping negroes to sell as slaves, a practice in which a few negroes acted as decoys, was a shocking
form of illicit traffic.[1] Huckstering, hawking and marketing required small capital and were suited to the negroes'
tastes. They were pursued chiefly by some of the more
enterprising who resided in the environs of the cities and
towns. Thus Baltimore in 1824 and 1831 had eighteen
hucksters, in 1841 thirteen, in 1850 twenty and in 1860
forty-one. Garden and dairy products, eggs and poultry
were the chief things disposed in this trade. In some communities fish and oysters were added to the list.

Another form of negro business enterprise was seen in
catering and restaurant-keeping. They were not open to
the same objections that were raised against negro grog-
shops.[2] On the contrary some of them were habitually
patronized by the whites, as they represented a proper exercise of a business in which the excellence of their managers was acknowledged. Passing mention should be made
of the cake-shops and booths that were often located on
vacant lots in the towns, or at convenient places on camp-
meeting and picnic grounds. Their keepers dispensed pat-
ties, other delicacies and sometimes more substantial foods.

[1] *Cf. 26 Niles Register*, p. 96.

[2] *Cf. Laws*, 1827, ch. 29; 1831, ch. 323; 1852, ch. 288; chapter on
Legal Status, *supra*, pp. 103-04; *Baltimore American*, May 21, 1859.

Catering for picnics and banquets and keeping ice-cream saloons were done chiefly by negroes, until near the middle of the nineteenth century when a part of such business in Baltimore fell to the whites. In some of the counties the best restaurants were conducted by negroes. One each at Chestertown, Easton and Princess Anne was favored by general public patronage and often graced by the presence of the élite circles of the Eastern Shore. The first chief steward of the United States Naval Academy at Annapolis was a free negro.[1]

Retail shop-keeping was more difficult for negroes to enter than either of the other forms of business mentioned. Nevertheless some negroes who had been employed at or about retail shops and others who had served apprenticeships for that purpose turned to merchandizing.[2] The city of Baltimore is here again the principal center of interest in the state. The earliest advertisement of a negro's business I have found in Maryland was that of the Union Blacking Shop advertised in the Baltimore American in the year 1809.[3] Its proprietor prospered well for one of his race.[4] His venture was followed by others by whom several different lines of goods were handled. The following table, compiled from the city directories, gives a partial indication

[1] Cf. Laws, 1847, ch. 133.

[2] Cf. Baltimore Indentures, Lib. WB no. 6, p. 127; Lib. WB no. 8, p. 1; Lib. WB no. 10, p. 366; Lib. DMP no. 16, p. 107; Baltimore Orphans' Court Minutes, Lib. 13, p. 76; Anne Arundel Orphans' Court Minutes, Lib. 217, p. 186.

[3] Issue of Jan. 31, 1809. The proprietor announced to his "friends and fellow-citizens" that he had discovered "a blacking, in point of utility and elegance, not to be surpassed in North America." He had also a powder for cleaning plate excelling any ever before offered to the public. Cf. his will in the Baltimore Wills, Lib. WB no. 10, p. 343; Lib. WB no. 11, pp. 603-05. He disposed of a moderate fortune, a part of which apparently came as a legacy in 1817. He was a leader among his people in the city.

of these activities.[1] Many of these were apparently unsuccessful. But failure was not a necessary consequence of engaging in merchandizing, for a respectable negro tobacconist
and cigar-maker in " Old Town," Baltimore, continued in
his chosen business from 1833 till as late as 1859.[2] Outside of Baltimore also were several respectable negro merchants. At Easton in 1819 a West Indian Negro was ad-
vertizing a variety of fruits, provisions, meats, hard and
soft drinks and sporting goods.[3] About ten years later his
creditors closed up his business and even sold the property
of the negroes' church to satisfy their demands. In the
last decade before the general emancipation several prominent negro merchants appeared. One was a well-to-do
tobacconist at Annapolis, a second a versatile variety store-
keeper, ship-owner, and mariner of Chestertown, a third a
prosperous merchant at Salisbury whose business seemed
to keep up well till he was prosecuted for having possession

[1]	*1819*	*1824-27*	*1831*	*1841*	*1850*	*1860*
Confectioners	0	1	1	2	8	17
Druggists	0	0	0	0	0	2
Feed stores	1	0	0	1	2	1
Flour merchant	0	1	0	0	0	0
Grocers	0	1	7	1	3	3
Milliners	0	1	0	1	3	0
Tobacconists	1	0	0	4	2	1
Wholesale dry goods dealer	0	0	0	1	0	0

[2] *Cf.* Varle, *View of Baltimore*, 1833, p. 162; *Md. Col. Jour.*, vol. ix,
p. 88. The firm name of Burley and Jones as dealers in feed occurred
in successive directories for a number of years.

[3] *Republican Star and Eastern Shore General Advertiser*, Dec. 7,
1819 to Feb. 1, 1820. Also Nov. 14 to Dec. 5, 1820, April 29 to May 6,
1823, and Sept. 13-20, 1835.

[4] *Talbot Land Records*, Lib. 48, p. 427; Lib. 49, pp. 400-02. A report
of long currency among the negroes was that "white clerks" in the
shop had robbed this store from the inside and ruined its proprietor.

of a copy of Mrs. Stowe's "Uncle Tom's Cabin" and
financially ruined. But all of these were eclipsed by the
career of Captain Robert Henry of Pocomoke City. Several
years before the war broke out he became a partner with
a southern gentleman in a general store. He also owned
and operated some small vessels plying in the trade between
Baltimore and points on the peninsula. He won a remarkable reputation for probity and enterprise and continued in his business until his death in 1898.

From the point of view of labor conditions the history
of Maryland free negroes may be divided into two periods,
one before and the other after the war of 1812-14. It has
been seen above that the systems of slavery and bond-servi-
tude prevailed in the province and that the latter had largely
passed into history when the revolution came on. After
the revolution for a time white labor seemed to decline,
while the growth of slavery, in numbers at least, continued
until after the beginning of the nineteenth century. During
that same period a great number of negroes were set free
from slavery. Those who were thus freed remained for
the most part in the communities where they had resided as
slaves and worked in the midst of the slaves in the manner
already described. Their employers generally wished them
well, advised, aided and encouraged them and sought to
give them a chance to prove their efficiency as free laborers. They were further favored by the prevalence of
slavery whose stigmatization of manual labor caused many
of the whites to retire before the advance rather than
attempt to compete with them directly. Wherever the
whites did not compete strongly, acute prejudices due to the
color line did not manifest themselves prominently. Ap-

¹Cross, *A Few Thoughts to Mr. Jacobs*, p. 4. Cf. Md. Col. *Jour.*,
vol. 2, p. 73; vol. 6, p. 74. *Letter of J. H. B. Latrobe.*

parently the negroes might have monopolized the pursuits of manual labor, had they used their opportunity to the fullest extent. As it was they improved their situation somewhat but the majority of their number were not strikingly superior to the slaves. It appeared, therefore, that they had not shared well in the boasted boon of liberty resulting from the gloriously achieved American independence. They seemed to remain essentially the same kind of economic labor force for whose employment and utilization the whites were still to be responsible.[1] Colonial conditions, as told in the growth of servile labor, were thus protracted for a generation after the revolution.

But this tendency did not prevail to the same extent over the whole of the state. As early as the time of the revolution the growing city of Baltimore was becoming a free labor center. Free negroes also had begun to congregate there, but by far the greater part of the growth of the urban laboring classes consisted of whites. That condition was permanent. On the other hand sixteen of the counties actually lost in numbers of whites, although after a time seven of these overcame such losses. And after 1820 all the counties on the Pennsylvania border and Anne Arundel, Somerset and Worcester gained appreciably more in whites than in free negroes. The causes of the changes are found in the industrial expansion that followed the Peace of Ghent. Industries were established affording unprecedented demands for labor for which whites were desired and efforts were made to check their migration to the frontiers.[2] At the same time European immigrants in large numbers were attracted to United States, part of them coming to Mary-

---

[1] *Cf. Letter of General Harper to E. B. Caldwell*, pp. 8, 10, 11; *Baltimore Sun*, Jan. 7, 1856.

[2] *History and Statistics of Maryland, Seventh Census of United States*, p. 20.

land.[1]   They settled chiefly in Baltimore and in the northern and western counties, 70 per cent of them in the cities
and towns.   They readily engaged in manual labor, and
owing largely to their lead white competition with negroes
began to grow.   In the course of time they demonstrated
their superiority in work which had once been done almost
wholly by negroes.[2]   As a consequence certain ominous dis-
placements of negroes with whites—particularly Germans
and Irish—took place in Baltimore.[3]   The increased immigration at the middle of the century brought into clearer
light the progress of the change.   In 1851 J. H. B. Latrobe
said :

In Baltimore, my home, ten years since, the shipping at Fell's
Point was loaded by colored stevedores.   The labor in the coal
yards was colored labor.   In the rural districts around Baltimore . . . free colored laborers, ten years since, got in the
harvests, worked the mine banks, made the fences, and indeed
supplied to a great extent, all agricultural wants in this respect.
Now all this is changed.   The white man stands in the black
man's shoes, or else is fast getting into them.[4]

In another instance the same man said: " In the rural district where I reside in summer, ten years ago, I could not
get a white man to work for me; now I can't get a black
man." [5]   Furthermore the whites became jealous of negro
competition in trades that had once been carried on mainly
by negroes.   In riots against negro laborers in Baltimore

---

[1] The immigration of foreigners in 1820-30 was 10,552; in 1831-40,
55,322; in 1841-50, 68,392.   Op. cit., p. 20.   In 1850, 12.85 per cent of
the whole white population were of foreign birth.

[2] Carey, Slavery in Maryland, p. 39; Md. Col. Jour., vol. ii, p. 203.

[3] 31 Niles Register, p. 305.   Md. Col. Jour., vol. ii, p. 103; vol. vi, pp.
71-73.   Genius of Universal Emancipation, vol. ii, p. 10.

[4] Md. Col. Jour., vol. vi, p. 71.

[5] 34th Ann. Report of American Colonization Society, p. 57.

they imitated the examples set in the northern cities.[1] To some persons who discerned what was happening these things seemed to portend the eventual exclusion of negroes from the labor field and their exile or destruction by natural causes.[2] But the demand for labor was generally sufficient to afford employment for the men of both races. This became true even in certain of the slave-ridden counties, where wages suddenly rose a few years before the war.[3] The change to white labor was neither sudden nor thorough-going, and it proceeded less rapidly in the rural districts than in the cities. The main body of the negroes were quite unperturbed about it. Their ignorance of causes and their experience with the white people and the government inspired them with confidence rather than fears for the future. They declined both to leave the state and to change radically from what they had been as a labor force.

[1] *Cf. Baltimore Sun,* July 5, 1858; June 28, 1859; *Md. Col. Jour.,* vol. i, pp. 49-50, 225-26. Also Douglass, *My Bondage and My Freedom,* pp. 311-12. Some negroes even left the state in order to avoid further contention, it was alleged. *40 Niles Register,* pp. 452-53.

[2] *34th Ann. Report of American Colonization Society,* p. 57; *Md. Pub. Docs.,* 1852 L, p. 4. *Maryland Scheme of Expatriation Examined,* p. 9. *Md. Col. Jour.,* nos. 17, 18, 19 (1838). The efforts to create a preference for white labor on purely racial grounds probably did not receive much encouragement, although there is no doubt that, other things being equal, a white laboring population would have been preferred to the then existing negroes. *Cf. Md. Col. Jour.,* vol. vi, p. 74. *31 Niles Register,* p. 305. *Letter of General Harper to E. B. Caldwell,* pp. 12, 15.

[3] *Baltimore Sun,* Jan. 3, 1855; Jan. 7, 1856; *Easton Gazette,* May 5, 1859.

CHAPTER VI

PROPERTY—ACQUISITIONS AND HOLDINGS

IN the preceding chapters it has been seen that the free negroes furnished an important part of the labor employed in Maryland industries. The extent of their liberties with respect to industry and property has also been shown. Their position was mainly that of employees and their share of what was produced was small. Their disposal of their wages was prodigal rather than provident, and hence they accumulated a smaller total of property than either their earnings or their numbers should have made possible. Nevertheless they had acquired some property in several of the counties before the general assessment of 1783, and after that time they increased its amount much more rapidly than their own numbers increased. As far as occasion offered, they used the same forms in acquiring and the same tenures in holding property that the whites used. As to acquisition the chief concern now is with the original acquisition by negroes as a result of production and of transfers from whites by sales, gifts and bequests.

Whatever a free negro produced as a result of his own investment and management became his own property. The forms of independent negro enterprises noticed in the preceding chapter thus became the means of procuring the ownership of property according to the customs of the whites. It seems probable that the major part of the accumulated property held by negroes was acquired as a result

174   [564

of such activities.[1] But for much of what they possessed
they owed thanks to the whites no less than they owed their
manumission to the same class. Wherever this was true,
the occasion for transferring things to them lay not in the
circumstances common to business transactions but in the
peculiar relations of the whites and negroes.

A part of the property was given for the purpose of providing for the support of old negroes and others who were
unable to labor for their own support. In certain statutes
that have been referred to above it was forbidden to manumit any negroes who were above the age of fifty years or
those who for any reason could not earn their living.
These laws also required masters to make sufficient provision for old and infirm slaves, failing to do which they
were liable to be placed under bond to provide such support.[2]
The enforcement of these rules, aided by the moral awakening that attended the revolution, obviously improved the
average treatment of superannuated slaves. For although
complaints of improper treatment and turning them adrift
were renewed for a time after 1825,[3] it was asserted that
such cases were exceptional in the middle of the century and
after. The wills furnished abundant evidence of appropriations of parts of estates for the negroes' benefit. In
1780, for instance, a citizen of Caroline County enjoined
upon his wife to " well cloth and maintain my old man
Pompey in sickness and health during life." And sixteen
years later in Queen Anne's a will ordered that two old

---

[1] The property assessed to negroes appeared much greater than the
sum total of recorded bequests and gifts discovered. Evidence from
individuals who had been acquainted with conditions before the civil
war corroborated this view.

[2] *Laws*, 1752, ch. 1; 1790, ch. 9; 1796, ch. 67. The bonding provision
was inserted in the last two of these enactments.

[3] *Genius of Universal Emancipation*, Oct. 7, 1826; *37 Niles Register*,
p. 340. *Cf.* note 5, *supra*, p. 49.

negroes should be kept in a decent manner.[1]   The practice
of thus making both the dwelling-place and the support of
old negroes a charge upon the general assets of estates prevailed in many of the wills.[2]   In others the appropriations
for the purpose were either to be derived from specified
property or to become special burdens upon particular legatees or heirs.[3]   The forty dollars a year to be given to an old
negro in Kent, in case he was not otherwise provided for,
represented about mean money value of such bequests.[4]   Provisions were also sometimes made to enable old negroes,
whether manumitted or not, to continue to occupy particular
places of abode and to continue the exercise of functions they
had been accustomed to on their masters' farms.[5]   But such
gifts were not sufficient in any case to aid greatly in building
up material fortunes.

The provisions noted were only such as the law demanded
for the sake of protecting the public interests and were less
often extended to slaves under the age of forty-five years

[1] Wills: Caroline, Lib. JR no. A, p. 42; Queen Anne's, Lib. WHN
no. 3, p. 193. Cf. Cecil Wills, Lib. 8, p. 74, in which the testamentary
provision is made in the form of an indenture.

[2] Cf. e. g. Wills: Baltimore, Lib. WB no. 6, p. 241; Lib. IPC no. 28,
p. 245; Anne Arundel, Lib. JG no. 1, p. 473; Baltimore County, Lib.
JLR no. 1, p. 92; Caroline, Lib. WAF no. A, p. 399; Cecil, Lib. 6, p.
297; Dorchester, Lib. THH no. 1, p. 38; Frederick, Lib. GME no. 3, p.
82; Harford, Lib. AJ no. 2, p. 244; Lib. TSB no. 6, p. 82; Howard,
Lib. WG no. 1, p. 56; Montgomery, Lib. WT of R no. 2, p. 343; Queen
Anne's, Lib. TCE no. 1, p. 104; Talbot, Lib. JP no. 6, p. 300; Washington, Lib. D, p. 195; Worcester, Lib. MH no. 27, pp. 19-20, 80.

[3] Wills: Baltimore, Lib. WB no. 12, p. 131; Frederick, Lib. RB no. 1,
p. 484; Harford, Lib. SR no. 1, p. 516; Howard, Lib. WG no. 1, pp.
105, 176, 251, 346; Kent, Lib. 10, p. 23; Montgomery, Lib. O, p. 436;
Talbot, Lib. JP no. 5, p. 77; Washington, Lib. D, p. 254; Lib. E, p.
274; Worcester, Lib. MH no. 7, p. 556.

[4] Kent Wills, loc. cit. Cf. infra, p. 181, on grants of annuities.

[5] Wills: Anne Arundel, Lib. TTS no. 1, p. 333; Caroline, Lib. JR no.
B, p. 138; Frederick, Lib. GM no. 1, p. 360; Harford, Lib. TSB no. 6,
p. 107; Talbot, Lib. JP no. 7, p. 83; Washington, Lib. E, p. 278.

who were able to work for their own support. Most slave owners gave to their freedmen but little more than was required of them. But there was a minority who felt that something more was required. To them the slaves were dependents who had had a part in building up the estates on which their labor had been spent and who as a consequence merited something more than mere pittances for what they had done. Their view was expressed by one in Dorchester County who wished " to do what is right and becoming " for his negroes but found himself " after an experience of thirty years as an owner, and a much longer period of anxious reflection, wholly at a loss to make a satisfactory disposition of them." [1] They were variously moved by moral obligation, by desire for fair play and even by " affectionate regard " on account of devoted service rendered by beneficiaries.[2] They knew both the hardships of the negroes and the weaknesses of their character and desired to make in their behalf provisions which would most effectively aid them in the struggle for their livings. A few individuals here and there over the state were also moved to take this course because of concubinage with negro women or of blood relationship with hybrid children.[3] As a consequence gifts and bequests of property to

---

[1] *Dorchester Wills*, Lib. THH no. 1, p. 4. This testator further wrote of his slaves that he deemed it an "imperative duty to treat them with kindness and forbearance and to strive . . . to enlighten them so as to prepare them for a higher scale or sphere of existence." He freed several, gave property to some and ordered that the rest be treated "with the kindness due to children." *Cf.* also *Wills: Talbot*, Lib. JP no. 5, p. 316; Lib. JP no. 9, p. 101; *Baltimore*, Lib. NH no. 25, p. 48.

[2] *Wills: Baltimore*, Lib. DMP no. 15, p. 453; *Frederick*, Lib. GME no. 2, p. 115; *Harford*, Lib. AJ no. A, p. 105; Lib. SR no. 1, p. 258; *Kent*, Lib. no. 5, p. 80; *Talbot*, Lib. JP no. 5, p. 316; Lib. JP no. 7, p. 83; *Washington*, Lib. E, p. 278.

[3] *Wills: Anne Arundel*, Lib. JG no. 2, p. 459; *Baltimore*, Lib. WB

manumitted negroes were common, and some property was sold to them at nominal prices and on easy terms of payment.[1]

Gifts and bequests were thus made in the same way as to whites. Accordingly there were grants of lands and houses and of various kinds of personal property. There were grants in perpetuity, grants for life and for specified terms of years, grants giving full rights of possession and disposal and grants in which only the incomes or annuities were to be received from designated property or invested funds. The following paragraphs will more fully set forth their character and give partial indications as to their amounts. Grants in perpetuity will be first considered and after them those in which rights of reversion were reserved to the estates concerned. Among grants in perpetuity were some which included whole estates. Their number and value, although small, were still sufficient to warrant mention here.[2] Of more importance were those of portions of

no. 7, p. 169; Lib. WB no. 11, p. 499; Lib. NH no. 26, p. 309; *Dorchester*, Lib. THH no. 1, p. 126; *Frederick*, Lib. GME no. 2, p. 669; *Harford*, Lib. SR no. 1, p. 13; *Washington*, Lib. E, p. 454. Other cases leading to suspicion of the same motive were the following: *op. cit.*, *Anne Arundel*, Lib. BEG no. 1, p. 321; *Baltimore*, Lib. WB no. 9, p. 334; *Frederick*, Lib. HS no. 1, pp. 39, 45; *Montgomery*, Lib. B, pp. 388-89; Lib. WT no. 2, p. 31; *Talbot*, Lib. JP no. 6, pp. 5-6; Lib. JP no. 7, p. 14.

[1] For cases of evident favors shown in the matter of prices, *cf. Baltimore Chattel Records*, Lib. GES, no. 26, p. 421; *Dorchester Deeds*, Lib. ER no. 10, p. 590; Lib. WJ no. 3, p. 89; *Harford Land Records*, Lib. JLG no. E, p. 300; Lib. HDG no. 35, p. 259; *Somerset Deeds*, Lib. LH, p. 64; *Worcester Deeds*, Lib. GMH no. 5, p. 208; Lib. EDM no. 2, p. 96. *Cf. Frederick Wills*, Lib. GME no. 3, p. 299; Lib. GM no. 1, p. 361.

[2] *Wills: Anne Arundel*, Lib. TTS no. 1, p. 547; Lib. BEG no. 1, p. 81; *Baltimore*, Lib. WB no. 12, p. 80; Lib. WB no. 15, p. 453; *Harford*, Lib. CWB no. 7, p. 226; *Frederick*, Lib. GME no. 2, p. 48; *Mongomery*, Lib. B, pp. 388-89. *Cf. Md. Wills*, Lib. CC no. 3, p. 632.

estates of which white legatees were the chief beneficiaries. A house and lot in Calvert street in Baltimore which were together assessed for taxation at $12093 in 1859 formed the most valuable single gift in this class I have found.[1] But inasmuch as these transfers generally took place in connection with the manumission of slaves, they were relatively less numerous in Baltimore than in the rural counties. In at least four instances in these counties tracts of more than a hundred acres each were willed to negroes;[2] tracts of smaller size and long-term leases were given much more frequently,[3] and in some instances in place of land money was left to purchase homes for negro beneficiaries. Besides these there were assignments of property to parents, or to other trustees, of children in whom the rights of ownership in fee were ultimately to be vested.[4] The great majority of the testamentary transfers, however, were bequests of personalty, conveying articles that would minister directly to personal wants or aid the recipients in acquiring a livelihood. Of the former were grain and pork, clothing, bedding, household goods, furniture and kitchen uten-

---

[1] *Baltimore Wills,* Lib. WH no. 26, p. 309. *Cf. Baltimore Tax Ledger,* 1859, no. 3, p. 49.

[2] *Wills: Anne Arundel,* Lib. EV no. 1, p. 88; *Kent,* Lib. no. 9, p. 149; *Montgomery,* Lib. B, pp. 388-89; *Queen Anne's,* Lib. TCE no. 2, p. 3.

[3] *Wills: Anne Arundel,* Lib. JG no. 1, p. 52; Baltimore, Lib. DMP no. 15, p. 453; Lib. DMP no. 21, p. 237; Lib. WB no. 9, p. 185; *Baltimore County,* Lib. JLR no. 2, p. 80; *Carroll,* Lib. JB no. 1, p. 39; *Cecil,* Lib. no. 9, p. 347; *Dorchester,* Lib. THH no. 1, p. 4; *Frederick,* Lib. TS no. 1, p. 45; *Queen Anne's,* Lib. TCE no. 2, p. 13; *Washington,* Lib. E, p. 234; *Worcester,* Lib. TT no. 8, p. 172. The Frederick County will cited in this note was that of John C. Fritchie, husband of one Barbara Fritchie.

[4] *Wills: Baltimore County,* Lib. JLR no. 2, p. 80; *Frederick,* Lib. TS no. 1, pp. 28-29; Lib. HS no. 2, p. 212; Lib. GME no. 2, pp. 356, 669; *Kent,* Lib. no. 19, p. 141; *Queen Anne's,* Lib. TCE no. 2, p. 3.

sils,[1] and of the latter barnyard fowls, swine, milk-stock, hoes, scythes, cradles, oxen, plows and gearings, looms, spinning-wheels and mechanics' tools.[2] Two negroes were to receive each a horse and dray, another the choice of his master's riding horses with bridle and saddle, and a few others such articles as jewelry, burnished shoe buckles, mahogany furniture, plate and guns.[3] In place of giving articles already in hand some testators set aside money for their purchase. A testatrix in Harford County in 1802 willed to a negro boy a hundred dollars to enable him to establish a business and twenty dollars pocket money besides.[4] Moreover there were unconditional gifts of money ranging from the debt of ten dollars forgiven by a creditor in Cecil to two thousand dollars to a single individual in Howard and five thousand dollars to a group of negroes in

---

[1] Wills: Anne Arundel, Lib. JG no. 39, p. 140; Lib. JG no. 1, p. 96; Lib. JG no. 2, pp. 351, 473; Baltimore, Lib. WB no. 9, pp. 23-24, 188; Caroline, Lib. JR no. B, p. 203; Lib. WAF no. A, p. 351; Cecil, Lib. no. 6, p. 115; Dorchester, Lib. THH no. 1, p. 139; Frederick, Lib. BB no. 1, pp. 72-73, 484; Lib. GME no. 1, p. 533; Lib. GME no. 2, p. 345; Harford, Lib. AJ no. 2, p. 466; Lib. AJ no. C, p. 103; Lib. R, p. 205; Howard, Lib. WG no. 1, pp. 101, 174, 175, 306; Kent, Lib. no. 9, p. 80; Queen Anne's, Lib. TCE no. 2, p. 305; Lib. WHN no. 3, p. 191; Talbot, Lib. JP no. 8, pp. 210, 384; Washington, Lib. D, p. 231; Worcester, Lib. MH no. 27, pp. 80, 286.

[2] Wills: Anne Arundel, Lib. JG no. 2, pp. 471-74; Lib. JG no. 1, pp. 83, 154; Lib. TTS no. 1, p. 89; Baltimore, Lib. WB no. 8, p. 101; Lib. WB no. 12, p. 251; Carroll, Lib. JB no. 1 ,pp. 79, 275; Frederick, Lib. HS no. 1, p. 230; Lib. GM no. 3, p. 134; Harford, Lib. AJ no. 2, p. 157; Howard, WG no. 1, pp. 174-76; Queen Anne's, Lib. WHN no. 3, p. 191; Talbot, Lib. JB no. 2, p. 297; Lib. JP no. 5, pp. 317, 257; Lib. JP no. 6, p. 372.

[3] Wills: Baltimore, Lib. WB no. 10, p. 402; Lib. DMP no. 13, p. 502; Lib. DMP no. 14, p. 119; Lib. WH no. 25, p. 307; Cecil, Lib. no. 8, p. 275; Dorchester, Lib. THH no. 1, p. 229; Howard, Lib. WG no. 1, p. 174; Talbot, Lib. JP no. 6, pp. 5, 6.

[4] Wills, Lib. AJ no. c, p. 103.

Washington,[1] and tradition tells hazily of gifts of still larger sums. The money was either given outright or in the form of annuities, the latter occurring more often at or near the city of Baltimore than anywhere else in the state. The annuities were to be paid in annual, semi-annual or quarterly instalments.[2] One in Queen Anne's amounted to ten dollars a year, while one in Baltimore amounted to five hundred dollars a year for five years. More often the amount to be paid was approximately that of a negro's wages. In place of definite annuities we find also bequests of securities, as stock of Baltimore City, bank stocks and savings deposits and funds to be devoted to their purchase. Of some of the legacies both principal and interest were to accrue to beneficiaries. In case the legatees were manumitted persons owing further service, the payments were to begin or to be made, when the manumission took effect. A few unemancipated servants were also offered the hire for their own labor.[5] Finally slaves were

[1] Wills: Cecil, Lib. no. 6, p. 362; Howard, Lib. WG no. 1, p. 99; Washington, Lib. D, p. 408.

[2] Wills: Anne Arundel, Lib. JG no. 2, p. 64; Baltimore, WB no. 6, p. 148; Lib. WB no. 9, p. 265; Lib. WB no. 10, p. 10; Lib. WB no. 11, p. 526; Lib. DMP no. 20, p. 10; Lib. DMP no. 20, p. 153; Lib. NH no. 6, p. 64; Baltimore County, Lib. JLR no. 1, pp. 133, 315; Lib. JLR, no. 2, p. 121; Queen Anne's, Lib. WHN no. 4, p. 103; Lib. TCE no. 1, pp. 407, 445; Talbot, Lib. JP no. 8, p. 427; Baltimore County Chattel Records, Lib. HMT no. 2, p. 371; Frederick, Lib. TS no. 1, p. 28.

[3] Wills: Queen Anne's, Lib. TCE no. 1, p. 445; Baltimore, Lib. WB no. 6, p. 148.

[4] Wills: Baltimore, Lib. WB no. 9, p. 186; Lib. no. 10, p. 10; Lib. DMP no. 13, p. 181; Lib. NH no. 26, p. 478; Lib. IPC no. 29, p. 136; Baltimore County, Lib. JLR no. 1, pp. 91, 285; Carroll, Lib. JB no. 2, p. 318; Frederick, Lib. GH no. 1, p. 250; Lib. GME no. 2, p. 356.

[5] Wills: Baltimore, Lib. DMP no. 13, p. 242; Kent, Lib. 8, p. 261. Under a will recorded in the Baltimore Wills, Lib. DMP no. 19, p. 491 (1842), a Delaware negro was to receive $1.50 a month for tobacco and sundries. Cf. also Wills: Caroline, Lib. JR no. B, p. 203; Kent, Lib. 11, p. 120; Queen Anne's, Lib. WHN no. 4, p. 304; Lib. TCE no. 2, p. 211.

bequeathed to be given or sold to their free consorts, to parents or to children in the same manner and for the same reasons indicated above in the chapter on the growth of the free negro population.[1] Apparently some slave-holders used this means of ridding their estates of the burdens of supporting worn-out negroes,[2] although some of the freedmen to whom burdens of their keep were shifted received from their manumittors material help in addition to their own freedom.[3]

Life estates and term estates were also mentioned above. In addition to the ordinary grounds for bestowing this form of bequest many testators were moved by fears that their negro beneficiaries were more likely to waste than to use economically things that were given to them in complete ownership. Although a few grants of usufructs were applied to ordinary articles of personalty,[4] they had to do chiefly with realty and income-bearing personalty. But usual freedom from rents on such grants did not apparently carry with it freedom also from tax payment,[5] although ad-

[1] *Supra*, pp. 59, 77-78. *Wills: Anne Arundel*, Lib. JG no. 2, p. 351; *Baltimore*, Lib. WB no. 9, pp. 184-86; Lib. NH no. 6, p. 351; *Baltimore Co.*, Lib. JLR no. 1, p. 371; *Cecil*, Lib. 6, pp. 230, 278; *Dorchester*, Lib. LLK no. 1, p. 18; *Frederick*, Lib. TS no. 1, p. 30; *Queen Anne's*, Lib. TCE no. 2, p. 13; *Washington*, Lib. D, p. 651; *Worcester*, Lib. TT no. 8, p. 256.

[2] *Wills: Caroline*, Lib. WGN no. B, p. 25; *Cecil*, Lib. 10, p. 7; *Frederick*, Lib. GME no. 1, p. 420; *Montgomery*, Lib. P, p. 315; *Washington*, Lib. D, p. 424.

[3] *Wills: Anne Arundel*, Lib. TTS no. 1, p. 52; *Queen Anne's*, Lib. TCE no. 2, p. 211; *Dorchester*, Lib. THH no. 1, p. 26; *Frederick*, Lib. GH no. 1, p. 19; *Montgomery*, Lib. O, p. 474. Some slaves were given to negroes to be used for profit, if desired. Cf. *Wills: Anne Arundel*, Lib. TTS no. 1, p. 481; Lib. JG no. 1, p. 83; *Baltimore*, Lib. WB no. 7, p. 179; *Montgomery*, Lib. B, pp. 388-89.

[4] *E. g. Wills: Frederick*, Lib. GME no. 3, p. 139; Lib. HS no. 3, p. 14.

[5] For cases of express exemption from tax payment and from other public burdens, *vide Wills: Baltimore*, Lib. NH no. 26, p. 477; *Caro-*

ditional bequests were frequently given to the recipients. Thus one negro in Dorchester was to have the privilege of cutting firewood and rail-timber from certain land without charge, and a negress in Talbot was to have ten dollars a year and a sufficient supply of firewood cut and duly delivered at the door of her life tenement.[1]   The munificent provision of a Baltimore County decedent consisted of the use for life of a house and as much land as the negro could cultivate, the privilege of getting fire-wood, two cows, four ewes, a sow, a horse and a life annuity of forty dollars.[2] On the other hand the life estates became the occasion frequently for imposing conditions and restrictions upon their holders.   The stated objects of such restrictions were varied.   In part they had to do with the manner of use.   In several cases they made occupation by the beneficiary essential to continued enjoyment of benefits and expressed or implied denial of the right to lease to any other parties.[3] In at least three instances the holders were to be warned that any attempt on their part to bargain away their allot-

---

line, Lib. JR no. B, p. 62; *Frederick*, Lib. GME no. 1, p. 71; *Howard*, Lib. WG no. 1, p. 91; *Kent*, Lib. no. 11, p. 328; *Worcester*, Lib. LPS no. 1, pp. 388, 400.   Under the law of this state the holder of the life estate paid the ordinary public burdens and at least a share of the special assessments levied upon the property.   *Cf.* Williams' case, *3 Bland's Chancery*, p. 253.

[1] *Wills: Dorchester*, Lib. THH no. 1, pp. 139, 233; *Talbot*, Lib. JP no. 9, p. 204.

[2] *Wills: Baltimore*, Lib. WB no. 10, p. 10.   *Cf.* nearly similar terms in the following: *Frederick*, Lib. HS no. 3, p. 14; *Talbot*, Lib. JP no. 5, p. 316.   *Cf.* also *Anne Arundel*, Lib. TTS no. 1, p. 150; *Baltimore*, Lib. WB no. 9, p. 265; Lib. NH no. 27, p. 31; *Frederick*, Lib. GME no. 3, p. 166; *Harford*, Lib. AJ no. C, p. 183; Lib. CWB no. 7, p. 62, and especially *Howard*, Lib. WG no. 1, p. 306.

[3] *Wills: Cecil*, Lib. no. 10, p. 428; *Dorchester*, Lib. LLK no. 1, p. 54; *Harford*, Lib. AJ no. C, p. 183; Lib. CWB no. 7, p. 62; *Washington*, Lib. D, p. 85; *Worcester*, Lib. LPS no. 1, p. 344.

TABLE I

Table Showing Property Assessed to Negroes in the Counties of Maryland

County	1793	1804	1813	1825-26	1832-33	1836-38	1841-42	1846	1852-53	1860
Allegany	2 180.66				8 181				15 5501	17 6656
Anne Arundel	8 1066.66 (1783)									98 58274 *
Baltimore Co.			10 571 (1818)	16 2830.46			61 16843		129 37801	
Baltimore City			59 7843	234 12718	44 13884	107 1571100		264 150135	338 289492.37	348 449138
Calvert										
Caroline			14 930	13 4406 (1822)	44 6100		98 20984		195 53308	184 59291
Carroll							29 9867		40 8579	35 8140.50
Cecil		11 1245.33	20 3347	16 2279	33 3031		47 19401		183 42367	146 37472
Charles	3 237.33 (1783)							67 19520 (1842)		
Dorchester				47 1025						
Frederick	3 49.66 (1798)		4 221 (1816)		81 3625 (1835)				178 53859.16†	291 86765
Harford									275 81712	167 45350
Howard									36 10056	32 10664
Kent	7 349.33	49 3794.88	53 7134	85 9152	76 7731		16 5436		128 58326	288 70702
Montgomery					72 1773		137 28937		43 9999	81 17142
Prince George's	2 143.185			89 5175 (1824)	96 4827		31 5371		237 66015	215 65227
Queen Anne's										
St. Mary's		88 6132.57					105 26588			
Somerset	13 1333.33 (1798)		15 1315	73 8009	88 12655		137 25498		201 54757	205 57298
Talbot	18 1766.30		108 5141.50	54 3188.58	86 3550.05		48 11615.40		169 31364	184 30133
Washington										
Worcester	5 762.66 (1783)									
Totals for counties represented	2066.65 (1783) 2439.47(1793)	12172.78	25710.50	48783.04	186732.05		320540.40		809136.54	1100191 ‡

NOTE—Small numbers in upper left-hand corners of spaces indicate numbers of property-holders counted.

* Three districts not accounted for. † Two districts not accounted for.

* Three districts not accounted for.

‡ Including estimates for counties of Baltimore and Dorchester.

TABLE II]

TABLE COMPARING PROPERTY HOLDINGS OF NEGROES AND WHITES, 1860

County.	Negro Holdings.	Total Holdings.	White Holdings.	No. of Free Negroes.	No. of White Population.	Per Capita Holdings. Negro.	Per Capita Holdings. White.	No. of Negro Holders.	Total Holders.
Allegany	$6,656	$5,532,040	$5,525,384	467	27,215	$14.25	*$203.02	17	......
Anne Arundel	58,274	7,523,161	7,464,887	4,864	11,704	11.98	637.80	98	......
Baltimore Co. (1852)	37,801	20,579,170	20,541,369	4,231	46,822	8.93	438.71	125	......
Baltimore City	449,138	127,899,370	127,450,232	25,680	184,520	17.49	690.71	348	......
Caroline	59,291	2,059,050	1,999,759	2,786	7,604	21.28	263	184	......
Carroll	8,140.50	8,425,298	8,417,158	1,225	22,525	6.64	373	35	3556
Cecil	37,411	7,784,770	7,747,359	2,918	19,994	12.82	387	145	......
Charles	......	4,615,380	......	1,068	5,796	......	......	......	......
Dorchester (1852)	53,859.16	5,191,732	5,137,873	3,848	10,747	13.99	*478	178	......
Frederick	86,765	21,314,727	21,227,962	4,957	38,391	17.50	552	291	......
Harford	45,350	7,186,029	7,140,679	3,644	17,971	12.44	397	167	3310
Howard	10,664	4,213,408	4,202,844	1,395	9,081	7.64	462	32	......
Kent	70,702	4,982,750	4,912,048	3,411	7,347	20.72	668	283	......
Montgomery	17,142	5,571,747	5,554,605	1,552	11,349	11.04	489	51	......
Prince George's	......	9,101,755	......	1,198	9,650	......	......	......	......
Queen Anne's	65,227	5,348,479	5,283,252	3,372	8,415	19.34	627	215	......
Somerset	57,298	5,376,265	5,318,967	4,571	15,332	12.53	346	205	......
Talbot	36,133	5,227,011	5,190,878	2,964	8,106	12.19	641	184	......
Washington	......	14,171,725	......	1,677	28,305	......	......	......	......
Worcester	......	4,788,921	......	3,571	13,442	......	......	......	......

* In Dorchester and Anne Arundel no allowance has been made for the fact that certain districts in each were not represented in the records used in compiling the data.

TABLE III

Negro Property Holders in Various Counties, 1859–1860

County.	Totals.	Holders of minima of $—— each.			
		$500	$1000	$2000	$5000
Allegany	17	....	....	....	....
Anne Arundel	98	31	14	5	1
Baltimore Co.................	125	18	9	1	....
Baltimore City..............	348	274	137	40	10
Caroline	184	24	11	2	1
Carroll...................	35	1	....	....	....
Cecil	145	11	4	....	....
Charles	....	....	....	....	....
Dorchester	178	7	3	1	....
Frederick	291	31	7	2	....
Harford....................	167	19	7	....	....
Howard....................	32	3	1	....	....
Kent ......,...............	283	14	6	2	....
Montgomery................	51	4	2	1	....
Prince George's............	....	....	....	....	....
Queen Anne's	215	28	7	1	....
St. Mary's.................	....	....	....	....	....
Somerset...................	205	27	6	2	....
Talbot	184	13	....	....	....
Washington	....	....	....	....	....
Worcester	....	....	....	....	....
Totals	2210	505	214	57	12

ments would lead to forfeiture.[1]   A will in Harford County exacted an annual rental of twenty dollars for a house, one in Talbot reserved the right to the fruit from certain trees, and one in Frederick forbade the clearing of the timber and the obstruction of the springs on a tract of land conveyed.[2] Some provisions again were designed to continue the exercise of supervision over the conduct of negro estate holders

[1] *Wills: Anne Arundel*, Lib. BEG no. 1, p. 111; *Harford*, Lib. AJ no. C, p. 183; *Queen Anne's*, Lib. TCE no. 2, p. 4.

[2] *Wills: Harford*, Lib. CWB no. 7, p. 62; *Talbot*, Lib. JP no. 6, p. 372; *Frederick*, Lib. GME no. 3, p. 166. *Cf.* also *Baltimore*, Lib. DMP no. 13, p. 229; *Harford*, Lib. TSB no. 6, pp. 55, 107.

by executors or major heirs. For instance, in Washington County the returns from the labor of two slaves were bequeathed to two other negroes, one of whom was the mother of two children. This mother was not to marry or to harbor as consort any negro until the youngest of her children had reached the age of thirty years.[1] Lastly there were the restrictions inherent in the administration of legacies by trustees. A few of these applied to realty[2] and money and to securities. An early instance was that of a trusteeship of a hundred pounds Maryland currency willed for the benefit of a " free negro woman " at Frederick in 1788.[3] It was followed by others all of which were in effect almost the same as annuities. Limited term estates differed from those for life chiefly in that their duration was fixed at the outset. In Cecil County in 1784 the usufruct of a house and lot was given to a negro for a period of three years,[4] and in the next quarter of a century a few other cases of the same kind occurred in Baltimore and Talbot Counties.[5] Gifts of slaves-for-terms-of-years

[1] *Washington Wills*, Lib. E, p. 390. *Cf.* also *Baltimore*, Lib. DMP no. 16, p. 389; Lib. IPC no. 28, p. 270; *Cecil*, Lib. no. 7, p. 156; *Dorchester*, Lib. LLK no. 1, p. 54; *Frederick*, Lib. GME no. 3, p. 4; Lib. GH no. 1, p. 514; *Harford*, Lib. CWB no. 7, pp. 36, 62; *Washington*, Lib. E, pp. 234, 390. Some of the conditions were set under the influence of fears that negro property rights were insecure under the law. *Cf. Wills: Anne Arundel*, Lib. EV no. 11, p. 88; *Worcester*, Lib. LPS no. 1, p. 400.

[2] *Wills: Anne Arundel*, Lib. JG no. 2, p. 417; *Baltimore*, NH no. 26, p. 477; *Baltimore County*, Lib. JLR no. 2, p. 80; *Worcester*, Lib. LPS no. 1, p. 344.

[3] *Wills: Frederick*, Lib. GM no. 1, p. 305. For other cases *vide Baltimore*, Lib. WB no. 11, p. 95; Lib. DMP no. 19, p. 322; Lib. NH no. 27, p. 225; *Baltimore County*, Lib. JLR no. 1, p. 348; *Cecil*, Lib. no. 9, p. 528; *Dorchester*, Lib. THH no. 1, p. 126; *Frederick*, Lib. GM no. 1, p. 361; Lib. GME no. 3, p. 166; Lib. HS no. 2, p. 336; *Montgomery*, Lib. WT of R no. 2, p. 31.

[4] *Wills:* Lib. no. 5, p. 11.

[5] *Wills: Baltimore*, Lib. WB no. 7, p. 211; *Talbot*, Lib. JP no. 6, pp. 5-6; Lib. JP no. 9, p. 437.

were made to yield incomes which, although of uncertain duration, were in effect much like those of incomes from other property.

A complete account of the property holdings of the free negroes is rendered impossible by gaps in the records,[1] and by the failure of the existing records to indicate with names all persons who were negroes. Presuming, however, that the tax records did mark as negroes nearly all the negro tax-payers, an attempt will be made to give an approximate statement. It has been seen that small amounts of property came into the hands of negroes in the province. The amounts of such holdings were apparently fluctuable but in the long run tended to increase as the negro population itself increased. At the general assessment of 1783 negro persons were accredited in certain districts of the counties of Anne Arundel, Charles, Queen Anne's and Worcester with taxable estates valued in the lists at $2066.65, and in three other counties ten years later twenty-seven negroes held property valued at $2439.47. The increases thereafter may be seen in Table I. In sixteen counties, including Baltimore City, these increases brought up the totals by 1860 to $1,100,191. Since the shares of the counties represented in these totals were unequal, any attempts to make them the basis for estimates for the amounts held in the counties not represented would seem to be hazardous. On that basis, however, a hypothetical computation will be attempted for the increase from the year 1793 to 1860. Dividing the period in half we find three counties represented in the column for 1793, nine in that for 1825-26 and sixteen for 1860. In order to attain the total given for 1825-26, the holdings in nine averaging the same as the three represented in 1793 would have had to increase 566 per cent; and in the same way in order to attain the total given for

[1] *Cf.* Bibliography, pp. 359.

1860, the holdings of sixteen counties would have had to increase 1164 per cent after 1825-26. The growth of negro property holdings was then one and one-half times as fast as that of the free negro population in the first period and more than ten times as fast in the second period.[1]

In certain of the counties the increases can be studied with less fear of discrepant results. The changes varied greatly in different counties. In Talbot in 1793 eighteen negroes were assessed in the aggregate $1766.30. By 1804 eighty-eight negroes held $6132.50 in assessed values, but a slump followed reducing the number of holders by 38.8 per cent and the aggregate holdings by 47.9 per cent by the year 1825-26. The recovery was delayed and despite the rapid growth of the aggregate after 1841 the county never regained the pre-eminence it had once had in negro property holdings.[2] In Frederick County in 1798 three negroes were assessed $49.66; in 1825-26 forty-seven were assessed $1025; and in 1860 two hundred and ninety-one were assessed $86765. The per-capita holdings in the two counties which had been $2.00 and $0.11 respectively in 1793 and 1798 became in 1860 $12.19 and $17.50 respectively. The case of Kent was nearly normal. There the forty-nine holders of an aggregate of $3794.88 in 1804 were succeeded by eighty-five persons holding $9152 in 1825-26, the slump that followed was less signal than in Talbot and the subsequent growth steadier. In the three counties the average holdings at the earlier dates given were $98.10, $16.55 and $77.43 respectively, and in 1860 $196.38, $298 and $249 respectively. The percentage increases in Kent

---

[1] The free negro population had increased approximately 396 per cent in 1790-1820, and 111.2 per cent in 1820-1860.

[2] Talbot County also experienced a decline in both white and slave populations before 1860.

and Talbot were less and those in Frederick greater than in the state at large.

The total assessments to negroes in the sixteen counties in 1860 were $1100191. As those of six rural counties are unaccounted for in this total, a pro-rated estimate added for these counties would give a grand total of $1360610. But since the average free negro population in five of those counties was less than half of that of the counties where negro property was most abundant, a deduction of at least $100000 from this figure is proper, leaving a remainder of $1260610. The free negroes constituted 12.21 per cent of the total population of the state, and 13.99 per cent of the free population. But of the total assessed property of the state they held not 13.99 per cent, but only 0.44 of one per cent, or 3.1 per cent of what a distribution according to numbers would have assigned to them. Their proportion of the total wealth was greatest in the counties having the least wealth and vice versa. In Carroll County, where they formed 4.9 per cent of the total population, they had only 0.09 of one per cent of the taxable wealth; in Frederick, where they formed 10.6 per cent of the population, they held 0.4 per cent of the wealth; while in Caroline, where they formed 25 per cent of the population, they held 2.8 per cent of the taxable wealth. In the counties represented in the table their per-capita holdings were on the Eastern Shore $16.12 and on the Western Shore $11.99. The highest per-capita occurred in the counties of Caroline, Kent and Queen Anne's, adjoining counties in the Eastern Shore and the lowest in Baltimore, Carroll and Howard, all west of the Chesapeake. Excepting for Baltimore City the proportion of negro property holders to total negro numbers varied but little from county to county.

In the rural counties the taxable wealth held by them varied from very small amounts of which the assessors

barely took notice[1] to the $6104 of Moses Coker in Caroline
and the $8059 of William Bishop of Annapolis.[2]

Table III, indicates that seventy-six negroes outside of
Baltimore City were each assessed at $1000 or more, and
that two hundred and thirty-one were each assessed at $500
or more. The average holding in these counties was valued
at $333.36; there was one taxable holding for every 20.6
free negro residents. In those counties whose tax records
distinguished the different kinds of property in detail the
larger holdings consisted chiefly of real estate, while the
smaller ones were made up of certain of the following:
small lots of land with inexpensive dwellings, horses, oxen,
cows, hogs, sheep, petty furniture, farming implements,
tools, and occasionally a carriage or gig, a watch, some plate
and along the water courses water-craft.[3] A few negroes
were assessed for notes, bank deposits and securities,[4] and

[1] In 1852-60, $50 worth was apparently the smallest amount listed to
one assessable person. *Cf. Somerset Tax Ledger*, 1852, *Dame's Quarter*, pp. 74, 100; *Frederick Tax Ledger*, 1853, Dist. no. 8, p. 112. For
smaller amounts listed in earlier assessments, *vide Kent Tax Ledger*,
1804-13, p. 115; *Somerset Records of Commissioners of Taxes*, 1810-12,
Pocomoke Hundred, name of Negro Tobias whose taxable estate was
listed at 10 pounds currency ($26.66).

[2] *Caroline Tax Ledger*, 1853-59 B, p. 20. *Anne Arundel Assessment
List*, Annapolis District, 1859. According to verbal reports a negro in
Worcester also held more than $5000 worth of taxable property. The
Land Records bear out that he was holder of different farms the
largest of which embraced 469 acres. *Vide Worcester Deeds*, Lib.
GMH no. 6, pp. 339, 341, 491; also Lib. EDM no. 4, p. 237. He was a
slaveholder and was reputed to have been a thriving farmer.

[3] *Vide Somerset Tax Ledgers*, 1852, especially those of the Dame's
Quarter, Lower, Potato Neck, and Tyaskin Districts. *Kent Assess-
ment Books*, 1852, Chestertown District. *Cf.* also *Cecil Land Records*,
Lib. JS no. 21, p. 270; Lib. JS no. 23, p. 308; Lib. JS no. 39, p. 321;
Queen Anne's Deeds, Lib. TM no. 1, p. 432; Lib. TM no. 2, p. 315;
Lib. TM no. 3, pp. 192, 559.

[4] *Frederick Tax Ledger*, 1853-66, District no. 2, pp. 17, 28, 37, 43,
195; District no. 8, pp. 14, 131. *Caroline Tax Ledger*, 1840-51, p. 333.

in Dorchester, Caroline Frederick and Somerset some were assessed for slaves.[1] In the city of Baltimore ten negroes were assessed at more than $5000 each, a hundred and thirty-seven at $1000 or more each and two hundred and seventy-four at $500 or more each. The largest amount assessed to an individual was $20506 to one, Thomas Green,[2] and the largest amount for a single piece of property was $12093 in a case referred to above.[3] There was but one taxed estate to every 73.8 negroes in the city, and the average value of the taxed estates was $1290.60, or four and seventy-seven one hundredths times as large as the average in the state as a whole. This property consisted chiefly of real estate, aside from which were furniture, work stock, carts and some plate and securities.

The unrestricted rights of negroes as to legal tenures of property have been stated. They were supplemented by squatter rights and rights on sufferance. The portions held under the several different tenures can here be stated only in general terms. The number of life estates, although never large, was sufficient to have accounted for at

Caroline Assessment Book, 1852-53, Lower, pp. 68, 71, 92, 104. *Queen Anne's Assessment Books*, 1852-53, District no. 3, names of Thomas, Taylor and Wright. *Cf. Dorchester Deeds*, Lib. ER no. 15, p. 116 ($750). *Harford Land Records*, Lib. HDG no. 37, p. 52 ($667). *Kent Deeds*, Lib. JNG no. 1, p. 119 ($500). *Queen Anne's Deeds*, Lib. TM no. 3, p. 559 ($40). *Worcester Deeds*, Lib. WET no. 2, p. 230 ($55).

[1] *Dorchester Tax Ledgers*, 1852-66, Cambridge District, p. 152. *Frederick Tax Ledgers*, 1853-66, Creagerstown, p. 112. *Liberty*, pp. 21, 112. *Urbana*, p. 46. *Woodsborough*, pp. 163, 178. *Somerset Tax Ledgers*, 1852-66, *Trappe*, p. 74. In 1841 negroes were assessed for $4600 worth of slaves in Somerset and $3450 in 1860. In Caroline the widely known Rixom Webb had been assessed $530 for three slaves in 1842. *Tax Ledger*, 1840-51, p. 333.

[2] *Tax Ledger*, 1859, no. 3, pp. 53, 410. This appears to have been the largest estate assessed to any negro in the state, although the writer was told of a larger one in the same city.

[3] *Supra*, p. 133.

least a small portion of the total taxable property given. It would be hazardous to attempt to say that this total was 5 per cent or 10 per cent of the whole at any time,[1] but as that total grew the percentage of it in life estates probably declined. If this is true, an increasing proportion of the real property was held in fee and under lease. It appears that in Baltimore City nearly all the real prooperty was held under the long-term leases. Outside the city, although such leases were not infrequent,[2] the greater part of the property was held in fee. As for these holdings it is important to know the extent to which they were hypothecated. It can be said that much of what they had, both of land and chattels, was mortgaged. Evidences of financial embarrassment, such as cases of insolvency,[3] and arrearages of taxes,[4] are not far to seek. But many releases from debt for other purposes than on account of slaves purchased for manumission were won by negroes.[5] Their management

---

[1] Cf. supra, p. 182, note 5, on tax payment by holders of life estates. Also 3 Bland's Chancery Reports, p. 253.

[2] Vide Dorchester Deeds, Lib. ER no. 18, p. 98; Lib. WJ no. 2, p. 586; Harford Land Records, Lib. HD no. 36, p. 257; Talbot Deeds, Lib. no. 57, pp. 66-67; Lib. no. 62, pp. 183, 317; Lib. no. 63, p. 99. For briefer terms of lease, vide Worcester Deeds, Lib. M, p. 473; Lib. AL, pp. 125-26.

[3] Vide Deeds or Land Records; Caroline, Lib. R, p. 365; Lib. U, p. 393; Cecil, Lib. JS no. 44, p. 192; Dorchester, Lib. ER no. 11, p. 615; Lib. WJ no. T, p. 454; Talbot, Lib. no. 53, pp. 118, 292; Lib. no. 54, p. 359; Lib. no. 55, pp. 249, 251; Lib. no. 58, pp. 273, 332; Lib. no. 60, pp. 43, 224, 374; Worcester, Lib. WET no. 2, p. 340; Lib. no. 6, p. 503; Kent Chattel Records, Lib. JR no. 1, p. 530.

[4] Vide published lists of delinquent taxpayers: Federal Gazette, Jan. 2, 1819, July 18, 1820; Frederick Examiner, Jan. 19, 1859; Maryland Republican, June 26, 1824; Nov. 5, 1825; Aug. 13, 1826.

[5] Deeds or Land Records: Frederick, Lib. HS no. 3, p. 328; Lib. HS no. 14, p. 360; Harford, Lib. JLJ no. 7, p. 7; Lib. ALJ no. 6, p. 426; Lib. WG no. 10, p. 61; Worcester, Lib. AB, p. 107; Baltimore Chattel Records, Lib. GES no. 26, p. 421; Lib. GES no. 18, p. 369.

in such matters was not so defective as some expressions of current opinion would have had it.

It is said that in some communities the opposition of the whites nearly precluded negroes from investing in land. In other places the negroes tended to segregate themselves and to form close settlements. They acquired small tracts of land and affected to develop separate community life. Inquiry in all the counties visited by the writer disclosed that outside of the municipalities whose population were chiefly whites the chief negro communities were at Georgetown Cross Roads in Kent and Sandy Springs in Montgomery. At the former the purchase of lots began at the end of the eighteenth century.[1] One Cornelius Comegys, grantor of most of the deeds, acted as patron. For a few years the number of settlers grew,[2] but for some reason anticipated enterprises failed to develop and the growth was permanently checked. In 1852, the year of the last general assessment here drawn upon, seventeen colored taxpayers were reported in the place, and among their number the highest individual valuation was $450.[3] The Sandy Springs settlement has become widely advertised through the account of it given in a bulletin of the United States Bureau of Labor.[4] Traditions of antiquity surround it. The land purchases there, taken for the most part from the "Charley Forest" tract, in so far as the Montgomery County records give evidence, began in 1848.[5] Its subse-

---

[1] Kent Deeds, Lib. BC no. 4, pp. 31, 413.

[2] Op. cit., Lib. TW no. 2, pp. 368, 534; Lib. TW no. 3, pp. 68, 308, 508, 519, 549; Lib. BC no. 5, pp. 28, 29, 73, 304; Lib. BC no. 6, p. 487.

[3] Kent Assessment Books, 1852, no. 3, pp. 3, 25, 37.

[4] The Negroes of Sandy Spring: A Social Study, Bulletin no. 32, 1901.

[5] Montgomery Land Records, Lib. BS no. 2, p. 26; Lib. JGH no. 1, pp. 40, 70. Cf. also Lib. JGH no. 2, pp. 25, 38, 39; Lib. JGH no. 3, p. 24; Lib. JGH no. 4, pp. 71, 78, 121; Lib. JGH no. 7, pp. 151, 170; Lib. JGH no. 8, p. 289. Clues to earlier grants were not discovered.

quent growth was apparently similar to that of the settlement in Kent County.   A third negro community was that
at Quaker Neck in Kent.[1]   Generally, however, the negroes
and the valuable property of the negroes were mingled with
or clustered about the population centers of the whites.   In
some of these a partial secondary segregation of negroes
took place, as was true in Friendship Street and in Busy,
Honey and Happy Alleys in the City of Baltimore.

The wills of the negroes are interesting.   Of more than
two hundred such documents found in seventeen of the
counties, including the city of Baltimore, twenty were recorded in Frederick, twenty-three in Queen Anne's and
sixteen in Talbot.[2]   Their authors seemed to feel appre-
hensions of restraint in providing for the disposal of their
estates.   They imitated both the forms and the kinds of
provisions employed by the whites.   They chose executors
and other trustees from men of both races.   They generally
followed the principle of equal division of their property
among the several heirs.[3]   The date of such partition was
sometimes postponed, as when a widow received a life interest in the whole of the property or in her thirds with
final division after her death.[4]   Specific provisions were
used to avoid equality and to cut off unfavored ones with
no shares or only nominal shares.   A Worcester negro

---

[1] *Kent Assessment Books*, 1852, District no. 1.   *Cf. Md. Col. Jour.*,
vol. x, p. 24.

[2] Some wills could hardly be identified certainly as those of negroes.
For instance, in the *Talbot Wills*, Lib. JP no. 5, p. 296 (1798), one
James Freeman signed with the mark and referred to his wife, named
Henny, but did not state that he was a negro.

[3] *E. g. Wills: Baltimore*, Lib. WB no. 11, p. 322; Lib. WB no. 12, p.
85; *Anne Arundel*, Lib. JG no. 39, p. 187; Lib. BEG no. 1, p. 414;
Somerset, Lib. JP no. 5, p. 95.

[4] *Wills: Baltimore*, Lib. DMP no. 16, p. 385; *Frederick*, Lib. GH no.
1, p. 384.

thus willed to each of certain children one shilling currency.[1]
Some testators showed favor to male rather than female
children. One at Baltimore gave his whole estate to his
sons.[2] Some willed that the daughters should receive nothing except in case all the sons died without issue.[3] In case
the natural heirs were unmanumitted slaves, they were incompetent in law to inherit property. Those belonging to negro
testators were generally freed, although a few were to be
treated like other property. Some that had belonged to
negroes who died intestate were freed by acts of the legislature and empowered to receive the property under the law
of descents.[4] But if as slaves they had belonged to other
owners such relief was impossible. Special provisions
were, therefore, made in order to secure the kind of dispositions desired by the deceased. Among them were trustee-
ships of executors or others set for one or more of the
following purposes: (1) to hold property for delivery to
beneficiaries upon the attainment of freedom;[5] (2) to manage the property and at the same time negotiate for the release of intended beneficiaries from slavery;[6] (3) to administer property for the benefit of children who obviously
were slaves without provision for freedom.[7]

[1] Wills: Lib. JP no. 5, p. 303; cf. Baltimore, Lib. WB no. 8, pp. 474-
75; Caroline, Lib. WAF no. A, pp. 65-66; Frederick, Lib. GME no. 2,
p. 366.

[2] Wills, Lib. DMP no. 21, p. 10.

[3] Wills: Baltimore, Lib. DMP no. 13, p. 93; Queen Anne's, Lib. STH
no. 1, pp. 20-21. Cf. Baltimore, Lib. DMP no. 21, p. 85.

[4] Vide supra, p. 78, note 3.

[5] Anne Arundel Wills, Lib. TTS no. 1, p. 333; Cecil Wills, Lib. no.
6, p. 530.

[6] Wills: Baltimore, Lib. WB no. 11, pp. 96, 604-05; Montgomery, Lib.
WT of R no. 2, p. 180.

[7] Wills: Anne Arundel, Lib. TTS no. 1, p. 233; Baltimore, Lib. WB
no. 9, pp. 374, 604-05; Washington, Lib. D, pp. 443, 494.

As shown by the following table the negroes had savings in two of the leading savings banks of Baltimore.

	Eutaw Savings		*Central Savings*
	1850	*1855*	*1860*	*1860*
Accounts open	23	67	117	325
Ditto closed	—	—	89	187
Ditto total	—	—	206	512
Amount total	$2,390.79	$9,156.29	$14,956.06	$5,871.69
Ditto ave.	103.95	136.66	126.97	18.07

CHAPTER VII

EDUCATION AMONG THE NEGROES

THE province of Maryland had made no general provision for the education of the youth. In some of the parishes the established church had conducted schools,[1] and just before the revolution the ministers and teachers of certain dissenting sects took up teaching with great ardor.[2] But a great deal of the instruction was imparted in private classes and schools and by tutors and governesses in the homes of the well-to-do. According to a clergyman of Charles County about two-thirds of the private teachers there in 1773 consisted of "indented servants and transported felons" whose time had been bought at low prices and who were employed and treated like common redemptioners.[3] For more advanced schooling children were sent

[1] Perry, *Historical Collections Relating to the Colonial Church*, pp. 215, 222, 224.

[2] Bacon, *Four Sermons Preached at the Parish Church of St. Peter's in Talbot County*, 1753, pp. 16, 139. In 1773 Reverend Jonathan Boucher of Charles County deplored the inactivity of the established church, while marking the "conduct of the various sectaries . . . springing up among us, like weeds in a neglected soil. They not only plant their schools in every place where they can have the most distant prospect of success; but they have conducted their interests with such deep policy, that . . . they have almost monopolized the instruction of the youth." *Causes and Consequences of the American Revolution*, 1797, p. 191. *Cf.* Scharf, *History of Maryland*, vol. ii, pp. 28-34.

[3] Boucher, *op. cit.*, pp. 183, 184, 189.

198 [588

to the mother country. And from the ranks of those thus educated " at home " were drawn many of the leaders and public servants of the colony.¹ This "very reproachful neglect of education" for the whites² was more than matched by the lack of provision for educating the negroes. The latter had come from a country that was almost " without history, literature or laws." They had lacked the incentives to intellectual endeavor there, and after being " forcibly transported to a state of slavery here,"³ were cut off from contact with any other people than their masters and their own kind. Their enlightenment was generally beneath consideration. Some of their number attended the services at the churches, some were given a modicum of religious instruction by the white ministers,⁴ and a few favored individuals received special instruction from their masters or other white friends. Yet in 1773 Reverend Jonathan Boucher wrote: " It is no necessary circumstance, essential to the condition of a slave, that he should be uneducated: yet this is the general, and almost universal, lot of slaves."⁵ For the free negroes the opportunities were hardly more favorable than for the slaves. Both classes alike were unenlightened. At the beginning of the nineteenth century more than half of the negro founders of negro schools and

---

¹ Sollers, " Education in the Colonial Period," in Steiner, *History of Education in Maryland*, pp. 13-14, 32.

² Boucher, *op. cit.*, p. 185. This writer applied to his people the remark of Diogenes to the people of Megara: "Seeing they took great care of their property, and paid little attention to the rising generation, he said, it was better to be one of their swine than one of their children."

³ *Cf. Eighth Census of United States, Population*, p. xi. *Cf.* Payne, *History of the African Methodist Episcopal Church*, p. 394.

⁴ Bacon, *op. cit.*, pp. 16, 147. Perry, *Historical Collections relating to the Colonial Church*, vol. iv, Maryland, pp. 304-07.

⁵ Boucher, *op. cit.*, p. 187.

churches used marks instead of writing their names in signing documents.[1]

The white people of the province were thus generally indifferent about educating the negroes. Although many remained in that attitude permanently, changes of far-reaching importance were ushered in by the awakening that came in the period of the revolution. There arose two different views, corresponding to the two rival views of the emancipation problem, and the adherents of both alike professed benevolence for the negroes. The first was that the negroes were to be educated in order to prepare them for eventual sharing in the citizenship of the commonwealth. Acting in the light of it the Quakers in their annual meetings at Baltimore in 1770, 1785 and 1793 and also in certain of their quarterly meetings enjoined upon the members of their congregations to instruct in useful learning all young negroes in their service.[2] The Methodists too, although at first engrossed with evangelization, gave the negroes some religious instruction,[3] and later took the lead in giving instruction through the day schools also. The second view was opposed to the education of the slaves,[4] and seeing that the free

---

[1] Of the six names attached to the first constitution of Bethel Church in 1816 two were written by their bearers. *Baltimore Chattel Records*, Lib. WG no. 20, p. 84. Substantially similar was the condition of the signatures in the case of the charter of the Sharp Street Church, *op. cit.*, Lib. AI no. 48, p. 349 (1832). In Frederick County at Mount Tabor in 1853 it was proposed to secure the services of a white person to act as secretary-treasurer of a negro church. *Frederick Records of Incorporation of Churches*, p. 186.

[2] *Extracts from Minutes of the Baltimore Yearly Meeting*, pp. 359, 360, 362, 367, 369, 370. *Minutes of Deer Creek Monthly Meeting*, 1801-19, pp. 273, 276, 358, 364.

[3] Matlack, *Anti-Slavery Struggle and Triumph*, p. 66.

[4] A plan was projected in 1818 at the state capital to educate some slaves. A local editor wrote about it: " If those who are at the head of this plan are actuated by pure and philanthropic motives, let them

negroes were so closely associated with the slaves, opposed also to the education of free negroes. Its adherents generally either regarded manumission as a doubtful boon, or felt that it would be impossible for white freemen and black freemen to dwell together in a state of peace.[1] To them it was sufficient to train negroes to do efficient manual labor and to give them instruction in those principles of Christianity whose inculcation would tend to make them obedient and peaceable, but to train them further was to risk implanting in their minds ambitions that could not be realized as long as they remained in Maryland.[2] They helped to bring about the omission of the educational provisions from the indenture contracts of negro apprentices.[3] And while they tolerated some instruction of negroes in private, and in scattered instances permitted a few negro children to attend the day schools of the whites, after the rise of the abolition movement in the northern states they suppressed negro schools and negro classes, whenever danger from them was apprehended. Their influence was exercised, however, most effectively outside of Baltimore City.[4]

exercise their charity on more useful objects." In the same issue of his paper occurs a letter from one signing himself "A. B." who was altogether opposed to the " education of slaves." He held that, if taught, they ought to be simultaneously freed. *Maryland Republican.* Aug. 8, 1818.

[1] *Genius of Universal Emancipation*, vol. i, p. 79. Cf. *General Harper's Letter to E. B. Caldwell*, pp. 15-16; Dr. Hall, *Address to the Free People of Color*, pp. 2-3.

[2] *Cf. Md. Col. Jour.*, no. 20, p. 80.

[3] *Supra*, pp. 138-39.

[4] There is a tradition that there was a statute that either forbade negro schools or forbade the education of negroes in Maryland. The author had found statutes, as those of 1821, chs. 139, 168; 1825, ch. 142; 1834, ch. 263; 1835, ch. 303; 1837, chs. 35, 163, providing for "free schools " and specifying that the children of white persons were to attend them, but no express exclusion of negro children was discovered. If such provisions were intended to exclude negroes, they were

The schools attended by the majority of colored pupils were Sunday schools. In the counties they were inconsequential, but in the city of Baltimore in 1838 nine Sunday schools were reported, seven of which had enrolled six hundred and twenty pupils; they had thirty-eight white and more than a dozen colored teachers.[1] Their brief sessions were divided between inculcating religious and moral precepts and teaching the elementary studies of the common schools; the line distinguishing them from the day schools was not, therefore, to be strictly drawn. Their beginnings were obscure. The annalist Griffith relates that in 1793 persons who were closing up the affairs of the Society for Promoting the Abolition of Slavery transferred to the religious people of color a building on Sharp Street which had been erected for the use of an African school.[2] Ten years later a deed conveyed to certain negroes a lot and building in the same street and bound them to use it as a school for " African children " and as a church for Africans of the Methodist Episcopal connection.[3] In the three following years the holders had paid for the property and erected a

violated in some cases. If there was a state-wide law precluding the education of negroes, it was grossly violated in Baltimore. *Cf.* Dr. Hall, *op. cit.*, p. 2. *The History of the Negro Race in America*, by Williams, vol. i, p. 385, states that " from the moment that slavery gained a foothold in North America until the direful hour that witnessed its dissolution . . . learning was the forbidden fruit that no negro dared taste. . . . Every yearning for intellectual food was answered with whips and thumbscrews." Again: " Positive and explicit statutes everywhere drove him away hungry from the tree of intellectual life; and all persons were forbidden to pluck the fruit for him, upon pain of severe penalties." As far as Maryland was concerned these statements were rhetorical rather than historical. Perhaps Maryland was the exceptional case.

[1] *Md. Col. Jour.*, 1838, p. 68.

[2] *Annals of Baltimore*, p. 128.

[3] *Baltimore Land Records*, Lib. WG no. 70, p. 521.

new structure upon it. The growth of the church and school led them in 1805 to make an appeal to the public for financial assistance. Aided by a committee of white and colored persons and a white person as treasurer they secured " subscriptions and individual donations " which enabled them to purchase adjoining property in 1811 at a cost of a thousand dollars. Thus relieved of the congestion that had been previously felt, they kept open schools for negro children almost uninterruptedly thereafter. The preaching and much of the teaching was done by white Methodists with whom the participants in this organization were linked in the church conferences. In 1828, however, a negro master from Fell's Point, named William Lively, was put in charge of the school. He gave it the name of the Union Seminary and projected a curriculum of liberal dimensions.[2] Its teachers were as well known and probably as well equipped as those of any like school in the city.[3] The allied congregation of Asbury Church also maintained a school in the eastern part of the city intermittently after 1831.[4]

The independent African Methodists also founded schools. At first they were handicapped because as contumacious separatists they were not heartily assisted by the white people and because their own membership lacked permanency.[5] The origin of their first school is likewise obscure, although it was obviously established soon after

---

[1] Op. cit., Lib. WG no. 115, p. 625. Cf. Baltimore American, June 6, 1805.

[2] Genius of Universal Emancipation, vol. ii, p. 120.

[3] Cf. Varle, View of Baltimore, p. 33; also Baltimore Chattel Records, Lib. AI no. 48, p. 347; Journal of Lambert Nicholson, p. 49; Baltimore City Directories 1840-41, 1849-50.

[4] Directories, 1831, name of Clement Burke, and 1841, name of John Fortie.

[5] Infra, pp. 217-18.

that at the Sharp Street Church.[1]   Before 1817 its sessions
were held in a rented building in Fifth Street and were probably more or less irregular.   Its manager and teacher was
the gifted Daniel Coker, pastor of the flock of dissident
Methodists who had formed Bethel Church.   In 1816 he
announced a Sunday school whose two-hour sessions were to
be open to all colored persons without charge.[2]   Although
his usefulness was once impaired by his expulsion from the
membership of the church, his reputation as a teacher increased and his school grew rapidly.   For a long time it
was aided but little by the whites, but it held public exercises
on festal days and through them endeavored to enlist the
interest of the benevolent-minded.[3]   In 1818 it took the
name of Bethel Charity School, having as such two teachers,
ninety-five pupils and a supporting committee of three white
and nine colored men.[4]   But in 1820 its organizer went as
a missionary with some emigrants to Liberia, leaving the
school to less energetic and less efficient hands.   Its growth
was checked, although it survived the general depression of
negro affairs that set in a few years later.[5]

This school from its foundation was a branch of the work
of Bethel Church.   In the forward movement that followed
the slump this active church became a missionary of the
educational idea among the churches of the Baltimore conference.   Through its leaders it recommended the members
of all the churches to get wisdom for themselves and by all
means to educate their children.   It moved the annual conference of 1837 to attempt to impose an educational test

---

[1] Handy, *Scraps of African Methodist Episcopal History*, pp. 11, 37.

[2] *Federal Gazette*, Aug. 16, 1816.

[3] *Federal Gazette*, May 31 and June 1, 1816; Feb. 4, 1819; Jan. 24, 1820.

[4] *Op. cit.*, Feb. 4, 1819.

[5] *Vide* Varle, *View of Baltimore*, p. 33; Handy, *op. cit.*, p. 38.

upon all candidates for its ministry.[1]   It built up its own
schools again under difficulties, and fostered the establishment of schools among the other churches also.[2]   In 1844
the annual conference heard reports from nine Sunday
schools with 869 pupils, three day schools with 128 pupils
and an educational society and at Washington, D. C., a
library of 45 volumes.[3]   As a result of the zeal incited by
that report the Bethel Church was authorized by the conference to establish a high school at Baltimore.   The resolution therefor was an expression of a pious wish whose
realization lay still in the future when another similar one
was passed in 1859.[4]   However, the historian Payne thought
that is was a step in the course that ultimately led to the
founding of a higher institution of learning for the negro
race.[5]

Other church societies likewise conducted schools for
negroes.   Foremost among them were the Presbyterians
who in 1818 had eighty-nine pupils in the Baltimore African

[1] Payne, *op. cit.*, pp. 49, 121, 141, 407.

[2] In 1837 it was said that it had a Sunday school of 160 scholars and
"a library of a thousand school books." A flood swept through its
building, ruined the library and caused a falling off of the attendance
to about 80 scholars. *Md. Col. Jour.*, p. 68. It still had nine colored
teachers at that time.

[3] The following data are taken from Payne, *op. cit.*, pp. 135, 139, 176.
For the year 1841 they are for Baltimore City alone, for the other two
years for the entire conference.

| | Sunday Schools | | | Day Schools | | |
	Number	Teachers	Scholars	Number	Teachers	Scholars
1841	2	19	208	1	1	50
1842	12	—	—	2	—	—
1844	9	—	869	3	—	128

If the data is reliable, it indicates more or less sporadic efforts.

[4] *Baltimore Sun*, May 6, 1859.

[5] Payne, *op. cit.*, pp. 182-83.

Association School in Paca Street,[1] and in 1838 two large negro Sunday schools.[2]   The school at the St. James Protestant Episcopal Church, founded in 1823, endured for a long period.[3]   A third school, conducted for years in the wing of a down-town Baptist church building, was aided by the abolitionists, Lundy and Garrison.   It was forced to seek new quarters, when the church moved from its old site in 1828.[4]   In Richmond Street was located the Providence African Catholic Asylum.   It consisted of a charity school and a boarding school for girls.   Its foundation had been due to the clergy of the Catholic Church and according to Varle received financial support from Negroes in Philadelphia.[5]

Of the other schools and classes formed in the city many were shortlived.   The most pretentious of them all was the Union Seminary of William Lively at Fell's Point.   In 1825 it announced the offer of day and night instruction in the branches of an " English Education," with Latin and French for those who desired them.   A few months later it also announced Sunday sessions of two hours each for women.[6]   In 1828 both teacher and name were transferred to the school of the Sharp Street Church.[7]   The city directories give the names of the following numbers of colored teachers in the years indicated in the following table.[8]   In

[1] *Federal Gazette*, Sept. 23, 1818.

[2] *Md. Col. Jour., op. cit.*

[3] *Cf. Baltimore Chattel Records*, Lib. WG no. 41, p. 389; Varle, *op. cit.*, p. 33; *Baltimore American*, Nov. 1, 1850.

[4] *Genius of Universal Emancipation*, vol. ii, p. 175.

[5] Varle, *op. cit.*, p. 33.

[6] *Genius of Universal Emancipation*, Oct. 8, 22, 29, and Nov. 5, 12, 19, 26, 1825, and Feb. 11 and July 16, 1826.

[7] *Op. cit.*, May 31, 1828.

[8] Other schools reported were a Sunday school conducted for years by

	1824	1827	1831	1841	1850	1860
Teachers	3	4	6	6	8	12
Musicians	—	—	—	—	5	6

certain of the counties also appeared a few temporary negro schools. But here the teaching of negroes came to be associated in the minds of the people with abolitionism and sinister designs. At Hagerstown, says a report, a day school was opened, but after a short time a hostile public forced its suspension for a period of fifteen years. A Quakeress held a night school in Kent County, a philanthropic slave-owner held one in Talbot, the notable colored Wayman family held one in Caroline and a mulatto named Hall one in Anne Arundel. It each instance the teacher was soon intimidated and the effort ceased. It was rumored, and by negroes at least believed. that a negro school-master at Cambridge had been spirited away by the " Georgia buyers." As preventives of negro schools these things were quite effective. The absence of such institutions. however, is to be attributed mainly to the weak financial position of the negroes and to a lack of real demand for such education. Certain well-to-do negroes in the counties sent their children to Baltimore to school rather than attempt to have them educated at home.

The duration of the average negro pupil's attendance at school was short. Opportunity for advanced study was thus lacking.[1] Most of the schools professed to do nothing more than teach the rudiments of knowledge. Reading, spelling. writing and arithmetic were the things that engaged their attention. The New Testament was the commonest

a white lady in Fortune Hall, a day school held in an upper room over an ice-house near Lexington Market, and that of the Quaker, Edward Needles, in Uhler's Alley back of his own residence. On the last, *vide Genius of Universal Emancipation*, Sept. 5, 1825.

[1] *Cf.* Handy, *op. cit.*, p. 15.

reading text after the beginner's book had been learned. Ability to read in it was an attainment worthy of remark.[1] Adding to the above-mentioned subjects a modicum of English grammar and geography we find what obviously constituted an "English education." Very few negro scholars took up the other subjects with profit, although in 1828 one school advertised that it would give instruction in several subjects that more commonly belonged to the academy and college.[2] The work of the schools was supplemented by a considerable amount of instructing of both slaves and free negroes by the whites with whom their duties brought them into close contact, by reading of papers and books, by curious-minded domestics and by the superior opportunities of the few who were sent to educational institutions in the northern states.[3]

[1] *Md. Col. Jour.*, p. 68. *Cf. supra*, pp. 136-39, educational provisions of indentures of apprenticeship; *Comly's Reading and Spelling Book*, Byberry, 1842, was one of the primers used.

[2] *Genius of Universal Emancipation*, May 31, 1828.

[3] *Cf. Md. Col. Jour.*, vol. ix, p. 88.

CHAPTER VIII

THE CHURCH AND THE NEGROES

THE principal organized moral force in the province of Maryland was the established Anglican Church. Its membership was confined to no particular social class but was substantially controlled by the land-holding slave owners. This class, although influenced somewhat by the missionary ideas of the day, had once hesitated to provide for the religious instruction of their negroes and to allow them to be baptized, because they feared that they had no legal right to hold baptized persons as slaves. A statute of the year 1671 which held that baptism should not be held to entail the manumission of a slave [1] obviated that as a ground of objection to preaching to negroes, but otherwise accomplished nothing towards missionary endeavor among them. From one parish it was reported that the masters were " so brutish " that they would not allow their negroes to be catechized or baptized.[2] In another parish, on the other hand, were masters who gave personal attention to the spiritual concerns of their slaves.[3] As a rule, however, they were willing to allow the clergy to teach the slaves, although they often regarded it as a fruitless task and would not themselves " be at the pains and trouble of it." [4] In

[1] *Archives of Maryland*, vol. ii, p. 272; vol. v, p. 267. *Laws*, 1715, ch. 44. *Archives of Maryland*, vol. xiii, p. 506.

[2] Perry, *Historical Collections Relating to the Colonial Church*, vol. iv, p. 304.

[3] *Op. cit.*, pp. 190, 203-04.

[4] *Op. cit.*, 305. *Cf.* also pp. 201, 203, 216, 240, 262, 292, 304, 307.

some parishes the clergymen warned them that " care should be taken about their slaves for the saving of their souls." [1] In 1724 the Eastern Shore clergy united in an appeal to the Bishop of London to enjoin upon the laity of their parishes the solemn duty of providing for the spiritual welfare of their negroes, and seven years later themselves undertook to work to that end in the course of a visitation to the people. [2] They preached as time and opportunity allowed, catechized many and baptized those who were deemed eligible for church membership. [3] In some communities the Quakers and Roman Catholics also had negro members of their churches. [4] But the efforts of all the churches were inadequate to the task of ministering in the way that some desired to all of the negroes in the province. The established church later, some thought, became unfitted for work of moral reformation, [5] and when the early Methodists came preaching, they reported that the negroes were treated as if they had no souls. [6]

The advent of the Methodists and the bearing of their activities upon the manumission movement have been related above. [7] They endeavored to preach the same gospel to all classes of the people. They fraternized with negroes in the churches. They established mixed congregations in which the two races worshipped " in harmony." Says Bishop Handy: " They sat on the same seats, and when they died,

[1] Op. cit., pp. 240, 262, 292, 296, 304.

[2] Op. cit., pp. 240, 292.

[3] Op. cit., pp. 192, 194, 195, 198, 208, 214, 215, 227, 262, 304, 306, 307. Among the new communicants were a family of free negroes in Kent Island, circ. 1724. Op. cit., p. 214.

[4] Op. cit., pp. 222, 227.

[5] Cf. Scharf, History of Maryland, vol. ii, pp. 28-34.

[6] Bangs, Life of Rev. Freeborn Garrettson, p. 144.

[7] Supra, pp. 47-51.

were buried in the same . . . . burial ground." [1] They
gave negroes a voice in the meetings and a role in the labors
of the church but were reluctant to ordain them as ministers.[2] " Black Harry," an illiterate but eloquent fellow,
traveled and preached with the founders of the Methodist
Church; he and Richard Allen of Philadelphia sat in the
Christmas Conference that met at Baltimore formally to
launch the Methodist Church of the United States.[3] It was
chiefly as local preachers, class leaders, exhorters and assistants [4] and faithful responders that they participated.
These things, however, gave them greater recognition than
they had ever received in the other churches. The Methodists, too, declared that it was " contrary to the Golden Law
of God . . . . and the unalienable rights of mankind . . . .
to hold . . . . in abject slavery . . . . souls that are capable of the image of God." [5] For a time they sternly insisted that their slave-owning members must manumit their
negroes or suffer expulsion from the church, and notwithstanding their weakening on that point still stood marked as
the friends of the oppressed. The negroes flocked to their
services and were received into their membership in unprecedented numbers. At the beginning of the nineteenth
century after many defections there were in the Baltimore

[1] *Scraps of African Methodist Episcopal History*, p. 22.

[2] *Op. cit.*, p. 23. Matlack, *Anti-Slavery Struggle and Triumph*, p. 73,
quoting Simpson, *Hundred Years of Methodism*, says negroes were
ordained as early as 1796.

[3] Handy, *op. cit.*, p. 23; Stevens, *History of the Methodist Episcopal
Church*, vol. ii, pp. 174-75; Payne, *History of the African Methodist
Episcopal Church*, pp. 88-89. Cf. mention of an " Ethiopian preacher
of very distinguished merit " in *Maryland Gazette*, May 9, 1774.

[4] *Class Records of the Light Street M. E. Church*, 1803-09 and 1819-23.

[5] *Suday Service of the Methodists of North America*, 1784. p. 15, *cf.*
Stevens, *op. cit.*, p. 199.

churches twenty-one classes of negroes whose membership was more than a third of that of all the classes in the City.[1] The two races thus labored together in building up the first two Methodist congregations in Baltimore.[2] But soon after the revolution the color line was drawn. The whites avoided too close association with the colored members and tended to control the organization without consulting them. The latter whose growing numbers seemed to entitle them to greater recognition, were over-awed and felt aggrieved.[3] Their increasing discontent wrecked the plan of continuing the worship in mixed congregations, and they, as the weaker party, were the ones to move out. Those who felt most keenly the discriminations withdrew and worshipped apart. Although some of their number returned to the mixed meetings, a considerable body held themselves aloof until after nearly a generation they established a separate organization of their own. The others who declined thus to secede were specially provided for within the parent church. Evidently it was to them that the abolition society

[1] *Class Records of Light Street M. E. Church*, 1803-09. Also Church Record of same, 1799-1837. In the classes in 1799 were numbered the following:

	Whites	Negroes
1799	531	290
1800	504	306
1803	——	412

In a manuscript history of the Sharp Street Memorial M. E. Church it is stated that in 1802 the Methodists of the city had 852 white and 482 colored members. In 1819 there were thirty negro classes in the city churches. *Records of the Light Street M. E. Church*, 1819-23.

[2] These two were the Strawberry Alley and Lovely Lane churches which have since become the Centennial and the First Methodist Churches. *Journal of Lambert Nicholson*, p. 41. *Cf.* Handy, *op. cit.*, pp. 22-23.

[3] Asbury, *Journal*, vol. ii, p. 280. *Cf.* Hamilton, *Colored Methodist Episcopal Church*, pp. 21-22.

gave possession of a building located on Sharp Street in 1792.[1] Separate class meetings were established and separate preaching services were held for them. In 1801 two of their number secured under deed of trust two city lots. According to the deed the profits from the sale of these lots were to be applied to " the purchase of some proper and convenient house for the accommodation of the members of the African Methodist Episcopal Church . . . . as a house of worship," and for such other purposes as the trustees might direct.[3] After a formal division of the congregations in 1802 the assets realized from the sale were invested by a self-perpetuating board of trustees in the property on Sharp Street which became the site of their church.[4] The deed to this property bound the trustees to hold it to " serve as a school for the education of black children of every persuasion " and for the benefit of the Africans in the city of Baltimore belonging to the communion of the Methodist Episcopal Church. The ministers of that church were to be allowed to preach in the building.[5] The negro members came to this fold with alacrity. The Lovely Lane Church was almost deserted by them.[6] The new congregation was managed as a member of the organic body of the churches of Baltimore until its incorporation in 1832 as a separate body. One staff of preachers served all the churches— white and colored —interchanging in all their duties as the

---

[1] Cf. Griffith, Annals of Baltimore, p. 128.

[2] Bangs, op. cit., pp. 144-45; Asbury, op. cit., p. 280.

[3] Baltimore Land Records, Lib. WG no. 142, p. 243; Lib. WG no. 71, pp. 124-25. The lots were to be sold within two years. Cf. Payne, op. cit., p. 89.

[4] Baltimore Land Records, Lib. WG no. 78, pp. 538, 643; Lib. WG no. 70, pp. 520-21. $1650 was realized from the sale of the lots and the purchased lot cost $1450.

[5] Op. cit., Lib. WG no. 70, p. 523.

[6] Journal of Lambert Nicholson, p. 41.

needs of the situation required.[1]   A substantial growth followed, and the Sharp Street Church became for a long time the principal negro church in the city. Asbury Chapel, founded in 1830, was united with it under the charge of one minister. Two other chapels were founded in 1834 and 1839 respectively.[2]   The racial segregation of the congregations proceeded more slowly outside of the city, but four separate chapels were founded in Dorchester County, four in Harford and one in Anne Arundel.[3]   They were located chiefly in communities where the independent African church did not take root.

The Wesleyan ideal of equality between the members of the laity did not long prevail in the Methodist churches of Maryland. The whites filled the positions of greatest responsibility, transacted the important business and administered the discipine. Before 1814 they also bore most of the expenses of the common enterprise of the two races. Dissatisfaction with this on their part, linked with unequal pastoral care in which there was discrimination against the negroes, threatened to disrupt the organization. In March 1814, however, the members adopted some articles " of peace and union . . . . among themselves and with the preacher." They agreed to have a minister to meet each of the classes in every church every quarter, to visit the sick as far as practical and prudential and to baptize the children in church, if they were well, but in private, if not. Finally they implored the African branch of the society

[1] *Records of Classes of Light Street Church*, 1803-09, cover page. *Cf.* Smith, *History of Sharp Street Station M. E. Church*, pp. 4-5.

[2] *Journal of Lambert Nicholson*, p. 41.

[3] *Dorchester Deeds*, Lib. WJ no. 3, p. 373 (1847) ; Lib. FJH no. 2, p. 601 ; Lib. FJH no. 4, pp. 95, 263 (1857 and 1859) ; *Harford Land Records*, Lib. HD no. 13, p. 300 (1830) ; Lib. HD no. 36, p. 69; Lib. HDG no. 37, p. 320; Lib. ALJ no. 9, p. 243 (1857) ; *Anne Arundel Deeds*, Lib. JHN no. 8, p. 576 (1859).

to prepare itself to bear its share of the expense of the preacher.[1] This modus vivendi apparently forestalled a more serious breach of relations but did not preclude discontent on the part of the blacks. They still felt that they had not been given the voice in church counsels that their numbers entitled them to, and that their own preachers, although licensed and given subordinate positions, were not being promoted to the higher ranks of the ministry. The Sharp Street and Asbury congregations were incorporated under negro trustees in 1832 but were still served by white pastors.[2] At intervals the negroes made known their displeasure, importuning the Baltimore Conference repeatedly to make a change. Finally on the eve of the general emancipation the larger pastorates of negro churches were opened to negro preachers and a separate annual conference established for the churches of Maryland and the District of Columbia.[3] Their relations to the white churches were thereby vitally altered, but not until long after the establishment of a thoroughly Africanized society by those who had held aloof from the parent church.

The independent African churches were founded by those who had felt most keenly the causes of separation just described. Methodist zeal was unable permanently to overcome the obstacles to equality and unity in the mixed society. The relations between races soon became again like their relations in the state generally. The results were a grievous disappointment to those negro members who on account of Methodist declarations had hoped for a different state of things.[4] Some felt that in a separate church of their own

[1] Records of Classes of Light Street Church, March, 1814.

[2] Nicholson, op. cit., p. 41; Handy, op. cit., p. 36; Payne, op. cit., p. 88; Reports of the Quarterly Conference of Frederick Circuit, 1805-46, p. 1.

[3] Nicholson, loc. cit.; Smith, op. cit., p. 6.

[4] Payne, op. cit., p. 9.

they might have the advantages of church life without white domination. In the summer of 1787 the seceders mentioned above held independent prayer meetings, discussed plans and finally projected a permanent organization.[1] However welcome this step to individuals of independent mind, the difficulties of those who participated in it had only begun. Their position was a hard one. They were financially embarrassed, their members were poor and had but little credit, they owned no lot or building and had to hold their meetings in an irregular manner. Their organization had been effected in a boot-black shop in a basement room.[2] For nearly a decade they met from house to house, as convenience dictated. In 1795 they consulted Bishop Asbury "about building a house,"[3] but without avail. About this time they first rented the property in Fish Street which has since become the Mecca of African Methodism. Arrears of rent, however, soon closed this place to them,[4] and again they met from house to house, until finally one of their number provided them a permanent room. Besides they had a shifting membership and a rudimentary organization. They had separated themselves from the mixed churches because they had been aggrieved at the whites' supremacy there, but they still desired to be within the Methodist Church. They manoeuvred to secure recognition as a part of it. In a conference with Bishop Asbury they

[1] Handy, op. cit., pp. 13, 24. The founding of this society was almost contemporaneous with that of a similar one at Philadelphia, it is said. Each one was independent of the other. Dr. Payne, op. cit., concludes that the secession at Baltimore preceded by three weeks the date of the lawsuit by which those at Philadelphia secured their "freedom". The latter, however, were first to procure title to church property.

[2] Handy, op. cit., p. 24.

[3] Asbury, Journal, vol. ii, p. 266.

[4] Handy, op. cit., pp. 14, 24. Cf. Baltimore Land Records, Lib. TK no. 279, p. 65.

presented a project for the launching of a distinct " African, yet Methodist Church." But their plan called for such a large degree of control of temporalities by the local stewards and trustees that it was rejected by the bishop.[1] They were regarded by the whites as a body of malcontents whose efforts to establish themselves separately were to be obstructed rather than encouraged.[2] They were held together by external pressure, and yet each new step seemed to render their separation less revocable. Their difficulties, to be sure, caused some to desert their ranks for the mother church and deterred others from coming out to them. But the roots of their dissent struck deeply, resolute spirits held on and defections from their number were more than made up by new recruits. Among the latter were Stephen Hill, a sturdy layman, and the talented Daniel Coker who became pastor.[3] Thus strengthened the church effected temporary arrangements for the reoccupation of the property in Fish Street and finally in 1817 to purchase it. The purchase contract bound them to make ten payments of $500 each in

[1] Asbury, *op. cit.*, pp. 266, 280.

[2] Handy, *op. cit.*, p. 24.

[3] This Daniel Coker, whose childhood name had been Isaac Wright, was born a slave in a Maryland county. He owed his early education, writes Bishop Handy, to his youthful master's refusal to attend school without the attendance of his servant. The latter was an apt pupil. He later stole away to New York, became a Methodist and was ordained by Bishop Asbury. Returning to Maryland, he concealed his identity, until he had been redeemed and formally manumitted. After a time at Baltimore he cast in his lot with the separatists, was sent by them to the Philadelphia conference in 1816, where he acted as secretary; was later expelled from the church; was restored and sent to Africa as a missionary with the first body of exiles carried away by the American Colonization Society. He acted as manager and teacher of Bethel Church school while in Baltimore. Cf. Payne, *op. cit.*, pp. 88-90; Handy, *op. cit.*, pp. 35-39; *Republican Star and Eastern Shore General Advertiser*, June 17,, 1820.

addition to the ground rents which were to be gradually extinguished as the principal itself was being paid.[1]

This purchase came at the end of a period of thirty years whose vicissitudes had tried and seasoned a group of staunch leaders. It was the last of three successive events which taken together had given Bethel Church permanency and a connection with an organized church outside. One of the other events was the organization of this church itself. The loose aggregation that has been described numbered 633 persons in 1816, according to Bishop Handy. In that year they adopted a constitution and elected trustees to act under the corporate name of the African Methodist Episcopal Bethel Society.[2] Amendments were added to the constitution in 1819, and owing to defective construction of the old an entirely new instrument was drafted in 1820.[3] The third event was the establishment of the African Methodist Episcopal Church. This event took place in Philadelphia in 1816 in a conference in which five churches were represented. To that meeting Bethel Church sent six of the sixteen delegates.[4] On April 9, 1816, Stephen Hill of Baltimore moved that " the people of Philadelphia and Baltimore, and all other places, who should unite with them, shall become one body under the name and style of the African Methodist Episcopal Church." His motion was seconded by Daniel Coker also of Baltimore and accordingly passed. The body next adopted the discipline of the Methodist Episcopal Church for temporary purposes, sav-

---

[1] The annual rental was at first $360. *Baltimore Land Records*, Lib. WG no. 140, pp. 599-601 ; Lib. TK no. 279, p. 65.

[2] *Baltimore Chattel Records*, Lib. WG no. 20, pp. 83-84.

[3] *Op. cit.*, Lib. WG no. 24, p. 233 ; Lib. WG no. 25, pp. 269-70.

[4] The other churches represented were located one each at Philadelphia, Attleborough, Pennsylvania, Salem, New Jersey and Wilmington, Delaware. Payne, *op. cit.*, p. 13.

ing that part relating to the presiding elders.[1]   The delegates then attempted to make Daniel Coker bishop, but he
declined the place and Richard Allen of Philadelphia was
selected and consecrated in his stead.   When its delegates
returned home the Bethel Church ratified the action of the
convention and thereby acquired a definite status in the
church world.

This church had begun to do missionary work before the
conference at Philadelphia.   It now zealously renewed its
efforts and its representatives found the people in many
places eager to become associated in the new connexion.
By 1817 three missions had been established and others were
appointed later.[2]   In 1820 was established the Baltimore
Annual Conference to which came representatives from
nearly all the congregations belonging to the new society in
the state.[3]   In the course of time churches also sprang up in
four more or less distinct groups outside of Baltimore.   We
shall first consider briefly these outlying churches and then
return to those in Baltimore.   (1) One group were the
churches of Southern Maryland and the District of
Columbia.   In 1818 there were two congregations in this
quarter, and in 1823 a third " under the African bishop and
conference " was mentioned as being in Anne Arundel
County.[4]   The church at Piscataway was practically closed
by an act of the legislature in 1828 which restricted its
meetings.[5]   The more active churches in this section were

[1] Payne, *op. cit.*, pp. 13-14; Handy, *op. cit.*, p. 15.

[2] Handy, *op. cit.*, pp. 25-26.

[3] Handy, *op. cit.*, pp. 50, 54. The Snow Hill church in 1818 had been
affiliated with the Philadelphia Conference.

[4] Handy, *op. cit.*, pp. 27-28; *Anne Arundel Deeds*, Lib. WSG no. 9, p.
425.

[5] *Laws*, 1828, ch. 151. It is not mentioned in the later lists given by
Payne, nor in those in the *Baltimore Sun*, May 6, 1857, and April 24,
1860.

in the federal district. (2) Western Maryland. In this part of the state progress was rapid. In 1822 a congregation at Frederick sent delegates to the annual conference, and in 1824 a second one was reported.[1] Others were founded, so that in 1833-34 the circuit, established with Frederick City as a center, was able to supply its chief preaching stations with preaching services only once a quarter. Long after the need had arisen a second circuit was established.[2] After much opposition and delay the Frederick and Hagerstown churches were promoted to the rank of stations at "full time."[3] (3) Harford and Cecil Counties. A missionary was assigned to three societies in Cecil County in 1818.[4] But only one of them, that at Port Deposit, endured under its original name. In 1824 there was in Harford County a circuit with four appointments and a total of a hundred and seventy-five members.[5] Two churches in Cecil and one in Harford acquired corporate property,[6] but the further progress here was less marked than that in any other part of the state where the connexion was established. (4) The Eastern Shore. Three congregations were established in Caroline and Talbot Counties in 1819, and were related to the elder of Baltimore, apparently as a circuit in 1821.[7] The next year three hundred and thirty members were reported, and two years still later

---

[1] Handy, op. cit., p. 28; Payne, op. cit., p. 42.

[2] Payne, op. cit., pp. 51, 99, 138.

[3] Op. cit., p. 156. Baltimore Sun, May 2, 8, 1855. The Frederick church was incorporated in 1855. Frederick Records of Incorporation of Churches, 1805-88, p. 78.

[4] Handy, op. cit., pp. 27-28.

[5] Payne, op. cit., p. 42.

[6] Land Records, Lib. GMcC no. 13, p. 31; Lib. HHM no. 19, pp. 278, 279, 566; Lib. HHM no. 1, p. 21; Harford, Lib. HDG no. 34, p. 408; Lib. HDG no. 36, p. 268.

[7] Payne, op. cit., pp. 20, 29; Handy, op. cit., pp. 28, 57.

five hundred and forty-three members in eight churches.[1] After that time progress was slow. The church at Easton nearly succumbed to financial difficulties,[2] and subsequently became at best the chief congregation in a circuit, while that at Denton, for a time a member of a circuit, became later a station supplied from the Baltimore station.[3] In addition to these scattered churches the Baltimore Annual Conference included churches in both Pennsylvania and Delaware; it sent a missionary to Hayti and exercised wide powers in planting the church in the newer states west of the Alleghanies.[4] The church at Snow Hill was apparently not affiliated with this conference.[5]

Baltimore City. The situation was more favorable for the growth of the negro churches in Baltimore City than in the counties. One of the three mission stations mentioned in 1817 was located at Fell's Point.[6] Although financially weak, its growth in numbers was substantial.[7] It was incorporated as the African Methodist Union Bethel Church

---

[1] Payne, op. cit., pp. 24, 42.

[2] This church had purchased property in 1820, but by some mishap the title became vested in one member of the board of trustees who was a merchant. When he became financially embarrassed in 1829, his creditors seized the church property. It was sold and soon re-conveyed to a new body of African trustees. Talbot Deeds, Lib. no. 42, p. 453; Lib. no. 48, p. 427; Lib. no. 49, pp. 400-02. For the charter of its incorporation, vide op. cit., Lib. no. 62, pp. 149-51.

[3] Payne, op. cit., p. 99; Baltimore Sun, April 24, 1860. Cf. also op. cit., May 8, 1855, and May 6, 1857.

[4] Baltimore Sun, May 2, 1855, April 24, 1860; Payne, op. cit., pp. 55, 210.

[5] Cf. Handy, op. cit., p. 54. Vide also Worcester Deeds, Lib. GMH no. 1, p. 468, and Lib. EDM no. 1, p. 250, on the purchase of church property by negroes in Snow Hill.

[6] Supra, p. 219.

[7] It had 426 members in 1842. Payne, op. cit., p. 139.

in 1844 and raised to the rank of a station about 1855.[1] In 1835 Bethel Church acquired the residual term of an extinguishable lease of a lot in order to get a mission site in the southern part of the city.[2] Although this mission also grew rapidly, no progress had been made in extinguishing the ground rent before 1848. At that time the property was assigned for a nominal sum to the trustees of the congregation who desired to build a new edifice.[3] About the same time it was incorporated as Ebenezer Church, soon became a station and took its place as an independent church.[4] The last of the new foundations before 1860 was Waters Chapel, situated between Bethel Church and Fell's Point. By 1847 it had become a well established mission and in 1856 engaged the services of a worker from the parent body. It was incorporated separately in 1859 and within three weeks thereafter acquired a site on Spring Street, paying at once eighty per cent of the purchase price.[5]

Bethel Church was a center of great activity also in its section. While it was giving financial assistance to those outside and contributing of its members to other churches in the city, its own interests at home developed steadily. Its final payment of the debt on its building site was made in 1838, twenty-one years after it had been con-

[1] *Baltimore Chattel Records*, Lib. TK no. 69, pp. 106-07; *Baltimore Sun*, May 8, 1855. It secured possession of its site in fee in 1856, price $800. *Baltimore Land Records*, Lib. ED no. 110, p. 346.

[2] The ground rent in this case was $264 a year and the purchase price $3860.66. *Baltimore Land Records*, Lib. TK no. 250, p. 289.

[3] Payne, *op. cit.*, p. 230; *Baltimore Land Records*, Lib. AWB no. 379, p. 113, and Lib. AWB no. 401, p. 35.

[4] *Baltimore Chattel Records*, Lib. AWB no. 76, p. 219. Cf. *Baltimore Sun*, May 8, 1855.

[5] *Baltimore Sun*, April 15, 1856; *Baltimore Charter Records*, Lib. GES no. 4, pp. 190-91; also *Baltimore Land Records*, Lib. GES no. 165, pp. 36, 38, 40.

tracted.[1] Its enduring power had been tested during the slump of negro affairs, and after the crisis was over, it entered upon a new era of expansion. A great revival in 1842 resulted in such an increase in membership that a project for a new building was mooted. Difference of opinion, however, led to its postponement for several years.[2] Another accretion of members came in *en bloc* five years later. In 1842 an independent Wesleyan Methodist society had been formed.[3] Unsuccessful financing had brought upon it a train of difficulties. The members therefore, applied to the Baltimore Annual Conference for admission to the African Methodist Church. After investigation the petition was granted without discussion. For three years the church attempted to continue as a separate organization, but at last allowed its membership to be merged in the other churches.[4]

About this time the proposal to build a new house of worship for Bethel Church was revived. The plan offered was to let the contract for the work as soon as a third of the necessary funds had been secured. The occasion of the vote to ratify became dramatic. At a preconcerted signal a band of supporters of the project grouped themselves about the altar to signify assent. A show of opposition by others was followed by a futile protest in the annual conference that followed. The plan, however, was enthusiastically carried and executed. Within a year after the vote the treasurer had in hand a fund of $5000; on August 2, 1847 a corner-stone was laid; and within another twelve-

---

[1] *Baltimore Land Records*, Lib. TK no. 279, p. 65.

[2] Payne, *op. cit.*, pp. 232-233.

[3] *Baltimore Chattel Records*, Lib. TK no. 64, p. 374. *Baltimore Land Records*, Lib. TK no. 329, p. 422. The annual rental on this congregation's property had been $173.50. *Cf.* Payne, *op. cit.*, p. 208.

[4] Payne, *op. cit.*, pp. 208-10. This body reported 337 members, a Sunday School of 159 and seven preachers.

month an imposing Romanesque edifice had been built and consecrated. The debt upon it was cleared away in the appointed period of eight years.[1] The consequences of this achievement were far-reaching, says Dr. Payne. It justly heightened the self-esteem of the builders, while to the rest of the community—whites and blacks—it appeared as a triumph of independent African enterprise. The imputations of indolence and vacuity cast upon the church by a critical public were modified, and in some quarters supplanted by a more friendly and judicious regard.

This period of outward progress was marked also by signal changes within the church. A reforming pastor had come in 1843. He found that two of the classes led by one elder had grown to about a hundred and fifty members each, and that others also were too large. He scented danger in such conditions and advised that the classes should be scaled down to the original Wesleyan number of twelve each. He soon carried through a resolution to that effect. His success and his conformity to the discipline and to Methodist traditions completely disarmed criticism of the step, but they stirred the wrath of the chief offender and estranged other workers whose confidence and support the minister could not regain. When he proposed to raise a building fund, opposition arose and the bishop was called from Philadelphia to mediate between factions. Less than a hundred dollars was subscribed.[2] In other ways also the church failed to co-operate, and when the pastoral term ended, the preacher's influence had been almost destroyed. His successor found discord among the members. At once upon his arrival he was advised by some to allow a return to the large classes. He declined and for a time held aloof

[1] Payne, op. cit., pp. 232-35. The total cost was about $16,000.

[2] Payne, op. cit., p. 233.

from alliance with either faction. In the course of the building operations in 1847, however, the church became the scene of a trial on a charge of " sowing dissensions," and a member was expelled for "outrageous conduct and an ungovernable spirit." [2] And when in the following year it was proposed to transfer the lot in south Baltimore to the trustees of the Ebenezer Church, five of the trustees of Bethel dissented. After a second vote on the matter they affected to acquiesce, but came late to the place appointed for signing the deed of transfer and became enraged because the pastor had already signed before they arrived.[3] In the quarterly conference a few months later they proposed to pass a set of resolutions which proved to be a firebrand. Other members objected that they were sowing discord and Pastor Payne declared that the enforcement of their proposed measures would drive a wedge between the church and the connexion outside. Counter resolutions protesting against their course were introduced and passed by a vote of 123 to 24. " Down went the five members' resolutions." [4] In February 1849 the chancery court of the city set aside the five trustees. Nothing daunted they continued their obstructions, until they were at last arraigned before the conference for discipline. They came to the meeting supported by wives and henchmen, some of whom were armed with bludgeons. The testimony was overwhel-

---

[1] Payne, *op. cit.*, pp. 233-34.

[2] *Bethel Quarterly Conference Records*, July 9, October, and November 12, 1847.

[3] Payne, *op. cit.*, p. 231.

[4] *Bethel Quarterly Conference Records*, Oct. 22, 1848. The counter resolutions recited that the church had already lived under its constitution for a generation and could continue so for ten generations to come; and that since the constitution had been in force their connexion had spread successfully into thirteen states of the union.

[5] *Op. cit.*, Feb. 9, 1849.

mingly against them : rejoinders were offered and the body
was about ready to vote. Suddenly two females rushed
forward to attack the conference officers. The pastor
eluded his assailant, but one of the secretaries was felled
speechless and a general melee followed. When the city
police officers had restored order, unclaimed weapons of
various kinds were strewn about the room.[1] Those who
were imprisoned gave bail in order to get free and the
trouble was renewed again. The conference again sat in
judgment and expelled the five members for " rebellion
against the spiritual and temporal government of the
church." The annual conference sustained the action of
the local conference and the affair was finally at an end.[3]
Its final settlement was followed by the withdrawal of the
elder who had resisted the reform of the class organizations
and forty-five of the adherents of the expelled trustees.
Acting together they became the nucleus of a new society
under the Methodist Protestant system.[4]

[1] Payne, op. cit., pp. 231-32. Baltimore Clipper, Feb. 24, 26, 1849.
Cf. also Clipper, Jan. 2, 1849, and Bethel Quarterly Conference Records, January 1849.

[2] Payne, op. cit. Payne states that for years there had been a
struggle between pastors and trustees for supremacy in the conference.

[3] Payne, op. cit., p. 236. The local church had prepared to resist the
reinstatement of the five members. Pastor Payne declared in the conference meeting that the time had come for every man to determine
whether he would " sustain the government of the African Methodist
Episcopal Church connexion." He therefore put the question: " Will
you sustain the government of the church against the spirit of rebellion?" Bethel Quarterly Conference Records, April 14, 1849. The
resolution against reinstatement ran in part as follows: " Believing as
we do that any such step would involve the church in a great and
crying evil, strengthening the hand of rebellion, and plunge our be-
loved Zion in war, tumult and bloodshed."

[4] Payne, op. cit., p. 232. For the charter of their church, vide Baltimore Chattel Records, Lib. AWB no. 78, pp. 252-53. Other churches
of the same order were chartered in 1859 and 1860. Baltimore Charter
Records, Lib. GES no. 4, pp. 166-68; Lib. GHC no. 4, pp. 175-77.

TABLE OF STATISTICS OF THE BALTIMORE ANNUAL CONFERENCE

	Congregations	Circuits	Stations	Pastors	Membership
1817	6	1	1	3	1066
1826	29	4	1	7	2403
1836	—	6	2	4	2052
1856	76	15	11	23	5279

Membership

Baltimore Churches		Bethel Church	
1816	633	1845	1302
1824	715	1850	1460
1842	980	1852	1504
		1860	1400

Compiled from data given in the volumes of Payne, Handy and of the *Bethel Quarterly Conference Records.*

The above table is incomplete, and yet it indicates that there was a substantial growth in the churches of the Baltimore conference. The decline in numbers in the years 1826-36 was due in part to the reaction that followed the first flush of success and in part to the same causes that counteracted the other interests of the negroes in that period. After that time the progress, although not unimpeded, was rapid. The preeminence of the churches in the city is notable. The free negroes there were about 30 per cent of all in the state, while before 1820 the city churches had nearly all, and in 1852 about 50 per cent, of the total church membership of the conference.

The history of the African Methodist Episcopal Church was one of progress. A chief cause of its success lay in that many negroes found in it a sphere in which they could act voluntarily. But its growth was not achieved without organization. In its government and customs it attempted to imitate the Methodist Episcopal Church whose discipline it adopted with slight alterations. The bishop resided in Philadelphia until 1852. The General Conference was composed of representatives from the different states meeting quadrennially. The authority of both alike extended over the Maryland churches, but in neither case was it confined to this state. Next below the General Conference was the Annual Conference. The Baltimore Annual Conference, although including some churches outside the state, and not including all those within the state,[1] was essentially the conference of the churches of Maryland. For years it met chiefly at Bethel Church, although later its entertainment was shared with the churches of Washington, D. C., and elsewhere. It was the chief formative agency with which concern is had here.

The Annual Conference was regularly composed of representatives of all the churches under its authority. In its early history, however, circumstances practically threw the conduct of its sessions into the hands of those from Bethel Church. It had thirty-two members in 1819 and thirty-nine in 1843, according to Dr. Payne. By 1859 it had increased to forty-one.[2] But for the change made in the rules governing its membership, it must have grown much larger than that. At the outset certain laymen were admitted because of their prominent part in the founding of the church and because of the paucity of qualified preachers to act in their stead.[3] The first three book stewards in the history of the conference were laymen. Local preachers were allowed seats in 1821 but no voice in the proceedings as against traveling preachers. But in 1827 a resolution was passed limiting the membership to ministers of, or above, the rank of licensed exhorters. After that time laymen and unlicensed ministers, although

---

[1] Payne, op. cit., p. 42; Baltimore Sun, April 15, 1856.

[2] Payne, op. cit., pp. 27, 138, 155; Baltimore Sun, April 29, 1859.

[3] Cf. Payne, op. cit., pp. 13, 19, 27, 29, 47.

[4] Op. cit., pp. 20, 23, 47. Cf. Handy, op. cit., p. 29.

not wholly excluded,[1] participated but little in the conference proceedings. In 1841 office-bearing laymen were admitted to seats but were denied any voice. Those admitted
to the later meetings were thus bishops, elders, deacons and
licentiates.[2] The presiding officer was the bishop, or in
his absence the senior elder present. The other officers were
the recording secretary, the book steward who was apparently a treasurer, a corresponding secretary, the head
of the book concern and the door-keeper.[3] Temporary
committees were appointed to investigate and report upon
matters which the whole conference could not take up at
first hand. Later on there appeared standing committees
having to do with the book concern, education, finance,
memorials, the post office and public worship.[4]

In the period of the early sessions of the conference the
members had been unused to yield obedience to persons of
their own color. The local preachers tended to be insubordinate, and many were disposed to evade the rules, to show
discontent, to tattle and act as tale-bearers.[5] The officers
likewise, " unaccustomed to command or to rule," bore
their part in a way that gave rise to complaint. As a consequence much time was wasted in enforcing the rules of
order. But several causes contributed to the improvement of conditions. For a time fines were imposed for
breaches of decorum. Unlicensed preachers were denied
the right to speak from the floor; the presiding officer was
given power to exclude non-members from the conference
rooms during the sessions; the book steward was ordered

---

[1] Payne, *op. cit.*, pp. 39, 57.

[2] *Op. cit.*, pp. 134, 135, 155, 182.

[3] *Op. cit.*, pp. 16, 27, 61, 189; also *Baltimore Sun*, April 29, 1859.

[4] *Op. cit.*, pp. 15, 46, 183, 210; Handy, *op. cit.*, p. 34; *Baltimore Sun*,
April 25, 1857.

[5] Payne, *op. cit.*, pp. 21, 28, 30, 52, 53.

not to allow an examination of his books without vote of the house; and members were forbidden to betray the confidential proceedings and were held responsible for their conduct both inside and outside the sessions.[1] Time too had a salutary effect. Petulance at restraint wore off and regard for the significance of their church produced a sobering sense of responsibility for its progress. One of its later sessions, reported for the *Baltimore Sun*, "might have been taken as a model for similar assemblages among those who have higher pretensions."[2]

The Baltimore conference exercised extensive powers. Within its own bounds it was practically autonomous. Guided by its own sense of what was proper, it determined its own membership and endeavored to meet the needs of every occasion. It freely took measures affecting the local churches below and apparently also the General Conference above. It made provisions for church extension both within[3] and without its own conceded jurisdiction. In the former it received church organizations into the connexion, adjusted the rank of each congregation as mission, member of circuit or station,[4] and prevented the transfer of one of its Pennsylvania circuits to another conference.[5] It also assessed the local churches for certain purposes. Apparently it did not venture too far without first ascertaining the wishes of those concerned, but it did make its power felt. It enforced the discipline upon the clergy, excepting the bishop. In a few instances it also inquired into the conduct of other members of the churches, gave such judgments as

[1] *Op. cit.*, pp. 15, 27, 42, 48, 53.

[2] *Baltimore Sun*, May 8, 1855.

[3] Payne, *op. cit.*, p. 210.

[4] *Op. cit.*, pp. 21, 22, 42, 157, 208-10; *Baltimore Sun*, May 2, 1855, and May 1, 1857.

[5] Payne, *op. cit.*, pp. 134, 157, 170.

the circumstances seemed to warrant and informed the interested churches of its action.[1] It selected the delegates to the general conference, excepting in 1839-47 when that duty was committed to the elders.[2] Acting in the wider arena it one time fixed the meeting-place of the general conference.[3] In 1822 in the interval between the general conference meetings it initiated steps for electing a bishop's assistant by taking a ballot whose result was not announced until after the Philadelphia Annual Conference had followed its example. The compiled returns were then published and an election declared. In 1821 it was at work determining the conference connections of churches situated west of the Alleghany Mountains, and in 1827 sought to determine the location of a mission station in the island of Hayti.[4] Its assumption of powers was limited only by its own resources and the needs of the church.

The development of a corps of ministers was also a function of the annual conference. Preachers coming from the regular Methodist Church were admitted to the same rank they had held in that body,[5] and those who had been thus admitted were promoted according to the Methodist plan. Owing to the backward state of negro education most of the candidates that offered were barely literate, or illiterate, and ignorant and poorly qualified for their calling. Although some were able to improve themselves creditably,[6] they found the task of preaching to impecunious parishion-

[1] Op. cit., pp. 15, 47, 247, 248-59; Handy, op. cit., p. 34.

[2] Payne, op. cit., pp. 20, 121, 211, 249, 317. Cf. Baltimore Sun, May 6, 1859.

[3] Payne, op. cit., p. 20.

[4] Op. cit., pp. 21, 22, 55; Handy, op. cit., p. 29.

[5] Payne, op. cit., p. 14. Cf. Baltimore Sun, May 2, 1857.

[6] Payne, op. cit., p. 53.

ers unfavorable to study. For two decades the church itself insisted but little upon the better preparation of its
ministers. But in the forward movement after 1835 ardent
champions of education arose. In 1838 Bishop Morris
Brown addressed the conference on the subject and prepared the way for the resolution of the following year which
imposed upon applicants an examination in the articles of
faith and religion.[1] At the instance of Reverend Daniel
Payne three years later the conference recommended all
ministers to study arithmetic, geography, grammar, history
and theology.[2] At its next meeting three candidates for
the ministry were examined. The majority of the examin-
ing committee recommended their acceptance; the one
member in the minority reported that they did not measure
up to the standard of the discipline and advised their rejection. A heated controversy ensued, one member ex-
citedly inquired whether it was necessary to know Hebrew,
Latin and Greek in order to be ordained. Education and
promoters of education were roundly denounced, until at
last the presiding bishop declared that, adhering to the discipline, he would ordain none of the applicants, even
though the conference might admit all of them.[3] Even before that time educational qualifications had been a criterion
for judging of the fitness of ministers. But it did not
suffice merely to turn down illiterates, because the interests
of the church required competent ministers and intelligent
laymen. Steps were, therefore, taken to promote education. There was a desire for a high school. In 1845 the
conference initiated the movement which led to the holding
of an education convention at Philadelphia.[4] In 1846 the

[1] *Op. cit.*, pp. 118, 121.
[2] *Op. cit.*, p. 141. *Cf.* Handy, *op. cit.*, p. 141.
[3] Payne, *op. cit.*, pp. 155-56. *Cf. op. cit.*, p. 117.
[4] *Op. cit.*, p. 182.

preachers were asked to form education societies in the churches and to foster the zeal for education among the people.[1] A decade later the members of the churches were advised to get wisdom, and, as in 1838, preachers were instructed to lead the minds of the people back to the subject. The moral and political elevation of their race, it was said, depended upon their enlightenment.[2] As a result of the agitation the desire for enlightenment was considerably furthered, the Sunday schools and day schools were strengthened, and private study, by those who had the opportunities for it, was stimulated. The standard of literacy for the ministry, although still low, was raised somewhat.

The financial organization of the annual conference was simple. In its early history its demands for money were small. It received a trifling sum from the fines imposed upon its members in the meetings,[3] but derived most of its funds from voluntary contributions. The total receipts reported in representative years were as follows:

1818	1825	1826	1836	1856
$437.90	$582.04	$498.30	$342.19	$577.91 *

* Exclusive of pastors' salaries.

After the depression of the thirties a reorganization of the finances resulted in the creation of separate funds for specific purposes. In 1842 a "regular collection" of two cents a month was ordered for ministerial support, and pastors were to see that it was taken in their respective churches on pain of expulsion, if they failed. Its fruits were $60.31 in 1842,

[1] *Op. cit.*, p. 197. *Cf.* also p. 118.
[2] *Op. cit.*, pp. 118, 406-07. *Cf. Baltimore Sun,* April 9, 1856 and May 1, 1857.
[3] Payne, *op. cit.*, p. 48.

$193.28 in 1855 and $122 in 1856.[1]   As early as 1854 there was a separate collection for episcopal support. In that year it amounted to nearly $200.[2]   The principal ordinary expenditures were for pastor's salaries. Of $472.04 collected for that purpose in 1825, 42 per cent went to the pastor of Bethel Church and the remainder was divided among five others.[3]

The foundation of the annual conference were the local churches. Each church held a quarterly conference to transact its own local business. The attendance at its sessions was a privilege of all members, but votes on some matters were confined to adults and on some others to free male adults. Although any member could initiate measures, its proceedings consisted mainly of matters presented by its officers, boards and committees. Excepting the naming of delegates to the annual conferences, its functions were of purely local import. Such things as elections and proposals affecting the church budget, poor relief and the administration of the discipline recurred often in the meetings. In cases affecting laymen it was competent to act. In cases affecting members who held seats in the annual conference, however, it was permitted to investigate and acquit, or to silence offenders and refer their cases to the annual conference.[5]

---

[1] Payne, op. cit., pp. 139, 317, 415.

[2] Payne, op. cit., p. 317.   For this fund $400 was voted in 1859. Baltimore Sun, May 10, 1859.

[3] Payne, op. cit., p. 46. Cf. Handy, op. cit., pp. 30, 73.

[4] Cf. Baltimore Chattel Records, Lib. WG no. 20, p. 84.

[5] Payne, op. cit., p. 24.   On June 28, 1850, Reverend Darius Stokes, chief steward of Bethel Church, was ordered by the quarterly conference to give up his office. Three months later he was declared " rebellious " for holding a " bush meeting " without permission of the elder in charge of the church, and was suspended for six months. Quarterly Conference Records, June 28 and September 27, 1850. He

Aside from this assembly of the whole church the chief local authorities were the pastor, the stewards and the trustees. The first was the chief personage. His duties included the conduct of the general church services, administration of the ordinances and the care of the flock. He visited the homes of the members, attempted to look to their comfort and spiritual welfare, and wherever meet, recommended cleanliness and decency. He nominated the stewards, directed the clerical members of the congregation, presided at the trustees' meetings and the quarterly conferences.[1] He attended the bishop, when the latter came into the parish, gave him all needful information as to the state of the church and on his own retirement gave like information to his successor.[2] Moreover, he was the leading representative of his church in the annual conference. Of the two advisory-administrative boards in the church the stewards stood first. They were nominated by the pastor from both ministerial and lay members and elected in the quarterly conferences. They assisted in the conduct of the church services and took charge of the collecting, disbursing and accounting for the funds for the support of the church and the pastor, and for sick and poor relief; they

objected to the manner of his suspension and continued to preach, baptize, bury the dead and officiate at the marriage altar. He was charged with contumacy and expelled from the connexion. *Op. cit.*, March 28, 1851. He appealed to the annual conference to have the action nullified, his petition was denied, but before adjournment of this body he was restored to "his official standing in the church." Payne, the historian, writes that both the deposition by the quarterly conference, the ratification by the annual conference and the restoration were alike irregular. *Op. cit.*, pp. 244-49.

[1] *Baltimore Chattel Records*, Lib. WG no. 25, p. 269; Lib. TK no. 69, p. 106; Lib. AWB no. 76, p. 219; Lib. GES no. 4, p. 190; *Bethel Quarterly Conference Records*, 1857-58, March 14, 1860; also Handy, *op. cit.*, p. 48.

[2] *Op. cit.*, p. 48.

aided the pastor in ministering to and encouraging the
people, in correcting disorders among the members and in
trying to realize the ideals of the church life.[1]   They sat as
members of the early annual conference meetings but in
1826 were deprived of their right to vote therein.[2]   The
chief steward was second in authority to the pastor.   The
trustees were composed of the pastor and elected members,
the latter holding their places for terms of from one to
four years each.[3]   Only free persons were eligible to their
membership.[4]   Their chief duties were to care for and
maintain in good condition the real property held by the
church and to transact all business matters appertaining
thereto.   They acted under the instructions of, and reported their doings to, the quarterly conference.

As the negro churches grew and multiplied, their interests
became more varied, and auxiliary societies with special
functions were founded.   At the annual conference meetings of 1843 and 1844 three temperance societies were reported.   In the latter year also an educational society was
reported, and a missionary society for the Baltimore conference was formed " as an auxiliary to the Parent, Home
and Foreign Society."[5]   In 1857 the report of the treasurer of Bethel Church contained an item of $101.00 for rent
paid by societies that had met in its building.   Some of these
were probably not church auxiliaries at all.[6]   At that time

[1] Handy, op. cit., p. 51. Cf. Discipline of the Methodist Episcopal
Church, 19th edition (1817), pp. 190-91.

[2] Payne, op. cit., p. 47.

[3] Frederick Records of Incorporation of Churches, 1805-80, p. 78.
Baltimore Chattel Records, Lib. WG no. 25, p. 269.

[4] Cf. references cited in note one, p. 183, and last note preceding.
Also Talbot Deeds, Lib. no. 62, p. 149.

[5] Payne, op. cit., pp. 157, 176, 183. For mention of societies, some
of which had quasi-religious objects, vide Md. Col. Jour., p. 68.

[6] Quarterly Conference Records, Feb. 13, 1857.

the church had among its members a sewing circle whose labors were devoted to charitable objects,[1] and in 1859 the annual conference set to work to found a preachers' aid society.[2]

Notwithstanding the strong attractions of the Methodist Church the Protestant Episcopal, Baptist, Presbyterian and Catholic churches each had a following among the negroes. The Episcopal church and school were under the pastoral care of a colored, ordained minister in 1823.[3]   In 1824 they united themselves under the name and style of St. James First African Protestant Episcopal Church, and in 1828 became an incorporated body.[4]   They denied the privileges of voting and office-bearing in their midst to any person not of African descent.   On account of its school this congregation was one of the best known among the negroes of the city.   At many other places in the state the negroes were received as communicants in the Episcopal churches of the whites.[5]   In 1837 a body of negro Baptists in Baltimore elected five " sober and discreet " members as trustees and became an incorporated church.[6]   Their charter divided the trustees into classes and provided for the selection of the pastor and for admitting members to the church.   In 1842 they purchased the lessor's rights in the lot on which their building had previously been erected.[7]   In 1854 a second Baptist church was chartered.   A part of its trustees were

[1] *Op. cit.,* 1857-58.

[2] *Baltimore Sun,* May 10, 1859.

[3] *Journal of the Conventions of the Protestant Episcopal Church, Maryland 1823,* p. 5.

[4] *Baltimore Chattel Records,* Lib. WG no. 41, pp. 343, 389; Lib. WG no. 37, pp. 166-67.

[5] *Journals of the Conventions. op. cit.,* 1823, p. 9; 1824, pp. 17-19, 20, 23, 24, 25; 1827, pp. 26, 27; 1828, pp. 29, 30; 1830, p. 38.

[6] *Baltimore Chattel Records,* Lib. TK no. 57, pp. 158-61.

[7] *Baltimore Land Records,* Lib. TK no. 322, p. 234.

selected by the Maryland Baptist Union Association of
the whites' churches. Otherwise its rules were similar to
those of its sister church.[1]   The Presbyterians exercised a
considerable influence among the negroes of Baltimore City
and organized one separate negro church.[2]   The Friends
had negro members in certain of their congregations, especially those of Baltimore City and Harford County.   The
Roman Catholics also received some negro members and
maintained for them a female society called the Oblates, or
Sisters of Providence.[3]   In 1853 a union church, calling itself
the Colored People's Congregation of Mount Tabor, was
chartered in Frederick County.   Its members were adherents of the German Reformed, Lutheran and Methodist
Episcopal Churches.[4]

[1] *Baltimore Charter Records*, Lib. ED no. 1, p. 393.   *Cf. Laws*, 1856,
ch. 262.   A free negro's will, recorded in the *Baltimore Wills*, Lib.
DMP no. 13, p. 46, mentioned an Ebenezer Baptist Church.

[2] *Md. Col. Journal*, p. 68.

[3] *Baltimore Wills*, Lib. IPC no. 28, p. 65.   *Vide* on the Friends, *op.
cit.*, Lib. DMP no. 19, pp. 268-69.

[4] *Frederick Records of Incorporation of Churches*, 1805-80, pp. 193-97.

CHAPTER IX

SOCIAL CONDITIONS

AT different points in the previous chapters there have been references to general social conditions. But there has been no attempt to emphasize as such the standard of life, unemployment, pauperism and mortality among the free negroes. Regarding these matters the evidence left by contemporaries is quite fragmentary, and much of what there is was recorded by biased persons. Nevertheless it seems necessary to give some account of them from such facts as are available. The first matter to be treated will be the negroes' home life, and in that connection attention will be devoted to dwellings, provisioning and apparel, to sanitation and medical attendance and to material relations and the social evil.

The buildings inhabited by the negroes were generally of mean character—often such as white persons could not be induced to occupy. A common type of rural dwelling was the low structure of one or two compartments built of logs. The tapering space underneath the rafters was often made to answer the demand for additional rooming space. The principal opening was the doorway, as window space was not highly prized. The chinks of the walls were not well daubed, and ceiled or lime-plastered walls did not generally prevail. For floors the bare earth, or in the region of severer winter temperatures, rough boards, did service. A ramshackle stove pipe, a hole in the roof or a chimney carried aloft the smoke from the hearth-fire. The room contained as furniture a few faded pieces such as safe, table, stools, a bedstead, or in its place a straw-tick, and a few other things. The floor was strewn with things that should have been placed elsewhere to be in order. Its aspect vied with that of the walls adorned with rags, leaf-tobacco, coon-skins, pot-hoops, spiders, kettles and other utensils. Dust, soot, smoke and soiled fingers had added their respective contributions to make the character complete. The appearance of the interior bespoke a poverty as to possessions, but even more poverty as to arrangement and care of what was there. The place served as kitchen, dining and living room, receiving and bed room. Into such quarters the master of the house huddled his family at night and barred the door to keep out the unknown terrors —and the fresh air. In Baltimore City the negroes' dwellings presented contrasts similar to those of the whites, although less extreme in degree. The buildings were rather more substantial than many of those used by the rural negroes but hardly furnished more comfort on that account.[1] Indigence and plenty occurred within a stone's throw of each other. On the one hand families crowded themselves into insufficient tenements whose reeking vermin and squalor were true signs of slums.[2] Winter cold and summer heat alike added to their discomforts. And on the other hand some well-to-do negroes in both the city and the country lived in better-class houses in a degree of comfort that would have done credit to many a white family.[3]

[1] Cf. 28 Niles Register, p. 100; also Baltimore Assessment Books, 1823, 12th Ward, p. 159.

[2] Cf. Buckler, History of Epidemic Cholera, 1849, p. 5.

[3] For contents of certain houses, cf. Baltimore Chattel Records, Lib. WG no. 29, p. 377; Lib. WG no. 30, p. 52; Harford Chattel Records, Lib. ALJ no. 1, p. 390; Worcester Deeds, Lib. GMH no. 1, p. 513; Lib. GMH no. 4, p. 258; Lib. GMH no. 7, p. 84.

The food and raiment of the free negroes was varied in amount and quality. The best fed of all were the well-to-do and thrifty whose women were skilful cooks and those who were numbered in the small gangs that worked for and hence ate in the kitchens of the well-to-do white farmers. When freemen served under indentures or under wage contracts by the year, they were provided for substantially like the slaves. The allowances for the slaves thus became a sort of standard to which free negroes aimed to attain when providing for themselves. The majority fared apparently about as well as did the slaves excepting sometimes in the winter season. Both free negroes and slaves varied their diet with garden vegetables and game, while many of both classes earned a part of what they lived on and foraged for the rest.[1]   In the matter of wearing apparel there was wide variety, although free negroes were generally garbed in such articles as were commonly allowed to slaves and apprentices.[2]   In addition to these, or in place of them, they wore many of the things that had been laid aside by their white employers. But to some negroes dress that pleased the fancy was valued above the necessaries. They therefore took pride in being nicely appareled, as

[1] *Vide* almost contrary opinion as to free negroes in Baltimore City about 1820-25, *28 Niles Register*, p. 100. *Cf.* also Griffith, *Annals of Baltimore*, p. 233, and *Md. Col. Journal*, no. 11.

[2] The "allowance" of clothing for a slave varied but little from county to county. For winter it consisted substantially of the following named articles given at Christmas time: for a male, Kersey coat and trousers, two shirts, a pair each of shoes and stockings, a cap and a handkerchief; for a female, Kersey petticoat and jacket, shift of linens, shoes, stockings, cap and handkerchief; and in the spring for a male, a change of shirts and a pair of trousers, and for a female a change of linens. But, as in the case of provisioning, time was often allowed to slaves to earn a little money to supplement these minimal supplies. *Vide supra*, p. 141, and Frederick Douglass, *Life and Times*, pp. 45-46.

witnessed their appearance on holidays and festal occasions. Domestic servants who were free were dressed in the same manner as were slaves acting in a similar capacity.

Although the negroes lived in a rude manner, they did not lack the social spirit. They loved to mingle in the crowds that gathered in the towns on Saturdays, holidays and market days and at picnics, churches, camp-meetings and other places. They also took delight in moving about among their friends and receiving the latter at their homes, whether such friends were slaves or freemen. Sometimes, however, there was a fear of slave-holders' wrath and, therefore, some restraint about entertaining and visiting slaves.[1] When not interdicted by the whites they held parties, and in the city of Baltimore cake-walks and balls at which the hilarity was unbounded.[2] Such affairs, however, were scrutinized by the peace officers and the patrollers and after 1831 were liable to be broken up summarily.[3] In Baltimore this regulation was supplemented by an ordinance requiring an official permit for holding any negro meeting excepting for certain approved purposes. But it was applied in a manner that allowed many social privileges to the law-abiding.

The marriage relations of the free negroes were in a state of disorder. The customs they had been used to in Africa were not followed here, because the conditions of the slave system had not admitted of it: the rules or practices had to be flexible enough to allow the owners to manage their slave property for their own advantage. The practices that sprang up in the province were perpetuated in the state and tended to prevail among the free almost as much as among

[1] Cf. Letter of General Harper to E. B. Caldwell, p. 8; H. Dels. Journal, 1829, p. 337, and 1830, p. 136.

[2] Baltimore Sun, Jan. 1, 1857, March 10, 1854, and May 11, 12, 1859.

[3] Laws, 1820, ch. 200, and 1822, ch. 85.

the slaves. The legal regulation of the marriage of the
slave lay entirely in the hands of the master. His consent
was necessary to its making and maintenance,[1] and he might,
therefore, dissolve it, in case he chose to sell or remove one
of the parties out of the community. As a consequence slave
marriages generally lacked the formalities and the deliberation that attended those of the whites. And although the
rule of one consort at time prevailed, there was widespread
disregard for the usual obligations of such consortships and
too little concern about the consequences of repudiating them.
The marriages of the free were raised but little above those
of the slaves, since they also lacked exact legal sanction.
When a free person consorted with a slave, marital obligations were not to be enforced at law, unless the slave party
had become the property of the free party. But inasmuch
as many of the reasons for holding these bonds inviolable
did not commonly obtain here, this question tends to be
mainly academic. Slaves and free persons did consort with
each other, and such objections as slave-owners made to the
practice were generally for other than legal and moral
reasons.[2] The children of slave mothers became slaves
and those of free mothers free persons, no matter what the
status of their husbands. The mixed marriages were,
therefore, not more formal than those of the slaves, although in one instance in Worcester County a license was
issued for a slave to marry a free colored woman.[3] In
case both parties were free, however, it was possible to have

---

[1] *Vide* illustration of this in Douglass, *op. cit.*, pp. 37-38.

[2] About the close of the revolution the Harford County Orphans'
Court threatened one, Jared Hopkins, with proceedings for contempt
because he had married a free woman to a negro slave. *Minutes*,
1778-97, p. 34. *Cf.* Douglass, *op. cit.*, pp. 37, 118-19.

[3] *Marriage Record*, May 31, 1811. On the matter of distribution of
property as affected by such marriages, *vide* chapter on Legal Status,
supra, pp. 105-06.

a regular marriage. Accordingly many marriage licenses were issued in favor of free negroes,[1] and often a ceremony followed. The effect of this was to add an element of deliberation and to impose a partial check upon utter license in this important matter. Thus, although whims, fancies and passion for novelty of marital connections were not ended, some beginnings were made towards the adoption of the whites' custom of establishing permanent households on the monogamous plan.

An emigrant from this country to Liberia stated that " the pure African has no conception of morality and virtue other than is drawn from the civilized beings with whom he is placed in contact." [2]   How much that conception was improved by the environment of the slave system depended upon circumstances. Those who were either exposed to the influences of unprincipled white men, or left most of the time to untaught negroes, remained much like their fathers had been. Chastity in either sex was at a discount, and both alike were impotent to prevent the invasion of this realm by non-African men. No evil to which they fell victim was more contemptibly condoned than this.[3]   It was deplorable, and yet it was not universal, because female domestics in some slave-holders' homes and the offspring of some free negroes were sacredly protected against being corrupted; and some were so schooled in the " precepts of morality and virtue " that they went undefiled to the marriage altar and maintained their repute for conjugal fidelity to the end of their lives.[4]

Second only to the love of the crowd was the negroes'

[1] Vide Marriage Records of Caroline, 1816-58, Dorchester, 1799-1859, and Worcester, 1795-1860.

[2] Md. Col. Journal, vol. i, p. 281.

[3] Cf. Douglass, op. cit., pp. 118-19.

[4] Op. cit., pp. 37, 118-19.

love of ardent spirits.   It asserted itself both early and late.
The account books of certain supply stores afford facts of
interest.   At Elk Ridge Furnace in 1767 a slave named
Sampson purchased four pints of rum for four shillings and
two and a half yards of cloth for four shillings sixpence;
other entries show that in the two preceding months he had
paid in four shillings for rum and eight for other articles.[1]
Another negro at the Cornwall Furnace in 1762 closed his
account amounting to sixty-seven pounds, seven shillings
and eleven pence half-penny for " store liquor and general
charges." [2]   And many others had small accounts for
liquors alone.   The detrimental effects of their consumption
were noticed before the end of the eighteenth century, and
legislation that has been noticed elsewhere [3] was enacted to
restrict or to prevent the sale of liquor to negroes on certain
occasions.   But verbal reports, corroborated by inferences
from legislative and other records, indicate that the consumption of liquors by negroes increased in the nineteenth
century.   The measures taken against their purchasing
the stuff were not of great avail, notwithstanding the desire
of many to check it.   They probably procured much of it
in compliance with the laws.   But in addition to this some
negroes were frequently " treated " to drinks by their employers, and others found means of getting theirs outside
the law.[4]   They were thus favored by portable dispensers
and by the clandestine purchasers of the farm products
which they stole and bartered away.   How much liquor

[1] *Ledger A of Caleb Dorsey & Co.*, p. 199. *Cf.* also pp. 48, 62, 132,
233.

[2] *Cornwall Furnace Ledger L.* p. 307, and *Journal N*, pp. 38, 108. *Cf.*
same journal, pp. 114, 115, 118, 121-27; also *Ledger A of Jesse Richardson*, 1790-91, pp. 24, 29, 31, 36, 77, 80; also *Patuxent Iron Works
Journal*, 1767-68, pp. 5, 7-10.

[3] *Supra*, pp. 103-04, chapter on Legal Status.

[4] *Supra*, p. 103, note 3.

they consumed it is impossible to calculate, but it seems beyond doubt that they constantly spent on this form of indulgence a considerable part of their earnings, and that many of the crimes they committed were due to its incitement.

Hygienic conditions about the negro dwellings have been already hinted at. The air in their poorly ventilated houses was not good, and cleanliness within was not general. Sanitation too was greatly neglected. Offal was imperfectly disposed of, cess-pools located without necessary regard for the demands of health, drinking water often carelessly provided and personal squalidness treated as a matter of course. Added to these things was the vermin which found a welcome in the conditions described. The sloth which allowed these things to spring up took little thought of measures to remove them. And in none of these particulars were there marked differences between the lot of slaves and that of freemen, saving that in some instances masters compelled their slaves to clean up the premises. As for medical attendance the slaves often enjoyed an advantage over freemen on account of the interest of masters in the health of their human stock. And yet it is said that many physicians endeavored faithfully to attend the cases of free negroes who were sick, whenever invited and needed. Nevertheless, the co-existence of these conditions along with others in the negro home was sufficient to impair their own health and the strength of their progeny to an appreciable degree.

The conditions described in the foregoing paragraphs affected the negroes first of all. Of themselves they were not of primary concern to the whites, but they had their counterpart in other conditions that were of concern to the latter. Such were those of unemployment, poverty and disease. The extent to which the free negro was kept employed was a source of constant anxiety to many of the whites. They had much to say about the subject. Their utterances generally agreed in pointing out weaknesses and disparaging the industrial character of the unenslaved negro. Because his personal resources consisted mainly of mere brawn, he lacked the power to think for himself, he had to have guidance and protection, and he was, therefore, forced to work in the lowest callings in which he received for his services smaller real wages than any other class of the people.[1] Attention was called to the disadvantages and the lack of incentives under which he labored through his exclusion from certain occupations to which white men were admitted without prejudice.[2] He had, moreover, no property or other independent sources of income from which to derive his living—his own labor alone generally stood between himself and starvation. But his sloth and indisposition to arduous work inclined him to be unproductive, and hence to lack the things necessary for his own support. He, therefore, tended to exert himself only so far as to get a meager subsistence.[3] His dependence upon the white man was scarcely less than that of the slave, and he was a burden to the state. Now some evidence to support these views was discoverable. It was magnified and generalized for political effect, and many quackish legislative proposals were based upon it,[4] but a closer examination of the subject shows that, although there was much improvidence,

---

[1] *Cf. e. g. Md. Col. Journal*, vol. i, p. 225, *28 Niles Register*, p. 100, and Hall, *Address to the Free People of Color*, p. 3.

[2] *Cf. supra*, pp. 151-53; also *Md. Col. Journal*, no. 19.

[3] In addition to the references given in the last note, *vide Md. Col. Journal*, vol. i, p. 279; vol. ix, pp. 277-78; *43 Niles Register*, p. 39; Griffith, *Annals of Baltimore*, p. 233; *Baltimore American*, March 5, 1832, and June 10, 1859; *Frederick Examiner*, March 24, 1858; *27th Annual Report of American Anti-Slavery Society*, p. 209.

[4] *Cf. infra*, pp. 263-64, chapter on Attempts to Check the Growth of the Free Negro Population.

honest toil was the chief resource of the free negroes for winning their subsistence.[1] With this view the less biased statements of contemporaries agreed.[2]

A favorite term with the critics of the free negro was the word "vagrant."[3] Clauses in several statutes, the first of which were inserted in 1796,[4] were enacted to prevent vagrancy on the part of adult free negroes, and to cause free negro children to be bound out to learn useful trades. The manner in which those laws were executed has been indicated elsewhere.[5] Complaints about vagrancy of negroes were perhaps more general before 1830 than after that time. For although it survived later in all parts of the state, it was, according to Governor Hicks, chiefly in the lower counties on both sides of the bay that the public suffered from it.[6] The reliable statistics that are available are confined to the almshouse reports of Baltimore County for the years 1851-1860. They show that in those years, excepting for the year 1855, 9.7 per cent of those committed to the almshouse as vagrants were negroes, whereas the proportion of free negroes in the total population of the county in 1850 was 13.6 per cent and in 1860 11.2 per cent.[7]

The chief data bearing upon pauperism among the

[1] Cf. on this Baltimore American, June 9, 1859, statement by Judge Pearce in the Slave-Holders' Convention.

[2] Vide Baltimore American, Feb. 2, 1860, letter from "Slave-Holder," and Feb. 16, 1860, memorial of citizens of Baltimore against the "Jacobs Bills".

[3] Cf. Md. Pub. Docs., 1841 H, pp. 3-5; Harper, op. cit., pp. 8-9; H. Dels. Journal, 1852, pp. 619, 623; 1853, pp. 120, 991 and 1055, and 1856, pp. 80, 137, 263, 323; also supra, pp. 95-97.

[4] Laws, 1796, chs. 30 and 67. Cf. 1797, ch. 56, 1804, ch. 96, and 1839, ch. 38.

[5] Supra, pp. 95 and 131-33 et seq.

[6] Inaugural Address, 1858, p. 13.

[7] Cf. Brackett, Negro in Maryland, pp. 221-22.

negroes are likewise confined to Baltimore County. As shown in the table below, the number of negroes in the county almshouse was relatively high in 1828, the date of the earliest report. But at that time it was said that the

TABLE SHOWING INMATES OF THE ALMSHOUSE OF BALTIMORE COUNTY

	White.	Colored.	Total.	Per cent Colored.	Per cent of Pop. Colored.	Per cent of Cfty Pop. Free Colored.
1828 . . .	4751	1204	5955	20.2	. . .	. . .
1830 . . .	5310	1278	6588	19.4	23.6	14.7
1835 . . .	5075	1029	6104	16.8	. . .	. . .
1840 . . .	4654	1502	6156	24.5	21.4	15.9
1845 . . .	5146	1386	6532	21.2	. . .	. . .
1849 . . .	5230	1389	6619	20.9	. . .	. . .
1850 . . .	5566	1008	6574	15.3	17.8	13.2
1855 . . .	6356	1123	7479	15.0	. . .	. . .
1860 . . .	8018	1069	9087	11.7	13.2	11.2

practice of setting free superannuated slaves aided to swell the ranks of the destitute free.[1] While in 1828-30 the percentage of negro inmates was greater than the free negro percentage of the total population of the county, after the middle of the century it declined, until in 1860 it exceeded the latter by only five-tenths of one per cent. In the three decades 1830-1860 the county's free negro population increased 12023. The average number of free negro inmates in 1828-33 was 1233.6, and in 1853-60 1177.4. The apparent improvement in the condition of the free negroes was no doubt offset in part by the peculiar forms assumed by private charities in their case. Verbal reports from several of the counties also concur in declaring that the ratio of negroes in the total number of inmates of the almshouses was small.

[1] 37 Niles Register, p. 340; Genius of Universal Emancipation, Oct. 7, 1826.

The following table gives the numbers of families helped by the Baltimore Association for the Improvement of the Condition of the Poor during the years 1857-60. The proportion of negro families in this instance exceeded that of the free negroes to the total population of the city.

	Families helped.	Negro families helped.	Negro per cent of total.
1857	4065	684	16.9
1858	5133	733	14.2
1859	3052	580	19.0
1860	3158	591	18.9
Total	15408	2598	16.7

It should be remarked that more than a third of all the white families helped through this agency in these years were those of foreign immigrants.

In addition to the charitable relief dispensed by the whites the negroes did much to help themselves and their own poor. Much of this was extended as individual relief, but some was given through relief societies. As early as 1821 a benevolent society of young men of color was in existence in Baltimore.[1] Others like it were either already at work or were founded soon thereafter, for in 1835 a committee of negro ministers reported that the colored people of the city had more than thirty " benevolent institutions " with a membership of from thirty-five to a hundred and fifty each, and that several of them had savings accounts bearing interest in the banks.[2] Among them were the African Friendship Benevolent Society for Social Relief which had

[1] *Federal Gazette*, Sept. 25, 28, 1821. Cf. *Genius of Universal Emancipation*, Oct. 7, 1826.

[2] *49 Niles Register*, p. 72.

four hundred dollars in funds at the time it was incorporated in 1833.[1] Others named by a writer in the *Baltimore Literary and Religious Magazine* in 1838 were the " Star in the East Association," the " Daughters of Jerusalem Association," the benevolent associations of caulkers, coachmen, mechanics, United Brethren and young men, and temperance, Bible and Sunday school societies.[2] Apparently most of these organizations endeavored in part to imitate the clubs and societies of the whites. They cultivated social life, endeavored to mutualize relief by giving financial and other assistance to their members in cases of sickness and distress, in burying the dead, *etc.*[3] The most pretentious of them were those of the Masonic order, the first permit for which was received from Philadelphia in 1825. The Friendship Lodge no. 6, then founded in Baltimore, was followed by two others with which in 1845 it was consolidated into the First Colored Grand Lodge of Maryland. Two years later was formed a second grand lodge which continued to maintain a separate existence, until in 1876 it was consolidated also with its senior sister society. Royal arch chapters also existed before the general emancipation but failed to administer successfully the higher degrees until 1865.[4] The laudable purposes of these organiza-

---

[1] *Baltimore Chattel Records*, Lib. TK no. 233, p. 325.

[2] *Md. Col. Journal*, no. 16, p. 68, reprinting article from the *Literary and Religious Magazine* vol. iii, p. 280. There were also a " Relief Society in Cases of Seizure," and a " Young Men's Mental Improvement Society " for the discussion of moral and philosophical questions. This writer named at least thirty societies and referred to still others whose names he could not give.

[3] *Op. cit.* Cf. also Lucas, *Picture of Baltimore*, 1833, p. 165.

[4] Gumshaw, *Official History of Freemasonry among the Colored People of North America*, pp. 165-71. Apparently these societies continued despite the statutory prohibition of negro secret societies in the act of 1842, ch. 281.

tions were no bar to suspicions that they might undertake to promote incendiary movements. There is no doubt that their activities were greatly obstructed by the legal restrictions upon negro meetings. And yet in the city of Baltimore, if not also in some other places, a tolerant policy enabled societies that were not secret to continue to pursue the objects for which they had been formed.[1]

The next subject to be treated is that of mortality. The statistics bearing upon it are not complete and are taken in part from *Niles Register* and from the newspapers. Several plague seasons will be first referred to and after them certain other years not marked by special causes of deaths. In the months of July and October 1819 a plague appeared in the city of Baltimore. The free negroes who then numbered about 14 per cent of the population of the county furnished 17.5 per cent of the deaths due to all causes.[2] In 1832 when another pleague occurred, the free negroes constituted about 14.5 per cent of the population of the county. In the month of August 46.3 per cent of the plague cases and 43.3 per cent of the deaths were those of negroes and in the following month 36.9 per cent of the deaths from all causes were those of negroes.[3] And whereas only about 63 per cent of the negroes were freemen, 88.8 per cent of those who died were freemen. And yet the percentage of fatalities among the cases reported was greater on the part of the whites than on that of the negroes. In May and June 1849 an epidemic of flagrant typhus visited the city. " It was confined almost exclusively to this race . . . . In rows of houses occupied by Germans, Irish and free blacks, it would invariably single out the latter, in many

---

[1] *Cf. Baltimore Sun*, Feb. 17, 1860, quoting *Cumberland Telegraph.* Also Brackett, *op. cit.*, pp. 203-05.

[2] *17 Niles Register*, p. 541, quoting report of Board of Health.

[3] The following table is compiled from reports published in *43 Niles*

instances seizing an entire family." [1]   Eighty-three cases
were sent to the almshouse, and of the thirty-nine victims
only one was a white person.   Finally in the midsummer
of the following year a cholera plague occurred at the almshouse.   At the time 27.3 per cent of the inmates were
negroes, while 27.7 per cent of the cases and 33.7 per cent of
the victims were of the same race.   Of the whites who were
attacked 50.8 per cent succumbed and of the negroes 67.4
per cent.[2]   In all of the cases the percentage of fatalities on
the part of the negroes was excessive.

The following tables compare the number of deaths of
the free negroes with those of the whites and the slaves in

Register, pp. 24, 44, 52, 71, 84, for the interval from September 1 to
October 4, 1832:

Week ending.	Number of deaths.				Total negroes.
	Total.	Whites.	Free negroes.	Slaves.	
Sept. 7	254	150	96	8	104
" 14	332	210	109	13	122
" 21	225	146	68	11	79
" 28	116	77	35	4	39
Oct. 4	89	58	29	2	31
	1016	641	339	38	375

Cf. op. cit., vol. 42, pp. 432, 451; vol. 43, pp. 2, 39; also *Baltimore
Republican*, Aug. 26, 27, 1832; *Baltimore American*, September 3, 4, 11,
18, 25, and Oct. 5, 1832.   On the cholera in the Eastern Shore, *vide
Centerville Times*, September 15, 1832.

[1] Buckler, *History of the Epidemic Cholera at the Baltimore County
Almshouse*, 1849, pp. 5, 12.

[2] *Op. cit.*, pp. 17-18.   Buckler gives the following data:

	Inmates	*Cases*	*Deaths*
Whites	407	112	57
Negroes	153	43	29

years not marked by special causes of death: (for Baltimore County)

Year.	Percentages.		Deaths.					
	Negroes in total popu-lation.	Free negroes in total negroes.	Total.	Whites.	Total negroes.	Slaves.	Free negroes.	Per cent negro.
1819	24.4 (1820)	59.2	2287	1716	571	. . .	. . .	24.9
1823	. . . . .	. . .	2108	1449	650	. .	. . .	31.3
1824	. . . . .	. . .	.	. .	416	48	368	. .
1829	23.6 (1830)	62.7	1849	1320	529	100	429	23.2
1843	21.6 (1840)	73.8	2520	1913	607	135	472	24.0
1849	16.7 (1850)	81.2	4576	3519	1057	266	791	23.09
1860	13.2	84.7	.	. . .	. .	. . .	. . .	. . .

Data from *Niles Register* and from *Baltimore American*, Jan. 24, 1850.

TABLE OF DEATHS OF NEGROES IN BALTIMORE COUNTY

	Total.	Slaves.	Free negroes.	Per cent free negroes.	Free negro per cent of total colored population.
1824	416	48	368	88.4	52.9 (1820)
1829	529	100	429	81.09	62.7 (1830)
1848	607	135	472	77.7	73.8 (1840)
1849	1057	266	791	74.8	. . . . . .
1853	879	67	812	92.3	81.2 (1850)
1854	841	106	735	87.3	. . . . . .
1858	808	135	673	88.3	. . . .
1860	853	104	749	87.8	87.4 (1860)

Assuming that these statistics are correct the decline of the free negro portion of the total population of Baltimore County was attended by an almost uniform percentage in the negroes' share of the total mortality. And among the negroes, although an excessive portion of the deaths were those of free negroes in 1824, the excess was later so far reduced that in spite of the plague of 1849 the balance at times even inclined in their favor. In the decade 1850-60 the death-rate of the free negroes of the county was but one and one-tenth per cent higher than the numbers of their class would have warranted.[1] For thirty-six of the years between 1818 and 1863 the death-rate among the negroes of the city of Baltimore was 3.1 per cent while that of the whites was 2.49 per cent.[2] It will be recalled that the major part of the free negroes resided in the city and the major part of the slaves in the rural portion of the county. The normal death-rate was probably higther in the city than in the county. Thus the grounds for the opinion that freedom was destructive to the negroes, in so far as they had to be found in the conditions in Baltimore, were nearly removed before the general emancipation.[3]

Comparing certain tables of mortality of the whites and negroes the United States Census stated that the two races had " different susceptibilities of the attacks of disease and different liabilities to death."[4] It is not to be thought on that account, however, that the negroes were more liable to diseases than the whites under similar circumstances.[5] And yet it was shown above that the death-rate both in

[1] The free negroes were 81.2 per cent of the county's negro population in 1850 and 87.4 per cent in 1860, or roughly an average of 84.3 per cent, while 83.2 per cent of the deaths were those of negroes.

[2] *Eighth Census of United States, Mortality and Miscellaneous Statistics*, p. 280.

[3] For some of the opinions referred to, *vide* C. W. Jacobs, *Speech to the Maryland House of Delegates in 1860. Cf. 28 Niles Register*, p. 100, and vol. 37, p. 340; also Griffith, *op. cit.*, p. 233.

[4] *Mortality Statistics, Eighth Census*, p. 280.

[5] Cf. *24 Niles Register*, p. 39.

normal times and in plague seasons was greater among the negroes. The excessive rate among the free negroes in 1824 and 1829 was partly due to the "unpleasant and oppressive fact" that "aged and infirm and worn-out negroes, from all parts of the state" had been turned out and allowed to go "to Baltimore, to live as they could, or die, if they must."[1] The excess that was not due to this cause was obviously the result of the operation of the combined forces of physical environment of negro homes, of dissolute habits and of the hardships and denials of the life they led. The approach to an equivalence in the rate as between free negroes and slaves in Baltimore in the years 1850-60 was probably due to improvements in the conditions.[2]

The reasons why the negroes thus fell short of the standards set by the whites will perhaps admit of restatement at this point. The negroes were of a race that was undeveloped in both the material and moral elements of civilization. They brought from their mother-land scarcely anything of culture that proved enduring here. Their material achievements in Africa were forgotten here, and of their striking moral characteristics none excepting their ignorance, their sensual natures and their lack of tense care for their own interests were permitted to express themselves. They had been suddenly thrust into the midst of an enlightened, ambitious and well-organized race. The community into which they came belonged to the white men: the fruits of its fields and the benefits of its institutions were for the white men. Other white men, if they came, were welcome bidders for a share in such advantages, but the men who were not whites had been fetched in for the benefit and convenience of the

---

[1] 37 *Niles Register*, p. 340, a conservative view, and *Genius of Universal Emancipation*, Oct. 7, 1826, a less conservative view.

[2] *Cf. Governor Hicks's Inaugural Address*, p. 13.

whites.[1] They were not prepared to adopt the manner of life of the white people, yet in many things they were compelled by moral and physical force to follow the lines laid down for them. They therefore underwent a severe course of training which began in them a process of remolding. This experience made distinctive other characteristics. Such were their depreciation of themselves and of other persons of their color, their lack of confidence in their own abilities, their deference and obsequiousness towards white persons and their lack of the sense of responsibility for the condition of affairs in general. Fidelity to the duties that engaged them, although often nobly exemplified, was a quality whose generality could not be safely asserted.

Freedom seemed to imply a measure of equality between free denizens of the community. Negroes were manumitted in order that they might be given a chance to realize freedom. Yet from acquaintance with the weaknesses of the slaves, the manumitters could hardly have been so blind as to have expected that the enfranchised negroes would rise to a plane of equality with themselves. Those who became free were generally ignorant of the meaning of their condition and of its possibilities. They still regarded themselves as " niggers," and hardly rose to a conception of sharing in the better things of life and becoming equal citizens in the state.[2] Ambitions to rival the white men's achievements

---

[1] Although this situation held less true in the nineteenth century than it had in the eighteenth century, the thought suggested by the statement given underlay a great deal of the anti-negro agitation. *Cf. 13 Niles Register*, pp. 177-78; *Baltimore American*, March 5, 1832; *Md. Col. Journal*, vol. i, pp. 279-80; vol. iv, p. 184; and Hall, *op. cit.*, pp. 2-3. Even the Methodist Church excluded negroes from the higher ranks of its ministry, until nearly forced to admit them.

[2] The exceptions to this were probably chiefly among those who came under abolitionist influence after 1830, but their reaction even in that case was hardly favorable to their elevation.

and to become "gentlemen" were at best vague on their part—they were fitted the rather mainly for the mean industrial rôle in which they everywhere appeared.[1] Their visual horizon was unwidened, and they seemed in many cases to have believed that their material condition would have been just as good in slavery as in freedom. Yet they cherished liberty as a relief from the toils of slavery, and too often had as a chief purpose the avoidance of labor such as they had undergone in slavery. In so far as they took this view, they allowed their own interests to fall into a condition of disorder and either abandoned themselves to the gratification of personal whims and appetites, or allowed the whole current of their lives to be determined by the demands of the whites.

The general tenor of contemporary accounts greatly disparaged the free negroes[2] and the possibilities of their achieving anything worth while. A great deal was said too about the impossibility of their getting recognition of such merits as they really possessed. But these things were not altogether true to fact. Both races of men were composed of good, bad and indifferent classes,[3] the last two being very numerous in each. Had the personal endowments been equal in both, there is no reason why many of the negroes might not have risen to good position. But many of the latent talents of the masses of both races wasted away without a chance for development. None of either race could rise from a low position without making the effort necessary

---

[1] Cf. Letter of General Harper to E. B. Caldwell, pp. 7-8.

[2] Niles Register, vol. 21, p. 119; vol. 28, p. 100; vol. 37, p. 340; Harper, op. cit.; Md. Pub. Docs., 1843 M, pp. 44-47; Debates of the Constitutional Convention of 1850, vol. ii, p. 222; Md. Col. Journal, vol. i, p. 281; Easton Gazette, May 7, 1859, and Frederick Examiner, June 1, 1859.

[3] Cf. Md. Col. Journal, vol. iii, p. 323.

for self-improvement.   The negroes, although landless and
denied entrance to many careers, were not barred from all
the good things of life, and merit on their part did not go
entirely unrewarded.   The social system did make invidious
discriminations against them in some matters, but nevertheless high character on a negro's part gained recognition as
an estimable achievement, even though its possessor wore
a black skin.   It was not true that a negro could at best
gain " a mere subsistence " in the state of Maryland.[1]   He
could provide well for his family, could have a home of his
own and could lead a fairly independent and respectable life.
The social system afforded a certain homage to him who
thus labored and prospered.   Negroes in general were not
" down " just because the hands of the white people were
against them—their obscurity as individuals was not wholly
due to causes lying outside of themselves.   Their humble
avocations fell to their lot, as to that of the masses of the
whites, because they were qualified chiefly for the kinds of
services called for therein.

Finally a word may be said in comparison of the free
negroes and the slaves.   The two classes shared the same
blood and the same standards of living.   Their identity in
these points was perpetuated through their constant consortship in the marriage relation.   The freedmen in de-
parting from slavery were usually unable to free themselves
from the influences of the life led by the slaves.   Hence
they tended to continue on the level of that life, such that it
seems certain that the average slave was better provided for
than was many a free negro.[2]   Had the 83942 free negroes
exchanged places with the 87189 slave negroes in 1860, but
little difference in the material welfare of the majority of

---

[1] *Cf.* assertion in *Md. Col. Journal*, vol. i, p. 279.

[2] *Cf. 28 Niles Register*, p. 100, and Harper, *op. cit.*, pp. 8-10.

either class would probably have resulted.[1] Reports came from different localities to the effect that one class or the other was superior. Some of them at least are quite credible, because of the uneven distribution of the better class of the negroes. Of such a condition Talbot County afforded an instance. Among its several districts that of Miles Neck had but few free negroes and Chapel a large number, but few of them in either case were of the superior class, while Easton, St. Michael's and Trappe each had a goodly number of the better class.[2] Apparently a similar condition obtained among the colored freemen of Dorchester, Frederick and Somerset counties also.

[1] *Cf. Baltimore American*, Feb. 14, 1860, for remarks by a slaveholder on the re-enslavement project of 1859-60.

[2] The assessment books for the year 1852 seem to corroborate the verbal report that this was true.

CHAPTER X

ATTEMPT TO CHECK THE GROWTH OF FREE NEGRO POPULATION

IT has been stated in preceding chapters that at the time of the revolution the presence of the slave population was viewed with anxiety. In order to check its growth the foreign slave trade was excluded from the ports of Maryland. At the same time the manumission movement began to swell rapidly the numbers of the free negroes. For about a generation both classes of negroes continued to increase. The free negroes were at that time formally almost upon a legal par with the whites. On the economic side, however, they had diverged but little from the condition of the slaves with whom socially they continued to be identified. They were generally treated with as much liberality as the whites felt safe in exercising towards them. But as they had failed to fulfil the obligations and to measure up well to the standards of freemen, it was not difficult to find objections to their continued enjoyment of the customary rights of freemen. They were eventually accused of causing the " evils " that afflicted the state,—they tended to supersede the slaves as the bone of contention in state politics. Proposals to the legislature affecting them, whether liberal or restrictive in tendency, were able to gain a hearing, although those of the latter sort were the more often carried. After the war of 1812 the whites who favored restriction endeavored to check the growth of the free negro class. The history of that endeavor will form the subject of this chapter.

At the beginning of the nineteenth century the white people of the state regarded themselves as the inhabitants of the land. The low position of the negroes was but the consequence of their residing in the white man's country.[1] Their environment, it was said, offered them no hopes for better things, but only increasing unhappiness and discontent. The colonial fathers had sought measures to check the slave trade through the Associations of 1774.[2] The wish that there might be a separation of the two races was cherished early, and plans for getting the negroes out were industriously devised.[3] But all efforts to secure the adoption of plans for the purpose were to fall unheeded, until in 1816 the negro population had grown in the states to about a million and a half, of whom 13 per cent were free. Then was founded the American Society for Colonizing the Free People of Color of the United States. The formation of this society was followed by the planting of branches in at least twenty-two of the states,[4] and by numerous auxiliaries. The continent of Africa was regarded as the fitting home for the negroes, and the United States government secured for the society possession of territory there which was made available for occupation by negro emigrants from the states.[5] Thus was opened the way through

[1] *Letter of General Harper to E. B. Caldwell*, pp. 7, 8; McKenney, *Origin, Progress and Necessity of African Colonization*, p. 9. Cf. *Md. Col. Journal*, vol. i, p. 242.

[2] MacDonald, *Select Charters*, pp. 363-64. McKenney, *op. cit.*, pp. 3-4. The Burgesses in Virginia petitioned the king of Great Britain to assent to an anti-slave trade law.

[3] McKenney, *op. cit.*, pp. 2-8; Washington, *Writings of Thomas Jefferson*, vol. v, pp. 563-64.

[4] *Colonization of the Free People of Color of Maryland*, 1832, p. 5; McKenney, *op. cit.*, pp. 12, 14. Cf. also *Republican Star and Eastern Shore General Advertiser*, Dec. 31, 1816.

[5] McKenney, *op. cit.*, p. 19. Cf. also *H. Dels. Journal*, 1818, p. 73, and Latrobe, *Maryland in Liberia*, p. 9.

which it was hoped that the negroes might be induced to pass away from the United States.[1]

The white people deemed themselves the arbiters of the destiny of the negroes. They were perhaps agreed at the time that slavery was not to be a permanent institution on American soil; and they were generally opposed to federal interference with slavery in the states. But they were far from being agreed as to how the state of Maryland should attempt ultimately to dispose of its negro citizens. In order to explain the state's course with regard to colonization it is necessary to take account of the different interests and sentiments of the people. First there were the tobacco producers and slave-holders who were domineering towards the others who did not share their interests. They regarded the social position of their class as a patrimonium which was to be passed on undiminished from generation to generation. In order to maintain the social order they preferred they were determined to protect and perpetuate slavery. They were sensitive about movements and proposals that might affect that cherished institution. They were opposed to free negroes, and hence to a manumission of slaves, but tended to favor colonization chiefly for the sake of getting rid of the free negro menace to slavery. Biding the fruition of the colonization scheme they favored measures to compel the free negroes to be industrious, in order that they might be peaceful and happy and be kept from exerting a baneful influence upon the slaves.[3] They favored severities or mild measures according as the objects in view might be best attained, for, they alleged, such measures would in the

---

[1] Washington, *op. cit.*, vol. vii, pp. 332-33.

[2] *Cf. H. Dels. Journal*, 1790, pp. 83, 102; 1791, p. 106; also *American Farmer*, series 3, vol. i, pp. 107, 187.

[3] *Md. Col. Journal*, vol. i, p. 160; *Md. Pub. Documents*, 1841 H, p. 4.

end prove themselves to be humane. By no means were the negroes to be allowed to attain a vantage ground which could warrant them in aspiring to equality with the whites. These views had been so often foisted upon the public that dissent from them appeared to be disloyalty to the best interests of the state. They therefore had great influence among the people. But they were the views chiefly of those who wished to maintain the old order of things prevailing in the non-progressive counties.[1] They had become the sentiments of a minority, but those holding to other views were not united in sentiment as were these. The grain growers and stock-raisers, referred to in an earlier chapter as turning to free labor, still held some slaves and often joined in the complaints against the free negroes. The manufacturing and trading classes and their employees tended to adopt the free labor point of view, although they were not distinctly hostile to slavery. These classes generally opposed harsh restrictions upon manumissions and upon free negroes. But they saw that the emancipation of slaves was in progress; they thought that in course of time it would be completed, and that it was the wisest policy to protect and to elevate the condition of the freedmen.[2] In some of their views they were joined by the conservative slave-holders, and they constantly acted as a check upon the advocates of harsh measures. From their number came certain leading champions of the colonization scheme. The small number of out-and-out abolitionists were a negligible factor.

In the three decades following the first federal census the free negroes of the United States increased from 7.8 per cent to 13.5 per cent of the whole negro population.

[1] Cf. Md. Pub. Documents, 1843 M, p. 46; 1845 G, p. 17; and Baltimore Gazette, March 17, 1832.

[2] Cf. editorial in 13 Niles Register, p. 82; also Easton Gazette, Jan. 22, 1842; Cecil Whig, Jan. 22, 1842; Md. Col. Journal, vol. i, pp. 122-23.

Those of Maryland increased from 7.2 per cent to 26.9 per cent, and from 13.5 per cent to 17 per cent of all free negroes in the union. The announcement of the colonization plan, although widely welcomed, was also greeted with jeers and hisses. Its promoters were accused of quixotism and utopianism on the one hand and of iniquitous desire to perpetuate slavery on the other.[1] Nevertheless the Maryland people furnished many of the leaders in establishing the American Colonization Society. They also organized auxiliary societies in Annapolis and Baltimore[2] and contributed liberally towards supplying the equipment of the first emigrant expedition to the African coast.[3] Their legislature had suggested that the federal government should acquire the territory mentioned above.[4] It later urged the federal government to aid and protect the interests of the American Colonization Society, and in 1826 itself made an appropriation of $1000 a year, which it continued until 1832 in order to promote the cause.[5] This "first efficient support" given to the society by any state government was held up to the other states as worthy of emulation.[6]

The primary aim of colonization was to remove the free negroes. On that account the House of Delegates hailed

---

[1] McKenney, *op. cit.*, p. 13; *Md. Republican*, Jan. 16, 1821; *Niles Register*, vol. xvii, pp. 201-02; vol. xviii, p. 298; and vol. xiii, p. 82.

[2] *Federal Gazette*, July 9, 15, and Aug. 6, 1817; Griffith, *Annals of Baltimore*, p. 223; McKenney, *op. cit.*, p. 14; *18 Niles Register*, p. 415; *Md. Republican*, Feb. 10, 1818; *Genius of Universal Emancipation*, series 2, vol. i, p. 149.

[3] McKenney, *op. cit.*, *Federal Gazette*, Jan. 1, 1820; *H. Dels. Journal*, 1825, p. 338.

[4] *H. Dels. Journal*, 1817, resolution no. 5, and 1819, p. 73.

[5] *Op. cit.*, 1825, Joint Resolution no. 547; *Laws*, 1826, ch. 172. *Cf. Repealing Act of 1832*, ch. 314; also *H. Dels. Journal*, 1829, p. 21.

[6] *Md. Republican*, March 10, 1827; *11th Annual Report of American Colonization Society*, p. 48.

it as "the hope of the Slaveholding states,"[1] and the state gave its financial support. The return derived by the country from the work of the organization, however, was small. The census of 1830 showed that in ten years the free negro population had increased by 33 per cent, becoming thereby more than 33 per cent of the total negro population. That increase alone exceeded by more than 200 per cent the number of negroes removed by the colonization society from the entire United States in the fourteen years of its career.[2] Proceeding at that rate the success of the enterprise was not assured, and the interest in it, writes Latrobe, was on the wane.[3] The Maryland leaders convinced of the practicability of the plan, when given a fair chance, desired increased facilities for accomodating emigrants from their state.[4] They were influenced also by events that took place outside the state. In the establishment of the American Colonization Society, some of its supporters, particularly in the northern states, had desired a clear avowal that the extirpation of slavery was the goal. But as that would have risked the loss of the necessary support of the slave-holders, it was left out.[5] These friends were pleased with the action taken by the society against the foreign slave trade and continued for a time hoping to give also an anti-slavery turn to its activities. But more than a decade had passed, and the southern leaders seemed less tractable to anti-slavery influences than they had been at the beginning. Maryland had even repulsed the two

---

[1] *Journal*, 1827, p. 342.

[2] McKenney, *op. cit.*, p. 19. Less than 4000 negroes had been removed through the work of the society up to 1830.

[3] *Maryland in Liberia*, p. 12. Cf. *Md. Col. Journal*, vol. i, p. 2, and *Baltimore American*, September 21, 1842.

[4] *Md. Col. Journal*, no. 1; *Baltimore American*, March 5, 1822.

[5] Cf. *Md. Col. Journal*, no. 1, and McKenney, *op. cit.*, p. 23.

leading anti-slavery agitators of the day and had practically
sealed the lips of their sympathizers within her borders.
The mask was off! and the meaning of colonization was
made clear! Many at the north withdrew from the society [1]
and joined the abolitionists who were just then rising into
prominence in the effort to encompass its defeat. The effect of these circumstances upon the Maryland people was
signal. It was said that the colonizationist leaders were
mainly members of the Whig party. Their argument now
ran that the colonization interest was being identified
with the slavery interest. That inasmuch as slavery was a
local institution, it was proper to leave it to the state to
work out its own problem. Extraneous interference, therefore, without the solicitation of the local people, was unwelcome.[2] Maryland, the chief sufferer from the free negroes,
had done a good part by the American Colonization Society,
and its work had been futile for her relief. It was able to
care for its own interests, and this state, although not in
opposition or rivalry with it, would attempt to care for her
own.[3] Moreover, in August 1831 occurred the Southampton massacre in neighboring Virginia.[4] The affair was at
once attributed to abolitionist machinations,[5] and rumors had
it that similar scenes were to be staged in Maryland. The

[1] McKenney, *op. cit.*

[2] *H. Dels. Journal*, 1829, p. 21. *Cf. Md. Col. Journal*, vol. i, p. 2,
and *Baltimore American*, Sept. 21, 1842.

[3] *Md. Col. Journal*, no. 1 (1835).

[4] Drewry, *Slave Insurrections in Virginia*, pp. 35-64; *41 Niles Register*, pp. 4, 19, 35; and *Village Herald*, Sept. 1831.

[5] *Cf.* Hart, *Slavery and Abolition*, pp. 217-20; Rhodes, *History of the
United States*, vol. i, pp. 56-57; Schouler, *History of the United
States*, vol. iv, p. 210; also *Snow Hill Messenger*, August 30, Oct. 18
and Nov. 1, 1831; also *Confession of Nat Turner*, advertised for sale
in *Hagerstown Torchlight*, Dec. 8, 1831. *Cf.* also *Cambridge Chronicle*, Sept. 3 and Aug. 27, 1831, and *Maryland Journal and True American*, Jan. 18, 1839.

horrors of St. Domingo were recalled, and the kingdom of slavery was thrown into a state of terror. The opportunity of those who favored restriction of free negroes seemed to have come. Colonization became quickly popularized.

In its session of 1830 the House of Delegates had declared the growth of the free negro population a grave matter.[1] In that of 1831 memorials came up from various quarters praying for action upon it. Several of them had desired the abolition of slavery, but for the most part they asked for more stringent police regulations to keep order among the negroes, for the curtailment of manumissions and for the removal of the free negroes from the state.[2] They were referred to the Committee on Grievances and Courts of Justice of which one Brawner, of Charles County, was chairman. Committees of the two houses met in joint conference before the House committee brought in its report. That report deplored the exodus of whites from the state and condemned the free negroes *carte blanche*. It declared that their presence was injurious to the prosperity of the people, that they were not only menacing to its " dearest interests and happiness," but that time was augmenting the evils. It was predicted that the time was drawing near when the " evils " could no longer be borne. It referred respectfully to the petitions for abolition but ignored them in its recommendations of " remedies " that it deemed necessary, if the state was to be saved from ruin.[3] A bill also

[1] *Journal*, 1830, p. 136.

[2] *Op. cit.*, 1831, pp. 106, 147, 148 (*Somerset Co.*), 154 (*Frederick* and two others), 167 (*Prince George's*), 201 (*Kent*), 223 (*Talbot* and *Queen Anne's*). Cf. *Baltimore Gazette*, March 17, 1832, and *61 Niles Register*, p. 216.

[3] *Baltimore Gazette*, March 17, 1832. Cf. *American Farmer*, 1829, p. 167, and *Village Herald*, Oct. 4, 1831. Regarding action proposed in Virginia two months earlier, *Niles Register*, in its vol. 41, p. 340, said: " The public attention, we think, is unfortunately chiefly called to the

was brought in. It repeated the prohibitions against the importations of slaves and the immigration of free negroes and proposed that every free negro in the state should be required to register annually in a public office and pay a fee of a dollar and a half therefor, failing which he was not to be allowed to work for any employer in the state; that every slave manumitted thereafter should be sold by the state as a slave for life, unless he left the state within three months, or unless his manumitters paid the sum of fifty dollars for his expatriation; and that no religious meetings of negroes were to be permitted without the presence of a white minister.[1] Its publication made a profound impression. The people had desired to have laws to check the growth of the free negroes but were not prepared to sanction what was here offered. The male members of the Light Street Methodist Church in Baltimore, moved " with alarm and deep solicitude " sent in a memorial reciting their objections to it. They asserted that the registry provision, if enforced as law, would almost certainly deprive many negroes of the right to earn an honest living; that the manumission tax would discriminate against manumission by slave-holders who were not able to pay it; that it would lead to defeat for the plan to prevent the growth of the negro population, inasmuch as the slaves increased faster than the free negroes; and that its stopping the mouths of the negro preachers would endanger the church's influence with their

free blacks. The elements of mischief we apprehend, are not so much in them as in the slaves. The first have some powerful motives to behave well, which cannot have influence over the second, when tempted to commit outrages on white persons." The Pennsylvania legislators were just then, January 1832, reported to have been resolving to resist the sending of free negroes from other states to reside in their midst. *Op. cit.*

[1] *Cf.* copies of the bill, *Baltimore American*, Feb. 24, 1832; *Maryland Republican*, Feb. 24, 1832; *Cambridge Chronicle*, Feb. 25, 1832; and *Maryland Journal and True American*, Feb. 28, 1832.

race. Finally, it contended that the "obligations of humanity and justice in reference to the colored population" demanded that radical measures that would imperil their interests ought not to be passed.[1] Protests against passing the bill also came from Centerville and other parts of the state.[2]

As a consequence the House omitted the provisions for the registry and for taxing manumissions, modified that on religious meetings and passed a materially altered measure.[3] The outcome of the efforts were two acts, one containing regulations for the free negro residents of Maryland,[4] and the other provisions regarding residence and colonization of manumitted slaves and of free negroes. The latter declared that slaves manumitted in future were to be removed from the state to some foreign colony, or to some place in the United States to which they would consent to go. It ordered the clerk of the county court and the register of wills in each county to send to the colonization society the names of all negroes whose manumissions were recorded in their respective offices, and the sheriffs to deliver the negroes to the colonization society to be sent away. But there were two exceptions: first, any negro whose going away would sever certain family ties might renounce freedom and remain in the state, and second, any negro who could procure a certificate of "extraordinarily" good character from the orphans' court of his county might remain in the state

[1] *Baltimore American*, March 5, 1832.

[2] The *Cambridge Chronicle* on March 10 expressed doubt whether the bill would be passed in its then existing form. Cf. *Village Herald*, March 13, 1832, and *Maryland Journal and True American*, Feb. 28, 1832. The latter takes an extreme position in favor of stringent measures. Also *Cambridge Chronicle*, March 17, 1832.

[3] *Easton Gazette*, March 10, 17, 1832.

[4] *Laws*, 1831, ch. 323. Its chief provisions are given in the chapter on Legal Status, *supra*, pp. 94-129.

for twelve months. Free negroes and slaves whose manumissions had been already recorded were to be transported, whenever they would consent to go.[1] These acts did not satisfy the rampant opponents of the free negroes, nor did the compulsory features of the colonizing clauses please the colonizationists. They were the result of a compromise. Nevertheless they marked an epoch in the policy of Maryland towards the negroes.[2]

Preparations were also made to give effect to the colonization statute. During the session of the legislature just referred to the Maryland State Colonization Society was formed and incorporated.[3] The colonization act included a clause authorizing an appropriation of $10,000 a year to the work and providing for a special tax levy to raise the funds to meet the charge.[4] It further empowered the Governor and Council to appoint a board of managers of three members to superintend the expenditure of the fund and to co-operate with the State Society in its colonizing labors. This board was to scrutinize the acts of the society, to procure and disseminate information about the Liberian colony and about certain other colonizing places,[5] to select

[1] *Laws*, 1831, ch. 281.

[2] A writer to the *Snow Hill Messenger* of May 28, 1832, considered the colonization plan to be of no probable avail at all. He would have sent the free negroes to the unoccupied southwestern country. He was opposed to chattel slavery, and at the time of writing was a candidate for a seat in the legislature.

[3] *Laws*, 1831, ch. 314. *Cf. Code of 1860*, ch. 283; *Md. Col. Jour.*, vol. i, p. 2; also Latrobe, *Maryland in Liberia*, pp. 12-13.

[4] *Laws*, 1831, ch. 281. Cf. Act of 1834, ch. 197, in which the school funds of the Western Shore counties were pledged to make good any deficits in the colonization funds of counties which should fail to impose the colonization tax. The appropriation was kept up until 1858. *Cf. op. cit.*, 1852, ch. 202.

[5] *16th Annual Report of American Colonization Society*, pp. 35-36; *Senate Journal*, 1839, p. 3; *Md. Col. Journal*, vol. iii, p. 322. *Cf. Laws*, 1831, ch. 281.

subjects for colonization from among those offering to go, to remove to Liberia, or elsewhere, those whom it selected, and once at their destination to aid them in procuring a living, until they should become self-supporting, and finally to render an account to the state government for the funds and the trust committed to its hands.[1] It made the State Society its agent for removing the negroes, and in that manner continued for three decades to patronize and support the work of removal. The legislature repealed the act making the appropriation for the American Colonization Society[2] and Maryland became free to pursue her own course for her own relief.

The methods and objects of the colonization society must be noted carefully, because they were sometimes misrepresented. It was not a scheme of coercion that they had in mind, even though the act of 1831 had authorized coercive expatriation of slaves manumitted after its enactment. Its realization was to be " the voluntary emigration of the free people of color."[3] The activities of the society were intended to prepare the territory in Africa for the occupation of the emigrants, to establish there such worthy negroes as would consent to go, allow them to manage their own affairs, both public and private, as soon as they could be placed in control and, as far as possible, to invest the place with such attractions for the negro as America possessed for the indigent European.[4] For a time, it was hoped the increase of the negroes could be taken away,

---

[1] H. Dels. Journal, 1832, p. 199; Md. Pub. Documents, 1834, Report on the Colored Population, pp. 2, 3.

[2] Laws, 1832, ch. 314.

[3] Md. Col. Journal, vol. i, p. 2. Cf. vol. iii, p. 322; vol. ii, p. 99; Baltimore American, Nov. 22, 1832; H. Dels. Journal, 1860, p. 584; and Laws, 1831, ch. 314.

[4] Md. Col. Journal, vol. iii, p. 2. Cf. op. cit., no. 1 (1835).

but hardly the entire number.[1] Beyond that point the society was to employ methods like those of an immigration agency. It was to advertise the country, to attempt to educate the negroes to regard Africa as their proper home and to facilitate their going and settlement there. It foresaw the need of supplies in the colony, the establishment of frequent intercourse with America in order to acquire them and an increasing disposition of negroes to inquire about and go to Africa. Finally, when the superiority of African residence for them had been fully discovered, they would seek to go eagerly. Emigration would thus grow rapidly and the local negro population would be decimated. By that time many of the slaves would have been manumitted and plans matured for the release and deportation of the rest. Thus slavery would be extinguished and the state wholly relieved of its African population.[2]

The success of colonization depended upon the assistance and cooperation of the white population in the removal and the willingness of the negroes to be deported. In order to enlist both classes in the work a traveling agent was employed, branch societies were founded and a journal established. Moreover, the church became an active ally in the cause. From the outset a traveling agent was kept in the field almost constantly. From 1833 to 1841 this agent was also the agent of the managers of the state colonization fund, but his salary and expenses were paid from the pro-

---

[1] McKenney, *op. cit.*, p. 13. *Cf. Maryland Scheme of Expatriation Examined*, p. 6; *9th Annual Report of American Colonization Society*, p. 7; and *Niles Register*, vol. xvii, p. 29, and vol. xxi, p. 265.

[2] *Cf.* Harper, *op. cit.*, p. 11; *Report of Managers of Colonization Fund*, 1834, p. 8; *H. Dels. Journal*, 1832, p. 26; *17 Niles Register*, p. 371; *Easton Star*, Jan. 8, 1850. And for critical views, *vide Md. Republican*, Jan. 16, 1821; *Maryland Scheme of Expatriation Examined*, p. 13; and *Wanderings on the Seas and Shores of Africa*, part 1, p. 29.

ceeds of voluntary contributions to the cause.[1]   The agent's office was amplified in 1841 and from 1856 to 1859 was divided between two persons.[2]   The duties of the agent consisted of visiting, making addresses and giving information about colonization to the people throughout the state, organizing branch societies, soliciting collections for the support of the work, canvassing for emigrants, receiving candidates for colonization and assisting them in their embarkation for Liberia.[3]   His work in some parts of the state was greatly assisted by the auxiliary societies which succeeded to the place of the local auxiliaries of the American Colonization Society.[4]   Owing to the zeal for colonization which had attended the legislation of 1832 several more such societies were organized.[5]   After the state convention of 1841 still others were formed.[6]   Among these were the Society of Enquiry of Govanstown and the Cambridge African Colonization Society, both of which were made up of negroes only.[7]   They were organized to facilitate the dissemination of intelligence and to promote the activities of the society in the respective communities.   They assisted somewhat in keeping alive interest and in raising funds to

[1] *Md. Col. Jour.*, vol. iii, p. 322; Latrobe, *op. cit.*, p. 59; *16th Ann. Report of Amer. Col. Society*, p. 35; *Md. Pub. Docs.*, 1840 no. 4, p. 4; *Maryland Republican*, Jan. 23, 1835; *Md. Col. Jour.*, vol. i, p. 9.

[2] *Cf. 60 Niles Register*, p. 227; *Md. Col. Jour.*, vol. ix, pp. 337-38.

[3] *Md. Pub. Docs.*, 1844, no. 4, p. 4; *Md. Col. Jour.*, vol. i, p. 5; vol. ii, p. 238; vol. v, pp. 247-48. *Cf. Laws*, 1831, ch. 231, sec. 3.

[4] *Supra*, p. 265. *Cf. Federal Gazette*, July 9, 1817; *Maryland Republican*, Feb. 10, 1818; *Fredericktown Herald*, April 9, 1825; *Genius of Universal Emancipation*, series 2, vol. i, pp. 149, 177, and *9th Annual Report of American Colonization Society*, pp. 53, 55. There had been at least eight auxiliaries before 1830.

[5] *Centreville Times*, June 23 and July 14, 1832.

[6] *Md. Col. Journal*, vol. i, pp. 1, 15, and *cf.* p. 93.

[7] *Op. cit.*, vol. ii, pp. 242-43; vol. vi, pp. 6-7. *Cf. 35th Annual Report of American Colonization Society*, p. 44.

pay expenses,[1] but evidently their careers were like that
of the Chestertown branch which was reorganized "three
of four times" within a term of five years.[2] The endeavor
to organize the whole people "in every town, village and
neighborhood" in the state[3] was far from being realized.
The chief effective organ of the movement was the central
state society itself, although some of the branches were intermittently quite active.

Aside from the traveling agents the press was the most
effective agency in spreading information. The newspapers
devoted approving articles to the subject and sometimes asserted that the free negroes would have to be removed from
the state,[4] in order to secure the permanent peace and prosperity of the people. The colonization society, however,
established in 1835 a sheet of its own, known as the Maryland Colonization Journal. It became a bi-monthly at the
end of 1836 and a monthly in 1838. Fifty-one issues appeared in all by the month of May, 1841. A change of
editors then came with the new impetus to the colonization
movement, and the journal entered upon a new era. It
became a sixteen-page octavo magazine and continued so
for twenty years. In spirit it was truly colonizationist,
avoiding alliance with the extremes of either pro-slavery or
anti-slavery.[5] It held colonization to be, not the means of

[1] 60 *Niles Register*, p. 227; *Maryland Republican*, April 4, 1829; and
Easton Star, July 8, 15, 1856.

[2] *Md. Col. Journal*, no. 11 (1837). *Cf.* also vol. vi, p. 5.

[3] *Baltimore Gazette*, May 15, 1832, and *Md. Col. Journal*, vol. i, p. 15.

[4] *Vide Baltimore Clipper*, quoted in *Md. Col. Journal*, 1840, p. 152,
and *Frederick Examiner*, March 24, 1858, and June 1, 1859.

[5] In 1847 the editor wrote: "We not infrequently receive letters from
our lower county subscribers wishing a discontinuance on the score of
our tendency to abolitionism. Then again we have an exchange refused
us in the north because our poor journal is but the 'tool of slavoc-
racy' in Maryland." Vol. iii, pp. 321-22.

riveting the bonds of the slaves, but of removing free negroes and manumitted slaves to a real home of freedom, until the state should have become free from both slavery and negroes. Its editor hugged throughout his delusions as to the practicability of colonization and as to convincing the negroes of its beneficence. " It was intended mainly as a vehicle of information respecting the Colony (Liberia) and the Colonists for the friends of the cause in the State and for the free people of color." [1] Its articles, therefore, dealt at length with the acts and proceedings of the colonization societies of the United States, with the removals of emigrant negroes, and with the condition of those who had taken up residence in the African settlements. They dwelt also upon the attitude of the whites towards the negroes and contrasted the dark features of negro life in the United States with its brighter prospects in Africa. As a journal it was well conducted and thus became an invaluable source of information about the colonization movement in Maryland.

These instrumentalities created by the movement were aided and re-enforced by the churches. Many members of the churches shared in the view that the " evils " caused by the negroes could best be remedied by separation of the two races. The missionary churches also found additional reason for favoring the movement, because it was carrying the means and elements necessary to the Christianization of Africa and was encouraging missionary work from the new colonies as a base.[2] It was repeatedly endorsed by " various Conventions, Conferences and Synods " of the several religious societies,[3] and ministers were urged to advocate its interests and to take collections for its support.

[1] *Op. cit.*

[2] *Md. Col. Journal*, vol. i, p. 197, and vol. ii, p. 177.

[3] *Op. cit.*, vol. vi, p. 1.

The Baltimore Conference of the Methodist Episcopal Church in 1852 alleged that its success would remove the evil of slavery whose existence had become a menace to the union between the states.[1] Church buildings throughout the state were commonly made the assembly halls for colonization meetings;[2] Christian missions and colonization were preached together from the pulpits; and from the ranks of the clergy were drawn nearly every one of the traveling agents of the society. The congregations of the churches too, although they often neglected the matter, took so many colonization collections that they were almost upbraided, when they failed to give regularly to the cause.[3] The negro churches were generally either lukewarm or opposed to the movement altogether.[4]

An effort was made to prevent every objection that could be raised against emigration to the colony. By authority of law the managers of the state fund and the colonization society combined resources to offer gratuitous transportation for negro emigrants, for the members of their families and their household goods, implements and utensils—due regard being promised for the safety and comfort of passengers *en route*. Dr. Hall wrote that the

Society's agent, the governor of the colony, will furnish them with a good dwelling-house for the first six months after their arrival . . . and will supply them during the same period with good provisions and necessaries of all kinds including medical

---

[1] *Op. cit.*, pp. 162-63.

[2] *Vide e. g.*, *Federal Gazette*, July 1, 1818; *Genius of Universal Emancipation*, series 2, vol. ii, pp. 94-95; *Village Herald*, May 29, 1832; *Baltimore American*, March 5, 1832; *Md. Col. Journal*, vol. vi, pp. 3-6; 60 *Niles Register*, p. 277; and *Political Examiner*, May 2, 1841.

[3] *Md. Col. Journal*, vol. vi, pp. 1-2. *Cf.* vol. i, p. 193; vol. ii, p. 177; vol. iii, p. 2; vol. v, p. 171; and *Md. Col. Journal*, series 1, p. 170.

[4] *Infra*, p. 292.

attendance, medicine and nursing, if necessary, during the six months—and all without pay or compensation of any kind. The agent, also, will give to each male (or female) adult or head of a family on their arrival five good acres of land adjoining that of the old settlers to be theirs forever, on condition that it is improved—and this, also, free of charge or expense.[1]

Larger tracts of land more remote were promised to those who showed ability to cultivate them, and money for building purposes was to be had at reasonable rates with the privilege of payment on the fructification of the settler's labor.[2]   Besides,

each adult male on arrival in the colony and signing the constitution will be admitted to all the rights and privileges of citizenship, will have the right to vote, to bears arms for the national defence, the right of trial by jury, etc., etc.   After two years an eligibility is acquired to any office in the colony.[3]

But these privileges were confined to those who had been *bona fide* residents of Maryland.[4]

One of the objects of Maryland's separate venture in colonization was to secure increased facilities for deporting emigrants.   For more than ten years the state society depended in part upon the vessels afforded by the American Colonization society,[5] and made up expeditions of its own, only when the number of emigrants from this state alone was sufficient to demand separate transportation.   It was

---

[1] *Md. Col. Journal*, vol. ii, p. 48.   *Cf.* also vol. iv, p. 72.

[2] *67 Niles Register*, p. 210.

[3] *Md. Col. Journal*, vol. i, p. 256.

[4] *Op. cit.*, vol. i, p. 308.

[5] McKenney, *op. cit.*, p. 22; *Report of the Board of Managers*, 1834, p. 11; *16th Annual Report of American Colonization Society*, p. 14, and *Md. Col. Journal*, vol. i, p. 5.

desired, however, to establish regular communication between the ports of Maryland and those of Liberia and to
build up a voluntary commerce, which, it was felt, would
provide adequate space for emigrants and their goods, place
the Liberian experiment upon its merits, and go far to dispel
the imputations that colonization had been conceived out of
hostility to the negroes' welfare.[1]   To accomplish this purpose it was suggested in 1838 that a packet service should be
established between Baltimore and Cape Palmas.[2]   The project was endorsed by the colonization convention in 1841,
and subscriptions were opened to get funds with which to
carry it into effect.[3]   The plan was not given practical form,
however, until in 1844 a Baltimore negro suggested that a
trading company should be formed among the colored
people.   At the next session of the legislature a charter act
was passed for the Chesapeake and Liberia Trading Company, about one fourth of the stock being subscribed by
Baltimore and Liberian negroes.[4]   After a further delay
on account of the Oregon boundary dispute the subscriptions were at last filled in, a keel was laid, and on December 3, 1846 a barque, especially constructed for this
service, sailed out of Baltimore harbor carrying thirty-nine
Maryland emigrants.[5]   It had been the design to allow the
negroes to take over the stock of the company that was held
by the whites as fast as they subscribed for it and to place
the whole enterprise in their hands.   The colonization
society made good its guarantee of freights and passenger

[1] *Md. Col. Journal,* vol. i, p. 8, and vol. ii, p. 365.

[2] *Md. Col. Journal,* series 1, no. 17.   *Cf. Maryland Republican,* Jan.
26, 1839, and *Md. Col. Journal,* vol. ii, p. 337.

[3] *Op. cit.,* vol. i, p. 15; vol. ii, p. 337; and 60 *Niles Register,* p. 227.

[4] *Laws,* 1844, ch. 195.   *Cf. Md. Col. Journal,* vol. ii, pp. 337-38; vol.
iii, p. 130, and vol iv, pp. 72, 76.

[5] *Op. cit.,* pp. 210, 241, 257, 274.

fares, and for several years the company paid substantial dividends,[1] but the negroes failed to increase their stock-holdings. Increased demands for service led to the charter-ing of vessels that were larger and to the sale of the com-pany's own boat. From that time forward the voyages were made as they had been prior to 1846.[2]

The object of colonization was to get the negroes out of the country. It was designed first of all to promote the in-terests of the whites.[3] It was held that the different elements of the mixed population would have to either be-come equals and therefore amalgamate, or remain unequal and be separated. Amalgamation was not to be thought of,[4] because of the extremely diverse characteristics of the two races: their fusion would surely drag down the one without elevating the other by way of compensation, and racial decay would follow. Aversion to that sort of con-tact and to such results rendered equality between the races impossible. The alternative was inequality, domination of one race by the other, which could not continue without provoking discontent and eventually internecine strife. Such a condition was inconsistent with the maintenance of republican government and had long been a disturbing factor in both state and federal politics.[5] Its perpetuation

[1] *Op. cit.*, vol. iv, pp. 76-77, and vol. vi, p. 275.

[2] In 1856 one, John Stevens, of Talbot County, gave the sum of $37,000 to build a packet for the Liberian service. He had planned to make the gift to the Maryland society, but after consulting with the managers decided to give it to the American Colonization Society, with provision for the carrying of Maryland emigrants under condi-tions. *Md. Col. Jour.*, vol. viii, pp. 130, 389. *Cf.* Latrobe, *op. cit.*, p. 83.

[3] *Cf.* Harper, *op. cit.*, pp. 6, 10, and Garrison, *Thoughts on Coloniza-tion*, p. 22, resolve passed by a negro meeting.

[4] *Cf. Report of Board of Managers*, 1834, p. 8; Harper, *op. cit.*, p. 6; and *Md. Col. Journal*, vol. i, p. 242.

[5] *Cf. Md. Col. Journal*, vol. i, pp. 241-42, and vol. vi, pp. 162-63. For several years the front page of the *Maryland Colonization Journal*

would lead to further trouble. Again, the fear of blind servile rebellions was ever present. The free negro, it was thought, made the slave long for freedom and inclined him to attempt to strike for it. Vicious free negroes were feared as the instigators of rebellions. Prudence and self-preservation, therefore, dictated that measures should be taken to forestall any such outbreaks. The free negro, moreover, was an injury to the white man's property. It was impossible to separate him from the slave upon whom his idleness, vice and precarious habits exerted a baneful influence. As a result of the association the slave tended to become restive, averse to labor and insubordinate; his usefulness for labor and, therefore, his value diminished.[1] The community of Maryland had been settled and brought to its then existing condition by the whites. It was a white man's country, and its constitutional liberty the heritage of the white man. The negro had no proper part in it.[2]

contained the following quotation from the pen of Jefferson: " Nothing is more clearly written in the Book of Destiny than the Emancipation of the Blacks; and it is equally certain that the two races will never live in a state of equal freedom under the same government, so insurmountable are the barriers which nature, habit and opinion have established between them." It was inserted first in September 1842, and removed in December 1849. Referring to it Dr. Hall wrote: ". . . . The black and white race (*sic*) can never live on terms of equality under the same government. This position is not only supported by the opinions of eminent politicians and philosophers of the present day, but all history declares its validity. On terms of equality, two distinct races of men cannot exist together. They never did, and never will. They must wholly part or wholly mingle. Amalgamation must take place—universal amalgamation of the Caucasian and the African race in these United States and both be swallowed up in a mongrel posterity:—or they must be separated—and the weaker and less energetic race seek a home in other lands, as has ever been the case in all ages of the world under like circumstances." Vol. i, pp. 241-42.

[1] Harper, *op. cit.*, pp. 8-10.

[2] *Cf.* memorial of certain negroes, *Baltimore Gazette*, Dec. 14, 1826, and duplicate in *Genius of Universal Emancipation*, ser. 2, vol. ii, pp. 94-95.

Could he be withdrawn and his place taken by the free white man,[1] he might have all the liberty possible in a state of his own and no longer be, as he was here, a source of danger both to the white man and himself.

In a secondary sense colonization was an altruistic enterprise—it looked to the welfare of the negroes also. The argument for emigration was most emphasized with this point. The negro was an unbidden guest in America, and for his own sake he ought to have been willing to go away. But his life in this country was to be portrayed in dark colors. He was nominally a free man, but his " freedom " had brought him into a position worse than slavery.[2] Social barriers which he could not surmount debarred him from elevating himself. The hands of the whites were against him to repress him and prevent the expansion of his intellect. The legitimate pursuit of honorable ambitions was denied him, a stigma rested upon his honest toil, and he was being displaced by white men in manual labor which had once been considered his own domain.[3] He was not to expect concessions of civil or social equality with the whites, because his color and his shortcomings had doomed him to everlasting inferiority. Every influence of his environment tended to degrade him, and his debasement, although at first compulsory, was becoming voluntary on his own part. The progress of the years served only to increase the evils from which he suffered.[4] A number of

[1] Cf. Harper, op. cit., p. 15, and Md. Col. Journal, vol. i, p. 242.

[2] Report of the Board of Managers, 1834, p. 8; also The Colonization of the Free People of Color of Maryland, p. 4.

[3] Report of Board of Managers, op. cit., pp. 8-9; Colonization of the Free People of Color of Maryland, p. 3; The Maryland Scheme of Expatriation Examined, p. 9; 34th Annual Report of American Colonization Society, p. 57; and H. Dels. Journal, 1860, p. 583.

[4] Harper, op. cit., pp. 6-8; Hall, Address to the Free People of Color of Maryland; Md. Col. Jour., vol. ix, pp. 290-91. Cf. Md. Col. Jour., vol. i, pp. 77, 274; vol. iii, p. 193; vol. vi, pp. 162-63; 63 Niles Register, p. 229.

negroes in Baltimore were induced to sign a statement declaring that " beyond a mere subsistence and the impulse of religion, there is nothing to arouse us to the attainment of eminence." [1]   Finally, looking to the future, Dr. Hall addressed all the free negroes in the state thus: " Shall your children also spiritually endowed with intellect and blest with enterprise grow up under the blighting influence that has cursed your hopes; will you, can you stay where this is the inevitable result?" [2]   The counsels of wisdom and of friendship alike dictated that the negroes should be so guided as to enable them to escape from their wretched lot here.

The colonizationist claimed that his plan was "to effect the most true good to the greatest number of human beings." If his argument was sound, the first step in ameliorating the condition of the negro lay in removing him from the white man's society [3] to one of his own.   In the latter he would not find the good things pre-empted by white men, and would suffer from no unequal competition with white men; he would be relieved of his sense of debasement and would find unrestricted opportunities to reach the full stature of manhood.   For his industry would fructify to his own advantage and places of honor and trust would be open to him.   It would become his duty to rear an independent state —a republic, if he chose—and to disseminate the blessings of liberty among the native Africans. [4]   He would thus

[1] *Genius of Universal Emancipation* 2 ser., vol. ii, pp. 94-95.

[2] *Md. Col. Jour.*, vol. iv, p. 16.   *Cf.* vol. i, pp. 307-08.

[3] *Cf. Md. Col. Jour.*, vol. i, pp. 19, 242; Harper, *op. cit.*, p. 8; *Baltimore American*, Dec. 6, 1842; *H. Dels. Journal*, 1860, p. 583.   Garrison, *Thoughts on Colonization*, p. 22, quotes certain Baltimore negroes who denied the philanthropy of colonization.

[4] Harper, *op. cit.*, pp. 18-19; *Md. Col. Jour.*, vol. iv, pp. 16, 362; vol. ix, p. 290.   And *cf.* vol. v, p. 297; vol. viii, p. 105; also *Carroll Co. Democrat*, May 18, 1854.

become a channel through which religion, science and the arts would be transported, and Africa would become enlightened and civilized by the return of its exiled children. Africa was the promised land of the American bondman, a great field of opportunity. Glorious the effort to regenerate her! Let the stolid negro take inspiration from the occasion! Let him rise up and transform his benighted people for their own sake! No man of whatever color was "a true friend to his country, a true friend to his race who would not labor" to consummate these objects.[1]

And a few years after the establishment of the settlement at Cape Palmas, the experiment was pronounced a success. It was reported that the colonists had prospered, and in 1844 that every family among their number was well housed.[2] They were free from the trammels of American society and were happy. To corroborate these reports letters from colonists were carried to their negro friends in Maryland inviting them to come on, and colonists returned in person to set at nought all doubts and misgivings about the reports.[3] The state society also at times carried over negroes who desired to see Liberia and gave them the option of remaining there or returning to Maryland without cost and without any other obligation to themselves.[4] We have seen above that dissension about ultimate emancipation disrupted the American Colonization Society, that enemies of its work arose among its original members and that Maryland with-

[1] *Md. Col. Jour.*, vol. i, p. 242. *Cf.* vol. ii, pp. 95, 238.

[2] *67 Niles Register*, p. 244; *Md. Col. Jour.*, vol. iii, p. 4.

[3] *Cf. op. cit.*, vol. i, pp. 82-84, 201, 272, 274; vol. ii, pp. 64, 80; vol. iii, p. 354.

[4] *Op. cit.*, vol. iii, p. 354. In making the invitation to the negroes to visit Liberia, the editor of the *Journal* wrote that in due time the packet would "again return to this port, and then, if you choose, you can return to your brush and razor strop, your curry comb, or your dray cart." *Cf.* also *Laws*, 1839, ch. 5, and *infra*, pp. 290-91.

drew support from it.   The opposition had been, as it were, mainly academic.   But Maryland's action, particularly the coercive clause in the colonization act of 1831, seemed to make colonization a buffer between anti-slavery and the slave institution.   And Maryland leaders did not deny that that was their intention.   As soon as this was understood " the colonization policy of Maryland . . . . became the point of virulent and opprobrious assault." [1]   It was an easy mark, because Maryland was accessible from the free states; and defeat for it here meant defeat elsewhere.   Two chief methods of attack were employed, first the broadside, and second personal appeals to the negroes to refuse to emigrate.   The chief publication in the crusade, entitled *The Maryland Scheme of Expatriation Examined,* by a Friend of Liberty, was issued from a Boston press in 1832. It asserted that colonization was no longer dependent upon moral suasion, but upon force,[2] and that there was left to the negro no other alternative than " bondage or exile." Colonization was designed to get rid of the free negro, thereby to deliver the proscribed institution of slavery from harassment by a class of people whose presence menaced it. Colonization policy was a salve to a public mind agitated about the sin of slavery, a purgatory for smiting consciences.   Its authors were cloaking the basest motives under the guise of philanthropy in order to postpone the final emancipation of the slaves.   The whole matter was one of " cold, calculating, selfish, bloody state policy; " it was settled hatred to the negro, " a scheme of most atrocious oppression."   It merited only execration from the public.[3] This pamphlet was followed in 1833 by the Thoughts on

[1] *Md. Col. Jour.,* vol. i, p. 5.

[2] P. 11.   *Cf. Md. Col. Jour.,* vol. i, p. 5.

[3] Pp. 5, 6, 13.   *Cf. Md. Col. Jour.,* vol. i, p. 5; vol. iii, p. 322; vol. iv, p. 362.

Colonization from the pen of the youthful Garrison who had suffered imprisonment for attacking slavery in Maryland. He labored to discover the condemnation of colonization in the writings of its advocates. In ten theses he assailed their motives and conduct.[1] These publications could not have directly reached many of the Maryland negroes, and their influence upon the whites who read them was in the main contrary to that desired by the writers. Nevertheless they became weapons in the hands of abolition emissaries.

In order to frustrate the efforts to execute the colonization plan it was necessary to deal directly with the negroes. And since they could not be well reached through the mails, the method of personal appeal was adopted. Traces of countervailing work were discovered soon after the traveling agents entered the field. The managing board reported in the colonization convention of 1841 that they had every reason to believe that their agents had been

tracked in their missions from place to place—their statements contradicted, their motives assailed, and the grossest falsehoods regarding them uttered by either the paid or the voluntary agents of abolition. Again and again, has the agent taken the names of whole families for emigration, who evidently, at the time of giving them, were wholly ignorant of abolition and its doctrines; and when he has afterwards visited them to collect

[1] The theses were in substance as follows: (1) Colonization is not pledged to oppose the system of slavery. (2) It apologizes for slavery and slave-holders. (3) It recognizes slaves as property. (4) It increases the value of slaves. (5) It is the enemy of immediate abolition. (6) It is nourished by fear and selfishness. (7) It aims at the utter expulsion of the free negroes. (8) It disparages the free negroes. (9) It denies the possibility of elevating the negroes in America. (10) It deceives and misleads the nation. He compiled excerpts from the utterances of colonizationists in such a manner as to give color to his own conclusions. Those whom he attacked would have agreed with him in all except these (6) and (10) and perhaps (7).

them for embarkation, they have refused to accompany him,
urging in excuse the well known arguments of the abolitionists:
and having their minds filled with hopes which it were madness
to believe could be realized, and statements so absurdly false as
to savour of the ludicrous, but for their mischievous and evil
intentioned source . . . . It was the usual remark of the agents
that it was only necessary for a colored man to declare publicly
his intention of emigrating, to make it certain that he would
never leave the state; for the declaration at once made him the
object of the countervailing efforts of the abolitionists.

The arguments of the last were of two kinds, suited to the
character of the individual addressed. To the ignorant, the
weak and timid, it was said that Africa was so unhealthy, that
to live there was impossible—that it abounded in serpents of
vast size and wild beasts, that would destroy the life the climate
spared—that the natives were warlike and ferocious, killing
and eating their enemies—and that they were constantly at war
with the colonists—that the accounts given by the colonizationists were all false—that they were in fact, slave traders—that
often, when their vessels with emigrants had cleared the Capes
of the Chesapeake, they ran down the coast to Georgia, and
there the emigrants were sold—or else they were carried still
further south, to unknown lands, to die by violence. To those
of the colored people who knew better than listen to these
absurdities, the argument assumed another shape, and the intelligent and the ambitious were told that all emigrants were
traitors to their race—that every emigrant to Africa diminished
by one the numerical force upon which they had to rely for
extorting from the fears, what they could not obtain from the
justice, of the whites—political and social equality—called
among the colored people, in common parlance, " their rights "
—that if Colonization could be destroyed by continued opposition from the coloured people themselves—for without emigrants it could not exist—then the whites would seriously consider how far they could yield to the other race an equal participation in all political and social privileges . . . The two sets of
arguments found hearers among the colored people, according

to the intelligence of the individual addressed; and being constantly urged for the last ten years, have formed the most serious obstacle in the way of the Society.[1]

From time to time thereafter additional deterrents were discovered. In one case it was reported that the emigrants would have to pay all the costs of the African colony, in another that the negroes' correspondence with their friends on the other side was tampered with in the mails, and in a third case that chattel slavery prevailed in Liberia as well as in Maryland.[2] It seems certain that these reports had not been either gratuitously conceived by the negroes or circulated by those interested in the success of the colonization movement. They probably came from beyond the borders of the state.[3]

At the beginning the negro was ignorant of the merits of the colonization plan, and perhaps apathetic about a change of country for himself. The things done both for and against emigration were intended to influence his decision. He was so easy to persuade that, in order to get his consent to go, it was only necessary to explain what his part in it was to be.[4] " It seemed to have grown into a general belief, on the part of the colored people, that their interests would be promoted by emigration."[5]   Up to 1832 it was not dif-

[1] *Md. Col. Journal*, vol. i, pp. 5-6. *Cf. Report of Board of Managers*, 1834, p. 14, and *H. Dels. Journal*, 1860, p. 583.

[2] *Md. Col. Journal*, vol. ii, p. 290, vol. vi, p. 18, and vol. viii, p. 306.

[3] In the *Colonization Journal* in 1837 it was reported that, while a body of emigrants was preparing to sail, " every stratagem practised by men kept in pay for the vile work of lying by wholesale, who pressed themselves unreasonably and unasked into the boarding houses of the emigrants, with the special design of weakening their confidence in the promises of the society." *Md. Col. Journal*, no. 13.

[4] *Report of Board of Managers*, 1834. *Cf. Md. Col. Journal*, vol. i, p. 5.

[5] *Md. Col. Journal, loc. cit.;* also *Address to the Friends of Colonization*, p. 10.

ficult, therefore, for the American Colonization Society to procure all the emigrants desired. And yet conflicting views had been expressed before that in two memorials adopted by negro residents of Baltimore City. The first one was passed in succession by large gatherings in the Sharp Street and Bethel churches in December 1826. It referred to the negroes as strangers, as " natives, yet not citizens," and absolved the white people from responsibility for their presence in the country. It deplored their condition in Maryland and affected to welcome the colonization plan as a source of relief from it. But its pretense of representing fairly the views of the negroes of the city was vehemently disputed, and its tenor was repudiated as having been given by members of the colonization society.[1] The second memorial voiced a lack of confidence in the society, a negro desire to remain in America, a depreciation of the " illiberal attacks " upon the moral character of the free negroes, and profuse regrets that the efforts of this benevolent enterprise had not been more in harmony with the Africans' wishes.[2] It desired an expression of sentiment from negroes in regard to the pretensions of the American Colonization Society. Although this memorial may have passed at the instigation of white persons, it had a ring of genuineness that was lacking in the other one.

So long as matters stood so, however, colonization seemed practicable, and the Maryland leaders anticipated a generous response to their appeals through the new state society. A small degree of unbiased interest by negroes kept alive their hopes throughout. But the policy of the state was brought into disfavor by its own eager supporters. The coercive clause of the colonization act overshot the mark. It pro-

---

[1] *Genius of Universal Emancipation,* ser. 2, vol. ii, pp. 94-95, 149-50. Duplicate of the memorial in *Baltimore Gazette,* Dec. 14, 1826.

[2] Garrison, *Thoughts on Colonization,* p. 22.

duced resentful feelings among negroes and caused some
to turn a deaf ear to the appeals that were made, and even
to offers of freedom to slaves on condition of emigration.[1]
The people also, including the society's agents, lacked tact
in their solicitation for emigrants. They assumed that it
would be necessary for the negroes voluntarily to relinquish
residence in this country;

that there was no other way to free the masters of slaves of
a nuisance which lessened the value of slave property; . . .
(and) instead of representing a return to the land of their
fore-fathers as the consummation of a providential interference
in favor of the colored man, it has been represented as necessary to the interests of the white man, enabling him to hold his
property in greater safety, while it would augment the value
of the slaves by withdrawing the competition of free colored
laborers.[2]

They had been dictatorial in bearing and had used unpalat-
able language.[3] These things had been done to gain the

---

[1] *Md. Col. Journal*, vol. ii, pp. 80, 99, 256. *Cf.* Jacobs, *Address on the
Free Negroes*, 1860, p. 29; *Dorchester Wills*, Lib. THH no. 1, pp. 40,
69; *Worcester Wills*, Lib. TT no. 8,, pp. 21, 545. *The Colonization
Journal*, vol. ii, p. 80, relates that in the summer of 1843 a negro who
had been manumitted about eight years before astonished his former
friends by returning to them " from Cape Palmas, and when they had
felt him all over, heard him talk of his new country and his friends, they
became satisfied that it was their old friend ' Ambrose', and that he
had not been sold to Georgia. All hands concluded at once to rise up
and get them out of this land. Several free families also embarked."

[2] Quoted from *Christian Advocate*, in *Md. Col. Journal*, vol. ii, pp.
98-99.

[3] *E. g.* " Go to Liberia and be saved — stay and be doomed, if not
damned." *Op. cit.*, vol. ix, p. 199. *Cf.* also *op. cit.*, vol. ii, p. 98; vol.
iii, p. 291, and *34th Annual Report of American Colonization Society*,
p. 57. In the last occurs the following: " It is the monition of history,
common sense tells us, that this people . . . must go from our midst."
Cf. also Garrison, *op. cit.*, pp. 21-22.

favor of the negroes whose consent was necessary to the success of colonization. They had not been done to give offence, yet they produced effects the opposite of those that had been desired. They "armed the ultra-abolitionists with weapons which they . . . . successfully wielded against the colonization cause and enabled them to wake up a hostile feeling among the colored people" against the work of the colonization society. Distrust, discontent and sometimes hatred of the native whites were the results.[1] The *Kent Bugle* in 1835 reported that the majority of the colored people were opposed to emigration.[2] In 1847 the Colonization Journal itself printed the opinion that "the almost unanimous voice of the colored people . . . . is opposed to emigrating, or to the colonization society,"[3] and two years later that "the fact that the colored people have founded an independent sovereignty on the coast of Africa . . . . is utterly abhorrent to the free colored people of these United States."[4]

A great many, probably half, of the negroes were un-touched by the appeals of the society. Many of the rest were affected by it so little that they were indifferent to its proposed changes for their welfare.[5] The rest were divided in sentiment, and their hesitation and hostility became serious obstacles to progress. In many places arose active negro opponents—wiseacres, black plantation and village "lawyers," preachers, exhorters and correspondents of the northern abolitionists. They were not to be halted by either fact or argument, and as instruments of the opposition to the movement they acquired a certain sway over the minds

---

[1] *Md. Col. Journal*, vol. ii, pp. 98-99.

[2] *Ibid.*, 1835, no. 2.

[3] *Ibid.*, vol. iii, p. 290.

[4] *Ibid.*, vol. iv, p. 362.

[5] *Ibid.*, vol. i, p. 255, and vol. vi, p. 17.

of their fellows.[1]   They were credited with causing changes of heart on the part of many who had once promised to emigrate.   Their antipathy manifested itself most strongly in the city of Baltimore, the chief center of colonization influence in the state.   For a long time the negroes there seemed to close their minds to any inquiry for facts about the society.   They furnished but a paltry share of the total number of emigrants.   They commiserated those who exiled themselves, and sometimes attended at the wharves at the time of embarkation of those who did go,[2] but they generally studiously refrained from any appearance of endorsement of such action.   In 1847, however, they sent a consignment of Bibles as a gift to the colonists,[3] but four years later, when a group of worthy negroes were to take passage from the port, not a negro church in the entire city was available to hold a service in their honor.[4]

But in the meantime there were some whose minds had not been befogged by the abolitionists nor unduly influenced by the colonizationists.   They were deeply interested in Liberia, although they did not in every case wish to become Liberians.   They accepted the invitation held out by the society to investigate the facts for themselves.   As early as 1832 in Somerset County a negro society debated the advisability of sending negro representatives to Africa to ascertain and bring back information as to the conditions there,[5] and at least one negro was at the time planning to make the trip.   The legislature lent encouragement by waiving the statutory provision against the return to the

---

[1] *Op. cit.*, vol. ii, p. 238.

[2] *Op. cit.*, vol. ii, p. 258; vol. iv, p. 33, and vol. vi, pp. 18-19.

[3] *Op. cit.*, vol. vi, p. 275.

[4] *Op. cit.*, vol. vi, p. 18.   *Cf.* also pp. 360-61, for account of a nearly similar incident at Frederick.

[5] *Village Herald*, July 10, 1832.

state of negroes who went to execute such errands.[1]   The
society also on its part repeatedly advertised its offer of
gratuitous passage to those who went in this manner and
carried back former emigrants who labored to lead others
to follow their example.[2]   In 1844 there suddenly appeared
at Govanstown a Society of Enquiry whose annunciation
was accepted as startling.   It had eighteen charter members
who had come together without instigation by the whites,[3]
in order to get " correct information as to the political and
religious advantages of the Liberian colonists."   Its worthy
secretary, a tobacconist in " Old Town," became a corre-
spondent of the Colonization Journal and a judicial inquirer
after the truth.[4]   In 1849 a Baltimore negro wrote that
hundreds of the colored people of the United States had
centered their hopes for civil enfranchisement in the
"Lone Star Republic" on the African coast.[5]   In 1851
twenty heads of families, most of them members of one
church in the city, covenanted among themselves to emigrate as soon as conditions favored.   Seven of the families
went in mid-summer that year.[6]   About the same time arose
the African Colonization Society in Cambridge.   Its members passed resolutions declaring their conviction that it

---

[1] *Laws*, 1839, ch. 5.

[2] *Md. Col. Journal*, vol. iii, p. 354; vol. iv, p. 17; vol. v, p. 297, and
vol. vi, pp. 6-7.

[3] *Op. cit.*, vol. ii, pp. 242-44.

[4] This man, Garrison Draper by name, educated his son in the common schools of Pennsylvania, at Dartmouth College and in certain law
offices in Baltimore and Boston. Thus equipped the young man emi-
grated and became a practising attorney at Cape Palmas. He died,
however, after a brief career. *Op. cit.*, vol. ii, pp. 287-88, 290, and vol.
ix, p. 88.

[5] *Op. cit.*, vol. v, p. 20.

[6] *Op. cit.*, vol. v, p. 361, and vol. vi, p. 33.

would be to their advantage to go to Liberia, but that they desired first to know more definitely the facts about the colony. They therefore deputed two representatives to make a tour of inspection there and report their findings on their return.[1] Accordingly Thomas Fuller and Benjamin Jenifer went away and non-plussed their friends by returning clothed and in their right minds. They made a simple report of what they had seen and expressed their intention to migrate with their families to settle in Africa.[2] These facts seemed to make a favorable impression, wherever they became known, but their effects were partly neutralized by the failure of Jenifer to emigrate.

Just in the middle of the century the turn of events intensified the interest in measures affecting the negroes. Agitation incited by the federal legislation on slavery had influenced the minds of the radicals of both the north and the south and had aroused fears of further trouble. The seventh federal census had shown a decided increase of 20.3 per cent in the free negro population of this state. The state's constitutional convention had signified a new refusal to admit the negroes to higher civil privileges.[3] About the same time the efforts to induce the negroes voluntarily to emigrate were redoubled, and negro interest in the matter seemed to become more widespread. In the spring of 1852 a number of negroes held some meetings in the school room of the St. James African Episcopal Church to consider the matter. They appointed a committee which issued a circular inviting the colored people of the counties to send delegates to a state convention in which the wishes of the

[1] *Op. cit.*, vol. vi, pp. 6-7, in part quoting the *Cambridge Chronicle.*

[2] *35th Annual Report of American Colonization Society*, p. 44. The report was also separately printed.

[3] *Debates of the Constitutional Convention of 1851*, vol. i, pp. 194-95. Cf. Harry, *The Maryland Constitution of 1851*, pp. 61-62.

whole colored population could be expressed.[1]   The call was heralded and commended in the newspapers, although its significance was deemed problematic.   Friends of colonization applauded the initiative in it and hailed it as the index of a change of mind on the part of the negro population.[2]   Enemies of colonization, feeling that they had nothing to gain by the new turn, opposed the proposal for the meeting.[3]

On August 25, 1852 an assembly of colored delegates was held in Washington Hall in Baltimore.   Representatives were present from six of the counties and from three separate quarters of Baltimore City.   They were "respectable in numbers, and highly so as to intellectual ability."[4] After the call to order a committee on permanent organization was authorized and announced.   The delegates from the counties had expected a hearty greeting from the Baltimore people.   The rabble of negroes who had dogged their tracks as they assembled, interposed objections and caused confusion, whenever they found opportunity.   A member from Kent begged protection from the police, as he had heard that his life had been threatened.   Some of those

---

[1] *Md. Col. Journal*, vol. vi, pp. 193-95.

[2] *Op. cit.*, vol. vi, pp. 195-98, 214-16, giving copies of newspaper reports and articles.

[3] *Op. cit.*, p. 225.

[4] Among these delegates were: from Baltimore, James A. Handy, owner of a woodyard, and later a bishop and historian of the independent African church; John Walker and Jacob Fortie who were schoolmasters; Darius Stokes, an influential local preacher.   From Kent, James Jones and William Perkins, who were merchants of eminent respectability at Chestertown; from Caroline, John Webb, a member of a well-to-do family of slave-owners.   From Dorchester, Reverend Thomas Fuller and Benjamin Jenifer, who had visited Africa in 1851, and Cyrus Sinclair, the principal butcher of the town of Cambridge; and from Talbot, Charles Dobson, a shoemaker.   There were in all forty-two delegates on the first day.   *Op. cit.*, pp. 225-26.

from Dorchester evoked applause by offering to go home, and the Frederick delegation proposed to follow their example. Other members labored to calm their fears and to induce them to remain in their places. Reverend Darius Stokes, of Baltimore, made a speech and was answered by a non-delegate who said he had come " to oppose and put down the Convention." There followed a lull in which the permanent officers were announced and a platform committee selected. Adjournment was then taken to await the committee's report. "A colored braggadocio mounted a bench, invoking the curses of Heaven on all concerned" in the meeting, and in the streets the retiring delegates were beset by a riotous mob. Several fights occurred, but the presence of the police prevented a general outbreak.[1]

On the second day several seats were vacant, and two new delegates reported from Caroline County. The platform committee recommended resolutions which embodied much of the colonizationist argument. They did not counsel emigration for every free negro resident, but would have had each one to accustom himself to the thought of ultimately leaving the state. They recommended the establishment of a bureau to acquire information for the benefit of enquirers,[2] and pointed to Liberia as the most eligible home for the American negro. The last mentioned item provoked a great deal of discussion, but led to no decisive result. On the following day a schoolmaster secretary offered substitute resolutions. They included the main substance of the committee report. They deplored the social degradation of the negroes as a crime against God; they looked to social improvement through the medium of intellectual culture and gave warning that, unless the negro

[1] *Op. cit.*, pp. 226-28.
[2] *Op. cit.*, pp. 229-30.

reached out after better things, he would continue in his wretched state. They pledged the members of the convention " each and every one " to make every effort for the improvement of themselves and their families to attempt to leave to their children a heritage of knowledge. They enjoined upon negro churches and ministers the duty of inculcating in their people's minds the need of enlightenment and of procuring the means of acquiring it. They further expressed the feeling that it was impossible to establish themselves on terms of equality with the white people, and that separation from the whites was " an object devoutly to be desired." Hence they differed from the committee's report in that they emphasized strongly the need of ameliorating the condition of their race in Maryland, whether to emigrate or not. The proposer made a strong address, and although several protests were made against different items in his draft, he got an unanimous vote of approval for it. Another resolve authorized the appointment of a committee to memorialize the legislature of Maryland with a view to secure " more indulgence to the colored people of the state, in order that they may have time to prepare themselves for a change in their condition, and for removal to some other land." [1] Adjournment was then taken to meet in Frederick in the following year.

This convention was noteworthy rather on account of what it was than for what it achieved. Its tenor and its utterances bespoke a high purpose. The conduct of its members was in strong contrast to that of the mob that opposed them. Their views on emigration to Africa, however, did not harmonize with those of the majority of their class, and hence their meeting together accomplished little except in giving momentary encouragement to the colonizationists.

[1] *Op. cit.*, pp. 233-36.

The first separate effort of the local society secured a hundred and forty-nine emigrants who were taken to the old colony at Monrovia in 1832.[1]   At the end of the year 1833 another body of eighteen others formed the nucleus of the first settlement in " Maryland in Liberia." [2]   During the first eight years the emigration proceeded at the rate of one hundred one and one-fourth persons per annum, of whom 78.1 per cent went to Liberia.[3]   During the next sixteen years the rate was thirty-eight and three-eighths persons per annum.[4]   In the twenty-four years the emigration had been equal to 5.6 per cent of the increase of the free colored population.   The character of those who went away, according to the reports, was excellent.   The managers apparently adhered to their early determination not to admit to the Maryland colony any negro who would not forego the use of ardent spirits, and in canvassing for candidates they attempted as far as possible to attract those who possessed the fibre of nation builders.   Notable among the early emigrants were several members of the Tubman family from the state of Georgia, but formerly of the Eastern Shore of Maryland, who were deemed to have the skill in husbandry that was needed,[6] and the family of George McGill, of Baltimore, members of which became leaders in the business and public life of the colony.[7]   In 1837 the spring expedition carried smiths, cobblers, tailors, weavers, turners and joiners, and that of 1853 smiths, brick-

---

[1] *16th Annual Report of American Colonization Society*, p. 14.

[2] *Md. Col. Journal*, vol. i, p. 67, and *Report of Board of Managers*, 1834, p. 11.

[3] *Senate Journal*, 1839, p. 3; *Md. Pub. Documents*, 1840, no. 4, p. 3.

[4] *Md. Col. Journal*, vol. viii, p. 135.

[5] *Md. Col. Journal*, no. 1 (1835), and Latrobe, *op. cit.*, pp. 32-33.

[6] *Md. Col. Journal*, vol. iii, p. 322.

[7] *Op. cit.*, vol. i, p. 274.

makers, tanners, farmers and a cooper.[1]   Among the others
were teachers, missionaries and an attorney.[2]   Preeminent
in a group who sailed in 1843 was James Lander, a well-to-
do boatman from St. Mary's County.   He led with him
eight and twenty children and grandchildren, besides the
child of a friend whom he had redeemed from slavery just
prior to taking passage.[3]   The expatriation of these persons
tended to lower the average quality of the free negro population, because it took away of the best and left the inferior behind.   However, the number who went was small,
and after the merging of the Maryland settlement in Liberia
proper, it declined still further.   The activity of the state
society dwindled, but its organization survived the war between the states, as administrator of the funds of a school
located at Cape Palmas.[4]

Colonization had been regarded as a means of relief from
the burden of the negro population.   Many persons who
had doubted that it would be effective apparently supported
it.   But when its coercive feature failed of execution, other
means of checking the growth of the " evil " were desired.
Certain radical proposals were urged upon the legislature in
1835-36,[5] but it declined to adopt them.   When the results
of the sixth federal census were published, the agitation
flamed up anew.   The " incubus " of the free negroes was
growing so rapidly, said one, that measures to counteract
it were imperative, whilst the preponderance of physical
strength left to the whites the " ability to enforce any

---

[1] *Md. Col. Journal*, no. 10, and vol. vi, p. 359.   *Cf. op. cit.*, vol. ii,
p. 238, vol. v, p. 361.

[2] *Op. cit.*, series 1, p. 138, and vol. ii, pp. 238, 288, and vol. ix, p. 88.

[3] *Op. cit.*, vol. i, pp. 290, 307.

[4] Latrobe, *op. cit.*, pp. 84-85.

[5] *H. Dels. Journal*, 1835, pp. 39, 53, 62, 66, 78, 139.   *Cf. Md. Col.
Journal*, 1836, no. 3.

legislative action on the subject." [1] A state colonization
convention was held in Baltimore in June 1841.   It resolved
to attempt to inaugurate a forward movement in colonization. [2] But it was too moderate.   A small number of anti-
free negro men met at Annapolis in September following [3]
and resolved to call a state convention of slave-holders to be
held in that city in January 1842.   The call was duly advertised, and on the appointed day delegates appeared from
all except four of the counties of the state.   Robert W.
Bowie, of Prince George's County, one of the great slave-
holders, was selected as chairman (the free negro population of Prince George's numbered only about one tenth as
many as its slaves).   Determined and thorough-going action was advocated, and a committee was selected to prepare "matter for the consideration of the convention."
When it was ready to report, the house had got into a hub-
bub about a reporter for an abolitionist newspaper who was
present. [4]   The long list of resolutions offered was length-
ened to twenty-five and passed.   The following proposals
for new legislation were embodied in them: to prohibit all
manumissions that were not to take effect at once; to avoid
all manumissions of negroes who should not leave the state
at once when set free; absolutely to exclude from the state

[1] *Md. Col. Journal*, vol. i, pp. 114, 120.

[2] *Op. cit.*, pp. 1-2.

[3] *American Farmer*, ser. 3, vol. iii, p. 149.

[4] The convention had passed an order to admit to the floor reporters
whom its members would vouch for.   A stranger was seen moving
from the floor to a committee room.   A crowd gathered about him, but
the police took him in charge.   On his person were found " incendiary" letters and papers, identifying him as reporter for the *Eman-
cipator* and *Spy* of Massachusetts.   His case was attended to in a local
court.   *Md. Col. Journal*, vol. i, pp. 115-16; *Baltimore American*, Jan.
15, 1842; *Easton Gazette*, Jan. 22, 1842, and Lovejoy, *Memoir of Reverend Charles T. Torrey*, pp. 91-99.

non-resident negroes and resident negroes who in going outside were doing other than attending personally some white person; to guard closely the movements of negroes from one county to another; to compel every free negro to be registered annually and to give security for his own good conduct; to repeal the clause in the act of 1831 allowing manumitted negroes to get certificates of good conduct from the orphans' courts; to order all free negro children at the age of eight years to be bound out to serve as apprentices until the age of — for males and females; to prohibit the sale of slaves to free negroes; to limit the negroes' tenures of real property to a maximum term of twelve months; to declare the presence of a run-away servant in premises occupied by a free negro to be prima facie evidence that the negro was aiding the fugitive to escape; and to sell into servitude outside of Maryland all negroes whose offences were punishable by imprisonment in the state's penitentiary.[1] A committee of five members was appointed to lay the report before the legislature and to petition for action to give effect to the wishes of the convention.[2]

The legislature was in session. The House Committee on the Colored Population, four of whose members came from Southern Maryland counties, had already begun work on a bill. Now, the membership of the convention had fallen more than seventy per cent below the number authorized in the summons that had called it into being and had represented mainly slave-holders. Neverthe-

---

[1] *Cf. Md. Pub. Documents*, 1841, copies of Resolutions; *61 Niles Register*, pp. 322-23 and 356-58, and *Md. Col. Journal*, vol. i, pp. 120-28.

[2] Full reports of the proceedings are given in *Md. Col. Journal*, vol. i, pp. 113-28. *Cf.* also *Baltimore American*, Jan. 14, 15, 17, 19, 1842.

[3] In December, 1841, the *Colonization Journal*, p. 111, had pointed out that "in the slave-holding counties of the state and in the slave-holding districts of all the counties, meetings are holden to appoint

less the report of the committee was of the same tenor as the report of the convention. It deprecated the growth and the idleness of the free negro population; it pointed to the state's liberality towards manumitting slave-owners and to its toleration of negro immigration as the causes of the increase. It declared that the power to manumit slaves was a licensed privilege which could be taken away without violating any rights under the state constitution. Although it anticipated objections to stringent measures, it submitted a bill containing drastic provisions that were designed to correct the "evils" and to meet the wishes of the slave-holders' convention.[1] Eighteen days later the House passed the bill by a vote of 40 to 31.[2]

The movement to enact the bill had thus gained a considerable momentum. Meanwhile the proceedings had been watched with intense interest throughout the state. The Colonization Journal expressed the hope that the subject would be "carefully weighed and maturely deliberated upon ere any measures were adopted."[3] It viewed the proponents as favoring "only one interest of the many, and that, at the expense of all the others;[4] that interest was a minority one and was itself not even fairly represented. The legislation proposed was unnecesary, because slave property was already "sufficiently protected by the statutes of

delegates to the Slave Holders' Convention," etc. Four of the counties failed to have delegates at the opening session, and Queen Anne's had reluctantly sent any representatives at all. Cf. Baltimore American, March 3, 1842, and American Farmer, ser. 3, vol. iii, p. 314.

[1] Md. Pub. Documents, 1841 H, and Baltimore American, March 1, 1842.

[2] Journal, p. 414.

[3] Vol. i, p. 111.

[4] Op. cit., vol. i, p. 159. Cf. Baltimore American, March 3, 1842, and Easton Gazette, Feb. 12, 1842.

the state." Agitation for further protection could only be injurious to both the white and colored populations.[1] The Cecil Whig declared that it would " censure the whole proceeding," if it was intended by means of it to perpetuate slavery.[2] The *Eastern Shore Star* on February 18, professed a neutral position regarding the convention's action, but hoped that the legislators would not inflict a new evil upon the state. Public meetings were held at Baltimore, Centerville, Chestertown, Easton and in the counties of Allegany, Anne Arundel, Caroline, St. Mary's, Washington and Worcester to oppose the passage of the bill.[3] The meeting in Queen Anne's expressed regret that there had been a distinct convention of slave-holders, because the " name was well calculated to excite jealousies . . . . of some who might not have an opportunity to participate in their proceedings." [4] According to Dr.Brackett twenty-six memorials and petitions were received by the lower house alone.[5] Many of them had arrived before the bill was passed. They together with others that arrived later were transmitted to the Senate,[6] where the measure was rejected by more than two-thirds majority.[7]

Another anti-negro movement had been defeated. But

[1] *Md. Col. Journal*, vol. i, p. 159.

[2] January 22, 1842.

[3] *61 Niles Register*, p. 368; *Md. Col. Journal*, vol. i, pp. 158-59; *Eastern Shore Star*, Feb. 8, 1842, and *Baltimore American*, March 3, 4, 1842.

[4] *Baltimore American*, March 3, 1842, quoting *Centerville Times. Cf.* also *American Farmer*, ser. 3, vol. iii, pp. 314, 341-43, 350.

[5] Brackett, *Negro in Maryland*, p. 245. *Cf. H. Dels. Journal*, 1841, pp. 205, 222, 237, 244, 265, 272, 273, 279, 286, 304, 308, 313, 335, 344, 394, 434.

[6] *Op. cit.*, pp. 450, 512. For additional memorials and protests to the upper house, *vide Senate Journal*, 1841, pp. 57, 63, 64, 111, 143, 163.

[7] *Senate Journal*, 1841, p. 200. *Cf. Cecil Whig*, March 12, 1842.

its causes, as seen in the conditions of industry and population in Southern Maryland and parts of the Eastern Shore, continued to operate. Charles County had been most affected of all. Between 1790 and 1840 its white population had declined 38.6 per cent, and its slaves 8.9 per cent, while its free negroes had a little more than doubled in number. Its total population had declined 22.26 per cent, its industries had grown stagnant; its condition stood out in strong contrast to that of the counties on the Pennsylvania border, and its people were sorely disturbed about it. Their representatives at Annapolis attempted to bring about legislative action to remedy the "evils" from which they were suffering. They made notable efforts in 1843 and 1845. They complained that the state had adopted a mistaken policy of toleration of the free negroes and asserted that that policy had completely failed. They erroneously represented that but for the city of Baltimore whose population had grown all Maryland should have been losing ground in numbers,[1] and speciously calculated that, if the changes then in progress were to continue, the free negro population would outnumber the whites within a half century.[2] They complained that the free negroes, who then composed 8.19 per cent of their county's negro population, had exhausted the fertility of their lands and lowered the level of competition in the trades, until white men had been nearly excluded from them, and that the negroes' advance had threatened to undermine the character of the whites and either to expel them from their own abode, or to rule them, if they remained in it. These negroes had not the enterprise that would improve agriculture and were living

[1] *Md. Pub. Documents*, 1843 M, p. 46. The increase of the whites outside of Baltimore County, 1790-1840 had been 35,103, that in Baltimore County 74,453.

[2] *Op. cit.*, 1845 G, p. 17.

under conditions that were unspeakably bad, yet their position was yearly growing more secure and menacing to all good interests.[1] The salvation of the state depended upon the correction of the "evils" that were due to their presence. The means of correction were to remove them from the state. Humanitarian objections to the proceeding would be silenced by the methods to be used in executing it and the moral improvement it would entail. Constitutional objections were not well-grounded, because free negroes were creatures of statute law and could be dealt with by the legislature without infringement of the constitutional rights of any persons under the jurisdiction of Maryland law. The report of 1843 in which this argument was made was accompanied by a project for a bill to authorize the removal of the free negroes from Charles County. It proposed to prohibit the manumission of slaves, to declare the free negroes the chattels of the state, to employ them and to accumulate from their wages a fund to pay the expenses of their deportation.[2] The delegates declined to pass this bill. It became a precedent, however, for others offered during the next two decades.

The negro question was brought up in the constitutional convention of 1850-51. In drafting a provision against the exercise of arbitrary authority against persons and property, the word " freeman " was objected to, because it was urged that its insertion might preclude action, in case the state should desire to banish a certain portion of its population. In order to remove doubts as to this point, an amendment was added to the clause declaring that it was not to be held to prevent the legislature from regulating and disposing of the colored population "as they may see fit."[3]

[1] *Op. cit.*, 1843 M, pp. 46-47.

[2] *Op. cit.*, pp. 46, 49, 51. *Cf.* also *op. cit.*, 1845 G, pp. 3-13.

[3] *Debates of Constitutional Convention of 1850*, vol. i, pp. 194-95, 197-98.

Earlier in the sessions a committee had been appointed to consider and report upon a plan for disposing of the free colored people. It was given wide scope and ample time to make its findings.[1] About four months later its chairman brought in a report. He reviewed the salient population changes of the state since the first federal census, noted the rise of the free negro class and the attempt to get rid of it by colonization, and characterized its members as " the veriest slaves on earth." The recommendation was that the new constitution should authorize the enactment of regulations that were substantially the same as those rejected in 1832 and 1842.[2] Subsequently this committee chairman made two attempts to induce the convention to act upon his proposals. As a response the consideration of the report was indefinitely postponed and the effort came to naught.[3] Adjournment was taken without action upon the subject, but there had been discovered a redoubtable champion of restriction of the free negroes. This champion was Curtis W. Jacobs who was to come into the lime-light a few years later.

Slavery in Maryland was dying a natural death. Apparently the people would have allowed that process to go on unhindered, had they been left to their own devices. But their geographical position sandwiched them in between the combatants for pro-slavery and anti-slavery, and partizans of either side were bidding for their support. As the abolitionists did not dare to work openly, the initiative in all public measures affecting the negroes was taken by the pro-slavery men. To certain of them the futility of former efforts was no deterrent—they were determined to preserve

---

[1] *Op. cit.*, vol. i, pp. 83, 207, 371, and vol. ii, p. 220.

[2] *Op. cit.*, vol. ii, pp. 220-23.

[3] *Op. cit.*, vol. ii, pp. 784, 865. *Cf.* Harry, *op. cit.*, p. 62.

Maryland as a " slave-holding state true to the interests of her Southern sisters and herself." [1]   The means of attaining the object was to make an end of free negroes.   The first steps were taken by men of the Eastern Shore, a section which had " suffered more than any other from the influences of abolitionism from abroad, and from free negroism" in its midst. [2]   Several slave-owners in Dorchester County in April 1857 organized a society, and sixteen months later voted in favor of a convention of Eastern Shore slave-owners.   In November 1858 a meeting in Worcester concurred in this desire and appointed Cambridge as the place of meeting. [3]   In answer to the call twenty-four delegates representing the five southern counties of Maryland in the peninsula met on November 3, 1859.   Their chief spokesman, one Stewart of Dorchester, regretted that they had been called together as a " Slaveholders' Convention," because the course of action they were to choose was to be for the benefit of all classes of the people alike.   At the next breath he declared that the manumission of the slaves had been a great error, because its effects had impaired the value of slave property.   And thus the poor free negro was again given his round of disparagement. [4]

The resolutions that were passed on the following day were quite pronounced in tone.   They stated that " free negroism and slavery are incompatible with each other, and

[1] *Cf. Md. Col. Journal*, vol. ix, p. 278.   In the *Baltimore American* of Feb. 7, 1860, an editorial stated that it had been supposed that the objects of the Slave-Holders' Convention of 1842 had been " forever put to rest in Maryland."

[2] *Md. Col. Journal*, vol. ix. p. 278.   *Cf.* also p. 273; *Frederick Examiner*, Nov. 10, 1858, and *Baltimore American*, June 1, 1859.

[3] *Easton Star*, April 14, 1857, Aug. 17, 1858; *Easton Gazette*, Oct. 30, Nov. 15, 1858, and *Baltimore Sun*, Sept. 21, 1858.

[4] *Md. Col. Journal*, vol. ix, pp. 275-76.

should not be permitted longer to exist in their present relations, side by side, within the limits of the state. That prompt and effective legislation upon this subject is absolutely essential to the interests of the people." They suggested that the negroes be presented with the alternative " of going into slavery, or leaving the state." They called for a general convention representing all the people to consider the subject, " not as slave-holders or as non-slave-holders, but as citizens of the commonwealth." They chose the second Wednesday of June 1859 as the time and Baltimore as the place of meeting. In the meantime the delegations of the several counties were to be selected and instructed as to how they should vote upon the things to be laid before them.[1] A large committee was selected to frame and publish an address to the people before the meeting should assemble.[2]

The Cambridge convention had propounded " the most complicated, important and embarrassing question that the General Assembly has had to deal with;" . . . . "the subject is an important one—deserving grave consideration and involving the deepest interest of our people," said influential county newspapers.[3] The situation was one of extreme delicacy. Many of those who sought to lead in common-

---

[1] The issue was to be squarely presented to the next General Assembly that it must either " provide for adequate relief for the injured or confess its inability to protect the domestic institutions of the community," said Mr. Stewart. *Op. cit.*, p. 276. For the resolutions, *cf.* pp. 278-79.

[2] *Op. cit.*, p. 279, and *Baltimore Sun*, Nov. 6, 1858. An editor in an Eastern Shore town wrote of the Cambridge meeting: " The only business transacted was the adoption of a series of resolutions which amounted to nothing." *Easton Star*, Nov. 9, 1858. Cf. *Easton Gazette*, No. 13, 1858. *The Baltimore Sun* of June 8, 1859, refers to a convention of slave-holders at Chestertown in the preceding year.

[3] *Frederick Examiner*, May 11, 1859. *Cf. Easton Gazette*, May 14, 1859.

wealth affairs knew not which road to take.   But a winter
intervened and allowed time for reflection and for exchange
of views before the date of meeting arrived.   Certain questions were cautiously discussed in the press,[1] one of them
being the questionable utility of an advisory convention
that could probably do no more than re-resolve as had the
one held in 1842.   To be sure it might serve to crystallize
public sentiment, if it could be brought to act without partizanship.   But were not the legislators competent to make
such additional arrangements as were necessary for the control of the free negroes?   What they could not do, could
not be accomplished by means of legislation.[2]   Another
question was as to the motives of the Cambridge meeting.
Demagoguery, it was said, had thrust its flaming brands into
the state from both the north and the south : this movement
seemed to be running to meet it.   A Democratic paper in the
Eastern Shore asserted that all the members of the publication committee of the Cambridge convention were old-line
Whigs, and accused them of trying to retrieve their lost
political fortunes by new agitations.[3]   The Frederick Examiner also scented partizanship and warned the movers
to beware.[4]   On every hand were sounded counsels for dis-
passionate action and avoidance of extremes and cautions
that competent remedies for the " evils " were not to be

---

[1] *Cf. Md. Col. Journal*, vol. ix, p. 274; *Frederick Examiner*, Nov. 10,
1858, and May 11, 18, 1859.

[2] *Cecil Whig*, June 4, 1859.

[3] *Centerville Advocate*, quoted in the *Cecil Whig*, Nov. 1858.   The
editor of the *Advocate* wrote that the composition of the committee
was such that the friends of slavery were made to witness its protection by those not its friends.   The horns of the devil were manifest in
this convention business.   And if the issue were drawn in that manner,
" may we not bid good-bye to the future welfare of this hitherto cherished institution among us "?   *Cf.* also *Easton Gazette*, No. 9, 1858.

[4] May 11, 18, 1859.

easily devised.   A careful execution of the Cambridge program might ameliorate the condition of the free colored
people; but there was danger that, in the effort to deal with
the offending class, unmerited injuries might be inflicted
upon the unoffending.   No one could foretell the consequences of a re-enslavement of the free, but it was at least
certain that there was no demand for a larger amount of
slave labor than the people had already in hand.   The other
alternative, expulsion, could in any event be carried out only
at great cost to the users of free labor.   And should it be
carried out, it would remove the best of the negroes, and
would leave a void that would soon be filled by eighty
thousand white people, probably free white Europeans.
These freemen in their turn would use their votes to
emancipate the slaves and would thus restore the very condition from which deliverance had been just achieved.[1]
The first delegates were chosen, not in the Eastern Shore,
but in Southern Maryland.   Four weeks before the appointed time of meeting only a few counties had chosen
their delegations.[2]   In the local convention in Talbot
County there was opposition to the " initiation of any
measures whatever," and three persons from as many separate districts declined to act as delegates to the Baltimore
meeting.   In Cecil the small group that assembled chose as
delegates several men who were not present at all.[3]   Baltimore City and Allegany County were alike dilatory, but
when the date of meeting arrived, delegations from nearly
all the counties were on hand.

[1] *Frederick Examiner*, April 20, May 11, 18, 25, June 1, 1859; *Baltimore American*, June 1, 1859; *Md. Col. Journal*, vol. ix, p. 274, and
American Sentinel, May 27, 1859.

[2] *Somerset Union*, April 26, 1859, and *Frederick Examiner*, April 20,
and May 11, 1859.

[3] *Easton Gazette*, June 4, 1859; *Cecil Whig*, May 28, 1859, and *Baltimore American*, May 30, 1859.

The roster of the convention contained the names of representatives of varied interests. At the outset the moderate elements gained control. As chairman E. F. Chambers, and as chairman of the resolutions committee J. A. Pearce, both of Kent County, were chosen. Orders were carried that the house should vote *en masse,* that the rules of the General Assembly should govern the proceedings, and that no resolution or proposal should be entertained by the chair without having first been duly reported through the committee on resolutions.[1] The committee listened to counsels of moderation and advices that subjects covered by existing laws were to be avoided and retired to make up its report. Upon its return the following day the chairman stated that many projects of resolutions had been laid be·fore the members, but that they had confined their attention chiefly to the consideration of two of them, viz., the proposed expulsion of the free negroes, and the better enforcement of the act of 1831 touching the manumission of slaves—they had ignored the re-enslavement proposal. As to the former, its execution would rid the state of about fifty per cent of its household and agricultural laborers and would inflict upon the people worse evils than any they had thus far suffered. Moreover, it would be harsh and oppressive and would violate public sentiment which was generally kind and just to the negroes. Therefore, they recommended that expulsion was inexpedient and uncalled for. They thought, however, that there ought to be laws to enforce order and to foster industry and productiveness on the part of the idlers, and that the act of 1831 ought to be reaffirmed and so amended as to give to its provisions

---

[1] *Md. Col. Journal,* vol. x, pp. 17-19. *Cf.* also *Baltimore American,* June 9, 1859; *Cecil Whig,* June 11, 1859; *Easton Gazette,* June 11, 18, 1859; *Baltimore Sun,* June 9, 1859; and *27th Annual Report of American Anti-Slavery Society,* pp. 206-07.

" active force and certain operation " and make it " either prohibit emancipation altogether, or compel prompt removal from the state of those emancipated." Finally they recommended that a committee of one member from each county should be appointed to submit the views of the convention to the legislature. Only one member of the committee had declined to concur in the report.[1]

At this point the leaders of the minority gained a hearing. Some of its number had come up to the place brimful of eloquence with which to electrify the delegates, and the galleries. Hard upon their arrival they had discovered that Baltimore City had chosen no delegation to greet them. When members for the city did appear, this group of the visitors tried to have them excluded and made futile endeavors to remove the assemblage to Frederick City.[2] They had lost innings also in the organization of the house and in the gag-rule on resolutions. They had expected to harangue the convention and to guide the committee in making up its report. Instead they had been treated to cautions against inflammatory utterances. They hinted that the majority had been intimidated by influences outside the state. They wanted unfettered expression—they would not be halted by what anybody was going to think of their action. They tried to open a debate. Instead they threw the body into a state of confusion and brought on an adjournment till the following day.[3]

Their opportunity came, however, after the presentation of the committee report. Their champion, C. W. Jacobs

---

[1] *Md. Col. Journal*, vol. x, pp. 18-19, 22-25; *Baltimore American*, June 9, 10, 1859; *Easton Gazette*, June 18, 1859. *Cf.* also *27th Annual Report of American Anti-Slavery Society*, p. 210, and *Baltimore Sun*, June 10, 1859.

[2] *Baltimore American*, June 9, 1859.

[3] *Op. cit.*

of Worcester, was the dissenting member of that committee. He produced a minority report and made a long speech. He proposed in effect that the right of manumission should be taken away, and that a limited period should be allowed, after which no free negro might remain in the state. During that period those who desired were to choose masters whom they would serve, or remove themselves. Otherwise after its expiration the officers of the law would take them up and sell them at low prices to non-slave-holders, or to slave-holders whose slaves did not exceed a certain fixed number. In the meantime the counties should be thoroughly policed to prevent insurrections.[1] The speaker claimed to be a Methodist and a great friend of the negro race. He had made a profound study of the negroes' condition and cultural capacity and had found that in the West Indies and in both the free and slave states of the American union, their freedom had meant their extermination. For welfare's sake slavery was " just as essential to the negro race as freedom . . . . to the white race." They were, moreover, dangerous competitiors in the labor market and a menace to social order. They were 90000 mill-stones about the necks of the Maryland people. They were not wanted as freemen anywhere, and a crusade was on to get rid of them. They would soon have to be restored to slavery or expelled! The chairman interrupted on a point of order, but the speaker gained a little more time and soon concluded. The house at once voted to limit all other speeches to twenty minutes each. It was also reminded that its committee's action had been nearly unanimous. The committee was then attacked by the minority for not proposing more stringent measures. Two Southern Maryland mem-

[1] *Baltimore American,* June 10, 1859, and *Md. Col. Journal,* vol. x. pp. 25-26.

bers attempted to introduce resolutions from the floor without committee. Higgling over points of order followed, and several excited members simultaneously demanded recognition by the chair. Quiet was restored for a moment. One member from Calvert flatly contradicted an opinion stated by his colleague. Mr. Jacobs spoke again but was little heeded. Dinner hour passed and the delegates grew eager to vote. Points of order, an attempt to bring on adjournment and rejection of the minority report followed each other in quick succession. Finally a resolution was passed to recommend the prohibition of manumissions, the majority report with this addition was passed and the body adjourned sine die.[1]

The radicals had been outwitted, but were not content to rest with it. In the last previous session of the General Assembly they had got permission to introduce a bill to provide for regulating the free negroes.[2] In the session beginning in January 1860 they got control of the Committee on the Colored Population with Mr. Jacobs as chairman. They were encouraged by the messages of the Governor and by several petitions [3] which called for decisive action. They made a long and biased report and introduced eight bills which embodied certain of the extreme ideas favored by the Cambridge convention.[4] The committee chairman

[1] *Baltimore American*, June 10, 1859; *Md. Col. Journal*, vol. x, pp. 26-40; *27th Annual Report of American Anti-Slavery Society*, pp. 206, 209-10, and *Baltimore Sun*, June 10, 1859.

[2] *H. Dels. Journal*, 1858, p. 46.

[3] *H. Dels. Documents*, 1860 B, p. 11; *Journal*, 1860, pp. 97, 101, 143, 291, 292, 293. The editor of the *Easton Gazette*, March 3, 1860, wrote that Mr. Jacobs had sought his seat in the legislature in order to be able to engraft his "peculiar and extreme views on the statute books of Maryland." Cf. *Baltimore Sun*, Jan. 14, 1860, and *27th Annual Report of American Anti-Slavery Society*, p. 211.

[4] *H. Dels. Journal*, 1860, pp. 294-95, 309-10, and *Md. Pub. Documents*, 1860 O.

made an extensive speech advocating their enactment.[1] Reports of these proceedings created a sensation and caused some negroes, especially at Cumberland, to prepare to abandon their residence in Maryland.[2] Public protests opposed the passage of the bills, however, and the committee itself was not united in supporting them. The House rejected the re-enslavement proposal and thus finally defeated its champion.[3] But it repealed the sections of the statutes authorizing the Board of Managers of the Colonization Fund and authorized the appropriation of seventy dollars for each negro over ten years of age, and half of that amount for each one under ten years, to be sent to Africa in future by the colonization society.[4] It prohibited manumissions, whether by will or by deed, and provided that free negroes above the age of eighteen years might renounce their freedom and choose their own masters. Children under five years of age, belonging to females who might

[1] He reiterated much of his former argument in the Baltimore Convention. He disparaged the free negroes again; attacked the labor theory of the abolitionists; reviewed the history of manumissions in Maryland; declared that the free negroes were the property of the state, and were without any civil rights; asserted that manumitters were afflicted with a diseased moral and religious sentiment; and closed with a metaphor about the upas tree spreading its branches into every county of Maryland and exhaling its deadly vapors at every hearthstone in the state. This speech was published in pamphlet form in 1860. For synopses of the " Jacobs bills," which became notorious, *vide Baltimore Sun,* Feb. 20; *Easton Gazette,* Feb. 11, 25; and *Somerset Union,* Feb. 21, 1860.

[2] *Baltimore Sun,* Feb. 17, 1860, quoting *Cumberland Telegraph.*

[3] *The Baltimore American,* Feb. 27, 1860, records that Mr. Jacobs abandoned his legislative seat after this reverse. *Cf.* also *op. cit.,* Feb. 7, 8, 10, 14, 16, 20, 21, 1860, and *Somerset Union,* Feb. 7, 14, 1860, and *Easton Gazette,* March 3, 1860.

[4] *Laws,* 1860, ch. 283. The aggregate appropriation in this manner was not to exceed $5000 in any one year. *Cf. Report of President of Maryland State Colonization Society, Senate Documents,* 1860 U.

thus renounce freedom, were to become slaves also, while
those over five years were to be bound out by the courts.[1]
Finally another act made provisions for hiring out certain
unemployed free negroes in eleven of the counties.[2] But
its final enactment was dependent upon a popular vote in
each of the counties concerned. The referendum was
taken in the fall of 1860 and resulted in an overwhelming
defeat, the smallest majority against it being 42 per cent in
Charles County.[3]

The people of Maryland had labored for three-quarters
of a century to construct a negro code. They had rejected
a multitude of proposals and yet had surfeited their statute
books with enactments that failed to reflect their wishes [4]
In those efforts they had often attempted to alter conditions
that were perhaps not to be remedied by legislation. At
any rate the restrictions they had set up were ineffective and
the complaints about it were only too well-grounded. The
true policy of the people, therefore, favored a mild treatment of the negro. It was dictated by a fair regard for
justice as well as by regard for the business interests of the
whites.[5] It was well adhered to notwithstanding the difficulties occasioned by the extreme advocates of pro-slavery
and anti-slavery. To be sure the negro was looked upon
as an inferior and was subjected to impositions. But his

---

[1] *Laws*, 1860, ch. 322.

[2] *Op. cit.*, ch. 232. For analysis of its details, *cf.* Brackett, *op. cit.*,
pp. 260-61. *Cf.* also *27th Annual Report of American Anti-Slavery
Society*, pp. 211-12.

[3] *Cecil Whig*, Nov. 10, 17, 1860; *Md. Col. Jour.*, vol. x, pp. 137-45,
253. *Cf.* Brackett, *op. cit.*, p. 262.

[4] *Cf. Frederick Examiner*, May 11, 1859; *Md. Col. Jour.*, vol. x, pp.
273-74, 278; *House Documents*, 1860 O, pp. 3-4.

[5] *Cf.* Cross, *A Few Thoughts to Mr. Jacobs*, p. 1; *Baltimore Sun*,
Feb. 20, 1860; *Easton Gazette*, Feb. 25, 1860; *Baltimore American*, Feb.
7, 1860.

foibles were borne with patience, and he was given a wide latitude to make the best of his circumstances. He was respected, wherever he made himself respectable, and was protected in his rights to an extent that was remarkable. The war between the states occurred too soon to allow the policy of prohibiting manumissions to be thoroughly tested.

CONCLUSION

In the foregoing chapters the endeavor has been to set forth the account of the introduction and growth of the negro portion of the population of Maryland, of its numerical and functional relations to the white people, of its eventual division into two formally distinct classes—slaves and free negroes—and its progress through changes in numerical relations until in 1860 those classes became substantially equal. The account has also brought out the methods of transferring individual negroes from the status of slavery to that of freedom, has shown the kaleidoscopic niches created for the free negroes by law and has emphasized the protective and exploitative points of view of both the formulators of the policies of the state government and the informal treatment meted out by the people to the free negro class. Further it has dealt with the industrial training of the young negroes, with the occupations and the quality of the labor of adults and with their wages and acquisitions of property; it has also dealt with the halting, restricted labors of a few persons for the education of negro children, with the emergence of numerous negro churches whose organizers timorously sought to impart a culture whose possession by negroes would not give offence to opponents of negro enlightenment; and with the standards of comfort and general well-being of the negroes. It has found that at least outside the city of Baltimore the freemen and the slaves were not widely different from each other. Finally, it has shown the jealousy of the whites towards and their lack of confidence in the integrity of negro

freemen as citizens and has narrated the futile endeavors to
prevent the increase of the free negroes and to induce those
already free to relinquish their residence in Maryland for
a home in Liberia.

In all phases of their life and activity the negroes formed
a nether crust of the social body. As a complementary
part in the industrial system their functioning was indispensable, but in determining the character of that system and
in fixing the relations of its parts to each other their voices
were unheard; while in the distribution of its benefits
their participation was confined to picking up crumbs from
the tables of " their betters." Their presence was not to
be allowed to impair any vital interest nor to restrict any activity of the whites, no matter what their own desires were,
no matter in what roles they appeared or in what form their
interests were involved. The *raison d'etre* of the state was
the promotion of the welfare of the whites. To discuss the
rightfulness of these conditions would be interesting. The
problem here, however, is to attempt the explanation, not
the justification.

The key to the early establishment of the negro element of
the population is found in the labor situation. The abundance
of cheap land on which marketable produce could be raised
gave rise to a demand for labor. The proprietor's policy
of peopling the province by offering colonists liberal treatment had led to the coming of many bond-servants and
others but had failed to attract enough settlers to satisfy
this demand. Moreover, the development of industries " at
home " in the later Stuart period afforded counter demands
there for the labor of the classes from which the colonists
had chiefly come. Of immigrants from the continent of
Europe Maryland had received only a minor portion and
before the treaty of Utrecht only a few thousand negroes.
As for the latter, although there was no clear apprehension

of the consequences of the increase of negro slavery, it can be said that the land-holders preferred not to receive any more, provided they could get whites instead. For the quality of the labor was inferior and besides they had scruples against holding in bondage for life any human beings and especially individuals who had received Christian baptism. But in their situation the alternatives to buying negroes were either leaving their fields unworked or operating with scant supplies of white labor, in either case allowing less scrupulous planters elsewhere to supply the tobacco and grain markets of Europe. The urgency of buying negroes accordingly appeared clear. Hence the bars were let down, negro labor flowed in faster than in the seventeenth century, and negroes became a large element in the population. Thus there were two distinct classes of servile laborers, the bond-servants who were mainly whites and the slaves who were negroes probably without exception.

The labor supply depended upon the importation of persons of these two classes. The policy of the laws of the province was to facilitate this supply and with this in view to make secure the rights of land-holders to the services of those in their employ. The province adopted for incoming laborers, therefore, the principle of perpetuating the status fixed upon them as individuals before they entered and applied it without apparent regard to the race or origin of those concerned. But it is notable that arrangements for emancipation were incidental to each of these systems. For bond-servants the arrangements occurred in the form of legally recognized contracts, or court decrees, whose provisions called for limited service and whose fulfilment brought freedom as a normal result. As most of the bond-servants were white persons, it followed that the execution of these contracts benefited mainly the whites. But as the slaves were negroes, and nearly all the negroes slaves, it followed that generally they gained no benefits under such rules. For slaves manumission depended upon the uncertain graces of masters who were invested with ownership rights unlimited as to time. Thus although it appeared that formally a consistent policy was adhered to, the effect was to discriminate between the races in making freedom grants. The discrimination thus established was maintained partly because its original causes did not disappear, partly because of the growing avidity of the planters and partly because slave-holders who observed industrial impotency on the part of negroes who had become free did not desire to increase the number of freedmen on that account. In the face of such circumstances the alternative of limited servitude with eventual freedom for negroes seemed to have less in its favor after the end of the seventeenth century than it had had before. The prevailing tendency was to make slavery co-extensive with the number of negro persons and negro freedom exceptional rather than normal throughout the provincial period.

Whether this discrimination was reasonable or not, the practice of manumission which set it at naught began long before the middle of the eighteenth century. Free negroes were the consequence. The rate of additions to their numbers was slow until the era of the revolution. Its acceleration then was provoked mainly by the falling demand for slave labor after the exhaustion of certain tobacco-producing soils, but was also due in part to the political and ethical awakening of the people. Moreover, as larger numbers of negroes, especially women, became free, their growth through natural causes was also facilitated. The increment arising from migration from the other states was not large. But the total result was that in the two and a quarter centuries between the first introduction of slavery and the general emancipation the free negro class grew from a very small number to 83942, thus becoming more than 49 per cent of the entire negro population of the state.

II

The mean condition of the free negro, although an accepted fact, was commonly deplored and often regarded as unjust to him. Its continuance disturbed the minds of many persons and led to the condemnation of those whites, especially the slave-holders, who were supposed to be responsible for it. It is not desired here to condone the faults of which the whites were guilty, but it is meant to attempt to explain further the conditions and causes that determined the course of negro history in this state. The chief matters of concern are to be the factors affecting the character and destiny of the negro, the progress made by the free negro before the general emancipation, the appraisement of the negro as a candidate for citizenship and the effect of his presence upon the state and society.

As a foreword to the discussion of the formative factors in the case of the negro we notice for a moment the prevailing providence of slave-owning parents for their children. They commonly endeavored, so far as their wisdom and resources permitted, to educate their offspring and to train them in the industrial arts and the manners and customs of the society of which they were to be a part. Thus the common-school branches of learning, the running of the farm, the care of the crops and farm animals, the management of the negroes, the observance of moral rules, the usages of intercourse in their particular social circle and the inculcation of Jeffersonian political doctrines each received its due measure of attention. Besides there was the endeavor to accumulate property to transmit as a complement to the mental equipment. And throughout all was

warmly cherished the belief that the better the parents performed their several parts, the better prepared would be the
offspring to play the role of citizens of the community.
The quickwitted, aggressive, powerful white citizenship
was the product of this endeavor.

Into the midst of such a citizen body was dropped the
negro freeman. He was removed from the savagery of
Africa by only a brief interval, and his experiences here
had been those of oppressed servant and menial. And yet
he was destined to be both free and a permanent part of the
population. His situation was critical. Before him was
the career in the community. He was either to be or not to
be a man among men. At any rate he was to meet the
competition of the strong white man, and, if he was to suc-
ceed, had to have a chance. The conditions under which
a fair chance was to be had were that his advantages in
industry and trade should not be less than those of his
competitor; that he should have trained faculties and the
use of supplies of land and capital adequate for his uses.
For this purpose it was meet that he should have due care
in nurturing and rearing and such a measure of the training
and discipline dispensed in the community as his case called
for. Indeed were he less responsive to stimuli than the
white, he ought to have been given the preference in order
to equalize the chances. Accordingly there should have
been provided adequate schools, supplied with books and
materials and manned by teachers who were prepared to
instruct and guide the negro youth to a high plane, to develop a brain-power and a skill in the industrial arts that
would match those of the whites. Moreover, in order to
assure access to land and capital, there should have been a
systematic sharing of the contents of estates to negroes as
well as to whites. With some such dispositions the inequalities between parties might have been reduced so that

at least the best qualities of each race could freely manifest themselves. So long as either race labored under a handicap to which the other was not subject, the complaint that it played its rôle poorly was open to objection. But as the negroes' own forbears had neither the minds nor the means to supply these advantages, it would have fallen to white friends or to the community to grant the necessary favors.

But the whites did not take this point of view. The bases of their thought about the matter are interesting. They were of European stock, mainly British, feeling themselves lords of the earth and the negro their servant. They had learned of the relationship of employer and employee from a past in which the latter was an under dog. And further they derived scant inspiration to desire to improve their labor system from what they observed of contemporary labor conditions either in Europe or the sister " free states." As for the negro he was in Maryland for no purposes of his own. His introduction as a labor quantity had been at a cost that had caused him to be figured into the capital account of the industrial system. He was a work animal and it was incumbent to treat him as such, to make outlays for his upkeep on a minimum basis rather than on one dictated by humanitarianism. Only so could uneconomic maintenance be avoided and the station of the human chattel preserved.

Furthermore, were the negro's position improved, were his intellect enlightened, it could only make him less contented. If slave, he would desire freedom, if already free, more freedom, hoping thereby to rise to equality with the whites. But freedom could not genuinely help him towards this, because nature had made him insuperably inferior to the white man by fixing hard and fast racial differences which could not be obliterated by amalgamation or otherwise. It was hopeless for him to try to gain power, either as lord or as peer of the whites, and the state ought not then to hazard such enlightenment as would give him the scent of power. Should it do so, the certain consequence would be discontent that would ripen into insurrection and race war in which he could but be felled and crushed. It were better not to mix matters so: it were better to preserve the status quo ante, that of the benighted, exploited, contented negro and of the domination and the enjoyment of the major portion of the fruits of the industries by the whites.

Imbued with these ideas, the governing classes determined to control the destiny of the negro but undertook no formal program of amelioration of his condition. In the last half of the eighteenth century, however, the decline of the demand for servile labor led to the conversion of many slaves into freemen. This process of change continued into the later decades and undermined the old system of control. At the same time it served to deepen the grave concern already felt about the growing negro population and to thrust into the foreground the problem of its disposal.

Long-sustained endeavors were made to recover the lost reins of power. The favorite expedient of their supporters was to attempt to restrict the right of owners to manumit their negroes. The statutes for this purpose form an interesting series. The first important one was designed to invalidate any grant of freedom that had not been made a matter of formal record. A later one, enforced for a generation (1752-90) denied the power to manumit by last will and testament. Still another laid penalties upon the master who allowed his negro to go about to work as a free person. Finally the act of 1832 affected to forbid any manumission excepting on condition of expatriation, while by that of 1860 manumission on any conditions at all was prohibited. In the meantime the colonization scheme had arisen, and although it attracted less ardent support than the restriction of freedom grants, was liberally helped by the state acting through both the American Colonization Society and the Maryland State Colonization Society. These two expedients had been designed to articulate hand in glove. They proved of little avail, however, the first because the people generally did not acquiesce in the spasmodic outbursts that led to the enactment of the extreme measures. As for colonization there was no rigid enforcement of the statute that was to supply the emigrants, while of the negroes who volunteered to go to Liberia, some came back to live " at home " again. The enterprise dwindled and died a natural death. The result of all the efforts was thus small. They did perhaps hamper the emancipation movement, which after all triumphed soon enough, but the failure to achieve their obvious intentions reflected discredit upon their framers. They also frittered away resources and energy that could better have been expended in ameliorating the negro's condition in the place where he was destined to stay. The growth of the free negro population proceeded apace in spite of them.

The governing classes failed to divine how the elevation of the negro could take place consistently with the maintenance of their own position. The defeat of the policies which they favored did not reconcile them to the growth of numbers and the advance of the other interests of the free negro class. Although they failed to plan for improvement, certain protective measures which they sponsored became constructive in effect. They were (1) that purporting to require the shiftless, vagabond free negro to be put to work, (2) the several statutes and clauses passed to penalize the negro who failed to keep his labor contract, and (3) that requiring the teaching of a useful trade to the negro child who had " no visible means of support." The first-mentioned was enforced occasionally in many communities and more or less consistently enforced inside and in the environs of the chief centers of population. Those of the second were of some avail in protecting injured employers but savored of peonage and like the first bore but lightly upon the training of laborers. The third was invoked commonly in all parts of the state, so that under its provisions were trained many of the most useful of the colored tradesmen and many other laborers. The persons to whom it was applied were regarded and treated as were slaves-for-terms-of-years saving that until about 1815-20 their masters were usually required to teach them the rudiments of learning.

Meager as was the provision for vocational training, it exceeded that for general education. Many of the negroes lived in communities whose schools were private, or if public, insufficient to preclude a common resort to the home governess among the well-to-do. Scholastic training above the " three R's," however, was a thing reserved for the favored ones among whom the negroes were not numbered. More advanced education for those who received it was commonly sought outside of the home community, or beyond the state borders. In some places, notably Baltimore City, the negroes were more highly favored. But in any case it was scant picking for them. Even in the metropolis the petty and generally evanescent schools they were privileged to attend did not accommodate many pupils nor advance any one very far. Some additional information was gained by those who attended church services, especially where white ministers of a teaching turn officiated. For the rest, the great majority of negroes, it lay mainly with the orders given by masters or overseers, with the experiences and conversation that befell and the things caught up by ear and eye while in service to impart enlightenment. None of these was calculated to raise the negro intellect to an independent thinking basis. It was for them rather to make mean beginnings that would not offend grievously the opponents of amelioration.

In each race were character-forming elements—good, bad and indifferent—by which careers were vitally affected. Those in the negroes were largely passive, and those in the whites more often active. The progress made by negro learners depended not only upon their receptive capacities but also upon the types of whites with whom they came into contact. For instance, the master who was alert, tactful and scrupulous about the consequences of his own acts sometimes diligently counseled and trained the negroes who were nearest to him in daily service. The effects of such care were frequently shown both in the general intelligence and in the moral integrity and earning power of the favored individuals. But such excellent masters could hardly have produced like results in the case of sluggard or vicious or otherwise non-tractable negroes. In them the timber for good citizens was not to be had, and their number was many. Furthermore, many masters themselves reached no high standard as trainers. Their chief defect was indifference to the elevation of the negro's condition. Generally they desired only that their own slaves should be merely pliant, effective chattels, not difficult of control. Owners of large gangs of slaves too had but little to do with most of their men. Besides there were the unbusinesslike, the vicious and dissolute all of whom were obviously unfitted to be trainers of citizens.

III

The needs of the negro and the chief obstacles in the way of their being met have been stated. How much progress could have been achieved, had the state undertaken seriously to elevate his condition is matter for speculation.[1] It should be noted, however, that the opposition to formal programs of amelioration did not prevent the private and informal agencies already mentioned from making for uplift. And as there were marked evidences of their effects, it is perhaps incumbent to attempt to estimate the progress made, although the hundred years with which this study has mainly to do was too short an interval for racial elevation to proceed very far. Quantitative measures of advance can not be given throughout.

The strength of the whites in numbers, in institutional development, in the essentials of civilization precluded the possibility of an internal *Kulturkampf*. The negro laid aside the things of Africa and henceforth achieved by imitation of the whites' models whose superiority he could not dispute. In all things he was directly or indirectly dependent upon guidance and counsel and often also on financial assistance of white friends. He often failed to make good copies of his models, failed to rise to the level of Caucasian excellence. But he ought not to be unduly disparaged for either the fact of imitation or that of the imperfections of his endeavors. It should be remembered that the achievements of the whites, whether in private or public enterprises, were also highly imitative and dependent upon teaching and counsel and the buoying support of the social nexus. They only appeared to be less so than those of the negro because (1) theirs was a case of like following like and (2) they generally showed the more thorough assimilation of teaching and practice of the two.

A vital part of this progress, a prerequisite to advance

---

[1] In making this remark it is not forgotten that supplies of trained teachers and probably also of capital to equip and support them could perhaps not have been had and that pedagogical and vocational methods were not available for the prosecution of such an enterprise.

in other ways, was the adaptation to the white man's social order. The speech, the objects and methods of production and consumption of goods, the manners and customs, the acceptance of the position of deference to and dependence upon superiors, all had to be learned. These things were received in the school of slavery, carried along by individuals who emerged therefrom into freedom and taught to the generations of children, both slave and free. The intimate relations between slaves and free negroes kept both on substantially 'the same level in all these matters. The lessons of slavery thus still held the freedmen in thralldom, but on account of differences in formal status the latter had distinct advantages over the slaves in respect to industrial activities and acquiring property and education.

Although it was in part an unconscious development, the free negroes followed the whites in growth of numbers. They consciously attempted to imitate in acquiring property. In the year 1755 the 1817 free negroes constituted 1.2 per cent of the entire population and 4 per cent of the negro population of the province. From available evidence it is concluded that they then had scarcely any mentionable property, had as incomes none save those of hired and bond servants, had in scattered cases acquired some rudimentary " learning " and had as organizations of their own nothing unless some primitive, clandestine societies.[1] In these several matters came changes that amounted to at least incipient progress, and we therefore note what had come into negro hands after the lapse of a century. By the year 1860 the free negro portion of the total population had risen to 12.2 per cent and that of the negro population to 49.05 per cent. The aggregate values of the properties held by negroes ap-

---

[1] Slaves had no legal property, had their keep as incomes, but probably at that time enjoyed as fully as freedmen the privileges of " learning " and club membership.

parently increased about 1500 per cent between 1813 and
1860. In the latter year they stood at about .44 of 1 per
cent of the total for the state. Although these were in
themselves sources of financial returns, there is also evidence
that the forms of annuities, life estates, interest and rents
yielded additional incomes to some, while personal earnings,
generally of small amounts, fell to those who worked for
them.

As to advance in living conditions the evidence is scanty,
but it seems worth while to state some inferential conclusions. It was reputed that the whites generally lived better
in the nineteenth century than they had lived before the revolution and that they also provided better for the slaves
than of old. It was common report also that the free
negroes "lived about as well as the slaves," and it seems
probable that they at least kept up with the improvements
in the lot of the latter. The individual, if inclined to lapse
to a lower level, could easily hire himself to a land-holder
for his "victuals and clothes." By this means he could
live at least as well as the slave, but generally he could get
something more than this minimum. Of resources once in
hand he so often made improvident uses that it was in
effect a pittance of poor stuff that he got when left to himself. And yet the growing incomes and increased power of
appreciation were factors making for improvement. Some
free families, it was known, lived quite well, although they
were a minority and their number increased but slowly.

On the side of education and institutions for culture there
had been notable advances. The jealous surveillance of the
repressionists had permitted a few schools and Sunday
schools to teach negro children to read and some to write
and do sums. Outside of Baltimore, however, such
agencies were practically nil, and yet there were a few
cases of negro school attendance even in country districts.

There was also much more of teaching the rudiments to those in service in the homes of the people. Advancing beyond this some teachers and preachers attained a fair minimum of education. One student of law in Baltimore passed successfully the examinations for admission to the bar. The level of intelligence as well as that of literacy was also raised. In this development the negro churches had a leading part. The first separate negro congregation arose in Baltimore about 1785-86. In 1860 there were at least twelve churches representing five or six different denominations in the city, while scattered about in the counties were some fifteen or twenty other churches and numerous congregations aspiring to be so-called. There was one independent African hierarchy which, however, did not belong wholly to the Maryland churches. The founding and maintenance of these churches and the financing and construction of certain of their buildings were activities of no mean sort. Besides involving business transactions that required resolution and dispensing comfort and culture to attendants they afforded for negro energies an outlet unvexed by white competition.

Although much could be said about moral conditions, it is with temerity that one ventures to write about moral advances. And yet the signs of progress in other lines already noted probably had their complement on the moral side. With this limitation, therefore, we may point to an increase in the integrity, trustworthiness, deference for law and order and in regard for parental and marital obligations. The evidences on which conclusions are based were dovetailed with deplorable contrary conditions. But the motive in making this statement is truth and not mere optimism.

IV

The gains thus noted had greatly changed the position of the negro in the course of a hundred years. They had not come about without mental reactions to the environment such as the eighteenth century had failed to bring about. The free negro class of 1860 was not a mere duplicate of an equal number of negroes of the provincial era. But yet the elevation of the negro had only fairly begun, and he still had much to do to rise in the scale of civilization to the level of his white neighbor. On this account there will now be given an appraisement of the negro and a comparison with the white man who for valid reasons deserved to be called the normal type of citizen of the commonwealth. The statement about each type will follow the same lines. The analysis will concern itself with the make-up and activities, accepting what were thought and done as the indices of the character. It assumes that society approved certain characteristics and disfavored their absence. It finds evidences of personal qualities in conformity or non-conformity to rules which society itself had ordained. These rules concerned themselves chiefly with the conventional, moral, economic, social and political phases of life. As affecting the individual no one of them stood apart from but rather complementary to the rest. Attention will first be given briefly to the white and then more at length to the negro. The main point of concern is the consideration of the qualities of the type, but at some points causes will also be discussed.

Regarding the white man it will suffice to give a general statement of the qualities that were ingrained in the average citizen. As a conventional being he applied to himself the common rules of decency, kept at least fairly to the usages and amenities of his station, had regard for those of others and had regard for women. As a moral person he appreciated the binding character of promises, of oaths and other obligations and knew that the maintenance of public order depended upon his acquiescence in it and his support of the public authorities in the discharge of their duties. He joined with others in reprobating sexual irregularities and in frowning upon unfairness and sharp practice in business transactions. In his opinion moral rules also affected economic practice in another way: they made it necessary for the normal man to get by honest means a respectable competence for himself and his household. He followed a calling for that purpose. He further attempted to utilize his income with some degree of economy to attain a reasonable standard of comfort and, had he a surplus over living expenses, to lay by something for the future. Socially he evinced a high regard for the sacredness of the home threshold and of the normal relations of husband and wife and parents and children. He objected to any intrusion into these precincts excepting for the sake of the protection of the home itself. Finally, he had an interest in the public affairs of the locality, the state and the union of states. He was a member of the Democratic party, or some other party; he supported it with his vote and, although sometimes blinded to the real issue in a contest, generally knew why he was called upon to vote and what were the promised consequences in case his party prevailed at the polls. In jury service also, in paying taxes and discharging other public duties he acted with a degree of realization of the responsibility that rested upon him. In some things he missed the mark of excellence, but of such as he were made the warp and woof of the social body.

The negro was different from this. He was the product of the raw material he had been in the low civilization of Africa made over in the melting-pot of servitude to men who were far more advanced than he was. What remained in him of the aboriginal dross had in this crucible been either burned away entirely or rendered plastic enough to fit without resistance into the molds that had been provided for it. He had become such as he was not because he was strong but because he was weak, because what was outstanding in him either served well the white man's purposes or failed to give offence that led to its suppression. The result was the cowering, self-depreciating, groveling, compliant and often pitiable creature the main lines of whose character are now to be sketched.

In his way the negro was a conventional person. Although hindered by lack of resources and the jealous vigilance of the whites, the barbaric love of ceremony and display constantly cropped out in his conduct. Keeping within limits it manifested itself in obsequiousness and in childish and imitative forms. This was especially true of him who had been a house-servant or lackey in a genteel family. The stride, mannerisms and speech of gentlemen and ladies were copied, and in some individuals the veneer thus taken on was converted into a fair measure of refinement. But field hands and common laborers, being in a different environment, learned less of these things. In saluting white persons generally negroes knew how to be meticulously careful and proper but in greeting their own kind were not so consistent. In many matters the degree of excellence varied a good deal. In the following the standards were commonly low: character and keep of abode, care of person, sufficiency and propriety of raiment, language and tone used in conversation, chivalry towards womanhood and regard for the feelings of others.

Some of the basic principles of the aboriginal moral code were similar to those of the European. As regarded truth-telling, fairness and honesty the European and the African were to an extent at one. But in the peculiar relations of the races here the African was subject to subtle influences.

He was expected to conform to the familiar principles. His labor, however, was being exploited for the benefit of the whites. That seemed unfair. The demand laid upon him was not reciprocated by the white man, and he had no power to make it so. He also found many other rules with which he had not been familiar in Africa. There were juristic laws, moral laws and customs, a whole system whose parts he did not understand, but evidently created to serve the white man's purposes. He was expected to keep certain of them also, although he did not know well how to do so. As a slave he had often been disinclined to a voluntary observance of rules, because he bore no responsibility for keeping things in order. He had been guided by inertia, by desire to curry his owner's favor or by fear of the roaring gutturals of the slave-driver. When legally free he did not become free from these impulses. He was a child: if trained he could be trusted, but not too far. He would readily incur obligations, and only less readily forget them. His unreliability in fulfilment was proverbial. It held in connection with labor contracts, engagements to pay in future, delivery of promised goods and fiduciary trusts. In other matters also his word was not dependable. He poorly understood the nature of an oath and thus in part destroyed the weight of his testimony in the courts. He was deficient in the moral parts necessary to labor efficiency. He depreciated the need of personal exertion to earn a living, slacked inordinately, imposed hard work upon women without scruple and often begged or stole to supplement meager earnings. For the white man's rule against adultery he had a loyalty that was higher than he would have had in Africa but many degrees below that of the Anglo-Saxon.

Reference was made above to ethical deficiencies as affecting the function of producer of goods. In no other point was the character of the negro more clearly revealed

than in his rôle in industry. His wants and means of supply were not like they had been in Africa. The trend of industry here was different and he had to adapt himself to the
change. For this he was plastic enough, as shown by his
survival and his continued service of the white man. But
the conditions of his importation, the intentions and manner
of his employment and the omission to give him adequate
training sufficed only to make of him an indifferent, unenter-
prising, undependable laborer. He had acquired at best
an ordinary technical skill, a low modicum of managerial
ability, scant bargaining power, knowledge mainly of the
poor economy of the slave system, little or no capital or
credit and little or no prudence that might set a rein
upon the impulses noted in the preceding paragraph. He
had had the experience of slavery but when free knew
not how to flee slavery. He feared to venture far from
the home community, from " old master " and his family.
The lure of cheap land on the frontier possessed no charm
for him. The tales of welcome and " freedom " in the free
states, or of full political rights in Liberia, linked with free
wage labor in either, did not move him.[1] He knew what
to expect, if he remained at home. He would be a " nigger." He would hire himself to a land-holder to work
from " Christmas to Christmas " for " victuals and clothes; "
or had he a patch of ground—life estate, lease or free-
hold—he would devote a part of his time to it and a
part to hunting possums and to other things. If in the
city, he would operate a dray-cart, shuck oysters, work on
the city streets, be a coachman, house-servant, waiter in an
eating-place, a barber or mechanic, or perhaps run a market-

---

[1] Between 1833 and 1859 only about 1450 negroes were carried from
Maryland to " Maryland in Liberia." In 1860 only a few negroes of
Maryland birth were residents of free states. Of these last a part
were runaway slaves.

garden in the suburbs. He might do well for one of his color but could hardly get employment excepting at manual labor, and even in that not on the job that was technically difficult and exacting and well-paid. As an active factor he was nearly excluded from financiering, brokerage and transportation, in manufacturing and merchandizing he had a meager part and in agriculture a somewhat larger one. His rôle was mainly passive. As a servant or laborer acting under direction he had part in many varied operations. But in practically all of them his efficiency was low and to his rating corresponded his wage. Of his utilization of his income to promote his own welfare account has already been taken.

The moral and economic qualities determined the position in social life and as regarded politics. In the first of these the interest centers in the home and family. In Africa the aborigine had not known the home, as edifice or as institution, as the Anglo-Saxon possessed it. While in slavery he learned many things about it and imbibed a certain desire to copy it. This desire grew with the advance of freedom, but its realization was accomplished with difficulty on account of lack of funds. What was gained depended in great part upon gratuities from white friends or upon what the negro acquired under white direction and assistance. What was had was the cabin, or in the city the tenement, with poor provision of floors, ceilings and furnishings and commonly unkempt and squalid. Its threshold did not screen from the world the elements of privacy and domestic felicity that belonged to the home. It was probably better than the average stable for the cattle but was not the place of security, of rest and enjoyment, the castle of the white man. The family also was defective. The imported slaves represented different nations of Africans whose marriage customs, while varying somewhat among themselves, differed strikingly from those in vogue among the whites. All alike had to confine their practices here to what slavery would admit of and besides sometimes to submit to the intrusions of incontinent white men. The result was, excepting in the case of those who adopted life-term monogamy, much confusion and irregularity of sexual relations. In effect adultery, concubinage, short-term unions generally without formal celebration, and infidelity were common. Birth without wedlock was the presumption at law, until the contrary was established by evidence. Desertion, breaking up of incipient homes and practical abandonment of children produced their demoralizing effects. Failure of home functioning allowed offspring to grow up without realization of sacred family relations, without being steeped in the home idea and with the knowledge that being " niggered " was the normal thing in this relationship also. The negro did not meet with, give and take with, go in and out with, exchange views and puns with nor go into the homes, societies and churches with those who were considered the " good people " of the community. The station he occupied was a nether one.

In each of the points of view above presented it has been possible to point to positive conditions. In the sphere of politics it is less easy to do so. The rude type of African political organization which did not protect its own people from abduction into slavery in foreign places need only be mentioned here. What it lacked of unfitting one for the exercise of political rights in an American commonwealth was supplied in full measure by the system of slavery on this side of the ocean. In that system the individual figured as a unit of capital, known to the law as was the ox. The property rights of the owner stood between him and all else. To be sure he had an exposure to the political system through the restraining and controlling laws, but it would be difficult to tell just the impress he received from such exposure. He learned at least to fear the constable and the policeman, to stand in awe of the justice of the peace and to know hazily of the governor and some other officials, noting betimes that all of them were whites. He became aware that in other ways also the white man enjoyed privileges that the negro did not possess, and that beyond his ken were other governmental functions that often affected him. But he was excluded from participation in them and bore none of the responsibility of the so-called " sovereign man." He did not even learn the habit of voluntary acquiescence in majority decisions. What was left to him was the position of passive denizen. He accepted it languidly and scarcely rose above it when manumitted; no more did the child of free parents rise above it. Each one accounted for his own low estate in terms of inferior physical power and inferior wits. The historian can hardly avoid agreeing that he was right.

On the basis of the statements in the preceding sections we come to the ultimate causes of the status of the negro. They were two in number, (1) the personal qualities accounted for in the above analysis, and (2) the course of action chosen by the whites. Those of the first were the more deep-seated and those of the second based upon them. No such things arose as permanent bars against the merging of the family stocks of those who had been white servants into the general population. But as conditions over which none had control such things did arise to plague the negro. They petrified racial distinctions, underlay racial antipathy and discriminations, begot fears of internecine strife and decreed the disqualification of one race to function on a par with the other. They limited the capacity of the negro to shuffle off the coil of servitude. To understand the second cause fully it is necessary to consider the original contact with the negro who had not been well known before. The whites inevitably marked the color and the other external differences but in their action were at the time probably motived by two things. One was the desire to make secure the rights to their new chattels and the other a disregard for the feelings of such chattels akin to that of the captor for his quarry. But in course of time these obstacles to a liberal policy could have been overcome, had not the characteristics of the chattels been as they were. The differences between the races were more than skin-deep, and the masters discovered this fact. Without them the normal tendency to deal with all servants merely as servants must have prevailed. Indeed in some cases a substantial equality of treatment was apparent. But in most cases it was impracticable to continue on that basis, and hence arose deliberate discriminations in the endeavor to establish a modus vivendi. To the whites it was a cause of self-preservation, and because it was so they took determined measures. If they were set against the negro, it was in the same manner in which a stronger race has often dealt with a weaker one in the history of different countries.[1] And yet in this case although the weaker did not supply the conditions of a normal citizenship, such a citizenship without political rights and with other modifications was accorded it.

V

For several generations the development of the mixed population had been under way. The alien stocks of white men who had come into the state had generally taken up work and easily assumed shares in community burdens. Their separateness seemed a terminable one. That of the negro, however, endured and brought difficulties. The rise of the free negro as a complement to the slave system added

[1] Cf. Ward, *Pure Sociology*, pp. 203-05.

to the embarrassments. His impotency precluded his real-
izing fairly upon the asset of freedom, thus defeating the
hopes of optimistic manumitters and perpetuating the un-
settling and dangerous inequality and separateness. It remains to inquire what were the effects of the presence of the
free negro upon the community. Such effects will be noted
as the economic, moral and legal, political and social.

   In some lines of activity and conduct the negro's achievements reached a fair degree of excellence, but there remained many points in which he was unable to rival the
white man. Inequality of attainments made inequality of
expectations inevitable and in due course also led to inequality of aims. Sporadic attempts made during the
several generations to bring the two races to a common basis
yielded but little fruit, and the close association with each
other made the inequality as patent to the one race as to the
other. In accordance with this realization there were
evolved in informal ways separate standards for the negro,
sanctioning his failure to measure up to those of the whites.
Differences in this point did not obtain in every matter, but
where they occurred, operated to impose restrictions or to
give liberties for the sake of the maintenance of peaceful
relations between the races. These separate standards were
one of the effects of the presence of the negroes.

   It has been seen that originally negro labor had been
accepted as a last resort because it was deemed inferior.
The later industrial changes that put slavery at a discount
also discounted all negro labor. They affected chiefly the
city of Baltimore and the counties bordering on the Mason
and Dixon Line. In these places were located in 1860 73
per cent of the whites, a little more than half of the free
negroes and less than a third of all the negroes in the state.
Of the total increase of the population after 1790 about 83
per cent and of that in these counties 93 per cent had been

whites. Thus the free negro afforded but a minor part of
the new labor supply of the whole state and still less of it
in these progressive counties. His importance was at a
mean in Southern Maryland, where slavery was most stead-
fast, and greatest of all in Anne Arundel County and seven
of the counties of the Eastern Shore. In many places the
dependence upon him was quite material. Whether the
quality of his labor was improved by emancipation is disputed. Some negroes got themselves free by dint of wits
and labor efficiency, and such qualities were constantly
brought into play by the hope of freedom. But neither did
their possession assure freedom to a slave nor freedom alone
suffice to make one an efficient laborer. In fact the formal
status of freedom, not industrial or moral or social qualities, was the chief mark to distinguish the average rural
free negro from his brother slave. Thus far the industrial
effect of gradual emancipation, as proceeding in this state,
was practically nil. But the increased activity of a minority
of superior free workers probably placed the level of the
free labor above that of the slaves. The negro figured as a
routine laborer and only to a slight extent as manager or as
introducer of new ideas. The course of industrial development was not, therefore, much affected by his participation
in it. Keeping to such a level he helped more than he hindered. But with such a labor force progress was hardly to
be made, because it would not adequately perform the new
operations of the new ventures that progress of necessity
consists in. It was frequently remarked that the counties in
which the dependence upon the negro was least were the
most progressive communities in the state.

The disqualification of the average negro for politics has
been remarked above. It resulted in his exclusion from the
suffrage in 1809 and subsequently also from party membership. Thenceforth he dreamed much of a better lot, his

foremost wish being probably to gain political and social equality. The significance of such a hypothetical change was appreciated but little, and he was measurably silent about it until stirred up by the missionary activities of the anti-slavery movement. He then chafed at his subordination and at the failure of his freedom to gain him anticipated recognition. His endeavors at political organization proved futile because of white interference. As a result his active influence was either nil, or if it had effect, tended to confine his movements within narrower limits. He was quite a creature of circumstances. But his very impotence caused the creation and injection into poliitics of a negro problem. It was first brought forward prominently by friends of negro amelioration within the sate. After failing to score in several innings, however, these friends were silenced because they feared to stir up trouble. The imported agitators, Lundy and Garrison, were forced to leave, but from without found means to continue their work. They were opposed from within and besides the negro problem, viewed from a different angle, was dealt with by the opponents of emancipation and amelioration. For a generation the public mind was deeply and recurrently agitated by machinations from both sides. The chief objectives of the actors in Maryland were to preserve the peace and protect property interests against impairment. The measures they employed were designed to stem the tide of manumissions, to prevent non-laboring negroes from eating up the land like grasshoppers, to colonize freed negroes in Africa and to counteract concerted movements of negroes at home. None of them was perhaps designed for the purpose of injuring the "black man." The chapter above on legal status reveals the ingenuity displayed by legislators in these matters. In public discussion and as a subject for legislative action no problem of the last generation of the slavery regime commanded more urgent attention than that of the free negro.

The effects upon morals and law, so far as they are dis-
tinguishable, were the legitimate fruitage of the subtle
forces arising from the mixed composition of the population.   Although the African and the European were of the
same genus and dwelt here in the same geographical sur-
roundings, they were molded by different forces.   Not only
did their hereditaments differ, but their environments differed also.   As to the manner in which either heredity or
environment affected different individuals there was the
greatest diversity.   But the latter at least tended to give
every advantage to the whites, while for the negro the portion assigned was to be exploited, repressed and precluded
from realization of good rather than nurtured and helped in
the way that would have made for his greatest improvement.   Its dole of a pittance of subsistence was character-
istic of its general provision for him.   The system that ensued became the established, the right order in the state.
The fact that two races were concerned gave it a peculiar
ethical cast only in so far as one of them suffered from
systematic impositions to which the other was not subjected.
But identity of policy and equality of enjoyments in disregard of race were hardly to be expected, no matter what
abstract justice would have decreed.   Environmental factors thus continued to make of the white a white and of the
black a "nigger," writing down low the plane on which the
latter had his being, maintaining the deplored inequality and
obstructing progress towards the coveted, hypothetical goal
of homogeneity of conditions.   The pathologic difference
in racial standards has been mentioned.   It made possible
the most flagrant breaches of usual moral rules without the
usual penalties.   This held true especially of offences committed against negroes by members of either race, but considerably less of those suffered by whites at the hands of negroes
and still less of those suffered by whites from whites.   It did

not fundamentally unsettle the reign of moral law, but it did inevitably entail a lower average of moral practice than an unmixed population of whites would have had. A tendency to a difference between standards also obtained in the administration of justice. In practice the courts frequently varied the rules applying to evidence, or to the defendant at the bar or to penalties on account of race. Sometimes the result was greater severity, sometimes greater leniency. It was unsatisfactory to do so, but so were the conditions that caused it. Finally a note of conscious moral flavor lay in that those who controlled the public policies of the state were determined to have no change in this regimen as long as they could prevent it.

To win esteem and to live in friendly relations with those who were themselves highly esteemed was deemed a worthy object of ambition: it was a goal to which the white man commonly attained on his social rung. In theory, at least, this goal was reached as a result of possession of personal qualities. The individual who was possessed of coarse voice, uncouth manners, of no personal force and no appreciation of niceties could hardly reach it. Neither could he who lacked a sufficient foundation on which to build towards it. The average negro was substantially such an individual and because he was so was unwelcome in any intimate connection with an average white person save as a menial. The line thus drawn against him was drawn during the prevalence of slavery and was a racial barrier, but it was not due to either slavery or physical ethnological differences. The free negro class had barely to appear to prove itself a disappointment and the line was continued against it also. Indeed it seems that if any change at all resulted from the rise of the new class, it caused a more strict definition of class boundaries, a more firm repulsion of the negro and an outcasting of any white man or woman who went across to the negroes. The inclination to disparage the Ethiopian, at home and abroad, was encouraged. It became habitual. With some persons it was made a matter of studied policy, in order to check manumissions and to prevent the growth of " free-negroism." The negro also was led to acquiesce in it and to despise himself. Such disparagement implied that in place of an equality basis of apportioning benefits between persons the negro was to wait until the white man was fairly supplied to see whether he would himself get anything at all. The perpetuation of such a handicap for the most needy part of the population was probably not sound social policy. Upon the whites the effects were, first, to cause at least a formal realization of race solidarity, and secondly, to intensify class lines within the ranks, although not to define the " poor whites " as rigidly as in certain of the sister slave states.

The free negro was an asset to the state, but an asset laden with many of the characteristics of liability. The managers of the corporate body to which he belonged would have been relieved, could they have written him as an item off their accounts. Nevertheless the sympathetic, personal attachment of many whites to individual negro servants, whether slave or free, was permanent.

BIBLIOGRAPHY

PAMPHLETS, ADDRESSES, LETTERS, *etc.*

Anonymous:

Address to the Friends of . . . Colonization, pp. 13. Baltimore, 1827.

Address of the Managers of the American Colonization Society to the People of the United States. Washington, 1832.

Address to the Non-Slaveholders of the South on the Social and Political Evils of Slavery, p. 58. New York, 1842-43.

A Few Thoughts to Mr. Jacobs, Chairman of the Committee on the Colored Population in the House of Delegates of Maryland. 1860.

Colonization of the Free People of Color of Maryland. Baltimore, 1832.

Colonization on the West Coast of Africa by . . . Mail Steamships, Report of Naval Committee, p. 82. Washington, 1851.

Essay on the Policy of Appropriations by the United States Government for . . . Liberating and Colonizing . . . Slaves. Baltimore, 1826.

Free Negroism, or the Results of Emancipation in the North and the West India Islands. New York, 1826.

Letter of a Baltimore Gentleman on Slavery, p. 12. Baltimore, 1841.

Letters of a Conservative Whig, from the Baltimore Patriot.

Loyalty and Devotion of Colored Americans in the Revolution and War of 1812, p. 24.

Proceedings against William Lloyd Garrison for a Libel, p. 32. Baltimore, 1847.

Slavery Indispensable to Civilization in Africa. Baltimore, 1855.

The Maryland Scheme of Expatriation Examined. Boston, 1834.

Wanderings on the Seas and Shores of Africa. New York, 1843.

Buckler, Thomas H., *History of Epidemic Cholera as it Appeared at the Baltimore City and County Almshouse ... 1849.* Baltimore, 1851.

Carey, Mathew, *Letters on the Colonization Society and Its Probable Results* (letters, legislative resolutions, speeches, etc.), p. 32. Philadelphia, 1832.

——, *Slavery in Maryland Briefly Considered,* p. 53. Baltimore, 1845.

Chambers, William, *American Slavery and Color.* London, 1857

Clay, Henry, *Address before the American Colonization Society at Washington, D. C.* Washington, 1827.

Cross, Andrew B., *Thoughts on the Expulsion of the Free Blacks from Maryland*, p. 4. Baltimore, 1860.

DeVinne, Daniel, *The Methodist Episcopal Church and Slavery*, p. 95. New York, 1857.

Dexter, Franklin B., *Estimates of Population in the American Colonies*, p. 10. Worcester, 1887. (Connecticut Almanac, 1891.)

Douglass, Frederick, *A Friendly Word to Maryland*, p. 16. Baltimore, 1864.

Easton, Reverend H., *A Treatise on the Intellectual Character and Civil and Political Condition of the Colored People of the United States and the Prejudice Exercised Against Them*, p. 54. Boston, 1837.

England, Reverend Bishop, *Letters to Honorable John Forsythe on Slavery*. Baltimore, 1844 (?).

Farquhar, W. H., *Annals of Sandy Spring, or Twenty Years History of a Rural Community in Maryland, 1863-83*. Baltimore, 1884.

Fuller, Richard, *Our Duty to the African Race*. (*Address before the American Colonization Society at Washington, D. C., 1851*. *Cf.* also *34th Annual Report of American Colonization Society*.)

Garrison, William Lloyd, *Thoughts on Colonization*, p. 76. Boston, 1832.

Hall, James, *Address to the Free People of Color of Maryland*, p. 25. Baltimore, 1859.

Harper, Robert G., *Letter to E. B. Caldwell, Secretary of the American Society for Colonizing the Free People of Color of the United States*, p. 24. Baltimore, 1818.

Hennighausen, Louis P., *The Redemptioners and the German Society of Maryland*. (2nd Annual Report of the Society for the History of the Germans of Maryland), p. 22. Baltimore, 1888.

Hicks, Thomas H., *Inaugural Address, as Governor of Maryland*. 1858.

Jacobs, Curtis W., *Speech on the Free Colored Population of Maryland*, p. 32. Annapolis, 1860.

Jones, C. C., *The Religious Instruction of the Negroes of the United States*. Savannah, 1842.

Johnson, Reverdy, *Speech in the United States Senate*. April 5, 1864.

Latrobe, J. H. B., *Letter to Thomas Sufferin on Colonization*, p. 48. Baltimore, 1851.

——, *Maryland in Liberia—A History of the Colony Planted by the Maryland State Colonization Society* (Maryland Historical Society, Fund Publication, no. 21), p. 138. Baltimore, 1885.

——, *Memoir of Benjamin Banneker*, p. 10. (*Cf.* Maryland Colonization Journal, new series, vol. 2.)

McKenney, W., *A Brief Statement of the Facts of African Colonization*. Baltimore, 1836.

Mayer, Brantz, *The Emancipation Problem in Maryland*, p. 4. Baltimore, 1862.

Martin, D., *Trial of Reverend Jacob Gruber*, p. 111. Fredericktown, 1819.

Muse, J. E., *Address on the Dominant Errors of Maryland Agriculture*. Baltimore, 1828.

Myers, E. H., *The Disruption of the Methodist Episcopal Church*. 1875.

Pinkney, William, *Speech in the House of Delegates of Maryland, 1788* (reprinted in *The Southern Platform*, Boston, 1858).

Potter, Richard J., *Narrative of Experience, Adventures and Escape*, p. 25, Philadelphia, 1866.

Raymond, James, *Comparative Economy of Free and Slave Labor*. Frederick, 1827.

Reeder, R. S., *Letter to Dr. S. W. Dent on the Colored Population of Maryland*, p. 26. Port Tobacco, 1859.

Ruffner, Henry, *Address to the People of West Virginia Shewing that Slavery is injurious to the Public Welfare*, p. 40. Lexington, 1847.

Stroud, George M., *Sketch of Laws Relating to Slavery in Several States of the United States* (extracts), p. 125. Philadelphia, 1856.

Tyson, Mrs. M. E., *A Sketch of the Life of Benjamin Banneker*. (Paper read before the Maryland Historical Society, October 5, 1854, by J. Saurin Norris), p. 19. Baltimore, 1854.

Van Evrie, ———, *Negroes and Negro Slavery*. Baltimore, 1853.

Wilson, Calvin Dill, "Negroes Who Owned Slaves," p. 12, *Popular Science Monthly*, November, 1912.

SECONDARY AUTHORITIES

Alexander, Alfred, *History of African Colonization*, p. 600.

An American, *Inquiry into the Condition and Prospects of the African Race in the United States*, p. 214. Philadelphia, 1839.

Ballagh, James C., *A History of Slavery in Virginia* (Johns Hopkins University Studies, extra volume no. xxiv), p. 160. Baltimore, 1902.

Bangs, Nathan, *Life of Reverend Freeborn Garrettson*, p. 335, New York, 1839.

Bozman, John L., *The History of Maryland from 1633 to 1660*. 2 volumes. Baltimore, 1837.

Brackett, Jeffrey R., *The Negro in Maryland. A Study of the Institution of Slavery* (Johns Hopkins University Studies, extra volume, no. vi), p. 268. Baltimore, 1889.

Browne, William Hand, *Maryland: the History of a Palatinate* (American Commonwealth Series), p. 292. Boston, 1895.

DuBois, W. E. Bughardt, *The Suppression of the African Slave Trade to the United States of America* (Harvard Historical Studies, vol. i), p. 335. New York and London, 1896.

Earle, Thomas, *Life, Travels and Opinions of Benjamin Lundy*, p. 316. Philadelphia, 1847.

Gaines, Wesley G., *African Methodism in the South; or Twenty-five Years of Freedom*, p. 305. Atlanta, 1890.

Gambrall, Theodore C., *Studies in the Civil, Social and Ecclesiastical History of Maryland*, p. 240. New York, 1893.

Garrison, W. P. and Garrison, F. J., *William Lloyd Garrison, the Story of His Life, 1805-1879*, 4 volumes. New York, 1885-89.

Griffith, Thomas W., *Annals of Baltimore*. Baltimore, 1824.

——, *Sketches of the Early History of Maryland*. Baltimore, 1821.

Gumshaw, W. H., *Official History of Freemasonry Among the Colored People of North America*, p. 392. New York, 1903.

Hall, Clayton C., *Baltimore, its History and its People*, 2 volumes. New York and Chicago, 1912.

Hamilton, F. M., *A Plain Account of the Colored Methodist Episcopal Church in America*, p. 136. Nashville, 1887.

Handy, Reverend James A., *Scraps of African Methodist Episcopal History*, p. 421. Philadelphia.

Hanson, G. A., *Old Kent: the Eastern Shore of Maryland*. Baltimore, 1876.

Harrison, Samuel H., *Social Annals of Talbot County*. Manuscript.

Harry, James W., *The Maryland Constitution of 1851* (Johns Hopkins University Studies, 20th series, nos. vii-viii), p. 84. Baltimore, 1902.

Hart, Albert B., *Slavery and Abolition, 1831-41* (American Nation Series), pp. 360. New York, 1906.

Hood, J. W., *One Hundred Years of the African Methodist Episcopal Zion Church*, p. 625. New York, 1895.

Hurd, John Codman, *The Law of Freedom and Bondage in the United States*, 2 volumes, pp. 617, 800. Boston, 1858-62.

Jacobstein, Meyer, *The Tobacco Industry in the United States* (Columbia University Studies in History, Economics and Public Law, vol. xxvi, no. 3), p. 208. New York, 1907.

Johnston, George, *History of Cecil County*, p. 548. Elkton, 1881.

Jones, Elias, *History of Dorchester County*. Baltimore, 1902.

McCormac, Eugene Irving, *White Servitude in Maryland* (Johns Hopkins University Studies, 22nd series, nos. iii, iv). Baltimore. 1904.

McMahon, John V. L., *An Historical View of the Government of Maryland*, 2 volumes. Baltimore, 1831.

McSherry, James, *History of Maryland*, pp. 437. Baltimore, 1904.

Mereness, Newton D., *Maryland as a Proprietary Province*, p. 530. New York, 1901.

Nell, William C., *Colored Patriots in the American Revolution*, p. 296. Boston, 1855.

Nicholson, Lambert, *Journal* (copied from the Records of the Sharp Street Station Methodist Episcopal Church, Manuscript).

Payne, Reverend Daniel A., *History of the African Methodist Episcopal Church*, pp. 498, Nashville, 1891. This writer, a bishop of the connexion about which he wrote, was long an active participant in the later events he has narrated.

Poole, W. F., *Anti-Slavery Opinions Before the Year 1800*, p. 82. Cincinnati, 1873.

Preston, Walter W., *History of Harford County*, p. 360. Baltimore, 1901.

Riley, Elihu S., "*The Ancient City*," a *History of Annapolis, in Maryland, 1649-1887*. Annapolis, 1887.

Ridgley, David, *Annals of Annapolis*. Baltimore, 1841.

Russell, John H., *The Free Negro in Virginia, 1619-1865* (Johns Hopkins University Studies, 31st series, no. iii). Baltimore, 1913.

Scharf, James Thomas, *The Chronicles of Baltimore: Being a Complete History of Baltimore Town and Baltimore City*, p. 756. Baltimore, 1874.

——, *History of Maryland from the Earliest Times to the Present Day (1879)*, 3 volumes. Baltimore, 1879.

——, *History of Western Maryland*, 2 volumes. Philadelphia, 1882.

Smedley, R. C., *History of the Underground Railroad in Chester and the Neighboring Counties of Pennsylvania*, p. 406. Lancaster, 1883.

Smith, J. H., *History of Sharp Street Station Methodist Episcopal Church*, p. 12 (?). Manuscript.

Spears, John R., *The American Slave Trade*. New York, 1907.

Steiner, Bernard C., *History of Education in Maryland* (United States Bureau of Education. Circular of Information, no. 2.) Washington, 1894.

Stevens, A., *A History of the Methodist Episcopal Church in the United States*, 3 volumes. New York, 1868.

Still, William, *The Underground Railroad*, p. 780. Philadelphia, 1872.

Todd, Reverend R. W., *Methodism in the Peninsula*, p. 343. ——, 1886.

Williams, George W., *History of the Negro Race in America, 1619-1880*, 2 volumes. New York, 1883.

Williams, Thomas J. C., *History of Frederick County, Maryland*, 2 volumes. Hagerstown, 1910.

——, *History of Washington County, Maryland*, 2 volumes. Hagerstown, 1906.

Directories, Guides, etc.

Boulden, J. E. P., *The Presbyterians of Baltimore: Their Churches and Historic Graveyards*. Baltimore, 1875.

Brief Sketch of Maryland, its Geography, Boundaries, History, Government, Legislation, Internal Improvements, etc., p. 256. ——, 1845.

Fisher, R. S., *Gazetteer of Maryland.* 1852.

Fry, W., *Directory for Baltimore.* 1810.

Gobright, John C., *The Monumental City, or Baltimore Guide Book,* p. 236. Baltimore, 1858.

Jackson, S., *Directory for Baltimore.* 1819.

Lucas, Fielding, *Picture of Baltimore.* Baltimore, 1833.

Matchett, R. J., *Directories for Baltimore, 1824, 1827, 1831, 1840-41, 1849-50.*

Mullin, J., *Directory for Baltimore.* 1799.

Thomson and Walker, *Directory for Baltimore Town and Fells Point.* 1796.

Varle, Charles, *View of Baltimore,* p. 166. Baltimore, 1833.

Woods, J. W., *Directory for Baltimore City.* 1860.

REPORTS OF CONVENTIONS, CONFERENCES, COMMITTEES, AND OTHER COMPILATIONS

African Methodist Episcopal Church.

    Minutes of Annual Conference for Baltimore District, 1851, 1855.

    Minutes of General and Annual Conferences, 1839-40.

    Minutes of Tenth General Conference at New York, 1852.

    The Budget. Annual Reports of the African Methodist Episcopal Church of the United States of America, 1816-1883, p. 152, Dayton, 1883. (Not what it purports to be upon the whole.)

American Anti-Slavery Society, Annual Reports of, 1834, 1837, 1855, 1860, 1861.

American and Foreign Anti-Slavery Society, Annual Report, 1850.

American Colonization Society, Annual Reports. 1818, 1826, 1828-29, 1833-35, 1838, 1841-43, 1845-49, 1851, 1852, 1861.

Board of Managers of Maryland State Colonization Society, Reports. 1834, 1835, 1850, 1852, 1853, 1856, 1858.

——, *General Report* of the same to January, 1850.

——, *History of Proceedings* of same to January, 1850. (*Cf. Maryland Colonization Journal,* new series, vol. v.)

Church Record, Light Street Methodist Episcopal Church of Baltimore, 1799-1837, 1 volume. Manuscript.

Class Record No. 6, do., 1803-09, 1819-23, 1 volume. Manuscript.

Colonization of the Free People of Color. United States, 19th Cong., 2nd Sess., H. R.

Jenifer, Benjamin and Fuller, Thomas, *Character and Condition of Liberia,* 1851. (Authors were members of the Cambridge Colored Colonization Society.)

Journals of Conventions of the Protestant Episcopal Church of Maryland, 1823-30.

Maryland Baptist Union Association. Report of 14th Annual Meeting, Baltimore, 1849.

Maryland State Colonization Society, Letter Book, 1841. Manuscript.

Massachusetts Anti-Slavery Society, Annual Reports, 1836, 1842, 1843.

Minutes of American Convention for the Abolition of Slavery at Baltimore, 1826.

Minutes of the Friends Meetings. (Manuscript):
Deer Creek Monthly Meeting, 1801-19, 1 volume.
Minutes for Sufferings, 1778-1841, 1 volume.
Nottingham Monthly Meeting, 1730-56, 1 volume.
Yearly Meeting at Baltimore, 1760-1815.

Minutes of Third Convention of Delegates from the Abolition Societies of the United States, 1796.

Proceedings of a Meeting of the Friends of African Colonization in Baltimore, Oct. 17, 1827, p. 17.

——, Ditto, for like Convention at Washington, D. C., 1842, p. 64.

Quarterly Conference Records, 1845-58, *Class Lists*, 1848-69 and *Financial Accounts*, 1850-66, of African Methodist Episcopal Bethel Church of Baltimore, 1 volume. Manuscript.

Quarterly Conference Records of Same, 1858-68, 1 volume. Manuscript.

Record of Membership of Same, 1825-54, 1 volume. Manuscript.

The Southern Platform: A Manual of Southern Sentiment on the Subject of Slavery. (Compilation of utterances of speakers, conventions, papers, etc.), pp. 95, Boston, 1858.

MISCELLANEOUS MATERIALS

Asbury, Reverend Francis, *Journal, 1771-1815*, 3 volumes, New York, 1821.

Alexander, J. H., *Index to Calendar of Maryland State Papers*, 1861.

Bacon, Reverend Thomas, *Four Sermons Preached at the Parish Church of St. Peter's in Talbot County*, 1753.

Balch, T., *Maryland Papers, Relating Chiefly to the Maryland Line during the Revolution, 1775-87*. (Seventy-six Society Publications, vol. iv), Philadelphia, 1857.

Banneker, Benjamin, *Almanac and Ephemeris of Maryland, Pennsylvania, Delaware, Virginia, Kentucky and North Carolina*. Baltimore, 1792, 1794, 1795, 1796.

Boucher, Reverend Jonathan, *A View of the Causes and Consequences of the American Revolution in Thirteen Discourses*. London, 1797.

Comly, (   ), *Reading and Spelling Book*, p. 169. Byberry, 1842.

Constitution and Bye-Laws of the Union Society of Journeymen Cordwainers of the City and Precincts of Baltimore, 1826.

Constitution of the Maryland Society for the Abolition of Slavery and the Relief of Free Negroes and Others Unlawfully Held in Bondage, pp. 8, Baltimore, 1789. (*Cf. Maryland Journal*, Dec. 15, 1789.)

Douglass, Frederick, *My Bondage and My Freedom*, pp. 464, New York, 1855.

Garrettson, Reverend Freeborn, *Journal.*
Hall, Clayton C., *Narratives of Early Maryland, 1633-84.* (*Original Narratives of American History*), New York, 1910.
Lovejoy, J. C., *Memoir of Reverend Charles T. Torrey who Died in the Penitentiary of Maryland,* p. 364. Boston, 1847.
Major, S., *Catalogue of Anti-Slavery Publications in America, 1750-1863.* (*Appendix to Annual Report of the American Anti-Slavery Society, 1864*), p. 19. 1864.
Maryland, its Resources, Industries and Institutions. (*Prepared for the Board of World's Fair Managers of Maryland by Members of the Johns Hopkins University and Others*), p. 504. Baltimore, 1893.
Mathews, Edward Bennett, *Bibliography and Cartography of Maryland.* (Maryland Geological Survey, Special Publication I, part 4.) Baltimore, 1897.
Memorial of the Free Colored People to the Citizens of Baltimore, December, 1826. (*Cf. Genius of Universal Emancipation,* 2nd series, vol. ii, pp. 94-95. Also *Speech of Honorable Henry Clay to the American Colonization Society at Washington, D. C.,* in January, 1827.)
Olmstead, Frederick Law, *A Journey in the Seaboard Slave States.* New York, 1856.
Payne, Reverend Daniel A., *Recollections of Seventy Years,* p. 335. Nashville, 1888.
Perry, William S., *Historical Collections Relating to the Colonial Church,* vol. iv, Maryland. Hartford, 1878.
Pitkin, Timothy, *A Statistical View of the Commerce of the United States of America,* p. 407. Hartford, 1816.
Seybert, Adam (M. D.), *Statistical Annals of the United States of America,* pp. 803. Philadelphia, 1818.
Sheffield, John Lord, *Observations on the Commerce of the American States,* p. 287. London, 1784.
The Sunday Service of the Methodists of North America. 1784.

NEWSPAPERS

(*Arranged according to locality of publication*)

Annapolis,
　Gazette, 1860.
　Maryland Gazette, 1745-46, 1746-48, 1752-56, 1761, 1767-69, 1773 1776-77, 1785-86, 1790-92, 1794-97.
　Maryland Republican, 1809-12, 1813-33, 1835-36, 1838-39.
Baltimore,
　American, 1799-1814, 1829-32, 1841-42, 1850-51, 1858-60.
　Clipper, 1837, 1849-50.
　Federal Gazette, 1796-1805, 1816-21, 1829, 1832.
　Maryland Journal and Baltimore Advertiser, 1773-78, 1783, 1788-94.
　Sun, 1837-1860.

Cambridge *Chronicle*, January, 1831–May, 1832.
Centerville *Times*, June, 1832–October, 1834.
Easton,
  Eastern Shore Star, 1841-44.
  Gazette, 1804, 1820, 1831-48, 1858-60.
  Republican Star, 1801-26.
  Star, 1844-61.
  Eastern Shore General Advertiser, 1806, 1814, 1818-19.
Elkton, *Cecil Whig*, 1841-46, 1848-61.
Frederick,
  Bartgis's Gazette, 1792-93, 1796-99.
  Bartgis's Republican Gazette, 1801-24.
  Examiner, 1841-44, 1857-60.
  Fredericktown Herald, 1813-22.
  Maryland Chronicle and Universal Advertiser, 1787.
  Political Examiner, 1839-41.
  Republican Citizen, 1837-38, 1848-56.
  Times and Democratic Advocate, 1837-38.
Hagerstown, *Mail*, 1828-31, 1849-50.
Princess Anne,
  Somerset Union, 1859-61.
  Village Herald, 1828-38 (lacking June–October, 1833).
Rockville *Journal* and *True American*, January, 1830–February, 1834.
Snow Hill *Messenger*, October, 1830–March, 1834.
Westminster,
  American Sentinel, 1855-60.
  Carroll County Democrat, 1854.

Periodicals Other than Newspapers

American Farmer, 1st series, 1819-33, 14 volumes; 2nd series (*Farmer and Gardener*), 1834-39, 5 volumes; 3rd series, 1839-43, 4 volumes; 4th series, 1845-59, 14 volumes.
Baltimore Literary and Religious Magazine (edited by R. J. Breckenridge and Andrew B. Cross), 1835-41, 7 volumes.
Genius of Universal Emancipation, 1st series, 1821-24, 3 volumes; 2nd series, 1825-29, 4 volumes; 3rd series, 1830-32, 2 volumes.
Gentleman's Magazine, 1764.
Maryland Colonization Journal, 1835-41, 1 volume. New series, 1841-61, 10 volumes. (*Cf.* chapter on "Attempts to Check the Growth of the Free Negro Population," *supra*, pp. 275-76.)
Maryland Historical Society, Fund Publications, 1867-86, 26 volumes.
——, *Publications*, 1844-45, 2 volumes.
Maryland Historical Magazine, 1906-14, 9 volumes.
Niles National Register, 1837-49, 26 volumes.
Niles Weekly Register, 1811-37, 52 volumes.

PUBLIC DOCUMENTS PRINTED

FEDERAL

1st Census of the United States, 1790. Maryland, Heads of Families. Washington, 1907.

4th Census of the United States, 1820. Washington, 1821.

Statistical View of the Population of the United States, 1790-1830. Washington, 1835.

6th Census of the United States, 1840. Compendium of Enumeration of the Inhabitants of the United States ... by Counties and Principal Towns. Washington, 1841.

7th Census of the United States, 1850. Report of Superintendent. Washington, 1852.

——, *History and Statistics of the State of Maryland According to ... the Seventh Census,* by J. C. G. Kennedy. Washington, 1853.

——, *Statistical View of Each of the States and Territories.* Washington, 1853.

——, *Mortality and Miscellaneous Statistics* (33rd Cong., 2nd Sess., H. R. Exec. Doc., no. 98). Washington, 1855.

8th Census of the United States. Population of the United States in 1860. Washington, 1864.

——, *Agriculture of the United States in 1860.* Washington, 1864.

——, *Statistics of the United States, Including Mortality, Property, etc. in 1860.* Washington, 1866.

Population of the United States at Each Census, 1790-1870. Washington, 1871.

10th Census of the United States. Agriculture, vol. iii, *Report on Tobacco.* Washington, 1883.

Report on African Colonization, by J. P. Kennedy, (27th Cong., 3rd Sess., H. R., Report, no. 283), pp. 1088. Washington, 1843.

The Negroes of Sandy Spring: A Social Study, by W. T. Thom. (United States Bureau of Labor, *Bulletin No. 32,* pp. 43-102.) Washington, 1901.

STATE OF MARYLAND

Archives of Maryland, 1637-1783, 33 volumes, Baltimore, 1883-1913.

Bacon, T., *Laws of Maryland at Large.*

Baskett, *Laws of Maryland, 1692-1715.* London, 1723.

Browne, William Hand, *Governors' Messages and Documents,* 1828-84, 29 volumes.

Court of Appeals of the State of Maryland, Reports, 1658-1860, 47 volumes.

Debates and Proceedings of the Constitutional Convention of 1850-51, 2 volumes. Annapolis, 1851.

Dorsey, C., *The General Public Statutory Law and Public Local Law of the State of Maryland, from the Year 1792 to 1839 Inclusive,* 3 volumes. Baltimore, 1840.

Herty, T., *Digest of the Laws of Maryland.* Baltimore, 1799.

House of Delegates, Committee on the Colored Population, Reports. (Md. Pub. Docs., 1834, 1839 Z, 1841 H, 1843 M, 1852 L, 1864 E.)

——, *Votes and Proceedings,* 1739-1824.

——, *Proceedings and Journal,* 1825-1861.

Index to the Journals of the Senate and House of Delegates of Maryland, 1777-1828, 3 volumes.

Kilty, W., *Laws of Maryland,* 2 volumes, Annapolis, 1799.

Maryland Chancery Reports, 1811-32, 1851-53, 7 volumes.

Maryland Public Documents, 1828, 1834, 1839, 1841, 1841-42, 1843, 1844-45, 1847, 1849, 1852, 1864.

Maxcy, V., *The Laws of Maryland with the Charter, etc., 1692-1800,* 3 volumes, Baltimore, 1811.

Proceedings and Debates of the Upper and Lower Houses of Assembly of Maryland, 1722, 1723, 1724, 1725. Philadelphia, 1725.

Scott, O. and McCollough, *Maryland Code... 1860,* 2 volumes. Baltimore, 1860.

Senate, Journal of Votes and Proceedings, 1777-1861.

Session Laws, 1727-1861.

Sharpe, Governor Horatio, *Correspondence,* 1753-71. (Archives of Maryland), 3 volumes. Baltimore, 1888-95.

CITY OF BALTIMORE

Ordinances and Resolutions of the Mayor and City Council. (Containing after 1828 the Mayors' messages and reports of the various city executive departments), 1794-1861, 28 volumes.

PUBLIC DOCUMENTS, MANUSCRIPT

STATE OF MARYLAND

Judgments of the General Courts for the Eastern Shore and Western Shore, 1779-99, 21 volumes.

Judgment Records of the High Court of Appeals, 1788-1818, 18 volumes.

Maryland Land Records, 1658-1854, 33 volumes.

Maryland Wills, 1635-1760.

Miscellaneous Executive Documents and Papers.

Provincial Court Judgments, 1679-1775, 68 volumes.

THE COUNTIES

Administration Accounts,
Carroll, 1 volume.

Assessment Books and Tax Ledgers,
    Allegany, 1833 and 1852, 21 volumes.
    Baltimore City, 1802-59, 112 volumes.
    ——, Assessment of Salaries and Incomes as per Act of 1841, ch.
      325, 6 volumes, 1843.
    Baltimore County, 1793-1852, 34 volumes.
    Caroline, 1822-60, 10 volumes.
    Carroll, 1837-60, 23 volumes.
    Cecil, 1795-1863, 11 volumes.
    Dorchester, 1852-60, 8 volumes (incomplete).
    ——, Negro Assessment Books, 1817-40, 2 volumes.
    Frederick, 1798-1865, 28 volumes.
    Harford, 1858-1864, 5 volumes.
    Howard, 1841-64, 2 volumes.
    Kent, 1804-65, 16 volumes.
    Montgomery, 1793-97, 1831-63, 4 volumes.
    Queen Anne's, 1824-60, 12 volumes.
    Somerset, 1793-1866, 62 volumes.
    Talbot, 1793-1863, 44 volumes.
Assessment Rolls of 1783 for certain districts in the counties of Anne
    Arundel, Cecil, Charles, Dorchester, Frederick, Somerset, Talbot
    and Worcester.
Charter Records,
    Baltimore City, to 1861, 5 volumes.
    Frederick, Incorporations of Churches, 1805-80, 1 volume.
Chattel Records,
    Anne Arundel (Bills of Sale), 1829-62, 4 volumes.
    Baltimore City, 1763-1861, 111 volumes.
    Baltimore County, 1851-61, 4 volumes.
    Carroll, 1837-64, 6 volumes.
    Harford, 1849-60, 3 volumes.
    Howard, 1840-60, 3 volumes.
    Kent, 1797-1861, 13 volumes.
Dockets of Criminal Courts,
    Carroll, 1837-62, 2 volumes.
    Dorchester, 1857-59, 1 volume.
    Harford, 9 volumes.
Freedom Certificates, Free Negro Books, or Records of Free Negroes,
    Anne Arundel, 1810-62, 3 volumes.
    Caroline, 1806-64, 4 volumes.
    Frederick, 1815-63, 2 volumes.
    Howard, 1840-61, 1 volume.
    Kent, 1849-63, 1 volume.
    Queen Anne's, 1806-26, 1848-63, 3 volumes.

Talbot, 1806-19, 1817-40, 10 volumes.
Washington, 1836-63, 3 volumes.
Indentures of Apprenticeship,
Anne Arundel, 1822-26, 1 volume.
Baltimore City, 1794-1861, 22 volumes.
Baltimore County, 1851-60, 1 volume.
Caroline, 1813-63, 8 volumes.
Carroll, 1837-73, 1 volume.
Cecil, 1794-1864, 3 volumes.
Frederick, 1794-1874, 7 volumes.
Howard, 1840-1907, 1 volume.
Kent, 1778-1860, 12 volumes. (In Kent the series is marked
"Bonds and Indentures". In certain other counties, as e. g.
Anne Arundel, Harford and Queen Anne's, many of the indenture
contracts were long recorded in the Orphans' Court Minutes,
and some in the Land and Chattel Records.)
Talbot, 1794-1864, 5 volumes.
Washington, 1806-1905, 5 volumes.
Judicial (or Judgment) Records of County Courts,
Charles (Deeds and County Records), 1662-1786, 73 volumes.
Frederick, 1748-50, 1763-66, 2 volumes.
Kent, 1714-15, 1732-34, 1739-41, 1756-62, 7 volumes.
Queen Anne's, 1730-1831 (incomplete), 9 volumes.
Somerset, 1671-1848 (incomplete), 70 volumes.
Talbot, 1810-68, 5 volumes.
Worcester, 1778-79, 1796-1860, 10 volumes.
Land Records, or Deeds,
Anne Arundel, 1665-1860, 86 volumes.
Baltimore City, 1659-1860, 693 volumes.
Baltimore County, 1851-61, 31 volumes.
Caroline, 1774-1861, 29 volumes.
Carroll, 1837-1861, 26 volumes.
Cecil, 1674-1864, 104 volumes.
Charles (extracts of Deeds), 1786-1828, 4 volumes.
Dorchester, 1669-1864, 77 volumes.
Frederick, 1748-1861, 173 volumes.
Harford, 1773-1862, 74 volumes.
Kent, 1648-1860, 61 volumes.
Montgomery, 1777-1862, 51 volumes.
Queen Anne's, 1707-1861, 46 volumes.
Somerset, 1660-1860, 74 volumes.
Talbot, 1662-1862, 69 volumes.
Worcester, 1742-1861, 69 volumes.

(Generally the best kept of any county records in Maryland and more or less thoroughly indexed, usually "both ways". In several counties they contain all land and chattel transfers recorded, and also manumission records, although in some, as *e. g.* in Kent in 1797, and Harford in 1849, separate series of Chattel Records were begun for the recording of all save instruments transferring real property.)

Levy Lists, Assessment Lists and Lists of Taxables,
    Anne Arundel, 1858-60. Districts nos. 1, 2, 3, 4, 8. (Rolls).
    Baltimore County, 1699-1705, 1828-53, 5 volumes.
    Caroline, 1860, 1 volume.
    Carroll, 1837-62, 4 volumes.
    Dorchester, 1853-57, 10 volumes.
    Queen Anne's, 1754-67, 1 volume.
    Talbot, 1813-65, 13 volumes.
Manumissions,
    Anne Arundel, 1816-44, 1 volume. (Marked "Deeds", Lib. C, no. 3.)
    Howard, 1840-61, 1 volume.
Marriage License Records,
    Caroline, 1797-1861, 2 volumes.
    Carroll, 1844-65, 1 volume.
    Frederick, 1778-1865, 1 volume.
    Talbot, 1774-1868, 4 volumes.
    Worcester, 1795-1819, 1 volume.
Minutes of Proceedings of Orphans' Courts.
    Baltimore City, 1777-1861, 32 volumes.
    Caroline, 1807-66, 10 volumes (Lacking, 1814-21, 1828-33).
    Carroll, 1837-61, 19 volumes.
    Dorchester, 1845-61, 2 volumes.
    Frederick, 1777-1861, 36 volumes.
    Harford, 1778-1864, 10 volumes.
    Howard, 1840-1862, 3 volumes.
    Kent, 1803-64, 7 volumes.
    Montgomery, 1779-1865, 10 volumes (Lacking 1835-40).
    Queen Anne's, 1778-1864, 17 volumes (Lacking 1791-99).
    Somerset, 1777-1864, 7 volumes (Lacking 1792-1810).
    Talbot, 1787-1861, 15 volumes.
    Washington, 1806-1859, 6 volumes.
    Worcester, 1833-61, 4 volumes (Lacking 1839-52).

(Usually well preserved and cared for, but of varying values for the purposes of this study.)

Wills,
    Anne Arundel, 1777-1861, 10 volumes.

Baltimore City, 1675-1861, 29 volumes.
Baltimore County, 1851-61, 2 volumes.
Caroline, 1777-1861, 5 volumes.
Carroll, 1837-69, 5 volumes.
Cecil, 1675-1862, 10 volumes.
Dorchester, 1852-61, 2 volumes.
Frederick, 1748-1860, 4 volumes.
Harford, 1774-1866, 7 volumes.
Howard, 1840-62, 1 volume.
Kent, 1669-1861, 15 volumes.
Montgomery, 1777-1861, 35 volumes. (In certain volumes are in-
   cluded records other than the wills.)
Queen Anne's, 1706-1861, 12 volumes.
Somerset, 1665-1859, 9 volumes.
Talbot, 1665-1862, 10 volumes (Lacking 1746-65).
Washington, 1777-1863, 5 volumes.
Worcester, 1742-1861, 12 volumes.

PRIVATE ACCOUNT BOOKS, JOURNALS AND LEDGERS

Seth Barton and Co., *Journal*, 1791-1801; *Ledger*, 1791-92.
E. T. Bourke, *Account Book*, 1828-34.
Briscoe and Lenham, *Ledger*, 1806-09.
Cornwall Furnace, *Journals*, 1752-53, 1754, 1756, 1758-59, 4 volumes;
   Ledgers, 1752-53, 1754, 1755-56, 1756, 1759-60, 1762-63, 6 volumes.
Douglass and Smoot (Vienna), *Ledger*, 1758-87.
Elk Forge, *Journals and Ledgers*, 1798-1832, 10 volumes.
Elk Ridge Furnace, *Journals*, 1758-72, 3 volumes.
Hopewell Forge, *Journals and Ledgers*, 1757-64, 5 volumes.
Kirby and Ready, *Ledger*, 1832-42, 1 volume.
Zachariah MacCubin, *Ledger*, 1789-1803, 1 volume.
Robert May and Co., *Journals*, 1798-1816, 3 volumes.
Merchant's Ledger (unmarked), 1832-37, 1 volume.
Patuxent Iron Works, *Journal*, 1767-94, 2 volumes.
Jesse Richardson, *Ledger*, 1792-93, 1 volume.
Richardson and Clayton, *Ledger*, 1791-92, 1 volume.
Savings Banks Accounts,
   Central Savings Bank (Baltimore), *Ledgers*, 1855-60.
   Eutaw Savings Bank (Baltimore), *Depositors' and Transfer Ledgers
      and Signature Books*, 1847-60.
   Fredericktown Savings Institution, *Ledgers B, C, D, E*, 1835-59,
      4 volumes.